YEAR C ■ 2001

# workbook
FOR LECTORS AND GOSPEL READERS

## Canadian Edition

*Susan E. Myers*

LTP
LITURGY
TRAINING
PUBLICATIONS

CCCB

The scripture quotations contained herein are adapted from the *New Revised Standard Version* of the Bible, © 1989 by the Division of Christian Education of the National Council of the Churches of Christ in the United States of America, and are used with permission. All rights reserved.

The lectionary texts contained herein are taken from the Lectionary of the Canadian Conference of Bishops, © Concacan, Inc., 1992, and are used with permission. All rights reserved.

WORKBOOK FOR LECTORS AND GOSPEL READERS 2001, CANADIAN EDITION © 2000 Archdiocese of Chicago. All rights reserved.
Liturgy Training Publications
1800 North Hermitage Avenue
Chicago IL 60622-1101
1-800-933-1800
fax 1-800-933-7094
orders@ltp.org
www.ltp.org

CCCB Publications
Canadian Conference of
Catholic Bishops
90 Parent Avenue
Ottawa, Canada K1N 7B1
1-613-241-7538
1-800-769-1147
fax 1-613-241-5090

Editor: David A. Lysik
Production editor: Bryan Cones
Cover art: Barbara Simcoe
Interior art: Steve Erspamer, SM
Original book design: Jill Smith
Revised design: Anna Manhart and Jim Mellody-Pizzato
Typesetting: Jim Mellody-Pizzato

Printed in the United States of America by Von Hoffmann Graphics Inc.

ISBN (USA) 1-56854-392-1
ISBN (CANADA) 0-88997-451-9
CWL01

# CONTENTS

Introduction . . . . . . . . . . . . . . . .iv

## ADVENT

1st Sunday of Advent
DECEMBER 3, 2000 . . . . . . . . . . . . .1

Immaculate Conception
DECEMBER 8, 2000 . . . . . . . . . . . . .4

2nd Sunday of Advent
DECEMBER 10, 2000 . . . . . . . . . . . . .8

3rd Sunday of Advent
DECEMBER 17, 2000 . . . . . . . . . . .11

4th Sunday of Advent
DECEMBER 24, 2000 . . . . . . . . . . .14

## CHRISTMAS SEASON

Christmas Vigil
DECEMBER 24, 2000 . . . . . . . . . . .17

Christmas Midnight
DECEMBER 25, 2000 . . . . . . . . . . .22

Christmas Dawn
DECEMBER 25, 2000 . . . . . . . . . . .26

Christmas Day
DECEMBER 25, 2000 . . . . . . . . . . .28

Holy Family
DECEMBER 31, 2000 . . . . . . . . . . .32

Mary, Mother of God
JANUARY 1, 2001 . . . . . . . . . . . . . .36

Epiphany of the Lord
JANUARY 7, 2001 . . . . . . . . . . . . . .39

## ORDINARY TIME

2nd Sunday in Ordinary Time
JANUARY 14, 2001 . . . . . . . . . . . . .42

3rd Sunday in Ordinary Time
JANUARY 21, 2001 . . . . . . . . . . . . .45

4th Sunday in Ordinary Time
JANUARY 28, 2001 . . . . . . . . . . . . .50

5th Sunday in Ordinary Time
FEBRUARY 4, 2001 . . . . . . . . . . . . .54

6th Sunday in Ordinary Time
FEBRUARY 11, 2001 . . . . . . . . . . . .58

7th Sunday in Ordinary Time
FEBRUARY 18, 2001 . . . . . . . . . . . .61

8th Sunday in Ordinary Time
FEBRUARY 25, 2001 . . . . . . . . . . . .65

## LENT

Ash Wednesday
FEBRUARY 28, 2001 . . . . . . . . . . . .68

1st Sunday of Lent
MARCH 4, 2001 . . . . . . . . . . . . . . .72

2nd Sunday of Lent
MARCH 11, 2001 . . . . . . . . . . . . . .75

3rd Sunday of Lent
MARCH 18, 2001 . . . . . . . . . . . . . .79

3rd Sunday of Lent, Year A
MARCH 18, 2001 . . . . . . . . . . . . . .83

4th Sunday of Lent
MARCH 25, 2001 . . . . . . . . . . . . . .89

4th Sunday of Lent, Year A
MARCH 25, 2001 . . . . . . . . . . . . . .93

5th Sunday of Lent
APRIL 1, 2001 . . . . . . . . . . . . . . . .99

5th Sunday of Lent, Year A
APRIL 1, 2001 . . . . . . . . . . . . . . .103

Palm Sunday of the
Lord's Passion
APRIL 8, 2001 . . . . . . . . . . . . . . .109

## PASCHAL TRIDUUM

Holy Thursday: Mass of the
Lord's Supper
APRIL 12, 2001 . . . . . . . . . . . . . . .122

Good Friday: Celebration of the
Lord's Passion
APRIL 13, 2001 . . . . . . . . . . . . . . .126

Easter Vigil
APRIL 14–15, 2001 . . . . . . . . . . . .138

Easter Sunday
APRIL 15, 2001 . . . . . . . . . . . . . . .155

## EASTER SEASON

2nd Sunday of Easter
APRIL 22, 2001 . . . . . . . . . . . . . . .162

3rd Sunday of Easter
APRIL 29, 2001 . . . . . . . . . . . . . . .166

4th Sunday of Easter
MAY 6, 2001 . . . . . . . . . . . . . . . . .171

5th Sunday of Easter
MAY 13, 2001 . . . . . . . . . . . . . . . .174

6th Sunday of Easter
MAY 20, 2001 . . . . . . . . . . . . . . . .177

Ascension of the Lord
MAY 24, 2001 . . . . . . . . . . . . . . . .181

7th Sunday of Easter
MAY 27, 2001 . . . . . . . . . . . . . . . .185

Pentecost Vigil
JUNE 2, 2001 . . . . . . . . . . . . . . . .188

Pentecost
JUNE 3, 2001 . . . . . . . . . . . . . . . .195

## ORDINARY TIME

Holy Trinity
JUNE 10, 2001 . . . . . . . . . . . . . . . .198

Body and Blood of Christ
JUNE 17, 2001 . . . . . . . . . . . . . . . .201

Birth of John the Baptist Vigil
JUNE 23, 2001 . . . . . . . . . . . . . . . .204

Birth of John the Baptist
JUNE 24, 2001 . . . . . . . . . . . . . . . .208

13th Sunday in Ordinary Time
JULY 1, 2001 . . . . . . . . . . . . . . . . .212

14th Sunday in Ordinary Time
JULY 8, 2001 . . . . . . . . . . . . . . . . .215

15th Sunday in Ordinary Time
JULY 15, 2001 . . . . . . . . . . . . . . . .219

16th Sunday in Ordinary Time
JULY 22, 2001 . . . . . . . . . . . . . . . .223

17th Sunday in Ordinary Time
JULY 29, 2001 . . . . . . . . . . . . . . . .226

18th Sunday in Ordinary Time
AUGUST 5, 2001 . . . . . . . . . . . . . .231

19th Sunday in Ordinary Time
AUGUST 12, 2001 . . . . . . . . . . . . .234

Assumption
AUGUST 15, 2001 . . . . . . . . . . . . .239

20th Sunday in Ordinary Time
AUGUST 19, 2001 . . . . . . . . . . . . .243

21st Sunday in Ordinary Time
AUGUST 26, 2001 . . . . . . . . . . . . .246

22nd Sunday in Ordinary Time
SEPTEMBER 2, 2001 . . . . . . . . . . .249

23rd Sunday in Ordinary Time
SEPTEMBER 9, 2001 . . . . . . . . . . .252

24th Sunday in Ordinary Time
SEPTEMBER 16, 2001 . . . . . . . . . .255

25th Sunday in Ordinary Time
SEPTEMBER 23, 2001 . . . . . . . . . .261

26th Sunday in Ordinary Time
SEPTEMBER 30, 2001 . . . . . . . . . .265

27th Sunday in Ordinary Time
OCTOBER 7, 2001 . . . . . . . . . . . . .269

28th Sunday in Ordinary Time
OCTOBER 14, 2001 . . . . . . . . . . . .272

29th Sunday in Ordinary Time
OCTOBER 21, 2001 . . . . . . . . . . . .275

30th Sunday in Ordinary Time
OCTOBER 28, 2001 . . . . . . . . . . . .278

All Saints
NOVEMBER 1, 2001 . . . . . . . . . . . .281

31st Sunday in Ordinary Time
NOVEMBER 4, 2001 . . . . . . . . . . . .284

32nd Sunday in Ordinary Time
NOVEMBER 11, 2001 . . . . . . . . . . .287

33rd Sunday in Ordinary Time
NOVEMBER 18, 2001 . . . . . . . . . . .291

Christ the King
NOVEMBER 25, 2001 . . . . . . . . . . .294

**The Author**

Susan E. Myers is a doctoral candidate in New Testament and early Christianity at the University of Notre Dame. She has degrees in theology and biblical studies, as well as experience in parish ministry and teaching. Susan's academic interests lie in all aspects of the beliefs, practices and prayer life of early Christians; her current research in early Christianity is concentrated in the region of eastern Syria. Her previous work with Liturgy Training Publications includes *At Home with the Word* (1997, 1998) and *Pronunciation Guide for the Sunday Lectionary* (1998). Susan brings to *Workbook for Lectors and Gospel Readers* a knowledge of biblical languages and exegesis, as well as knowledge of and participation in the pastoral and liturgical life of the Christian church.

# INTRODUCTION

## The Ministry of Proclaiming the Word of God

You were probably encouraged to become a lector in your parish or community by someone who knows you well and appreciates your love of God, or by someone who has witnessed your skills at public speaking. Or perhaps you volunteered for this ministry, moved by God's Spirit to share your gifts with others. Whatever brought you here, you are now part of the team of those who minister at liturgy. Some ministers have visible positions, such as the music director, the presider or the choir members, while others labor quietly behind the scenes: the members of the liturgy committee and its director, those responsible for the decor and presentation of the worship space, bread bakers, ushers and church maintenance crew members. Even the work of the pastoral ministers—RCIA catechists, religious education instructors, counselors, youth ministers, those involved in sacramental preparation—all comes together in the liturgy, the central event of our life as a church. It is through our gathering for prayer and praise that we celebrate who we are as God's people. When we come together for liturgy, we encounter God—in one another, in the sacramental actions (such as baptism or eucharist), and in the proclamation of the word of God.

You have the task of making God present in the liturgy of the word for your community. God has been among us in the past, especially in the person of Jesus. The prologue to the gospel of John says it best: "In the beginning was the Word, and the Word was with God, and the Word was God. . . . And the Word became flesh and lived among us." The Greek for "word" in this passage is *logos*, which can mean "reason"; it is what goes on in God's "head" and "heart." *Logos* can also mean "word," and that is how it is usually translated in this passage. It is the communication of the thoughts of God.

Jesus is God's word incarnate, but God's word is also spoken through others. God has spoken in the past through leaders and prophets, evangelists, apostles and many others. Today God speaks also through you as you proclaim in the assembly God's word as communicated through the individuals who composed the scriptures.

When the word of God is proclaimed in the assembly, it challenges and comforts, encourages and admonishes. Your task is to proclaim a living Word, not simply words on a page. When we read or hear the scriptures, we become part of the story they tell. We are part of the chosen people of God, struggling to understand God and ourselves, striving to be faithful, repenting when we fail. We are disciples of Jesus, following him and learning from his teachings. We are members of the Christian communities served by the evangelists and letter-writers of the New Testament. The word of God shapes our lives, teaching us, changing us, bringing us into an encounter with God.

In the liturgy, the Christian community depends on you, the lector or gospel reader, to mediate an encounter with God. In order to do this effectively, you must make the text come alive for your listeners. The job of making God present is an awesome responsibility, one that requires commitment and time. But do not worry. The Spirit of God will guide you in your ministry. You have been chosen.

## Preparing to Proclaim

You can begin to bring God into your assembly by experiencing God's presence yourself, communicated through the words you are asked to read. Spend time with the selection you will proclaim. Read it several times. Pray about it. Allow God to speak to you through it.

Learn about the reading. The commentaries in this *Workbook* are intended to help you understand something about the purpose of the author who wrote the passage, as well as the historical setting out of which the passage arises. You might wish also to turn to your Bible and read the verses that precede and follow your selection, so that you can better understand its context. It might be helpful as well to read any introductory material in your Bible about the book from which the selection is taken, or consult a Bible commentary. The more you know about the reading, the more effectively you can share it with others.

Do not worry if the text does not completely make sense to you. Biblical scholars have long argued about the precise meanings of some passages and continue to find new information that adds to our understanding of the text. In addition, do not be alarmed if you find the reading confusing or bothersome. "There is nothing comfortable about the Bible" if we are truly engaged with it, as Thomas Merton has said. Remember that God has communicated this word to fallible human beings who sometimes inserted some of their own interests and biases into the text. Trust that God is bigger than any uncertainty or difficulty you have with the reading. If you are open to the movement of the Spirit of God in your life, you will enable the Spirit to move in your listeners in ways beyond your imaginings.

Preparation to proclaim the word of God ideally takes place in a group setting. Participants, usually other lectors and gospel readers, gather to discuss and summarize the readings, to practice together and to provide practical tips for one another. The sessions are most effective if a skilled leader directs them. If group meetings of lectors are not the norm in your parish, you might want to suggest that a group be formed or offer to organize one yourself. If you are unable to prepare with others, practice individually, but always try to have another person listen to you and offer suggestions at least once.

When you practice, it can be especially enlightening to have yourself videotaped or, if that is not possible, to create an audio tape of the reading. You will learn a great deal about your posture and vocal inflection, your phrasing and your pace by hearing and seeing yourself on tape. Always prepare with the microphone in the church and, if possible, with the same lectionary from which you will be reading. This *Workbook* is not suitable for use in the assembly; an elegantly bound lectionary, carried in procession, is the appropriate choice. Check also with your liturgy director or the presider for any special instructions, such as a choral refrain or other interlude, especially if you are preparing to read on a special feast day.

A microphone amplifies your every sound. It must clearly project your whispers, but not be too loud for forceful proclamation. Know how to adjust the microphone, how far away to stand from it and when to lean forward slightly or back away. Some microphones are very sensitive and should not be approached too closely. Especially avoid the popping of "p" and "b" sounds or the hissing of "s" and "z" that microphones tend to produce. Practice making these sounds subtly but clearly, so that your congregation will understand you but not be distracted by unwelcome noises. It is important that someone else listen to you and give you feedback when you are practicing with the microphone.

## The Proclamation of God's Word

It is natural to approach the task of reading before an assembly with a bit of trepidation. Such nervousness, if controlled, can be to your advantage. God's word is powerful and active, and your energy can be channeled into a more effective proclamation. You are not giving a history lesson or telling a story but proclaiming the movement of God throughout history for the benefit of your listeners. The process of reading the scriptures does include some teaching, but you stand in the dual role of teacher and disciple. Most of all, you stand before your community as a believer. Proclaiming the word involves an active sharing of faith between the reader and the assembly; your community will sense your energy and will communicate back to you its trust in God's fidelity and love.

## INTRODUCTION

Despite the power of God's word, many of us adopt a monotone whenever we read before an assembly. Reading the word of God is unlike any other public proclamation, but it requires some of the same skills that are necessary for effective speeches, oral interpretation or debate. For many of us, the time we are most likely to put great expression into our oral reading is when reading children's books to a captive audience. Try adopting some (but not too much) of the inflection and exaggeration of reading to a child in your public proclamation. Although you may feel you are adding too much emphasis and inflection, it probably sounds quite differently to your listeners.

A small minority of people tend to exaggerate when reading in public. Although most of us need to "ham it up" more than might make us comfortable at first, we all need to remember that we are not entertaining. Proclaiming the word of God is a formal task, one requiring dignity and restraint. Avoid anything that might draw attention to you and away from the word you proclaim. This is not a performance but a noble ministry, entrusted to you by God and by your community.

Be careful, then, how you communicate through your body language. Stand erect and hold your head high. Move slowly and deliberately.

Plan your phrasing and know when you will pause. Be certain that you can pronounce all of the words you will read. Enunciate clearly; this is especially important in a church with a great deal of reverberation. If you do stumble while reading, correct yourself and then continue without drawing undue attention to your error. Your composure will allow the dignity of God's word to be retained.

When you approach the microphone, pause and wait for any activity in the assembly to die down. Take a moment to compose yourself. Be sure that you have the attention of your entire assembly before you begin. Proclaim in a strong voice, "A reading from . . ." and then pause. At the end of the reading, be sure you do not swallow "The word [or gospel] of the Lord." Instead, pause before the phrase and then proclaim it as something in which you take great pride. Your community will remind you through their response that they are as involved in this proclamation as you. If returning to your seat, move slowly and with dignity.

Eye contact is essential in a reading before an assembly. If you have practiced the reading well, you will be able to address your listeners directly during important phrases, and glance back at your text during pauses. You might want to keep your finger at the spot from which you are reading so that you do not lose your place, if you can do this without drawing attention to your movements. But remember that this is a reading of God's word, not a speech; there is no need for constant eye contact.

Trying to establish some eye contact can aid in achieving another objective of most readers: slowing down. In order for the members of your community to reflect on what you are proclaiming, they need time to digest the message. Many of us, in our nervousness, rush through a reading and return to our seats hurriedly. In everything you do, act slowly and deliberately, as is fitting for a proclamation of the majestic word of God. Your goal is to capture your assembly's attention so completely that its members will be transfixed by your words, experiencing God in their midst. Those who have the habit of reading along in a missalette or worship aid will leave the printed word behind and truly listen, with ears attentive to God's voice speaking through yours.

Your physical appearance should convey your respect for your ministry. Dress comfortably but nicely. Remember that you are not trying to draw attention to yourself, either by dressing shabbily or by trying to turn the liturgy into a fashion show. Before the liturgy begins, check your appearance in a mirror one last time so that you do not have to worry about how you look prior to or during the reading. And know that it is very difficult for your community to concentrate on your words if you have a tuft of hair sticking straight up during your proclamation.

Throughout everything, be confident. Know that you are not only capable of the task before you but have the guidance of the Spirit of God to assist you. If you are focused on God's word and have prepared well, you will be the vehicle through whom God speaks to your community.

### Workbook for Lectors and Gospel Readers

*Workbook* includes the scripture readings for Masses on Sundays and feast days. It does not include the psalm selection, since that is properly sung, not proclaimed in the same manner as the readings.

# INTRODUCTION

Be sure that you know if you are to read a shorter version of the passage than that provided here. Shorter options are available for especially long readings, but this *Workbook* always gives the longer form.

The commentaries provided for each reading are intended to provide background information for the minister of the word. Historical and literary information is stressed, as well as suggestions for making your proclamation of the reading most effective. Understanding the reading is a first step toward proclaiming it.

Included to the left of the readings are margin notes with specific suggestions for your proclamation, as well as occasional information that will explain certain words and phrases or ancient practices. Pronunciations of difficult words are provided as well; refer to the pronunciation key that follows this section. Consult the *Pronunciation Guide for the Sunday Lectionary*, available from Liturgy Training Publications, for additional terms that are unfamiliar to you.

The italics evident in the text are intended to indicate an appropriate emphasis on certain words. Not all of the italicized words are to be stressed to the same degree. Instead, the italics provide a guide to the rhythm of the passage; truly significant words will need to be given added emphasis. The italics are provided as a service to readers, but there are other legitimate ways to convey the meaning of the text. If after careful preparation you find that another pattern of stress seems to communicate more effectively God's word as you understand it, feel free to adopt that pattern.

Since you will be reading from a lectionary and not from this *Workbook*, lectionary numbers are provided for each Sunday or other day in order to facilitate the location of the readings in the lectionary. You may wish to practice with the lectionary from which you will read as well as from this *Workbook*, since the layout of the reading might differ from that printed here. Anything you can do in order to be more confident in proclaiming the word will allow you to communicate God's presence more effectively.

## Pronunciation Key

Most consonants in the pronunciation key are straightforward: The letter B always represents the sound B and D is always D, and so on. Vowels are more complicated. Note that the long I sound (as in kite or ice) is represented by *ī*, while long A (skate, pray) is represented by *ay*. Long E (beam, marine) is represented by *ee*; long O (boat, coat) is represented by *oh*; long U (sure, secure) is represented by *oo* or *yoo*. Short A (cat), E (bed), I (slim) and O (dot) are represented by *a, e, i* and *o* except in an unstressed syllable, when E and I are signified by *eh* and *ih*. Short U (cup) is represented by *uh*. An asterisk (\*) indicates the schwa sound, as in the last syllable of the word "stable." The letters OO and TH can each be pronounced in two ways (as in cool or book; thin or they); underlining differentiates between them. Stress is indicated by the capitalization of the stressed syllable in words of more than one syllable.

| | |
|---|---|
| bait = bayt | thin = thin |
| cat = kat | vision = VIZH-\*n |
| sang = sang | ship = ship |
| father = FAH-<u>th</u>er | sir = ser |
| care = kayr | gloat = gloht |
| paw = paw | cot = kot |
| jar = jahr | noise = noyz |
| easy = EE-zee | poison = POY-z\*n |
| her = her | plow = plow |
| let = let | although = awl-<u>TH</u>OH |
| queen = kween | church = church |
| delude = deh-L<u>OO</u>D | fun = fuhn |
| when = hwen | fur = fer |
| ice = īs | flute = fl<u>oo</u>t |
| if = if | foot = foot |
| finesse = fih-NES | |

## Bibliography of Recommended Works

### Guides for Proclaiming God's Word

Connell, Martin. *Guide to the Revised Lectionary.* Chicago, Illinois: Liturgy Training Publications, 1998.

*Lector Training Program: This Is the Word of the Lord.* Audio tapes and booklet. Chicago, Illinois: Liturgy Training Publications, 1988.

*The Lector's Ministry: Your Guide to Proclaiming the Word.* Mineola, New York: Resurrection Press, 1990.

Lee, Charlotte I., and Galati, Frank. *Oral Interpretation*, 9th ed. Boston, Massachusetts: Houghton Mifflin, 1997.

Myers, Susan E. *Pronunciation Guide for the Sunday Lectionary.* Chicago, Illinois: Liturgy Training Publications, 1998.

*Proclaiming the Word: Formation for Readers in the Liturgy.* Video. Chicago, Illinois: Liturgy Training Publications, 1994.

Rosser, Aelred R. *A Well-Trained Tongue: Formation in the Ministry of Reader.* Chicago, Illinois: Liturgy Training Publications, 1996.

———. *A Word That Will Rouse Them: Reflections on the Ministry of Reader.* Chicago, Illinois: Liturgy Training Publications, 1995.

———. *Guide for Lectors.* Chicago, Illinois: Liturgy Training Publications, 1998.

### General Reference Works on the Bible

Boadt, Lawrence. *Reading the Old Testament: An Introduction.* New York, New York/Mahwah, New Jersey: Paulist Press, 1984.

Brown, Raymond E. *An Introduction to the New Testament* (The Anchor Bible Reference Library). New York, New York: Doubleday, 1997.

*Collegeville Bible Commentary, Old Testament Series.* Diane Bergant, general editor. Collegeville, Minnesota: The Liturgical Press, 1985.

*Collegeville Bible Commentary, New Testament Series.* Robert J. Karris, general editor. Collegeville, Minnesota: The Liturgical Press, 1991.

*The Collegeville Pastoral Dictionary of Biblical Theology.* Carroll Stuhlmueller, general editor. Collegeville, Minnesota: The Liturgical Press, 1996.

*The New Jerome Biblical Commentary.* Raymond E. Brown, Joseph Fitzmyer and Roland E. Murphy, editors. Englewood Cliffs, New Jersey: Prentice Hall, 1990.

*New Testament Message: A Biblical-Theological Commentary.* Wilfrid Harrington and Donald Senior, editors. Collegeville, Minnesota: The Liturgical Press, 1980.

*The Women's Bible Commentary*, expanded edition. Carol A. Newsom and Sharon H. Ringe, editors. Louisville, Kentucky: Westminster/John Knox Press, 1998.

### Commentaries on the Gospel of Luke

Fitzmyer, Joseph A. *The Gospel according to Luke.* Garden City, New Jersey: Doubleday, 1981.

Kodell, Jerome. *The Gospel according to Luke.* Collegeville, Minnesota: The Liturgical Press, 1985.

LaVerdiere, Eugene. *Dining in the Kingdom of God: The Origins of the Eucharist according to Luke.* Chicago, Illinois: Liturgy Training Publications, 1994.

LaVerdiere, Eugene *Luke* (New Testament Message). Collegeville, Minnesota: The Liturgical Press, 1990.

# DECEMBER 3, 2000

## 1ST SUNDAY OF ADVENT

*Lectionary #3*

### READING I Jeremiah 33:14–16

**A reading from the book of the prophet Jeremiah**

Raise your voice in hope and encouragement. This is a solemn promise made by God.

The *days* are surely *coming*, says the Lord,
when I will *fulfil* the *promise*
I *made* to the house of *Israel*
and the house of *Judah*.

Stress words dealing with justice and righteousness. This is no ordinary ruler, but one who will make all things right. Lower your voice a bit, and speak in a more relaxed, assured tone.

In *those* days and at *that* time
I will cause a *righteous Branch* to spring *up* for *David*;
and he shall execute *justice* and *righteousness* in the land.

Pause before the final line, then read slowly and carefully. "In those days" even the name of Jerusalem will be changed to reflect the justice of God.

In those days *Judah* will be *saved*
and *Jerusalem* will live in *safety*.
And *this is* the name by which it will be called:
"The *Lord* is our *righteousness*."

READING I In the time of the prophet Jeremiah, Jerusalem was besieged and eventually conquered by the Babylonians. Many of the leading members of the community were sent into exile. Jeremiah is remembered as a prophet of doom, warning of the impending fall of the kingdom of Judah.

Despite Jeremiah's harsh words, the book of Jeremiah also offers messages of hope and comfort. In Jerusalem's darkest days, shortly before the Babylonians conquered it, Jeremiah defies the prevailing wisdom and offers hope. God will not forsake this people, he says. Instead, God's righteousness will prevail, put into action by a descendant of the royal house of David.

Christians believe that Jesus fulfills the hopes spoken by Jeremiah. Proclaim this brief passage with eagerness for justice, confident that it is available in Christ.

**1ST SUNDAY OF ADVENT ■ DECEMBER 3, 2000**

## READING II     1 Thessalonians 3:12—4:2

These are Paul's words of endearment to the Thessalonians. Speak lovingly.

**A reading from the first letter of Paul to the Thessalonians**

*Beloved*:
May the Lord make you *increase*
and *abound* in *love* for one *another* and for *all*,
just as *we* abound in love for *you*.
And may he so *strengthen* your hearts in *holiness*
that you may be *blameless* before our *God* and *Father*
at the *coming* of our Lord *Jesus* with all his *saints*.

Give strong emphasis to such terms as "holiness" and "blameless."

Pause before and after "that." Then read the next line (up to and including "God") a little more quickly, as an aside.

Finally you conclude the thought begun at the start of the paragraph. Raise your voice a bit and speak this line slowly and firmly. Close with a reminder that this is not a new teaching.

*Finally*, brothers and sisters,
we *ask* and *urge* you in the Lord *Jesus* that,
as you *learned* from *us* how you ought to *live* and to *please* God,
as, in fact, you *are* doing,
you should do so *more* and *more*.
For you *know* what *instructions*
       we gave you through the Lord *Jesus*.

---

READING II  One of the ways we prepare during Advent for Christ's coming is by personal spiritual discipline. When Christ lives in us and inspires our words and actions, we more truly become the people God calls us to be. This is precisely what Paul exhorts the Thessalonians to do as well.

Paul expects Christ to return soon in glory, and he wants the Christians in his communities to be ready for that day. He instructs them to live holy and pure lives so that God might be pleased with their conduct. When their hearts overflow with love, they will be blameless before God. Paul is not chastising the Thessalonians, who look to him for leadership and guidance, but he does remind them that they have more to learn about living upright lives. Paul offers himself

and the others who have ministered to the Thessalonians as models of Christian living.

Reflect on someone who has inspired you to lead a better life. Resolve to offer that same service to the people around you. And as you read these words encouraging holiness to the members of your community, pray that eventually all hearts might abound in love for one another.

DECEMBER 3, 2000 ■ 1ST SUNDAY OF ADVENT

## GOSPEL Luke 21:25–28, 34–36

**A reading from the holy gospel according to Luke**

Jesus spoke to his *disciples* about his *return* in *glory*.
"There will be *signs* in the *sun*, the *moon*, and the *stars*
and on the *earth distress* among *nations*
*confused* by the *roaring* of the *sea* and the *waves*.
People will *faint* from *fear* and *foreboding*
of what is *coming* upon the *world*,
for the *powers* of the heavens will be *shaken*.

"*Then* they will see 'the *Son* of *Man* coming in a *cloud*'
with *power* and *great glory*.
Now when these things begin to take *place*,
stand *up* and *raise* your *heads*,
because your *redemption* is drawing *near*.

"Be on *guard* so that your hearts are not weighed *down*
with *dissipation* and *drunkenness*
and the *worries* of this *life*,
and that *day* catch you *unexpectedly*, like a *trap*.
For it will come upon *all* who live on the *face* of the whole *earth*.
Be *alert* at all times,
*praying* that you may have the *strength*
to *escape* all these things that will take *place*,
and to *stand* before the *Son* of *Man*."

---

**Begin slowly and emphasize the various locations of the "signs." Pause briefly after "earth" before continuing with greater urgency.**
**Let some anxiety enter your voice.**

**With this line your voice should change. Speak slowly and with awe.**

**Offer these words as encouragement to your listeners. Speak with confidence.**

**Pause before beginning this section, and earnestly urge your community to reflect on matters of great importance.**

**Read this line quickly, as if the day is sneaking up on those who hear your words.**

**These final lines are key to this reading. Slow down and speak with encouragement and hope.**

---

GOSPEL **One of the comings of Christ we pray for during Advent is Christ's return as judge of the world. For the early Christians, the hope that Christ would soon return in glory was alive and active. Believing that he was truly the Messiah, the chosen one of God who sits at God's right hand, the earliest Christians believed that Christ would return to bring judgment.**

**Jesus' words in today's passage from the gospel of Luke suggest that the last days will be a time of terrible tribulation for most**

**of the world. Jesus asserts that the entire cosmos will be changed, and a sense of impending doom will prevail. For Christians, however, the last days will be a fulfillment of their hopes, if they live faithfully the life to which they have been called.**

**Jesus describes the glorious vision of the righteous judge, using words from the prophet Daniel. The members of Luke's community are instructed to welcome the last days with outstretched hands rather than cower in fright, as do those without hope. For Jesus' followers, the day will bring ransom and redemption, not fear. But this will**

**be so only if they follow the exhortations in the final paragraph, keeping themselves pure and eagerly awaiting Christ's return.**

**In Advent, we too recall that there is more to life than our daily concerns. As we prepare for the celebration of Christmas, we must also prepare our hearts for Jesus' presence in them, and our lives for our own final judgment. Proclaim this reading as encouragement to your community to look toward that day with eagerness rather than loathing, ready to stand before God in purity and hope.**

# DECEMBER 8, 2000

# IMMACULATE CONCEPTION

*Lectionary #689*

## READING I  Genesis 3:9–15, 20

**A reading from the book of Genesis**

When the *man* had *eaten* from the *tree*,
the Lord God *called* to him, and said, "Where *are* you?"
The man said, "I heard the *sound* of you in the *garden*,
and I was *afraid*, because I was *naked*; and I *hid* myself."

God said, "Who *told* you that you were *naked*?"
Have you *eaten* from the *tree*
of which I commanded you *not* to eat?"
The man said,
"The *woman* whom you gave to be *with* me,
*she* gave me *fruit* from the tree, and I *ate*."
Then the Lord God said to the *woman*,
"What *is* this that you have *done*?"
The woman said,
"The serpent *tricked* me, and I *ate*."

The Lord God said to the *serpent*,
"Because you have *done* this,
*cursed* are you among all *animals*
and among all wild *creatures*;
upon your *belly* you shall *go*,
and *dust* you shall *eat*
all the *days* of your *life*.

---

**Begin slowly. Allow God's question to sound genuine. In this story, God shows human attributes, even ignorance about what has happened.**

**The man is embarrassed.**

**God understands the situation now; let your voice express some indignation.**

**Adam sounds like a child trying to pass blame.**

**The woman's words also try to avoid responsibility.**

**Speak God's words firmly but without overemphasis.**

---

READING I   The stories in the early part of Genesis tell great truths about life. Today's reading gives an account of how sin entered the world and explains why human life can be difficult. Although God creates humans to dwell in paradise, this story indicates that we often overstep the boundaries of what is good for us, with dire results.

The story opens with a discussion between God and the man. When confronted with the truth of what he has done, the man instantly tries to blame the woman; the woman, in turn, points to the serpent. The

sin was a social action; it was something the pair chose to do together. But they are embarrassed when it becomes known and want to deny it.

God directs the punishment at the snake. The author attempts to explain the natural world: The reason that snakes crawl and that humans and snakes have a natural aversion to one another is the result of what happened in the garden. In fact, the whole story suggests that everything wrong in the world is the result of the choice of human

beings to reach beyond themselves, to act in ways that are reserved for God.

The final verse of the reading accords the woman great honor and is the reason this passage is chosen for today's feast. In a play on words ("Eve" means "life"), the woman is said to be the mother of all the living. This is somewhat similar to the promise of descendants given to Abraham; having many children was considered a great blessing to the Hebrews.

Mary, the new Eve, chose right instead of wrong and restored life where there was

DECEMBER 8, 2000 ▪ IMMACULATE CONCEPTION

enmity = EN-mih-tee

I will put *enmity* between *you* and the *woman*,
and between *your* offspring and *hers*;
he will *strike* your *head*,
and *you* will strike his *heel*."

The tone changes here; pause. Read this last verse with a bit more warmth and hope.

The man named his wife *"Eve,"*
because she was the *mother* of all the *living*.

---

### READING II    Ephesians 1:3–6, 11–12

**A reading from the letter of Paul to the Ephesians**

Open with a resounding word of praise. Read this as a joyous proclamation of honor to God.

*Blessed* be the *God* and *Father* of our *Lord* Jesus *Christ*,
who has *blessed* us in Christ
with *every spiritual blessing* in the heavenly *places*,
just as he *chose* us in Christ before the *foundation* of the *world*
to be *holy* and *blameless* before him in *love*.

The tone changes a bit with the second paragraph, becoming more explanatory.

He *destined* us for *adoption* as his *children*
through Jesus *Christ*,
according to the good *pleasure* of his *will*,
to the *praise* of his glorious *grace*
that he freely *bestowed* on us in the *Beloved*.

Our response to God's goodness is to offer praise and thanksgiving.

In *Christ* we have also obtained an *inheritance*,
having been *destined* according to the purpose of *him*
who accomplishes *all* things
according to his *counsel* and *will*,
so that *we*, who were the *first* to set our *hope* on *Christ*,
might *live* for the *praise* of his *glory*.

---

death. She reversed the downward spiral begun in Genesis by bearing the one who offers life to all. Because of her willingness to trust even what she did not understand, God truly made her the "mother of all the living."

READING II  In a tone of praise and thanksgiving, the author of the letter to the Ephesians reflects on the many blessings God bestows on humanity in

Christ. These are not mere physical blessings but are of a heavenly cast, and they have been intended from the beginning. Even before creation, God chose us to be adopted children. The human choice to thwart God's plan for us, recounted in the first reading, was undone even before it occurred. God chooses us to inherit all the blessings that rightfully belong to Christ.

The goal of all this—indeed the goal of all creation—is to offer praise to God, who makes it all possible. Because of God's tremendous love for us, God blesses us with

an abundance that we could never claim to deserve. The only response possible is praise and gratitude.

Speak these words with a tone of great sincerity. Emphasize terms such as "blessing" and "bestowed" to stress the lavish generosity of God. Then lift your voice in praise, and give glory to God!

## IMMACULATE CONCEPTION ▪ DECEMBER 8, 2000

---

**GOSPEL**  Luke 1:26–38

**A reading from the holy gospel according to Luke**

The angel *Gabriel* was sent by *God*
to a town in *Galilee* called *Nazareth*,
to a *virgin* engaged to a man whose name was *Joseph*,
of the house of *David*.
The virgin's *name* was *Mary*.

And he *came* to her and said,
"*Greetings*, favoured one! The *Lord* is *with* you."

But she was much *perplexed* by his words
and *pondered* what sort of *greeting* this might *be*.
The angel said to her, "Do not be *afraid*, Mary,
for you have found *favour* with *God*.
And now, you will *conceive* and bear a *son*,
and you will name him *Jesus*.
He will be *great*, and will be called the *Son* of the *Most High*,
and the *Lord God* will give to him
the *throne* of his ancestor *David*.
He will *reign* over the house of Jacob *forever*,
and of his *kingdom* there will be no *end*."

Mary said to the angel,
"How can this *be*, since I am a *virgin*?"

The angel said to her,
"The *Holy Spirit* will come *upon* you,
and the *power* of the *Most High* will ov*ershadow* you;
therefore the *child* to be born will be *holy*;
he will be called *Son* of *God*.

---

**Pause slightly after "name" to give emphasis to Mary's name.**

**Speak these words with joy, but also with a sense of their importance.**

**Jesus' name is significant. Emphasize it.**

**Mary is puzzled.**

---

GOSPEL Although today's feast celebrates the conception of Mary, the gospel reading is an account of the conception of Jesus. Stories about Mary's own origins are relatively late, but she is remembered for her important role in giving life to the true life-giver. As we prepare our hearts for receiving Christ this season, this reading is appropriate and honors Mary for her trusting "Yes!" to God.

The story is familiar but deserves all the attention, preparation and fresh presentation one might give to any text. It is the story of a young girl who experiences a most extraordinary event—the appearance of an angel—and is given an even more extraordinary promise.

The angel Gabriel begins by indicating the favor God has bestowed on Mary and explains what this means: Her child will be given both honor and a mission. The name of this child—Jesus—bears special import. In Hebrew, the name means "he will save." The angel does not tell Mary what Jesus'

saving actions will involve, only the glory due him. The pain that Mary will come to know remains shrouded in the dark silence of her womb.

Mary's question ("How can this be?") brings us back to the situation at hand. The angel explains that this is no ordinary child but will be called holy. Indeed, he will be the ruler in the line of David for whom Israel has longed. Writing long after Jesus' humiliating death and triumphant resurrection, the author knows that the reign of this child will not be earthly, nor will he be enthroned in a

DECEMBER 8, 2000 ■ IMMACULATE CONCEPTION

And now, your relative *Elizabeth*
in her *old age* has *also* conceived a *son;*
and this is the *sixth* month for her who was said to be *barren.*
For *nothing* will be impossible with *God."*

Then Mary said,
*"Here* am *I,* the *servant* of the *Lord;*
let it *be* with *me* according to your *word."*
Then the angel *departed* from her.

**Pause before concluding. Then read Mary's words with solemn conviction.**

palace. But in him the hopes of Israel find true and lasting fulfillment.

Mary is confused, perhaps frightened, but in the end her response is firm: Yes, Lord, whatever you will. Her humble response to this awesome message is an inspiration for all times. She simply, quietly, opens her heart to God's word and accepts her role in birthing the savior. Her trust in God's goodness will lead her down paths she could never have imagined.

As we honor Mary today, it is appropriate to remember her for her strength and conviction, the characteristics attributed to her in the gospel of Luke, from which most of our knowledge of Mary comes. Only a few verses after the conclusion of this story is Mary's Magnificat, a song of praise to God for turning the world on its head. Not only has God chosen a young Jewish girl to bear the hope of the world, but God has brought down the wealthy and powerful, giving honor to the lowly and disenfranchised. God is to be found not in palaces but in the humble hearts of those who have nothing.

Read this story as though for the first time. Allow the characters to come to life for you and for your assembly. And honor Mary by presenting her as the quietly forceful woman of conviction she was.

## DECEMBER 10, 2000

# 2ND SUNDAY OF ADVENT

*Lectionary #6*

### READING I    Baruch 5:1–9

**A reading from the book of the prophet Baruch**

> Speak joyfully and urgently. This is a time for rejoicing, not for sorrow.

Take *off* the garment of your *sorrow* and *affliction*, O Jerusalem,
and put on *forever* the *beauty* of the *glory* from *God*.

> Let your voice reflect wonder at the beauty of these garments. But also emphasize the theme of justice, from which the clothing is fashioned.

Put on the *robe* of the *righteousness* that comes from *God*;
put on your *head* the *diadem* of the *glory* of the *Everlasting*;
for *God* will show your splendour *everywhere* under heaven.
For *God* will give you *evermore* the name,
"*Righteous Peace, Godly Glory.*"

> Raise your voice with excitement, as though you are encouraging someone with spectacular news.

*Arise*, O Jerusalem, *stand* upon the *height*;
*look* toward the *east*,
and see your *children* gathered from *west* and *east*
at the *word* of the *Holy* One,
*rejoicing* that God has *remembered* them.

> The humiliation of defeat and exile is reversed.

For they went *out* from you on *foot*,
led away by their *enemies*;
but *God* will bring them *back* to you,
carried in *glory*, as on a royal *throne*.

> The author recounts how God has changed the desert terrain to prepare the way for the exiles' return. Speak with wonder at God's care for the people.

For *God* has *ordered* that every high *mountain*
and the everlasting *hills* be made *low*
and the *valleys* filled *up*, to make level *ground*,
so that *Israel* may walk *safely* in the *glory* of *God*.
The *woods* and every fragrant *tree*
have *shaded* Israel at God's *command*.

---

READING I The book of Baruch reflects back on the experience of the Babylonian exile of the Hebrew people. The Babylonians were able to conquer Jerusalem and take its leaders into captivity because of the sinfulness of the chosen people. But the Israelites learned from their experience. Today's passage joyfully recounts how personified Jerusalem is decked out in glory and awaiting her children as they return from their exile.

While the people were held captive in Babylon, Jerusalem lay in ruins. The image here is of a woman in mourning, wearing sackcloth. But she is told to leave her garments of sorrow behind and dress in splendid royal robes and a crown. Her clothes are not merely rich and beautiful, though; they are the garments of righteousness and God's glory, and they will give Jerusalem her new name, a sign of her restored existence.

Today's reading pictures a woman, Jerusalem, looking out from the heights at her children, the exiles, returning to her. God brings them back in glory, making the traveling easy, an honor that would be accorded royalty. It is a day of great rejoicing, and God's righteousness is evident.

It can be difficult to imagine Israel's experience of exile. Perhaps it helps to think of refugees driven from their homeland and yearning to return. Here, God's people are coming home to their beloved Jerusalem. In Advent, we are coming home, too. We journey through this season of darkness, yearning for the light. But we have hope that we will be restored, for we know that God's promises are true. Read this selection in joyful expectation of that glorious day when

DECEMBER 10, 2000 ■ 2ND SUNDAY OF ADVENT

**Close with a confident proclamation of God's goodness and righteousness.**

For *God* will lead Israel with *joy*,
in the *light* of his *glory*,
with the *mercy* and *righteousness* that come from *him*.

---

### READING II    Philippians 1:3–6, 8–11

**A reading from the letter of Paul to the Philippians**

**Offer this as a prayer for your own community. Speak earnestly and with joy.**

My *brothers* and *sisters*,
I *thank* my *God* every time I *remember* you,
*constantly* praying with *joy*
in *every* one of my *prayers* for *all* of you,
because of your *sharing* in the *gospel*
from the *first* day until *now*.

**Raise your voice a bit, and speak more boldly.**

I am *confident* of *this*,
that the one who *began* a good work among you
will bring it to *completion* by the *day* of Jesus *Christ*.

**Stress "long." Pause before continuing.**

For *God* is my *witness*,
how I *long* for all of you
with the *compassion* of Christ *Jesus*.
And *this* is my *prayer*,

**Speak forcefully, slowly and confidently from here to the end.**

that your *love* may *overflow* more and more
with *knowledge* and full *insight*
so that in the *day* of *Christ*
you may be *pure* and *blameless*,
having produced the *harvest* of *righteousness*
that comes through Jesus *Christ*
for the *glory* and *praise* of *God*.

---

**God's reign will be universally recognized, and justice and righteousness will prevail.**

READING II   Paul was very fond of the community in Philippi, as this reading makes clear. Here he expresses in a range of emotions how he feels about this church that he nurtured and guided. He is thankful for its members, confident of their progress in the faith, and longs to see them grow more and more in love and understanding. In that way, they will produce the "harvest of justice" that gives glory to God.

During Advent we reflect on God's promises, which we believe are fulfilled in Jesus. At the same time, we recognize that God's promises in Christ have yet to be fully realized, and we joyfully await and work toward the time when God's righteousness will be evident to all.

Paul speaks of the same reality in his words to the Philippians. Christ has begun the "good work" in them, but it must be brought to completion. They, as we, are an Advent people, on a journey to greater recognition of the love of God. Paul prays that

their love may increase. It is a fitting prayer for any community.

Offer this message to your own listeners with all the hope, joy and confidence that Paul expresses. Reflect on the ways that your community lives the gospel, and speak tenderly in gratitude for such action. Pray also that each member of your assembly will continue to grow in love and will contribute to an abundant harvest of righteousness.

GOSPEL   The gospel of Luke places Jesus squarely in the center of world history. Jesus is not simply a fringe

# 10

2ND SUNDAY OF ADVENT ■ DECEMBER 10, 2000

The first half of the reading is background historical information.
Tiberius = tī-BEER-ee-uhs
Pontius Pilate = PON-shuhs Pī-luht
Judea = joo-DEE-uh
Herod = HAYR-uhd
Galilee = GAL-ih-lee
Ituraea = ih-too-REE-ah
Trachonitis = trak-uh-NĪ-tis
Lysanias = lī-SAY-nee-uhs
Abilene = ab-uh-LEE-nee
Pause after "Caiaphas," then proceed slowly and forcefully. This is the turning point of the passage.
Annas = AN-uhs
Caiaphas = KĪ-uh-fuhs
Zechariah = zek-uh-RĪ-uh

Brighten your tone with this line.
Exhort your community to "prepare."

Close with a sense of joy and fulfillment.
This is what we are hoping and waiting for!

## GOSPEL  Luke 3:1–6

### A reading from the gospel according to Luke

In the *fifteenth* year of the reign of Emperor *Tiberius,*
when *Pontius Pilate* was *governor* of *Judea,*
and *Herod* was ruler of *Galilee,*
and his brother *Philip*
ruler of the region of *Ituraea* and *Trachonitis,*
and *Lysanias* ruler of *Abilene,*
during the high *priesthood* of *Annas* and *Caiphas,*
the *word* of *God* came to *John* son of *Zechariah* in the *wilderness.*

He went into *all* the region around the *Jordan,*
proclaiming a *baptism* of *repentance* for the *forgiveness* of *sins,*
as it is *written* in the book of the *words* of the prophet *Isaiah,*
"The *voice* of one *crying out* in the *wilderness:*
'*Prepare* the way of the *Lord,* make his paths *straight.*
Every *valley* shall be *filled,*
and every *mountain* and *hill* shall be made *low,*
and the *crooked* shall be made *straight,*
and the *rough* ways made *smooth;*
and *all flesh* shall *see* the *salvation* of *God.'*"

---

character but alters the world and history forever. At the same time, he is the answer to the hopes of Israel. For this reason the author also stresses Jewish history in this section, detailing the rulers of the various regions and the high priests of the Jewish temple. Jesus fulfills the expectations of the Hebrew people and answers the unrecognized need of the entire world as well. He is indeed the savior of all the world.

After situating the story of Jesus within history, the narrative turns to the person of John the Baptist. He is neither ruler nor priest, but one who fulfills the words of the prophets. His role is to prepare for the coming of God. In a rough, mountainous region, the claim that all roads will be made level testifies to the importance of the person who is expected. The Lord is to be treated like royalty.

What John proclaims, however, is a "baptism of repentance for the forgiveness of sins." The most effective way to prepare for the Messiah is to repent. The person who receives John's baptism expresses a sincere sorrow for sin and a resolution to change, to turn a stone heart into one of flesh.

We spend Advent waiting, preparing. We prepare in practical ways for the celebration of Christmas, with its feasting, exchanges of gifts, and time spent with loved ones. But we also prepare our hearts, creating a place for Jesus to dwell and examining our lives to prepare for that final day when we will meet God face to face. How can we best straighten the roads and level the paths, so that God may more easily come to us? John suggests one way: turning away from sin and starting fresh.

## DECEMBER 17, 2000

# 3RD SUNDAY OF ADVENT

*Lectionary #9*

### READING I   Zephaniah 3:14–18a

Zephaniah = zef-uh-NĪ-uh

**A reading from the book of the prophet Zephaniah**

Raise your voice and proclaim this with joy.

*Sing* aloud, O daughter *Zion; shout,* O *Israel!*
*Rejoice* and *exult* with *all* your *heart,*
O *daughter* of *Jerusalem!*

There is comfort in these words.

The *Lord* has taken *away* the *judgments against* you,
he has turned *away* your *enemies.*
The *king* of Israel, the *Lord,* is in your *midst;*
you shall fear *disaster* no *more.*

Speak this as a promise of God's goodness.

On that *day* it shall be said to *Jerusalem*:
Do not *fear,* O *Zion;*
do not let your *hands* grow *weak.*
The *Lord,* your *God,* is in your *midst,*
a *warrior* who gives *victory;*

Again, lift your voice and exult in God's love.

he will *rejoice* over you with *gladness,*
he will *renew* you in his *love;*
The *Lord,* your *God,* will *exult* over you with loud *singing*
as on a *day* of *festival.*

---

**READING I** Today, Gaudete Sunday, we raise our voices in praise of our God, who promises to come to us soon! The exultant words of the prophet Zephaniah ring in our ears, and we believe that the promises proclaimed here are addressed to us as well.

Zephaniah lived in a time when the kingdom of Judah enjoyed political independence; it was not responsible to any superior foreign power. It was a time of religious renewal as well, and much of Zephaniah's prophecy was directed toward this need. Today's reading, however, celebrates the new people formed by God. On the day when all God's people respond in faithfulness, God will cease to judge them and will proclaim them victorious.

As we approach the shortest days and darkest time of the year, when we are busy with the many demands of this season, it is good to be reminded that God is on our side. Proclaim this passage with enthusiasm and a tone of comfort, so that your community can be reminded of God's tremendous love for them. And rejoice! God is in our midst.

**3RD SUNDAY OF ADVENT ▪ DECEMBER 17, 2000**

---

**READING II**  Philippians 4:4–7

**A reading from the letter of Paul to the Philippians**

*The passage begins on a strong note. Be sure that you have the attention of your listeners before beginning. Then proclaim these words with all your energy.*

*Read this line slowly and with promise.*

*These words are meant to strengthen your community. Read them with sincerity and encouragement.*

*Pause, then continue with assurance of the peace available in God.*

*Rejoice* in the Lord *always;*
*again* I will say, *Rejoice.*

Let your *gentleness* be known to *everyone.*
The *Lord* is *near.*
Do not *worry* about *anything,*
but in *everything* let your *requests* be made *known* to *God*
by *prayer* and *supplication* with *thanksgiving.*

And the *peace* of *God,*
which *surpasses* all *understanding,*
will guard your *hearts* and your *minds* in Christ *Jesus.*

---

**GOSPEL**  Luke 3:10–18

**A reading from the holy gospel according to Luke**

The *crowds,* who were gathering to be *baptized* by *John,*
     asked him,
"*What* should we *do?*"
In *reply* John said to them,
"Whoever has *two* coats must *share* with anyone who has *none;*
and whoever has *food* must do *likewise.*"

*John's replies are solemn and demanding. Speak them slowly to allow their importance to sink in.*

Even *tax* collectors came to be *baptized,*
and they *asked* him,
"*Teacher,* what should *we* do?"

---

READING II  Paul reveals his fondness for the Philippian community in the words that begin our passage, words that fairly sing out, "Rejoice!" This proclamation reflects this Sunday's name, "Gaudete" Sunday (*gaudete* means "rejoice" in Latin). Paul is proud of the Philippian church and commends the members of the community on their kindness. He further encourages them to offer their concerns to God in prayer and thanksgiving; in this way the community will come to know God's

own peace. Paul expects the second coming of Christ to occur soon, and encourages his churches to be ready for it.

Reflect with fondness on your own community and the ways in which it makes God's presence known in the world. Then proclaim to your assembly the exultant message: Rejoice! Read the rest of the passage with gentle encouragement, so that your listeners will know that they can truly turn to God with every need.

At this hectic time of year, we need to hear the promise of peace for our hearts. Strive to do what Paul advocates—to let go of anxieties and trust in God—so that you can communicate a sense of joyful peace to your assembly.

GOSPEL  John the Baptist was a popular preacher, a messenger of reform and renewed commitment to God. As today's gospel illustrates, he preached justice and proclaimed the dawn of a new

DECEMBER 17, 2000 ■ 3RD SUNDAY OF ADVENT

He said to them,
"Collect *no more* than the amount *prescribed* for you."
*Soldiers* also asked him,
"And *we*, what should *we* do?"
He said to them,
"Do *not* extort *money* from *anyone* by *threats*
        or false *accusation*,
and be *satisfied* with your *wages*."

As the people were *filled* with *expectation*,
and *all* were *questioning* in their *hearts* concerning *John*,
whether he might be the *Messiah*,
John answered *all* of them by saying,
"*I* baptize you with *water*;
but one who is more *powerful* than I is *coming*;
I am not *worthy* to *untie* the *thong* of his *sandals*.
*He* will baptize you with the *Holy Spirit* and *fire*.
His *winnowing* fork is in his *hand*,
to *clear* his *threshing* floor
and to gather the *wheat* into his *granary*;
but the *chaff* he will *burn* with unquenchable *fire*."

So, with many other *exhortations*,
John proclaimed the *good news* to the *people*.

**Stress the contrast between John and Jesus.**

**Let your voice grow in strength as John describes the one who is coming.**

**Pause after "fire," then conclude on a quieter note.**

age. To those who have plenty (two coats instead of one!), he notes the importance of sharing with those in need. People in positions of power—tax collectors, soldiers— are not to use their positions for their own advantage but are to accept only their due. The people hearing this are "filled with expectation." The vast majority of the people at the time were struggling to survive, burdened by extremely high taxes and living in uncertainty. John proclaims that things can change.

The followers of John and those of Jesus were apparently rivals for the attention of the masses. But in today's gospel, John makes it clear that he is not the one for whom the Hebrew people are waiting. One who is even greater than John is coming. John's baptism is with water only, but the Messiah will baptize with the Holy Spirit and fire. Finally, John speaks of a coming judge who will bring fire and burn what is not worthy or useful.

There is both comfort and challenge in this message. Offer this gospel to your assembly as a reminder to live justly, with concern for the powerless, in order to be counted among the righteous.

**DECEMBER 24, 2000**

# 4TH SUNDAY OF ADVENT

*Lectionary #12*

## READING I    Micah 5:2–5a

**A reading from the book of the prophet Micah**

The *Lord* says to his *people*:
"*You*, O Bethlehem of Ephrathah,
who are one of the *little* clans of *Judea*,
from *you* shall come *forth* for me
one who is to *rule* in *Israel*,
whose *origin* is from of *old*, from ancient *days*."

*Therefore* he shall give them *up* until the time
when she who is in *labour* has brought *forth*;
then the *rest* of his kindred
shall *return* to the *people* of Israel.
And he shall *stand* and *feed* his *flock*
in the *strength* of the *Lord*,
in the *majesty* of the *name* of the *Lord* his *God*.

And they shall live *secure*,
for *now* he shall be *great* to the *ends* of the *earth*;
and he shall be the one of *peace*.

---

Bethlehem = BETH-luh-hem
Ephrathah = EF-ruh-thuh

Pause, then alter your voice slightly to indicate that the quote has ended.

Speak warmly as you read this image of a ruler who acts as a shepherd. This is the legacy of David, the shepherd who became the greatest ruler of Israel.

Read firmly and slowly, with a sense of majesty. Conclude with a strong voice to emphasize the idea of peace.

---

READING I    The prophet Micah was active during the time of Assyrian threat against the kingdom of Judah. Micah offers this prophecy of hope in the Davidic line to a people fearing catastrophe. His advice is to trust that God will work through the royal family, bringing a ruler who will know how to care for the people. In fact, Jerusalem did not fall to the Assyrians.

This prophecy has special meaning for Christians, who look to Jesus as its fulfillment. A descendant of David whose "origin is from of old," he is the king Israel awaits and will rule as a shepherd, lovingly guiding his flock. Jesus' reign is universal, and with it comes profound peace.

As our Advent preparation draws to a close, this passage offers hope and comfort to an expectant people. Speak it with a sense of gratitude and wonder. Tiny, insignificant Bethlehem is the source of the greatest of all gifts to the world! Finally, close with a firm, confident proclamation that in Jesus is true peace.

DECEMBER 24, 2000 ■ 4TH SUNDAY OF ADVENT

## READING II    Hebrews 10:5–10

**A reading from the letter to the Hebrews**

When *Christ* came into the *world*, he said,
"*Sacrifices* and *offerings* you have not *desired*,
but a *body* you have *prepared* for me;
in *burnt* offerings and *sin* offerings
you have taken *no pleasure*.
Then *I* said,
as it is *written* of me in the *scroll* of the *book*,
'*See*, God, I have *come* to do your *will*, O God.'"

When Christ said,
"You have neither *desired* nor taken *pleasure*
in *sacrifices* and *offerings*
and *burnt* offerings and *sin* offerings"
(these are offered according to the *law*),
then he added,
"*See*, I have *come* to do your *will*."
He *abolishes* the first
in order to *establish* the second.

And it is by God's *will* that we have been *sanctified*
through the *offering* of the *body* of Jesus *Christ*
once for *all*.

---

**Lift your voice as you begin the quotation. The author places the words of Psalm 40 in Jesus' mouth.**

**The passage is still quoting the psalmist. The "I" is now understood to be the statement of Jesus. Slow down for these lines, so that the significance of Jesus' claim to be doing God's will can be heard.**

**That is, the sacrifices of the Jewish law are no longer relevant, since Jesus has fulfilled the will of God.**

---

READING II   In a book that repeatedly refers to the work of Christ in terms reminiscent of the cult of Israel, this passage from Hebrews claims that the offerings of the past are abolished. There is only the pure offering of Christ, given "once for all," unique and universal in its impact. The author presents Christ speaking the words of a psalm that rejects ritual sacrifice in favor of doing God's will.

This mention of God's will reminds us of Jesus' words in the Garden of Gethsemane just before his betrayal and arrest: "Not my will, but yours." In Christ is summed up the will of God; he was obedient even to the point of death. This reminder of Christ's obedience to death connects our celebration of Advent and Christmas to that of the Triduum. The incarnation, the coming of God into the world in human form, is fulfilled in the triumph of the cross and the glory of the resurrection.

Keep in mind Jesus' sacrifice on the cross as you read this difficult passage. By doing so, you will remind your assembly that the central Christian feast is not Christmas but Easter. The purpose of Christ's coming into the world—which we celebrate on Christmas—was to die and, by his death and resurrection, to conquer death forever.

# 4TH SUNDAY OF ADVENT ▪ DECEMBER 24, 2000

## GOSPEL  Luke 1:39–45

**A reading from the gospel according to Luke**

*Mary* set *out* and went with *haste*
to a Judean town in the *hill* country,
where she entered the house of *Zechariah*
and greeted *Elizabeth*.

When *Elizabeth* heard Mary's *greeting*,
the child *leaped* in her *womb*.
And Elizabeth was *filled* with the Holy *Spirit*
and *exclaimed* with a loud *cry*,
"*Blessed* are *you* among *women*,
and *blessed* is the *fruit* of your *womb*.
And why has this happened to *me*,
that the *mother* of my *Lord comes* to me?
For as *soon* as I heard the *sound* of your *greeting*,
the *child* in my *womb leaped* for *joy*.
And *blessed* is *she* who *believed*
that there would be a *fulfilment*
of what was *spoken* to her by the *Lord*."

*Convey Mary's haste by speaking somewhat quickly, but not at the expense of clarity. Continue at a normal, relaxed, pace.*
Zechariah = zek-uh-RĪ-uh

*Give great emphasis to "leaped" and "filled." This is exciting news!*
leaped = lept

*Speak these familiar words slowly.*

*Elizabeth's question is humble and genuine. Raise your voice in question for the first "me," not the second.*

*Offer this as a real blessing from one joyful expectant mother to another who has trusted completely in God.*

---

GOSPEL  Last Sunday's gospel spoke of John's role as forerunner of the Messiah. Although John preached a message of radical newness and of righteous actions, he was pointing to the one who would be given dominion and power to judge the world. Today, in a passage from earlier in the same gospel, John has his first encounter with Jesus. Even in his mother's womb, John recognizes the superiority of Mary's child, and he is overjoyed at the coming of the Christ to the world.

This story's first encounter, however, occurs between the two pregnant women, filled with joy and hope. In her ecstatic blessing of Mary, Elizabeth speaks for all who await the coming of the Lord and expresses her wonder at the presence of God on earth. It is this wonder that we experience as we come ever closer to the celebration of God's coming to earth as one of us.

Immediately following today's passage in the gospel of Luke is the Magnificat, Mary's beautiful song of praise. In it she envisions a world in which the wealthy and powerful are cast down, while the lowly are

exalted. In this she anticipates the teaching of John and of Jesus. Her child brings a righteousness that will transform the world.

Take care to proclaim this passage with the exuberance and awe that Elizabeth felt.

DECEMBER 24, 2000

# CHRISTMAS VIGIL

*Lectionary #13*

**READING I** Isaiah 62:1–5

**A reading from the book of the prophet Isaiah**

The Lord says this:
"For *Zion's* sake I will not keep *silent*,
and for *Jerusalem's* sake I will not *rest*,
until her vindication *shines out* like the *dawn*,
and her *salvation* like a burning *torch*.

"The *nations* shall see your *vindication*,
and all the *kings* your *glory*;
and you shall be *called* by a *new* name
that the *mouth* of the *Lord* will *give*.
You shall be a crown of *beauty* in the *hand* of the *Lord*,
and a royal *diadem* in the *hand* of your *God*.

"You shall no *more* be termed 'Forsaken,'
and your *land* shall no more be termed 'Desolate';
but *you* shall be called 'My *Delight* Is in *Her*,'
and your *land* 'Married';
for the Lord *delights* in you,
and your *land* shall be *married*.

"For as a young *man* marries a young *woman*,
so shall your *builder* marry *you*,
and as the *bridegroom rejoices* over the *bride*,
so shall your *God* rejoice over *you*."

*Let your voice be heard loud and clear;
you are the prophet's mouthpiece.*

*Jerusalem will shine forth in splendor for
all to see. Proclaim these words with
great joy.*

*diadem = DĪ-uh-dem*

*Pause briefly before and after the words in
quotation marks so that they can be heard
as names.*

*Let tenderness fill your voice.*

**READING I** Written at the end of the exile in Babylon, this passage declares the importance of the holy city Jerusalem for the Hebrew people and the renewed blessings God will bestow on it. The exile was understood as a punishment for wrongdoing; the destruction of Jerusalem and the temple gave witness to the barrenness of its former inhabitants. But all that is over; what matters now is that God has forgiven the sins of the people and

Jerusalem is to be restored to glory. The vindication of the city and its inhabitants is for all the world to know and see.

Jerusalem's "new name" is significant; the name of something indicates its very essence. Jacob's name was changed to Israel as a sign of the change in his life; Jerusalem's new titles indicate that the status of the city (and of the people who reside within it) has changed. Perhaps the most famous instance of assigning names of particular significance occurs in the story of the prophet Hosea, whose children bear

names that reflect their mother's faithlessness (and by implication the faithlessness of Israel). However, their names are altered in the end to represent the conversion of Israel after God woos the people into a new committed relationship of love.

The former names of Israel in today's passage are reflected also in an earlier passage of the book of Isaiah (54:1–8). There, exiled Judah is called barren and is compared with a desolate woman. Although the terms can also be applied to agricultural

CHRISTMAS VIGIL ▪ DECEMBER 24, 2000

Antioch = AN-tee-ahk

Raise your voice over the crowd, just as Paul must have done.

Paul gives a brief history of Israel, concentrating especially on David and God's favor to him.

Although the Davidic dynasty no longer rules Israel, God's promises to David are realized in the person of Jesus.

Speak with humility and conviction.

## READING II    Acts 13:16–17, 22–25

**A reading from the Acts of the Apostles**

When *Paul* arrived in *Antioch*,
he stood *up* in the *synagogue*,
held up his hand for *silence*, and began to *speak:*

"You *Israelites*, and *others* who fear God, *listen.*
The *God* of this people *Israel* chose our *ancestors*
and made the people *great* during their *stay* in the land of *Egypt*,
and with uplifted *arm* he led them *out* of it.

"When God made *David* their *king*,
in his *testimony* about him he said,
'I have found *David*, son of *Jesse*, to be a man after my *heart*,
who will carry out *all* my *wishes.*'

"Of this man's *posterity God* has brought to Israel a *Saviour*, *Jesus*,
as he *promised*;
*before* his coming
*John* had already proclaimed a *baptism* of *repentance*
to *all* the people of *Israel.*
And as John was *finishing* his work, he said,
'What do you suppose that I *am*?
*I* am *not* he.
No, but one is coming *after* me;
I am not *worthy* to untie the *thong* of the *sandals* on his *feet.*'"

---

devastation, the introduction of a woman into the imagery and the play on the word for "married" reflect the status of women in Hebrew society. Marriage and children were seen as the greatest blessings a woman could receive, and the lack of them could be understood as punishment. But the use of terms related to commitment and the close bond of family ties is especially appropriate when applied to God's relationship of love and commitment with the chosen people.

Today's passage affirms the honor that will be given Jerusalem. It will be crowned and revered as royalty, espoused to God. The wedding of a monarch was always cause for great celebration in antiquity (as it often is today) and the passage reflects that joy. The desolation of old is left behind, and the bridegroom (God) professes delight with the bride. The restored Jerusalem will enter into a new and deeper relationship with God, one marked by the passion of newlyweds.

Allow the joy of this passage to ring out in your words. Just as Christians joyfully celebrate the union of divine and human in

the person of Jesus, so also the Hebrew people knew that they were to be intimately united with God. Let the newness of the marriage you announce remind your hearers of the renewed relationship possible with God, based as it is on the new covenant inaugurated by Jesus.

READING II The author of the Acts of the Apostles always depicts Paul proclaiming the gospel first in the

DECEMBER 24, 2000 ■ CHRISTMAS VIGIL

## GOSPEL Matthew 1:1–25

**A reading from the holy gospel according to Matthew**

An *account* of the *genealogy* of Jesus the *Messiah*,
the son of *David*, the son of *Abraham*.

*Abraham* was the *father* of *Isaac*,
*Isaac* the father of *Jacob*,
*Jacob* the father of *Judah* and his *brothers*,
*Judah* the father of *Perez* and *Zerah* by *Tamar*,
*Perez* the father of *Hezron*,
*Hezron* the father of *Aram*,
*Aram* the father of *Aminadab*,
*Aminadab* the father of *Nahshon*,
*Nahshon* the father of *Salmon*,
*Salmon* the father of *Boaz* by *Rahab*,
*Boaz* the father of *Obed* by *Ruth*,
*Obed* the father of *Jesse*,
and *Jesse* the father of King *David*.

And *David* was the father of *Solomon* by the *wife* of *Uriah*,
*Solomon* the father of *Rehoboam*,
*Rehoboam* the father of *Abijah*,
*Abijah* the father of *Asaph*,
*Asaph* the father of *Jehoshaphat*,
*Jehoshaphat* the father of *Joram*,
*Joram* the father of *Uzziah*,
*Uzziah* the father of *Jotham*,
*Jotham* the father of *Ahaz*,
*Ahaz* the father of *Hezekiah*,
*Hezekiah* the father of *Manasseh*,
*Manasseh* the father of *Amos*,

---

Take a deep breath before beginning this long list of Jesus' ancestors. Take your time as you read, and convey the importance of family in what could otherwise be a wearying selection.

Perez = PAYR-ez, Zerah = ZEE-rah

Tamar = TAY-mahr

Hezron = HEZ-ruhn

Aram = AYR-uhm

Aminadab = uh-MIN-uh-dab

Nahshon = NAH-shuhn, Salmon = SAL-muhn,

Boaz = BOH-az, Rahab = RAY-hab

Obed = OH-bed

Pause briefly before beginning the next section.

Uriah = yoo-RI-uh

Rehoboam = ree-huh-BOH-uhm

Abijah = uh-BI-juh

Asaph = AY-saf

Jehoshaphat = jeh-HOH-shuh-fat

Joram = JOHR-uhm

Uzziah = uh-ZI-uh

Jotham = JOH-thuhm

Ahaz = AY-haz

Hezekiah = hez-eh-KI-uh

Manasseh = muh-NAS-uh

Amos = AY-m*hs

---

Jewish synagogue, turning to the Gentiles only after being rejected there. Paul himself gives us a quite different picture of his mission. Whatever the historical reality, the speech in today's reading provides Paul with the opportunity to indicate that the new revelation in Jesus is the fulfillment of God's promises to David. Jesus does not simply arrive in the world from nowhere, but was born into a people chosen by God and given

protection and guidance through many travails. God promised eternal favor to the descendants of David.

Although the Davidic monarchy suffered through exile, foreign occupation and defeat, the Jews continued to hope that a descendant of David would arise and restore the people to right relationship with God. In today's speech, Paul indicates that Jesus is that descendant, the savior of Israel. And it was John, the revered preacher of repentance, who declared Jesus to be the one for whom Israel was waiting.

Read this passage as a claim that God's promises are always kept. Allow John's humble words to inspire you and your listeners, so that you may celebrate the manifestation of God in the world in humility and joy.

GOSPEL In today's passage, Matthew's author offers a message similar to that of Paul in Acts. Jesus came into the world as part of a particular people and a particular family. It is this particularity that

CHRISTMAS VIGIL ■ DECEMBER 24, 2000

Josiah = joh-SĪ-uh

Jechoniah = jek-oh-NĪ-uh


**Pause briefly before beginning the next section.**

Salathiel = suh-LAY-thee-uhl

Zerubbabel = zuh-R**OO**B-uh-b*l

Abiud = uh-BĪ-uhd

Eliakim = ee-LĪ-uh-kim

Azor = AY-zohr

Zadok = ZAY-dok

Achim = AH-kim

Eliud = ee-LĪ-uhd

Eleazar = el-ee-AY-zer

Matthan = MATH-uhn


**This is the announcement for which your assembly has been waiting. Slow down and proclaim it solemnly.**


**Pause again before beginning the story about Joseph. Proceed with an animated voice.**

*Amos* father of *Josiah*,
and *Josiah* the father of *Jechoniah* and his *brothers*,
at the time of the *deportation* to *Babylon*.

And *after* the deportation to *Babylon*:
*Jechoniah* was the father of *Salathiel*,
*Salathiel* the father of *Zerubbabel*,
*Zerubbabel* the father of *Abiud*,
*Abiud* the father of *Eliakim*,
*Eliakim* the father of *Azor*,
*Azor* the father of *Zadok*,
*Zadok* the father of *Achim*,
*Achim* the father of *Eliud*,
*Eliud* the father of *Eleazar*,
*Eleazar* the father of *Matthan*,
*Matthan* the father of *Jacob*,
and *Jacob* the father of *Joseph* the husband of *Mary*,
of whom *Jesus* was born,
who is called the *Messiah*.

So all the generations from Abraham to David
      are fourteen generations;
from *David* to the deportation to *Babylon*, *fourteen* generations;
from the deportation to *Babylon* to the *Messiah*,
      *fourteen* generations.

Now the *birth* of Jesus the *Messiah* took place in *this* way.
When his mother *Mary* had been engaged to *Joseph*,
but before they *lived* together,
she was found to be with *child* from the Holy *Spirit*.

is often baffling to non-Christians: How could God be present in such ordinariness? But that is what Christians claim, as we acknowledge Jesus' human ancestry and proclaim that he truly is one of us.

The long genealogical list establishes Jesus as one who inherited both the blessings and the struggles of the Hebrew people. His lineage is traced back to Abraham, the original recipient of God's promises of favor and protection. He is the descendant of David as well, whose royal house was to endure forever. Jesus' ancestors survived

the exile in Babylon, the humiliation of being deported to a foreign land, and the joy of returning home again. Jesus received all the hopes and dreams of his people at his birth: the covenant established with Abraham; the Davidic dynasty; the struggles for independence from foreign powers. Jesus was fully human and profoundly Jewish.

While Luke emphasizes the role of Mary in the story of Jesus' conception and birth, the gospel of Matthew focuses on Joseph.

Joseph is the noble one, unwilling to embarrass Mary, found pregnant before their marriage, and willing to accept God's will without fully understanding it. The divine messenger who appeared to Mary in Luke appears instead to Joseph in Matthew with the astonishing news of an unusual conception. To Joseph is given the command to name the child Jesus, which means "he will save" in Hebrew.

Just as in the gospel of Luke, the purpose of the story of Jesus' conception and

DECEMBER 24, 2000 ■ CHRISTMAS VIGIL

The Jewish law suggests that infidelity on the part of a betrothed woman is to be punished by stoning. Joseph, although he believes that Mary has been unfaithful, does not seek to disgrace her or hold her subject to such a penalty.

Her husband *Joseph*, being a *righteous* man
and *unwilling* to expose her to public *disgrace*,
planned to *dismiss* her *quietly*.
But *just* when he had resolved to *do* this,
an *angel* of the *Lord appeared* to him in a *dream* and said,
"*Joseph*, son of *David*,
do not be *afraid* to take *Mary* as your *wife*,
for the child *conceived* in her is from the Holy *Spirit*.
She will bear a *son*,
and you are to name him *Jesus*,
for he will *save* his *people* from their *sins*."

All *this* took place
to *fulfil* what had been spoken by the *Lord*
through the *prophet*:
"*Look*, the *virgin* shall *conceive* and bear a *son*,
and they shall *name* him *Emmanuel*,"
which means, "*God* is *with* us."
When Joseph awoke from *sleep*,
he *did* as the angel of the Lord *commanded* him;
he *took* her as his *wife*,
but had *no* marital *relations* with her
until she had borne a *son*;
and he named him *Jesus*.

[Shorter: Matthew 1:18–25]

the angel's message is to assert Jesus' otherworldly origin. He is, as later Christians would articulate, fully human, descended from Abraham and David, and at the same time fully divine, conceived of the Holy Spirit. The author adds a final note, claiming that these events fulfill the scriptures, and quotes from the prophet Isaiah. This child is the manifestation of God on earth: Emmanuel.

Because of the long list of obscure names, this passage can be difficult to read. It is important to learn the pronunciations well and to practice them carefully. However, it is always more important to be confident in

your proclamation than to do it without error. If you stumble or forget a pronunciation, try not to draw attention to your error, but continue as though nothing had happened. It is better to keep your listeners' attention focused on the gospel than to distract them by your efforts to correct your mistakes.

The list of names is divided into three sets. Pause between the sets in order to provide a break for your listeners and to emphasize the structure of the passage. There is also a natural rhythm to the genealogical list; be sure that you do not allow your voice

to become sing-song. This can happen when a reader becomes bored and does not focus on communicating the intent of the passage: to demonstrate Jesus' origins.

The account of Joseph can be told as a tender story of commitment and honor, as well as an indication of the special character of this young child. As we celebrate this Christmas the incarnation of the divine Son of God, this story draws us into the events of 2,000 years ago. Offer it as a meditation on trust in God and a proclamation that, in Jesus, God is truly with us as never before.

# DECEMBER 25, 2000

# CHRISTMAS MIDNIGHT

*Lectionary #14*

## READING I    Isaiah 9:2–4, 6–7

**A reading from the book of the prophet Isaiah**

*Speak these words warmly and joyfully.*

The *people* who walked in *darkness*
have *seen* a great *light*;
those who *lived* in a land of deep *darkness*—
on them *light* has *shone*.
You have *multiplied* the *nation*,
you have *increased* its *joy*;
they rejoice *before* you
as with *joy* at the *harvest*,
as people *exult* when dividing *plunder*.

For the *yoke* of their *burden*,
and the *bar* across their *shoulders*,
the *rod* of their *oppressor*,
you have *broken* as on the day of *Midian*.

*Midian = MID-ee-uhn*

*Begin anew, quietly but joyfully, then increase in volume and intensity until you fairly shout with joy the titles given to the ruler.*

For a *child* has been *born* for us,
a *son given* to us;
*authority* rests upon his *shoulders*;
and he is named
Wonderful *Counsellor*, Mighty *God*,
Everlasting *Father*, *Prince* of *Peace*.

*Continue with confidence and conviction.*

His *authority* shall grow *continually*,
and there shall be *endless peace*
for the throne of *David* and his *kingdom*.

---

READING I  **Coming soon after Isaiah's promise that a child would be born who would be Judah's answer to threats of doom, this passage from the book of Isaiah seems to rejoice in the birth of that child. Isaiah was deeply committed to the promise made to David that his royal line would last forever. When Assyria first threatened and then defeated and dissolved the northern kingdom of Israel, Isaiah placed his hope in God's commitment to the Davidic monarch. He assured the king that God would never forsake Judah.**

**Today's reading celebrates the royal line and may have been used at the enthronement of a king, asserting that this "child" of God was able to embody the best qualities of his ancestors and would rule as an ideal monarch. However it was used historically, it came to represent the Jewish hope in a messianic savior that enlivened the thought of subsequent generations and provided fertile ground for the establishment of Christianity.**

**Christians have long held this passage as a favorite text, a hymn celebrating the qualities of Jesus the Christ. Indeed, as we gather during the darkest days of the year, we**

**proclaim that it is precisely through the birth of a child that a piercing light, one that can never be extinguished, has shone through the darkness. We rejoice that the burdens placed on our shoulders are removed through the actions of this one sent by God. And we claim that he is precisely the fulfillment of all hopes for a Davidic king, for a royal Messiah. Even Solomon's wisdom cannot compare with his counsel; David's victories pale next to the heroic activity of God through him; he has inspired the patriarchs, the**

DECEMBER 25, 2000 ■ CHRISTMAS MIDNIGHT

He will *establish* and *uphold* it
with *justice* and with *righteousness*
from this time *onward* and *forevermore.*
The *zeal* of the Lord of *hosts* will *do* this.

---

### READING II    Titus 2:11–14

**A reading from the letter of Paul to Titus**

The *grace* of *God* has *appeared*, bringing *salvation* to *all*,
training us to *renounce impiety* and worldly *passions*,
and in the present age to live lives
that are self-*controlled*, *upright*, and *godly*,
while we *wait* for the blessed *hope*
and the *manifestation* of the *glory* of our great *God* and *Saviour*,
Jesus *Christ*.

*He* it *is* who *gave* himself for us
that he might *redeem* us from all *iniquity*
and *purify* for himself a people of his *own*
who are *zealous* for good *deeds.*

---

**The meaning of Christmas is that God's graciousness is evident on earth.**

**That is, for Jesus to come again.**

**This is why he came to earth.**

---

"fathers" of Israel, from the beginning; and his rule is marked by peace and justice. But his dominion is not that of any human king; he will rule forever in glory.

This familiar text is a joy to read in the assembly. Recall the exuberant majesty of Handel's *Messiah* as you share the source of Handel's inspiration. Let your words echo with joy and hope as you proclaim the fulfillment of God's promises in the God-child born in Bethlehem.

READING II  A fitting text for Christmas, this selection from the letter to Titus celebrates God's glory manifested in Jesus. We celebrate today not simply the babe in the manger but the entry of God into human history in the person of Jesus. This great gift, the incarnation of God, brings salvation to all. We know that Jesus' willingness to suffer and die, and his defeat of death, are the central salvific events in history. But today's passage suggests that salvation becomes a reality because of God's

willingness to become human, to share in our struggles and our joys, our hopes and our dreams.

The gift God gives in being willing to become one of us also provides moral instruction. The passage suggests ways in which to live upright lives, adopting values that are instilled when we accept and give thanks for the gift of Jesus and look forward to his return. The gift of salvation comes first; righteous deeds follow.

**CHRISTMAS MIDNIGHT ■ DECEMBER 25, 2000**

Augustus = aw-GUHS-tuhs

Quirinius = kwih-RIN-ee-uhs

Because Jesus was raised as Joseph's adopted child, he was considered of the same ancestral line as Joseph. Thus, he was of the royal line of David.

Jesus was born in abject poverty.

The appearance of an angel and a bright light must have been terrifying. Try to convey some of that fear in your voice.

## GOSPEL   Luke 2:1–16

**A reading from the holy gospel according to Luke**

In those days a *decree* went out from Emperor *Augustus*
that all the *world* should be *registered*.
This was the *first* registration
and was taken while *Quirinius* was governor of *Syria*.
*All* went to their own *towns* to be *registered*.
*Joseph* also went from the town of *Nazareth* in *Galilee* to *Judea*,
to the city of *David* called *Bethlehem*,
because he was *descended* from the *house* and *family* of *David*.
He went to be registered with *Mary*,
to whom he was *engaged* and who was expecting a *child*.

While they were *there*,
the time came for her to deliver her *child*.
And she gave *birth* to her firstborn *son*
and wrapped him in bands of *cloth*,
and laid him in a *manger*,
because there was no *place* for them in the *inn*.

In that region there were *shepherds* living in the *fields*,
keeping *watch* over their flock by *night*.
Then an *angel* of the *Lord* stood *before* them,
and the *glory* of the Lord shone *around* them,
and they were *terrified*.

---

This short passage can be difficult to read because of the long sentence in the opening section. Practice dividing the sentence according to parts, but do not rush the intervening material. Close with a sincere hope that your assembly will eagerly choose the good deeds desired by God.

GOSPEL   As one of the best-loved passages in the New Testament, today's gospel has the ability to inspire children and adults alike. It is far more than a

story about a cute baby, although the birth of this child is central to its proclamation. But the implications of the birth are far-reaching.

The author of the gospel begins this section with a historical note, although there are problems with its accuracy. However, the point of providing such information is to indicate that the birth of this lowly child, wearing rags and sleeping in an animal's food trough, changes all of human history. The claims made about him are not about some fictitious figure, but about a real person, born at a particular time and place. The

unattended birth of a baby in a stable inaugurates a new age in God's dealings with humanity and a new era of world history.

The journey of Joseph and Mary to Bethlehem, home of King David, is another way of claiming Jesus' royal ancestry and identifying him as the fulfillment of God's promises to David. This child will change human history, but he was sent precisely to answer the hopes of a particular people, the Jews.

DECEMBER 25, 2000 ■ CHRISTMAS MIDNIGHT

**Speak reassuringly.**

**Slow down and proclaim this announcement with great solemnity.**

**Raise your voice in joyful song.**

**Be careful of your phrasing here; pause after "Joseph" (so that Mary and Joseph do not appear to be lying in the manger!).**

But the angel said to them,
"Do *not* be *afraid*; for *see* —
I am bringing you *good news* of great *joy* for all the *people*:
to you is *born* this *day* in the city of *David* a *Saviour*,
who is the *Messiah*, the *Lord*.
*This* will be a *sign* for you:
you will find a *child* wrapped in bands of *cloth*
and lying in a *manger*."

And *suddenly* there was with the angel
a *multitude* of the heavenly *host*,
praising *God* and *saying*,
"*Glory* to *God* in the highest *heaven*,
and on *earth peace* among those whom he *favours*!"

When the angels had *left* them and gone into *heaven*,
the *shepherds* said to one *another*,
"Let us *go* now to *Bethlehem*
and *see* this thing that has taken place,
which the *Lord* has made *known* to us."
So they went with *haste* and found *Mary* and *Joseph*,
and the *child* lying in the *manger*.

Just as the angel Gabriel appeared at the annunciation, so also a host of angels appears at Jesus' birth, offering praise to God for the wondrous event. But, as the rest of the gospel of Luke will make clear, the earth-shattering, life-changing, heart-warming event is one quite contrary to all expectations. The great Davidic ruler for whom Israel was waiting is born poor and unknown in a stable. The announcement of his birth by a heavenly host, proclaimed as good news of joy for all people, is heard only by lowly,

illiterate shepherds. The first visitors to the Messiah, the Savior and royal child, are not wealthy rulers or powerful elite, but unassuming guardians of sheep.

All expectations are turned upside down. No palace welcomes the Davidic ruler, no precious ointment caresses the skin of the anointed one of God. If we want to see Christ in others, perhaps we need to look first in the homeless shelters and drug rehabilitation clinics, on street corners and in prisons. From birth to death, those are the types of places Jesus frequented.

This is an exciting gospel to share with the members of your assembly. Try to read it as though for the first time. Share the quiet joy of the baby's birth, the exultation of the angels and the excitement of the shepherds. On this day is born a Savior, Christ the Lord.

## DECEMBER 25, 2000

# CHRISTMAS DAWN

*Lectionary #15*

### READING I    Isaiah 62:11–12

**A reading from the book of the prophet Isaiah**

The whole world will know the salvation given to Jerusalem. (Zion is another name for Jerusalem.)

The Lord has *proclaimed* to the *end* of the *earth*:
"Say to daughter *Zion*,
*See*, your *salvation* comes;
his *reward* is with him,
and his *recompense before* him.

Your voice may become slightly quieter here, but still joyfully reassuring.

"They shall be called 'The Holy *People*,'
'The *Redeemed* of the *Lord*';
and *you* shall be called 'Sought *Out*,'
'A *City* Not *Forsaken*.' "

### READING II    Titus 3:4–7

**A reading from the letter of Paul to Titus**

Pause briefly. The next line can be spoken a little faster; it is parenthetical.

When the *goodness* and loving *kindness*
     of God our *Saviour* appeared,
he *saved* us,
*not* because of any works of *righteousness* that *we* had done,
but according to his *mercy*,

Slow down as you describe baptism, through which Christians receive the Spirit. Pause briefly after "Holy Spirit."

through the *water* of *rebirth* and *renewal* by the Holy *Spirit*.

---

**READING I** The end of the Babylonian exile brought about the joyous return of the Hebrew people to their beloved Jerusalem. The renewed city, rebuilt and restored, was the fulfillment of the people's hopes and the sign of God's favor bestowed on them. Although the exile was often understood as punishment for lack of faithfulness, the restoration of Jerusalem was proof of God's favor and Israel's vindication after the exile.

The song of joy in today's reading proclaims God's delight in the holy city, here called Zion, and in the people returning to

dwell there. A name formerly appropriate for the city is changed: Zion is no longer "forsaken" but is now once again the dwelling place of many. These are the holy people, the redeemed of God. They have completed their time of exile and now can rejoice to return to their beautiful homeland.

Christians see the salvation of God offered most fully in the person of Jesus. It is he who makes us a holy people. Share this brief selection with your community as a song of praise and thanksgiving for what God has done for us in Jesus the Christ.

**READING II** This passage from the letter to Titus addresses the question of salvation in a uniquely Christian manner. It clarifies that salvation is a gift and does not result from any human actions. Instead, it is something God offers purely out of love for us, and it is effected through baptism. It is appropriate on this feast of the birth of the Savior that we reflect as well on our own rebirth in the waters of baptism.

Through baptism the Spirit of God is offered, a Spirit who gives us the strength to call out to God, not as a foreigner or a guest, but as a member of the household of God.

DECEMBER 25, 2000 ■ CHRISTMAS DAWN

This *Spirit* he poured *out* on us *richly*
through Jesus *Christ* our *Saviour*,
so that, having been *justified* by his *grace*,
we might become *heirs* according to the *hope* of eternal *life*.

---

### GOSPEL    Luke 2:15–20

**A reading from the holy gospel according to Luke**

When the angels had *left* them and gone into *heaven*,
the *shepherds* said to one *another*,
"Let us *go* now to *Bethlehem*
and *see* this thing that has taken *place*,
which the *Lord* has made *known* to us."

So they went with *haste* and found *Mary* and *Joseph*,
and the *child* lying in the *manger*.
When they *saw* this,
they made known what had been *told* them about this *child*;
and all who *heard* it were *amazed*
at what the shepherds *told* them.

But Mary *treasured* all these words
and *pondered* them in her *heart*.
The shepherds *returned*, *glorifying* and *praising God*
for *all* they had heard and *seen*,
as it had been *told* them.

---

**The shepherds are eager and curious.**

**Be careful of your phrasing here; pause after "Joseph" (so that Mary and Joseph do not seem to be lying in the manger!).**

**Speak with amazement in your voice.**

**Speak quietly and warmly about Mary, then enthusiastically as you describe the shepherds again.**

---

We are heirs, recipients of the gift of life willed to us as children of God.

Offer this passage to your assembly as a confirmation that it is chosen by God. Read it with confidence and conviction.

GOSPEL   This morning's gospel passage picks up and continues where the passage for the Mass at midnight left off. The shepherds have received from the angels the joyous announcement of the birth of a child, a child who is proclaimed as the anointed one of God, Savior and Lord. In eagerness, they visit the child and share the angels' announcement with those they meet, including Mary and Joseph. The words of the angels are greeted with astonishment and awe. The earlier scene, with splendid light and a chorus of angels' voices, continues to inspire. For the gospel writer, everything about this event is amazing.

It is unlikely that Mary would find something new in the words of the shepherds; what is more interesting is what she does with the good news: She ponders it in her heart. The shepherds, on the other hand, praise God and continue to proclaim the glad tidings.

Inspire the members of your assembly to join with the shepherds in going forth filled with wonder at the goodness of God, who did not deem it undignified to be born in a stable, to walk the earth as a human, to live among the poor and downtrodden. Convey as well the priceless treasure we celebrate today, so that the entire assembly might join with Mary as she ponders the good news in her heart.

## DECEMBER 25, 2000

# CHRISTMAS DAY

*Lectionary #16*

### READING I    Isaiah 52:7–10

**A reading from the book of the prophet Isaiah**

*Speak in a gentle, peaceful tone, building as you approach the end of the sentence.*

How *beautiful* upon the *mountains*
are the feet of the *messenger* who announces *peace*,
who brings good *news*,
who announces *salvation*,
who says to *Zion*, "Your *God reigns*."

*The guards on the towers are awaiting the coming of God to Jerusalem (here called Zion).*

*Listen!* Your *sentinels* lift up their *voices*,
together they *sing* for *joy*;
for in plain *sight* they see
the *return* of the *Lord* to *Zion*.

*Speak with exuberance.*

Break forth together into *singing*,
you *ruins* of *Jerusalem*;
for the *Lord* has *comforted* his *people*,
he has *redeemed* Jerusalem.
The Lord has *bared* his holy *arm*
before the *eyes* of all the *nations*;
and all the *ends* of the *earth* shall *see*
      the *salvation* of our *God*.

*Let your voice become quieter but still filled with conviction.*

---

**READING I** Announcing the end of the exile in Babylon and the restoration of Jerusalem, a messenger runs along the mountaintops, shouting out the good news that God rules over all the earth. During the Babylonian exile, it must sometimes have seemed that God was no longer in power and could not save the people of Judah, living in captivity. But the Persians under King Cyrus defeated the Babylonians, confirming the hopes of those who trusted in God.

The beautiful passage that forms today's reading also announces the end of the exile through the words of the guards in the towers above the city and even through the stones of the ruined city of Jerusalem. God was understood to be with the people as they returned to their beloved homeland. Throughout the exile, God remained with the people and now joins them in coming home, restored as well to the proper divine dwelling. It is time for rejoicing.

As Christians, we too rejoice that God is present in the birth of a child, which we celebrate today. We cry out in joy as we sing the good news that God reigns, confident that all the earth can come to know the salvation offered by our God.

Allow the joy of the speakers in the passage to fill your heart and your voice, so that the community may see and proclaim the wonders of God. Encourage the members of your assembly to see God's activity not only in Jesus but also in the story of the Hebrew people and in their lives today. God is active throughout all of human history.

DECEMBER 25, 2000 ■ CHRISTMAS DAY

## READING II    Hebrews 1:1–6

**A reading from the letter to the Hebrews**

Long *ago* God *spoke* to our *ancestors*
in many and various *ways* by the *prophets*,
but in these *last* days he has spoken to us by a *Son*,
whom he appointed *heir* of all *things*,
*through* whom he also created the *worlds*.

He is the *reflection* of God's *glory*
and the exact *imprint* of God's very *being*,
and he *sustains* all things by his powerful *word*.
When he had made *purification* for *sins*,
he sat *down* at the right *hand* of the *Majesty* on *high*,
having become as much *superior* to *angels*
as the *name* he has *inherited* is more *excellent* than *theirs*.

For to *which* of the angels did God ever say,
"*You* are my *Son*;
*today* I have *begotten* you"?
Or again,
"I will be his *Father*,
and he will be my *Son*"?
And again,
when he brings the *firstborn* into the *world*, he says,
"Let *all* God's angels *worship* him."

These terms and images were once applied to Lady Wisdom, and the pre-existent Son is presented in much the same way that Wisdom is elsewhere.

The terminology recalls the actions of the Jewish high priests, offering expiation for the sins of the people in the temple.

Hebrews quotes several Old Testament passages; three are included here. The first (Psalm 2:7) was originally applied to a king, seen as God's son; the second (2 Samuel 7:14) designated the descendant of David; and the third (Deuteronomy 32:43 in the Greek version) comes from a song of Moses. Proclaim these words as statements of Christ's greatness.

READING II The opening verses of the letter to the Hebrews lay out the principal themes that will be addressed in the work. In terms similar to those in today's gospel, this passage declares that Christ the exalted Son reflects God's glory and was present at creation, referring to his salvific actions and his enthronement in heaven. This is one of the strongest statements in the entire New Testament regarding the preexistence of the Son, and it paves the way for development of the doctrine of the Trinity.

Initially, a contrast is made between the way in which God formerly communicated, through the prophets, and God's communication in the final age, through the Son. With amazing succinctness, the passage declares the special status of this Son, the one who is declared "heir of all things" and is above even the angels; he is, in fact, the imprint of the very essence of God.

The author goes on to discuss Christ's exaltation at the right hand of God. Here his superiority to the angels is revealed. He, unlike the angels, is called "Son."

The richness of this passage can make it difficult to proclaim. Be sure to read it slowly and deliberately, pausing briefly after each phrase so that the complexity of the passage will be clear to your listeners. Read the quotations as expressions of God's word and, as the author intends, proclamations of the greatness of Christ.

CHRISTMAS DAY ■ DECEMBER 25, 2000

## GOSPEL     John 1:1–18

**A reading from the holy gospel according to John**

*Speak very slowly, so that your listeners can follow the progression of thought.*

In the *beginning* was the *Word,*
and the Word was with *God,*
and the Word *was* God.
He was in the *beginning* with *God.*
*All* things came into being *through* him,
and *without* him not *one thing* came into *being.*
What has come into being in him was *life,*
and the *life* was the *light* of all *people.*

*The image shifts here: The one through whom the world was created is also light for all people.*

The light *shines* in the *darkness,*
and the *darkness* did not *overcome* it.
There was a *man* sent from *God,* whose name was *John.*
He came as a witness to *testify* to the *light,*
so that *all* might *believe* through him.
He *himself* was not the *light,*
but he came to *testify* to the *light.*

*Change your tone and tempo to indicate the shift in subject. Make your voice lighter and less serious.*

The *true* light, which enlightens *everyone,*
was coming into the *world.*
He was *in* the world,
and the world came into being *through* him;
yet the *world* did not *know* him.
He *came* to what was his *own,*
and his own *people* did not *accept* him.

*Slow down again, and speak with regret in your voice.*

---

GOSPEL   The beautiful hymn that forms the prologue to John's gospel is a complex literary work. It is at once a hymn of creation, perhaps originally celebrating Wisdom as the cocreator of the world, and at the same time a proclamation of the incarnation. In its present state, it declares that the Word *(Logos)* presided at the creation of the world, bringing life and light to all people. The light is then personified and identified with Jesus, the Word

made flesh, who is the only Son of God. Within this broad framework are inserted two digressive statements about John the Baptist, the one who gives witness to the coming of the light.

"In the beginning" recalls the creation story of Genesis, but the creation story is more complex than it appears at first, for with God at the beginning was the *Logos,* through whom God fashioned the world. The Greek term, usually translated "word," means a single word or story, or communication itself. It also signifies reason and intellectual capacity. To declare that the

"Word was with God and the Word was God," then, is to speak of the communication of God's thought processes; the Word is divine, as intimately connected with God as a person's thought and speech are with that person.

After the digression concerning John the Baptist, the author resumes the discussion of the light. To explain to the original readers of the prologue (and to us today) why not everyone became a disciple of Jesus, the author claims that "his own" did not recognize or accept him. Surely this is

DECEMBER 25, 2000 ■ CHRISTMAS DAY

**Speak with hope and wonder.**

But to all who *received* him,
who *believed* in his *name*,
he gave *power* to become *children* of *God*,
who were *born*, not of *blood*
or of the *will* of the *flesh*
or of the *will* of *man*,
but of *God*.
And the *Word* became *flesh* and lived *among* us,
and we have seen his *glory*,
the *glory* as of a father's only *son*,
full of *grace* and *truth*.

**Communicate the awe of witnessing the glory of Christ.**

**Again there is a digression, as John is said to declare the superiority of the Word-made-flesh. When the text begins again, it continues with the same awe as before.**

John *testified* to him and cried out,
"This was *he* of whom I *said*,
'He who comes *after* me ranks *ahead* of me
because he was *before* me.' "

From his *fullness* we have all *received*,
*grace* upon *grace*.
The law *indeed* was given through *Moses*;
*grace* and *truth* came through Jesus *Christ*.
*No* one has ever *seen* God.
It is *God* the only *Son*,
who is *close* to the Father's *heart*,
who has made him *known*.

*[Shorter: John 1:1–5, 9–14]*

**The passage closes with a statement of the closeness of the Son to God; the revealer knows intimately the one he reveals.**

an argument by the Jewish-Christian evangelist against the other Jews who did not follow Jesus. But, says the author, those who do follow Jesus become children of God, a relationship made possible because of the Word's special role as the very Son of God.

The claim that the divine could become flesh defies all human reason. The chasm between divine and human, especially evident to one unaccustomed to Christian claims, is great. But as Christians we believe

that this *Logos* of God, active in creation and the bearer of life, was born as a human and lived on earth. A God who may at times appear remote has become one of us. The awesome wonder of the incarnation is ultimately beyond our understanding; we proclaim this with faith and gratitude, and with amazement at the tremendous love of a God who would share fully in our human life.

What a wonderful celebration of the incarnation you offer to your community as you read this awe-inspiring and poetic passage. Allow the sections about John to stand

as the parenthetical statements they are; lower your voice a bit and increase your speed slightly in order to convey this. Meditate upon this gospel reading, so that the wonder it evokes in you can be heard as you proclaim it in the assembly.

## DECEMBER 31, 2000

# HOLY FAMILY

Lectionary #17

### READING I 1 Samuel 1:11, 20–22, 24–28

**A reading from the first book of Samuel**

Elkanah = el-KAY-nah

Express clearly the depth of Hannah's sorrow and longing.

*Hannah*, wife of *Elkanah*, had no *children*;
she *prayed* to the Lord and made this *vow*:
"O *Lord* of *hosts*,
if only you will look on the *misery* of your *servant*,
and *remember* me, and not *forget* your servant,
but will *give* to your servant a male *child*,
then I will set him *before* you as a *nazirite*
        until the *day* of his *death*.
He shall drink neither *wine* nor *intoxicants*,
and no *razor* shall touch his *head*."

nazirite = NAZ-uh-rīt
A nazirite was one who was set apart, dedicated to the service of God. The vow was usually temporary, but Hannah presents Samuel as a nazirite for life.

There is a sense of triumph and joy here. Pause after "Lord" before continuing with the story about Elkanah.

In *due* time Hannah *conceived* and bore a *son*.
She named him *Samuel*, for she said,
"I have *asked* him of the *Lord*."
*Elkanah* and all his *household*
went up to *offer* to the Lord the yearly *sacrifice*,
and to pay his *vow*.
But *Hannah* did not go up, for she said to her husband,
"As *soon* as the child is *weaned*, I will *bring* him,
that he may *appear* in the *presence* of the *Lord*,
and *remain* there *forever*;
I will offer him as a *nazirite* for all *time*."

Hannah speaks confidently. But pain must have filled her heart at the thought of separating from her son. Begin by speaking in a subdued voice, then grow in strength as you repeat Hannah's vow.

READING I After the period when the judges ruled Israel, Samuel was recognized as the leader of the people. In fact, he anointed both the first king, Saul, and the successful and beloved King David. Today's story tells of the faithfulness and integrity of Samuel's mother, Hannah.

Hannah prays to God and asks for a son, promising to dedicate the child to God's service at the temple at Shiloh. True to her word, Hannah consecrates the child Samuel to God as soon as he is old enough to be

separated from her. She turns Samuel over to the priest, so that he might serve in the temple and grow in wisdom. Hannah was later blessed with other children, but it was her first child who was destined for greatness in Israel.

The trust Hannah displays is inspiring. Although her heart longs for a child, she has confidence that she can plead her case before God. Earlier in the story, Hannah

believes the word of Eli the priest and sets aside her sadness as soon as a child is promised to her. Finally, she allows Samuel to be raised by someone else, even though he is still young when she presents him in the temple. She is confident that God will provide for him.

Hannah keeps her word as well. No one but God had heard her vow. It would have been easy for her to forget it once she bore her beloved son, but her integrity is too

DECEMBER 31, 2000 ■ HOLY FAMILY

Shiloh = SHĪ-loh

Eli = EE-lī

These words are addressed to Eli, the priest of the temple. Speak with confidence to communicate the strength and fortitude of this remarkable woman.

When she had *weaned* him,
she took him *up* with her,
along with a *three*-year-old *bull*,
a measure of *flour*, and a skin of *wine*.
She *brought* him to the house of the Lord at *Shiloh*;
and the child was *young*.
Then they *slaughtered* the bull,
and they brought the child to *Eli*.
And she said,
"Oh, my *lord*! As you *live*, my lord,
*I* am the woman who was *standing* here in your *presence*,
praying to the *Lord*.
For this *child* I prayed;
and the Lord has *granted* me the *petition* that I *made* to him.
Therefore I have *lent* him to the *Lord*;
as *long* as he *lives*, he is *given* to the Lord."
She *left* him there for the *Lord*.

### READING II    1 John 3:1–2, 21–24

**A reading from the first letter of John**

Begin in a tone of amazement at the tremendous love of God.

See what *love* the Father has *given* us,
that we should be called *children* of *God*;
and that is what we *are*.
The reason the *world* does not *know* us is
that it did not know *him*.

Pause before and after "Beloved," and speak warmly. Continue in a warm tone, and add a bit of wonder to your voice as you contemplate what is yet to be.

*Beloved*,
we are God's *children now*;
what we *will* be has not yet been *revealed*.

great to allow that. Still, it must have been heartbreaking for her to part with her young son. We can imagine her tender caresses and gentle words during the few years when Samuel remained in her care. Hannah's trust in God and her own dedication to the Lord give her the confidence to keep her vow.

Hannah's faithfulness and trust were matched only by those qualities in Mary, the mother of Jesus. Mary also trusted the

promises made to her and taught her son to love and serve God. Hannah and Mary are examples of dedicated women who created families that were truly holy. As you proclaim this passage, keep in mind your own family's struggles to be holy, and let your voice reflect wonder and admiration at the deep devotion displayed by Hannah.

READING II The Christian community is a "holy family," for we are all children of God. As if that is not enough, the author of this reading goes on to say that there is even more that awaits us. When God is revealed, we will be not only children of God but truly like God!

In an intricate weaving of themes, the passage proceeds to an exhortation to right behavior. We can boldly ask God for what we need and be assured that God hears us

HOLY FAMILY ■ DECEMBER 31, 2000

What we *do* know is *this*:
when he is *revealed*, we will be *like* him,
for we will *see* him as he *is*.

*Beloved*,
if our *hearts* do not *condemn* us,
we have *boldness* before God;
and we *receive* from him whatever we *ask*,
because we *obey* his *commandments*
and do what *pleases* him.
And *this* is his commandment,
that we should *believe* in the *name* of his *Son* Jesus *Christ*
and *love* one *another*, just as he has *commanded* us.
All who *obey* his commandments *abide* in him,
and *he* abides in *them*.
And by *this* we know that he *abides* in us,
by the *Spirit* that he has *given* us.

**Speak more boldly.**

**Emphasize the commands of faith and love.**

**Slow down, concluding with peaceful confidence.**

---

## GOSPEL    Luke 2:41–52

**A reading from the holy gospel according to Luke**

**The story opens as a straightforward narrative.**

Now every *year* the *parents* of Jesus went to *Jerusalem*
for the festival of the *Passover*.
And when he was *twelve* years old,
they went up as *usual* for the *festival*.

When the festival was *ended* and they started to *return*,
the boy *Jesus* stayed *behind* in *Jerusalem*,
but his *parents* did not *know* it.

---

precisely because we keep the commandments of God. Most important is the command to have faith, to believe in the revelation of God in the person of Jesus, and to love one another. And the result of believing in Jesus is the deep peace that comes with resting or abiding in God. The Spirit, whose life in our hearts assures us that we are abiding in God, brings us that peace.

In proclaiming this passage, proceed slowly, so that your listeners can follow the progression of thought. Speak with warmth

and confidence, in order to assure your community that it is indeed part of the family of God. And offer this message in an encouraging tone, so that God's peace might truly dwell in your assembly.

GOSPEL    The story of the boy Jesus in the temple is a story that brings understanding nods from almost any parent. A child who runs off without warning, whose precociousness amazes adults, and who simply cannot understand why anyone would be upset by an unexplained

absence—there are many such children in the world! In some ways, the family of Jesus is not so different from many "holy families" that argue and misunderstand, that struggle to live in harmony, and that love deeply and tenderly.

Of course, not all children are comfortable discussing divine law with religious leaders, as Jesus is. Placed between the story of his birth and the beginning of his ministry, this account provides a transition to the adult world in which Jesus will soon find himself. He is still a child, obedient to

DECEMBER 31, 2000 ■ HOLY FAMILY

**Let a bit of tension and anxiety be heard in your voice.**

*Assuming* that he was in the group of *travellers*,
they went a day's *journey*.
Then they started to *look* for him
    among their *relatives* and *friends*.
When they did not *find* him,
they *returned* to Jerusalem to *search* for him.

**Speak with astonishment.**

After *three days* they found him in the *temple*,
sitting among the *teachers*,
*listening* to them and asking them *questions*.
And all who *heard* him were *amazed*
at his *understanding* and his *answers*.
When his parents *saw* him they were *astonished*;
and his *mother* said to him,

**Let Mary's reproach convey how upset she must have been.**

"*Child*, why have you *treated* us like this?
*Look*, your *father* and I have been *searching* for you
    in great *anxiety*."
He said to them,

**Jesus responds with little concern for his parents' anxiety.**

"*Why* were you *searching* for me?
Did you not *know* that I must be in my Father's *house*?"
But they did not *understand* what he *said* to them.

**Read this with tenderness, close the passage in a strong, confident tone.**

Then Jesus went *down* with them and came to *Nazareth*,
and was *obedient* to them.
His mother *treasured* all these things in her *heart*.
And Jesus *increased* in *wisdom* and in *years*,
and in *divine* and human *favour*.

---

his parents, but his concerns are those of an adult with a message.

    The portrait of Jesus' parents in this passage is fascinating. Although Joseph's name is not mentioned, both parents are portrayed as law-abiding, faithful Jews attending a feast in Jerusalem. The journey would have taken several days, but they made the trip annually, as the law commands. Since they are part of a large kinship group, they assume Jesus is safe with

relatives or friends when they notice his absence. Then they search high and low, as any parents would, for their beloved child.

    When they find him, it is Mary who speaks. She reproaches her son, as so many mothers do, for his thoughtlessness. Yet in the end, she holds the event and his response in her heart, pondering its meaning and wondering at the depth of devotion to God displayed by the child she bore. Her heart has yet to be pierced by the intense pain it will know when she witnesses the torture and death of her beloved son.

    Offer this selection to your community as encouragement for each family's journey. Give as much life as possible to the speakers and to the contrast between Mary's concern and Jesus' lack thereof. Being a holy family is hard work, and it is comforting to know that Mary, Joseph and Jesus had to struggle with it just as we do.

# JANUARY 1, 2001

# MARY, MOTHER OF GOD

*Lectionary #18*

## READING I    Numbers 6:22–27

**A reading from the book of Numbers**

The *Lord* spoke to *Moses*:

The family of Aaron had priestly responsibilities in ancient Israel.

"Speak to *Aaron* and his *sons*, saying,
'*Thus* you shall *bless* the Israelites:
You shall *say* to them,

Speak this blessing over your assembly with warmth and encouragement.

"'The *Lord bless* you and *keep* you;
the *Lord* make his *face* to *shine* upon you,
and be *gracious* to you;
the *Lord* lift up his *countenance* upon you,
and give you *peace*.'

"So they shall put my *name* on the *Israelites*,
and I will *bless* them."

READING I — Today we celebrate Mary, the mother of Jesus, but we also gather as a people beginning a new calendar year. Offer the blessing in this reading over your community as it begins a new year in the hope that God will indeed look with kindness on this people.

This blessing is priestly in character. It is extremely ancient and is still being used today in many Jewish and Christian congregations. The blessing itself consists of three parts. The first asks God to provide for and protect the people. The second poetically refers to God's "face" and asks that it be turned toward God's chosen ones, a way of asking for God's benevolence and graciousness. God's face shines like the sun, giving warmth and attention to the beloved of the Lord. The third part asks that God may bring peace to the people.

Speak the introductory words and conclusion with firmness; this is God's command. But look upon your assembly with fondness as you warmly pray the words of the blessing.

READING II — Paul wrote these words to remind the Galatians of their newfound status as Christians. He claims in an earlier passage that the Galatians were like slaves to sin prior to their reception of faith, lacking the freedom to act rightly. But when the Son came into the world, he freed us, allowing us to be called children of God.

For Paul, slavery was a fact of life. He freely refers to it to make his point. Because

JANUARY 1, 2001 ■ MARY, MOTHER OF GOD

---

**READING II** Galatians 4:4–7

**A reading from the letter of Paul to the Galatians**

When the *fullness* of time had *come,*
God sent his *Son, born* of a *woman,*
*born* under the *law,*
in order to *redeem* those who were under the law,
so that we might receive *adoption* as *children.*

And because you are *children,*
God has sent the *Spirit* of his *Son* into our *hearts,* crying,
"*Abba! Father!*"
So you are no *longer* a slave but a *child,*
and if a *child* then also an *heir,* through *God.*

**God's Son was born of a woman, subject to the law of Moses.**

**As proof of their new status, Paul appeals to the Galatians' own prayer: They call upon God as "Abba," the address of a child to its father.**

of the history of our nation, however, the mention of slavery brings to mind painful memories and unresolved tensions. Read this passage with sensitivity to the feelings of your listeners. At the same time, remind them of their status as Christians; they are truly God's children, free to approach God in intimacy and trust.

GOSPEL This selection was also used as the gospel reading for Christmas Mass at dawn. See that commentary for a fuller discussion.

Today's gospel reminds us of the wondrous event of the incarnation. It recalls the birth of a child who will inspire countless people to change their lives and acknowledge God's goodness. This is a child who will grow to be a preacher and teacher, and who will live his life in total obedience to God. This child will become a symbol of the overturning of the old order and a completely new offer of life from God. Finally,

this child will one day be proclaimed as one so intimately united with God that the child himself is divine.

The central mood of this passage is one of wonder. Awe-inspiring events accompany the birth of Jesus, astonishing all who hear the shepherds' tales of angelic splendor. The shepherds themselves are transformed, inspired to sing God's praises. More importantly, Mary quietly reflects on the events of the day and the words of the visitors.

Added to the gospel that was used on Christmas is the account of Jesus' circumcision, a detail that reveals the importance

MARY, MOTHER OF GOD ■ JANUARY 1, 2001

## GOSPEL    Luke 2:16–21

**A reading from the holy gospel according to Luke**

When the angels had *left* them
the *shepherds* said to one *another*,
"Let us *go* now to *Bethlehem*
and *see* this thing that has taken place,
which the *Lord* has made *known* to us."

**Pause after "Joseph," so that it does not seem that Mary and Joseph are lying with the baby in the manger!**

So they went with *haste*
and found *Mary* and *Joseph*,
and the *child* lying in the *manger.*
When they *saw* this,
they made known what had been *told* them about this *child;*
and all who *heard* it were *amazed*
at what the shepherds *told* them.
But Mary *treasured* all these words
and *pondered* them in her *heart.*

**Raise your voice to convey the excitement of all who heard the message.**

**Speak quietly and reflectively.**

The shepherds *returned, glorifying* and *praising God*
for *all* they had heard and *seen,*
as it had been *told* them.

**Again, raise your voice in joy and wonder.**

After eight *days* had passed,
it was time to *circumcise* the *child;*
and he was called *Jesus,*
the *name* given by the *angel*
before he was *conceived* in the *womb.*

of the Jewish law for his parents. They faithfully perform all the rituals required of them. The account of the circumcision also reminds us of the words of the angel to Mary at Jesus' conception. He is given the name that indicates what he will do: In Hebrew, the name Joshua (in Greek, Jesus) means "he will save."

Although this passage was used only a few days ago on Christmas, many in your assembly might not have heard it yet. Read it as though for the first time, emphasizing

the awe of all involved, and especially concentrating on the tender trust of Mary as she ponders the significance of her son.

## JANUARY 7, 2001

# EPIPHANY OF THE LORD

*Lectionary #20*

### READING I   Isaiah 60:1–6

**A reading from the book of the prophet Isaiah**

Sing out with joy and wonder at the splendors the author describes.

Lower your voice just a bit, then build to the end of the sentence.

*Arise, shine,* for your *light* has *come,*
and the *glory* of the Lord has *risen upon* you!
For *darkness* shall cover the *earth,*
and thick *darkness* the *peoples;*
but the *Lord* will arise upon *you,*
and his *glory* will appear *over* you.

*Nations* shall come to your *light,*
and *kings* to the brightness of your *dawn.*
Lift up your *eyes* and look *around;*
they all gather *together,* they *come* to you;
your *sons* shall come from far *away,*
and your *daughters* shall be carried on their nurses' *arms.*

Let your voice be filled with joy.

Then you shall *see* and be *radiant;*
your *heart* shall *thrill* and *rejoice,*
because the *abundance* of the sea shall be *brought* to you,
the *wealth* of the *nations* shall *come* to you.
A *multitude* of *camels* shall *cover* you,
the young camels of *Midian* and *Ephah;*
all those from *Sheba* shall come.
They shall bring *gold* and *frankincense,*
and shall proclaim the *praise* of the *Lord.*

Midian = MID-ee-uhn
Ephah = EE-fah
Sheba = SHEE-buh

---

READING I  The early Christians kept the feast of the Epiphany as the celebration of the incarnation and the manifestation of God to the world in the person of Jesus. The celebration of Christmas came later and is still secondary for many of the world's Christians. In today's feast we proclaim that God's glory is made known to all. This brings with it a responsibility to ensure that all peoples are welcome, that all needs are met.

The first reading is a joyous proclamation about the splendor of the holy city of Jerusalem. It is a beacon of light in a world

of darkness, splendid and radiant as the sun. Its brightness guides not only its own sons and daughters (the people of Israel returning from exile) but even provides light for foreigners, who stream to the city, praising God and bearing riches from their own lands.

This selection also recognizes the responsibility Israel had to be a light to the nations, telling others of both the expectations and the blessings of God. Christians believe that the promises made to Israel are fulfilled in Jesus and that he is most fully the light for the nations. Jesus is like Jerusalem,

radiant in glory, guiding all peoples and receiving gifts of wealth and honor.

Cry out with joy and excitement as you share this passage with your community. Let it inspire your listeners to rejoice in the splendors of God, now revealed in Jesus. Encourage them to be welcoming to all people, friend and foreigner, in order to become a new Jerusalem, shining for all to see.

READING II  Paul's ministry was marked by controversy. Among the earliest followers of Jesus (all conscientious Jews, as was Jesus himself), there

EPIPHANY OF THE LORD ■ JANUARY 7, 2001

---

### READING II    Ephesians 3:2–3a, 5–6

**A reading from the letter of Paul to the Ephesians**

The author claims that Paul's ministry to the Gentiles was undertaken in response to a revelation.

*Surely* you have already *heard*
of the *commission* of God's *grace* that was *given* me for *you*,
and how the *mystery* was made *known* to me by *revelation*.

Close with strong emphasis on the equality of all in God.

In former *generations*
this *mystery* was not made known to *humanity*
as it has *now* been *revealed* to his holy *apostles* and *prophets*
by the *Spirit:*
that is, the *Gentiles* have become *fellow heirs*,
members of the *same body*,
and *sharers* in the promise in Christ *Jesus* through the *gospel*.

---

### GOSPEL    Matthew 2:1–12

**A reading from the holy gospel according to Matthew**

There were people in the ancient Middle East who were known for their knowledge of the movement of stars. The gospel writer has them in mind here.

In the time of King *Herod*,
after Jesus was born in *Bethlehem* of *Judea*,
*wise* men from the *East* came to Jerusalem, asking,
"Where is the *child* who has been born *king* of the *Jews*?
For we observed his *star* at its *rising*,
and have come to pay him *homage*."

Herod the Great was a ruthless, greatly disliked puppet king. He jealously guarded his power and was afraid that he would be ousted from his throne.

When King Herod *heard* this, he was *frightened*,
and all Jerusalem *with* him;
and calling together
all the chief *priests* and *scribes* of the *people*,

---

arose a dispute about who could be saved. Paul and others argued that the salvation offered in Christ was available to all, regardless of race or religious heritage. The original view held that Jesus had come to his own people, the Jewish nation, and that it was necessary to be Jewish in order to be his follower. The letter to the Ephesians, written by an admirer of Paul, insists that God's blessings are for all; Gentiles together with Jews are recipients of the promises made to Israel and fulfilled in Jesus.

Today's passage recalls the ministry of Paul in establishing and serving churches composed primarily of non-Jews. The author uses the Pauline image of the body. Gentiles are pictured as a limb of the body of Israel. By being part of the same body, Gentiles are able to inherit all that belongs to the Israel, all that has been promised by God to the chosen people.

Since most of us are non-Jewish followers of Christ, we are the direct recipients of this Epiphany message. But just as the Jewish followers of Jesus were challenged to accept Gentiles, so also we cannot truly claim to follow Jesus unless we proclaim him to all the world without regard to race or class or appearance.

Your task is to present this challenge to your listeners by reading the concluding lines of the passage with special forcefulness. Encourage them to appreciate both the abiding nature of God's promises to the Jewish people and the inclusiveness that we must offer to others.

GOSPEL  High drama now greets us as we turn from the adorable child in the manger and the choirs of angels celebrating his birth to the scheming of the

JANUARY 7, 2001 ■ EPIPHANY OF THE LORD

he *inquired* of them where the *Messiah* was to be *born*.
They told him, "In *Bethlehem* of *Judea*;
for so it has been *written* by the *prophet*:
'And *you*, *Bethlehem*, in the land of *Judah*,
are by *no* means *least* among the *rulers* of Judah;
for from *you* shall come a *ruler*
who is to *shepherd* my people *Israel*.'"

**Convey Herod's cunning.**

Then Herod secretly called for the *wise* men
and *learned* from them the exact *time*
when the star had *appeared*.
Then he sent them to *Bethlehem*, saying,
"*Go* and search *diligently* for the child;
and when you have *found* him,
bring me *word* so that *I* may also go and pay him *homage*."

**They begin to "follow" the star at this point. Express the wonder and joy the wise men felt.**

When they had *heard* the king, they set *out*;
and *there*, *ahead* of them,
went the *star* that they had seen at its *rising*,
until it *stopped* over the place where the *child* was.
When they saw that the star had *stopped*,
they were *overwhelmed* with *joy*.

On entering the *house*,
they saw the *child* with Mary his *mother*;
and they knelt *down* and paid him *homage*.
Then, opening their *treasure* chests,
they offered him *gifts* of *gold*, *frankincense*, and *myrrh*.

And having been warned in a *dream* not to return to *Herod*,
they left for their *own* country by *another* road.

---

king, who attempts to keep anyone from honoring this child. One of the reasons for the change in tone is the change in authors. Up to this point we have been reading the nativity story primarily from the gospel of Luke; we now turn to the gospel of Matthew. But it is also time to recognize the demands placed on us by that sweet babe, for Epiphany is a challenging feast. There is great joy in the proclamation that God is made known to the entire world in Christ Jesus, and great challenge to us to be as open and accepting of those who are different from us as the child Jesus was of his visitors.

The story is familiar, yet it has a timeless quality. People of great wealth and education, able to see the signs of the times concentrated in a single star, come to honor a poor, unknown baby born to parents far from home. Naturally they begin by seeking him in a palace, since they recognize that he is to be the king of the Jews. When King Herod attempts to trick them, they accomplish their mission and return home, thwarting his jealous plot.

On this feast of Epiphany, we celebrate the mission of these foreign people, who carried news of God's presence in Jesus back to their homelands. The significance of Jesus, unrecognized so often by his own people during his ministry, is clear to those who have never met him before.

Proclaim this gospel as the exciting story it is. Allow your voice to enliven it, so that it will appeal to children and adults alike. And let the story challenge your listeners to become more inclusive people, more accepting of those who are unfamiliar or foreign.

JANUARY 14, 2001

# 2ND SUNDAY IN ORDINARY TIME

*Lectionary #66*

### READING I    Isaiah 62:1–5

**A reading from the book of the prophet Isaiah**

*Open with great enthusiasm.*

The Lord says this:
"For *Zion's* sake I will not keep *silent,*
and for *Jerusalem's* sake I will not *rest,*
until her vindication *shines out* like the *dawn,*
and her *salvation* like a burning *torch.*

*Express with your voice the awe one feels when beholding something of great beauty. Pause at the end of the sentence. Speak earnestly and reassuringly.*

"The *nations* shall see your *vindication,*
and all the *kings* your *glory;*
and you shall be *called* by a *new* name
that the *mouth* of the *Lord* will *give.*
You shall be a crown of *beauty* in the *hand* of the *Lord,*
and a royal *diadem* in the *hand* of your *God.*

"You shall no *more* be termed 'Forsaken,'
and your *land* shall no more be termed '*Desolate*';
but *you* shall be called 'My *Delight* Is in *Her*,'
and your *land* 'Married';
for the Lord *delights* in you,
and your *land* shall be *married.*

*This closing section should be proclaimed with tenderness and deep joy.*

"For as a young *man* marries a young *woman,*
so shall your *builder* marry *you,*
and as the *bridegroom rejoices* over the *bride,*
so shall your *God* rejoice over *you.*"

---

READING I   Exulting in Jerusalem's glory, this passage was written at the end of Israel's exile in Babylon. While the leading citizens of Jerusalem had been away, longing to return to their beloved city, the city itself had been lying in ruins. Now, however, God declares the importance of Jerusalem and the blessings that will be bestowed on it. Jerusalem will shine like the dawn; it will be as radiant as jewels. The splendor of God's chosen people, as depicted in the city itself, will be evident to all.

This passage was used also at the Christmas Vigil (see that commentary for further discussion). Its use today continues our celebration of Epiphany. On Epiphany, we proclaim that God's glory is manifest to all the world. This passage from Isaiah declares that the city of Jerusalem shines forth in splendor as a sign of God's greatness and love for the people of the city.

There are two aspects of this reading that require special emphasis today: Raise your voice joyfully as you proclaim the greatness of God, seen in the splendor of

Jerusalem; and speak tenderly of the tremendous love and commitment of God toward this people, imaged in the love of newlyweds.

READING II   This beautiful passage from Paul on the gifts of the Spirit is a celebration of what it means to live in a Christian community. Despite great diversity and different outlooks, there is one Spirit, who inspires all activity for the sake of the common good. Our challenge is to recognize

JANUARY 14, 2001 ■ 2ND SUNDAY IN ORDINARY TIME

## READING II    1 Corinthians 12:4–11

**A reading from the first letter of Paul to the Corinthians**

**Paul is trying to teach his community; speak accordingly. Proper stress is particularly important in this opening line. Give emphasis to "gifts," "services," and "activities," and especially to the word "same" throughout this section.**

**The Spirit is not given simply for personal use but for the entire community.**

**Although there is a similar presentation given to many of these gifts, each is unique. Try to provide some variety in your proclamation, so that each one stands out. Pause briefly after each gift.**

There are varieties of *gifts*, but the *same Spirit*;
and there are varieties of *services*, but the *same Lord*;
and there are varieties of *activities*,
but it is the *same God* who activates *all* of them in *everyone*.

To *each* is given the *manifestation* of the *Spirit*
for the common *good*.
To *one* is given through the Spirit the utterance of *wisdom*,
and to *another* the utterance of *knowledge*
according to the *same* Spirit,
to another *faith* by the same *Spirit*,
to another gifts of *healing* by the *one Spirit*,
to another the working of *miracles*,
to another *prophecy*,
to another the discernment of *spirits*,
to another various kinds of *tongues*,
to another the *interpretation* of tongues.

**Pause before proclaiming this line slowly and with a strong voice.**

*All* these are activated by *one* and the same *Spirit*,
who allots to *each* one *individually* just as the Spirit *chooses*.

## GOSPEL    John 2:1–12

**A reading from the holy gospel according to John**

There was a *wedding* in Cana of *Galilee*,
and the *mother* of Jesus was there.
*Jesus* and his *disciples* had *also* been invited to the *wedding*.

both our own gifts and those of other members of our communities, in order to build up the entire community as lovingly and effectively as possible.

Paul continually needed to reprimand the members of the Corinthian community and guide them in their faith development. It was not that the Corinthians were faithless or wayward. Often the problem was precisely one of excessive enthusiasm. In worship, some were given spectacular signs of God's power in their lives, such as speaking in tongues or prophesying God's messages. Paul must remind them that these are gifts

from God and should not be sources of personal pride. In addition, others also manifest God in their activities, even if their gifts are more subdued. Paul asserts that God, the source of all charisms, is one. There is one Spirit, one Lord (Jesus), one God. And the gifts given by the Spirit are given for the good of all.

Offer this message to your community as a reminder to appreciate the gifts of every member, young and old, male and female, whether rich or poor, educated or not. It is an assurance to those who do not see themselves as an integral part of the community

to know that their presence and their particular skills are essential for the church. And it is a reminder to those in leadership positions and those with more noticeable gifts that everything comes from God and that their gifts are no greater and no lesser than anyone else's.

GOSPEL The gospel of John is filled with more symbolism and deeper meaning than first appears. In the story of the wedding at Cana, a simple account of an extraordinary event takes on

## 2ND SUNDAY IN ORDINARY TIME ■ JANUARY 14, 2001

**Jesus' mother is given few words here. How do you think she intends this? Express it as you imagine her speaking.**

**Although Jesus' words are not meant to be harsh, he is asserting his authority over his mother's. Do not overemphasize "woman," but focus on the rest of the question.**

**Her words here are confident and decisive.**

When the *wine* gave out, the mother of Jesus *said* to him,
"They have no *wine*."
And Jesus said to her,
"*Woman*, what concern is that to *you* and to *me*?
My *hour* has not yet *come*."
His mother said to the servants,
"Do *whatever* he *tells* you."

Now *standing* there were six stone *water* jars
for the Jewish rites of *purification*,
*each* holding about a hundred *litres*.

**Jesus is in charge. Although his words are few, they are spoken with authority.**

Jesus said to the servants, "*Fill* the jars with *water*."
And they filled them up to the *brim*.
He said to them, "Now *draw* some *out*,
and take it to the chief *steward*."
So they *took* it.

When the steward *tasted* the *water* that had become *wine*,
and did not *know* where it *came* from

**This line is parenthetical. Speak it somewhat quickly.**

(though the servants who had *drawn* the water *knew*),
the steward called the *bridegroom* and said to him,

**There is amazement and perhaps a bit of reproach in his comment.**

"Everyone serves the *good* wine *first*,
and then the *inferior* wine after the guests have become *drunk*.
But *you* have kept the good wine until *now*."

**Speak with certitude.**

Jesus *did* this, the *first* of his signs, in *Cana* of *Galilee*,
and revealed his *glory*;
and his disciples *believed* in him.

**Capernaum = kuh-PER-nee-*m**

*After* this he went down to *Capernaum* with his *mother*,
his *brothers*, and his *disciples*;
and they *remained* there a few *days*.

---

even greater meaning when examined in light of the gospel as a whole. As the concluding lines claim, this first "sign" of Jesus is intended to display his glory. It is also an inspiration to faith.

Jesus responds to his mother's observation by asserting that his hour has not yet come. The "hour" in John's gospel is always that of Jesus' death on the cross, which manifests his glory. The story of Cana is thus linked with Jesus' sacrifice on the cross, suggesting that the water become wine

should be interpreted in the same light. The "sign" that most fully reveals Jesus' glory is the shedding of his blood on the cross. And the eucharistic wine is Jesus' blood, shed for all. For this reason, Christian art has long linked this story with the eucharist.

The jugs in which the water is poured are those used in Jewish ceremonial washings. Such purification rituals were—and are—very important for law-abiding Jews. Since Jesus himself is linked with the wine, the use of these jars for holding the wine suggests that salvation comes out of Judaism, with its extensive religious observances. At

the same time, the new wine is better than what was originally served, as the steward observes. The new life brought by Jesus, himself fully Jewish, is superior to that available under the Jewish law.

Although this story is familiar, there is much here that is exciting to proclaim. Meditate on the passage's significance so that you will be able to proclaim it with a sincerity and exuberance.

# JANUARY 21, 2001

# 3RD SUNDAY IN ORDINARY TIME

*Lectionary #69*

### READING I    Nehemiah 8:1–4a, 5–6, 8–10

**A reading from the book of Nehemiah**

All the *people* gathered together
    into the *square* before the *Water* Gate.
They told the scribe *Ezra* to bring the book of the *law* of *Moses*,
which the *Lord* had given to *Israel*.
Accordingly, the priest *Ezra* brought the *law*
    before the *assembly*,
both *men* and *women*
    and all who could *hear* with *understanding*.
This was on the *first* day of the *seventh* month.
He *read* from it *facing* the square before the *Water* Gate
from early *morning* until *midday*,
in the presence of the *men* and the *women*
and those who could *understand*;
and the *ears* of all the people were *attentive*
to the *book* of the *law*.
The scribe *Ezra* stood on a wooden *platform*
that had been *made* for the *purpose*.

And Ezra *opened* the book in the *sight* of *all* the *people*,
for he was standing *above* all the people;
and when he *opened* it, all the people stood *up*.

---

**Stress the length of this reading.**

**Lighten your voice and speak enthusiastically to stress the attentiveness of the people.**

---

READING I    Ezra was a leading figure in the period following the rebuilding of the Jerusalem temple. The temple had been destroyed by the Babylonians and the leading members of Judean society taken into captivity in Babylon. When they returned, they set about building another temple and, as this passage attests, again devoted themselves to God. Ezra was instrumental in helping the people purify themselves, encouraging them to set aside any customs they had acquired from other peoples during the exile.

Ezra reads the law God gave to Moses to the gathered people. It is not entirely clear how much of the Pentateuch (the first five books of the Hebrew Bible) Ezra read, but it must have included some materials dictating proper conduct and ritual. It was certainly complex, since the Levites needed to interpret it so that the people could better understand it.

The response of the people is interesting. They stand transfixed, listening attentively to Ezra's words. When Ezra holds the sacred book for them to see, they bow down to worship God. But they also weep, whether

in sorrow at their own failings or because they are touched by the words. Since Ezra tells them to act joyfully and to feast, it appears that they react in sorrow. At the same time it was the people who asked Ezra to read the law in the first place, and they listen for hours on end. They are eager to learn what they must do in order to serve God fully.

This attentiveness and love for the word of God is what we all wish for our own assemblies. Your task is to act as Ezra did, holding your listeners in rapt attention while

**3RD SUNDAY IN ORDINARY TIME ■ JANUARY 21, 2001**

*Let the enthusiasm of the people be heard.*

Then Ezra *blessed* the Lord, the great *God,*
and all the people *answered,* "Amen, Amen,"
    *lifting* up their *hands.*
Then they *bowed* their *heads*
and *worshipped* the Lord with their *faces* to the *ground.*

*Ezra read the law in Hebrew, and the Levites either offered instruction or translated Ezra's words into Aramaic, the language of the people.*

So the *Levites* read from the book,
from the *law* of *God,* with *interpretation.*
They gave the *sense,* so that the people *understood* the *reading.*
And *Nehemiah,* who was the *governor,*
    and *Ezra* the priest and *scribe,*
and the *Levites* who *taught* the people
said to all the *people,*

*Speak comfortingly.*

"This day is *holy* to the Lord your *God;*
do not *mourn* or *weep.*"
For all the people *wept* when they heard the *words* of the *law.*

Then Ezra said to them,
"Go your *way,* eat the *fat* and drink sweet *wine*
and send *portions* of them to those for whom nothing is *prepared,*
for *this* day is *holy* to our *Lord;*
and do not be *grieved,*
for the *joy* of the Lord is your *strength.*"

---

## READING II    1 Corinthians 12:12–30

**A reading from the first letter of Paul to the Corinthians**

*Throughout this reading, give slight emphasis to the word "one" wherever it appears.*
*Speak firmly and decisively.*

Just as the body is *one* and has many *members,*
and all the *members* of the body, though *many,* are one *body,*
so it is with *Christ.*

you share God's word with them. You do this by the way you speak and move, and by the enthusiasm you bring to the reading. After all, hearing God's law is cause for rejoicing; it is not burdensome or tiring. Ezra declared that the day when Israel heard God's law was holy; it was a day for celebrating. Listening to God's word can be enlivening for us as well.

Today you are Ezra, sharing the word of God with the members of your assembly. Be sure you have their attention before you

begin. Express with amazement the attentiveness of the crowd, and convey their sincerity as they hear the law. Proclaim with vigor the words of Ezra to go forth and celebrate. Let this instruction ring in the ears of your hearers today.

READING II   Paul's beautiful metaphor of the church as a body whose parts must work in harmony picks up on last Sunday's reading. There Paul discussed the gifts of the Spirit, which God gives to each person in order to edify the entire community. It would be helpful to go back and read

that passage first before continuing to prepare today's reading.

Just as the physical body has many parts, so also the community of Christians comprises many different people, each with different abilities and interests. But the one Spirit of God gives all of these various gifts. We become filled with this same Spirit in baptism. We must spend the rest of our lives appreciating our own gifts and the fact that the Spirit enlivens those around us, however different their skills and interests may be.

JANUARY 21, 2001 ■ 3RD SUNDAY IN ORDINARY TIME

**Imagine a foot or an ear actually talking, and read this section with that in mind. Then your voice will express the foolishness of claiming that some members are more important than others.**

For in the *one Spirit* we were all *baptized* into one *body*
—*Jews* or *Greeks, slaves* or *free*—
and we were *all* made to drink of *one Spirit*.

Indeed, the body does not consist of *one* member but of *many*.
If the *foot* would say,
"Because I am not a *hand*, I do not *belong* to the body,"
that would not make it any less a *part* of the body.

And if the *ear* would say,
"Because I am not an *eye*, I do not *belong* to the body,"
*that* would not make it any less a *part* of the body.
If the whole *body* were an *eye*,
where would the *hearing* be?
If the whole *body* were *hearing*,
where would the sense of *smell* be?

**Now speak solemnly and slowly.**

But as it *is*,
God *arranged* the members in the *body*,
each *one* of them, as he *chose*.
If all were a single *member*, where would the *body* be?
As it *is*, there are *many* members, yet *one body*.
The *eye* cannot say to the *hand*, "I have no *need* of you,"
nor again the *head* to the *feet*, "I have no need of *you*."
On the *contrary*,
the *members* of the body that *seem* to be *weaker*
     are *indispensable*,
and those *members* of the body that we think less *honourable*
we clothe with *greater* honour,
and our less *respectable* members are treated with *greater* respect;
whereas our *more* respectable members do not *need* this.

---

Paul provides a compelling argument for recognizing the various gifts each person has. There can be no question that the parts of the body must work in concert with one another in order for the entire body to function. No part is insignificant, and no part is so great that it can take the place of the others. As Paul says, if everything were an eye, how would we hear or smell? Even the parts of the body that embarrass us are given honor, even honor greater than the other, less embarrassing parts.

Think of what this means when applied to the Christian community! Each task is necessary and noble, no one is insignificant, and no one can claim superiority over anyone else. And think of someone in your community who causes you embarrassment. Far from being shunned, that one is to be given greater honor! This message is both encouraging and challenging.

Paul was responding to a tendency in the Corinthian community to value some gifts, such as speaking in tongues, over other, less spectacular ones. Paul's hierarchy reverses their expected order, placing

the gift of speaking in tongues in the last position. How do you think Paul would respond to the hierarchies in our churches today? If he were to look at your community, would he be assured that all members were exercising their gifts? Would he need to correct some who consider themselves more important than others?

Proclaim this passage with sincerity and respect for each gift from God and for each member of your community. When Paul directly addresses the Corinthians ("you are the body of Christ"), offer these words to your

**3RD** SUNDAY IN ORDINARY TIME ■ JANUARY 21, 2001

**Offer these words with earnest compassion.**

But *God* has so arranged the *body*,
giving the *greater* honour to the *inferior* member,
that there may be no *dissension* within the *body*,
but the *members* may have the same *care* for one *another*.
If *one* member suffers, *all* suffer *together* with it;
if one member is *honoured*, all *rejoice* together *with* it.

**This is a key line. Give it great emphasis. It is only when all members of the community are truly appreciated that we can claim to be the body of Christ.**

Now *you* are the body of *Christ*
and individually *members* of it.
And God has appointed in the *church* first *apostles*,
second *prophets*, third *teachers*;
then deeds of *power*, then gifts of *healing*,
forms of *assistance*, forms of *leadership*,
various kinds of *tongues*.

**Speak the questions slowly, although the negative answer to each is readily apparent. The passage ends rather abruptly. Read the final lines slowly, then provide a lengthy pause before returning to your seat.**

Are *all* apostles? Are all *prophets*?
Are all *teachers*? Do *all* work *miracles*?
Do *all* possess gifts of *healing*?
Do *all* speak in *tongues*? Do all *interpret*?

*[Shorter: 1 Corinthians 12:12 – 14, 27]*

---

### GOSPEL   Luke 1:1–4; 4:14–21

**A reading from the holy gospel according to Luke**

Since *many* have undertaken to set down an orderly *account*
of the *events* that have been fulfilled *among* us,
just as they were handed *on* to us by *those*
      who from the *beginning*
were *eyewitnesses* and *servants* of the *word*,

**Pause before and after "from the beginning."**

---

own listeners. Finally, pray that you might touch their hearts so that the value of each member of the community might be known and the oneness envisioned by Paul created.

GOSPEL Today we begin in earnest this liturgical year's journey through the gospel of Luke. We have heard from Luke before, during Advent and Christmas, and we shall occasionally read from other gospels in the months ahead, but

it is the gospel of Luke that will predominate in our gospel readings during Ordinary Time.

The gospel of Luke opens, as does today's gospel reading, with an introduction that sets the stage for the rest of the two-volume work, the gospel of Luke and the Acts of the Apostles. The author writes in relatively polished Greek and uses many of the techniques employed in the Greek tradition of history writing. Although others have written similar accounts, our author claims to have researched the material and gained trustworthy witnesses before putting this information in writing. Indeed, all of the

gospels are compositions written long after the events they record. Decades of oral tradition preceded the composition of even the earliest gospel. This two-volume work is dedicated to a certain Theophilus, whose name means "lover of God."

After the introductory paragraph, the lectionary skips to the beginning of Jesus' ministry. (The intervening material is the story of Jesus' birth and childhood.) The author paints a rosy picture of Jesus' popularity and influence. Ironically, today's passage

JANUARY 21, 2001 ■ 3RD SUNDAY IN ORDINARY TIME

**Theophilus = thee-OF-uh-luhs**

**Pause after "instructed" before beginning again on a strong note.**

I *too* decided,
after investigating everything *carefully* from the very *first*,
to write an orderly *account* for you, most excellent *Theophilus*,
so that you may know the *truth*
concerning the *things* about which you have been *instructed.*

*Jesus, filled* with the power of the *Spirit,*
returned to *Galilee,*
and a *report* about him *spread*
        through all the surrounding *country.*
He began to *teach* in their *synagogues*
and was *praised* by *everyone.*

When he came to *Nazareth,*
where he had been brought *up,*
Jesus went to the *synagogue* on the *sabbath* day,
as was his *custom.*

**Jesus seems to have chosen this passage. The entire gospel presents him as the fulfillment of it. Read the passage slowly and forcefully.**

He stood up to *read,*
and the *scroll* of the prophet *Isaiah* was *given* to him.
He *unrolled* the scroll
and found the *place* where it was *written:*
"The *Spirit* of the Lord is *upon* me,
because he has *anointed* me to bring *good news* to the *poor.*
He has *sent* me to proclaim *release* to the *captives*
and recovery of *sight* to the *blind,*
to let the *oppressed* go *free,*
to *proclaim* the year of the Lord's *favour."*

And Jesus rolled up the *scroll,*
gave it *back* to the *attendant,* and sat *down.*
The eyes of *all* in the synagogue were *fixed* on him.

**Speak this final line slowly and with great solemnity.**

Then Jesus began to *say* to them,
*"Today* this *scripture* has been *fulfilled* in your *hearing."*

ends immediately before the synagogue crowd in Nazareth turns against Jesus and tries to throw him off a cliff.

Jesus reads a passage from the prophet Isaiah in which the anointed of the Lord speaks, proclaiming good news to those who have been without favor. The poor, the captives, the blind, the prisoners—all those who are in pain, struggling and often rejected— will have their situations reversed. Indeed,

the entire gospel of Luke is about change in the present reality, when what is expected is turned on its head. By reading this passage, Jesus not only offers himself as the anointed one of God, the fulfillment of God's promises, but also as a revolutionary. He is a preacher of a new world order in which the disenfranchised find favor and the despised are chosen.

Your proclamation of this passage sets the tone for much of the rest of this liturgical year. Let Jesus' words be forceful and

prophetic, offering hope to those without hope. In this way, you may be able to offer the downtrodden in your own community the hope to carry on, knowing that Jesus came for their sake.

# JANUARY 28, 2001

# 4TH SUNDAY IN ORDINARY TIME

*Lectionary #72*

**READING I**    Jeremiah 1:4–5, 17–19

**A reading from the book of the prophet Jeremiah**

**Speak tenderly.**

Now the *word* of the *Lord came* to me saying,
"Before I *formed* you in the *womb*, I *knew* you,
and before you were *born*, I *consecrated* you;
I *appointed* you a *prophet* to the *nations*.

**Jeremiah is to be a prophet not only to the chosen people but to all nations.**

**The tone becomes more ominous here, as a battle ensues.**

"Therefore, *gird* up your *loins*;
stand *up* and *tell* the people *everything* that I *command* you.
Do not break *down* before them,
or I will break *you* before them.
And *I* for *my* part have made you today a fortified *city*,
an iron *pillar*, and a bronze *wall*,
against the whole *land*—
against the *kings* of *Judah*,
its *princes*, its *priests*, and the *people* of the *land*.

**Lighten your voice a bit, and speak encouragingly.**

**End on a strong note.**

"They will *fight* against you;
but they shall not *prevail* against you,
for *I* am *with* you, says the Lord, to *deliver* you."

---

**READING I**    The prophet Jeremiah's message often resonates with us because it flows from his own struggles with his ministry. He argues with God about his capabilities, but he also responds faithfully, even when threatened with death. Often remembered as a prophet of doom, he advised the king of Judah to accept foreign control in order for Judah to survive. Just as Jerusalem was about to be conquered by the Babylonians, Jeremiah offered encouraging words, stressing God's commitment to this people.

Today we read part of Jeremiah's call to ministry. Even before he was born, he was set aside for this task. God chose him not only to go to the people of Israel but to the Gentiles as well.

The task ahead of Jeremiah is daunting. There will be some who will oppose his message. But God will provide not only words but strength for the prophet. Even though he will challenge the most powerful people of the land, God assures Jeremiah that he will not be conquered.

The prophets of our own time know well what it is like to feel opposition, to take on the strong and powerful. But we can see in them (whether Martin Luther King Jr., Mother Teresa, Dorothy Day, or others) the iron will to resist and continue to proclaim God's love for all, even—and especially—the outcast.

The call of Jeremiah also has much in common with the beginning of Jesus' ministry. Jesus was chosen before he was born and sent to all the nations. He experienced conflict and resistance to his message. But we believe that God delivered him, that he has not been conquered despite all appearances to the contrary.

JANUARY 28, 2001 ■ 4TH SUNDAY IN ORDINARY TIME

## READING II    1 Corinthians 12:31—13:13

**A reading from the first letter of Paul to the Corinthians**

Brothers and sisters,
*strive* for the *greater* gifts.
And I will *show* you a still more *excellent* way.

If I *speak* in the tongues of *mortals* and of *angels*,
but do not have *love*,
I am a noisy *gong* or a clanging *cymbal*.
If I have prophetic *powers*,
and understand all *mysteries* and all *knowledge*,
and if I have all *faith*, so as to remove *mountains*,
but do not have *love*, I am *nothing*.
If I give away *all* my *possessions*,
and if I hand over my *body* so that I may *boast*,
but do not have *love*, I *gain* nothing.

*Love* is *patient*; love is *kind*;
love is not *envious* or *boastful* or *arrogant* or *rude*.
It does *not* insist on its own *way*;
it is not *irritable* or *resentful*;
it does not rejoice in *wrongdoing*,
but *rejoices* in the *truth*.
It *bears* all things, *believes* all things,
*hopes* all things, *endures* all things.
*Love* never *ends*.

But as for *prophecies*, they will come to an *end*;
as for *tongues*, they will *cease*;
as for *knowledge*, it will come to an *end*.

---

**Start each sentence on a hopeful note, then lower your voice with the words "but do not have love."**

**Pause, then begin again slowly, building in volume, speed and intensity as you proceed.**

**Pause. Stress the contrasts in the following lines.**

---

As you proclaim today's reading, keep in mind the prophets in your own community or your own life. Speak tenderly to them, and offer them God's supportive words, so that this reading might be a source of strength for all who must challenge the powerful in order to work for justice.

READING II This intensely beautiful passage on the greatest gift, love, is an inspiration for all who read it. Although it is often used at weddings, it is directed to all of us.

There were several competing factions in the Corinthian community, and some members claimed to have greater gifts than others. These more spectacular charisms, such as speaking in tongues and prophesying God's messages, were the cause of much boasting. This teaching on love proclaims the goal of the Christian life and serves as a challenge to those who would claim superiority.

Paul begins by declaring that spectacular spiritual gifts are useless unless they are grounded in love. Without love, everything else is lost. This is not a "warm and fuzzy" or romantic love, but a deep, abiding commitment to another. This love truly desires the best for the other and strives to make that a reality. The second section of the reading includes several statements about what love is (and is not). Proclaim this section even more slowly than usual, allowing each line to sink in. The conciseness of Paul's message reveals the depth of what he is expressing.

Paul goes on to speak of the lasting nature of love. Even if all else fails and

**52**

4TH SUNDAY IN ORDINARY TIME ■ JANUARY 28, 2001

---

prophesy = PROF-uh-sī

For we *know* only in *part*, and we *prophesy* only in *part*;
but when the *complete* comes, the *partial* will come to an *end*.
When I was a *child*, I *spoke* like a child,
I *thought* like a child, I *reasoned* like a child;
when I became an *adult*, I put an *end* to childish ways.

For *now* we see in a *mirror*, *dimly*,
but *then* we will see *face* to *face*.
*Now* I know only in *part*;
*then* I will know *fully*, even as I have been fully *known*.

**Close very slowly, stressing each of the three terms, and especially emphasizing the final word.**

Now *faith*, *hope*, and *love* abide, these *three*;
and the *greatest* of these is *love*.

*[Shorter: 1 Corinthians 13:4–13]*

---

### GOSPEL    Luke 4:21–30

**A reading from the holy gospel according to Luke**

Jesus, *filled* with the *power* of the *Spirit*,
came to *Nazareth*, where he had been brought *up*.
He went to the *synagogue* on the *sabbath* day, as was his *custom*,
and *read* from the prophet *Isaiah*.
The eyes of *all* were *fixed* on him.
Then he began to say to them,

**This is a solemn declaration. Speak slowly and forcefully.**

*"Today* this *scripture* has been *fulfilled* in your *hearing*."
All spoke *well* of him
and were *amazed* at the gracious *words*
     that came from his *mouth*.
They said, "Is not this *Joseph's* son?"

**Try to convey the peoples' questioning of Jesus' teaching. How could the son of someone they knew have such authority?**

---

passes away, love will remain. In the future, when all is brought to perfection in God, nothing of the things of this world will remain except love. All other gifts are imperfect, poor reflections of a greater reality. But love, together with faith and hope, will endure. And, as Paul says, the greatest of these is love.

Proclaiming this passage is both a joy and a challenge. Do not rush through it, but give each word due weight. Resist sentimentality, but read with seriousness and

dignity. The passage has a natural rhythm to it, but be careful not to become sing-song. With plenty of practice and attentiveness to the message, you will be able to offer your listeners an eloquent lesson in love.

GOSPEL   Today's gospel picks up and continues last Sunday's and repeats some of it. Jesus claims that he fulfills the prophecy of Isaiah, in which the poor and disenfranchised receive blessings. This challenges Jesus' contemporary social reality, but the opposition he meets is directed

primarily at his inclusion of non-Jews in his mission.

The Jewish people of Jesus' time based their self-understanding and social outlook on the knowledge that they were chosen by God. God established precepts, and Israel responded, sometimes faithfully, sometimes only with great struggle. But the very existence of this people was the result of God's initiative in establishing a covenant relationship with the Hebrew people. The Hebrew

JANUARY 28, 2001 ■ 4TH SUNDAY IN ORDINARY TIME

**Capernaum = kuh-PER-nee-\*m**

**This paragraph is a direct challenge to the divine favor that many claimed for Israel.**

**Elijah = ee-LĪ-juh**

**Zarephath = ZAYR-uh-fath**
**Sidon = SĪ-duhn**

**Elisha = ee-LĪ-shuh**
**Naaman = NAY-uh-muhn**

**Express clearly the anger of the crowd.**

**Jesus, blessed with divine protection, emerges unscathed. Speak with wonder, but also with certainty.**

Jesus said to them,
"Doubtless you will *quote* to me this *proverb,*
'*Doctor,* cure *yourself!*'
And you will say, 'Do *here* also in your *hometown*
the things that we have *heard* you did at *Capernaum.*'"

And he said, "*Truly* I *tell* you,
*no* prophet is *accepted* in the prophet's *hometown.*
But the *truth* is,
there were many *widows* in Israel in the time of *Elijah,*
when the *heaven* was shut up *three years* and *six months,*
and there was a severe *famine* over all the *land;*
yet *Elijah* was sent to *none* of them
except to a widow at *Zarephath* in *Sidon.*
There were also many *lepers* in Israel
in the time of the prophet *Elisha,*
and *none* of them was *cleansed* except *Naaman* the *Syrian.*"

When they *heard* this,
*all* in the *synagogue* were filled with *rage.*
They got *up, drove* Jesus out of the *town,*
and led him to the *brow* of the *hill*
    on which their town was *built,*
so that they might *hurl* him off the *cliff.*
But Jesus *passed* through the *midst* of them and went on his *way.*

prophets likened the covenant between God and Israel to a marriage, which required total exclusion of all other parties. Israel was not to turn to other gods, and God was to remain always faithful to the chosen people.

Jesus' emphasis on the generosity of God to those outside the Jewish community, then, comes as a shock to his hearers. He speaks of God turning aside from the needy within Israel and acting compassionately

toward foreigners. On top of the outrageousness of the message, the one preaching it is a local boy, returning as an upstart after a little travel. Jesus' hearers find this unbearable, and they seize him and attempt to harm him. But his role as the anointed one of God extends beyond his preaching. God's power protects him, and he is given further opportunity to spread his revolutionary message.

There is drama in this passage, making it exciting to proclaim. In speaking Jesus'

words, try to provide a sense of the opposition he faces. Read the closing paragraph with energy, expressing the anger of the people, before ending on a peaceful note.

FEBRUARY 4, 2001

# 5TH SUNDAY IN ORDINARY TIME

*Lectionary #75*

## READING I    Isaiah 6:1–2a, 3–8

**A reading from the book of the prophet Isaiah**

Uzziah = uh-ZĪ-uh
Let your voice be filled with wonder as you describe the heavenly scene.

seraphs = SAYR-uhfs

In the *year* that King *Uzziah* died,
I *saw* the *Lord* sitting on a *throne, high* and *lofty;*
and the hem of his *robe filled* the *temple.*
*Seraphs* were in attendance *above* him;
each had six *wings.*
And one called to *another* and said:

Cry out in praise of God.

"*Holy, holy, holy* is the *Lord* of *hosts;*
the whole *earth* is *full* of his *glory.*"
The pivots on the thresholds *shook* at the *voices*
of those who *called,*
and the house *filled* with *smoke.*

Speak in despair and with humility.

And I said:
"*Woe* is *me*! I am *lost,*
for I am a man of *unclean lips,*
and I live among a *people* of unclean *lips;*
yet my *eyes* have seen the *King,* the Lord of *hosts*!"

There is hope in the action and words of the seraph.

Then one of the seraphs *flew* to me,
holding a live *coal* that had been taken from the *altar*
with a pair of *tongs.*
The seraph touched my *mouth* with it and said:
"*Now* that this has touched your *lips,*
your *guilt* has *departed* and your *sin* is blotted *out.*"

READING I  The call of Isaiah emphasizes the unworthiness of the human being in the presence of God. The setting is the heavenly court, where angels cry out in praise of God. There is majesty and an awesome power evident in this vision of God's abode.

Isaiah responds in fear-filled acknowledgement of his imperfections. No one is allowed to stand in the presence of God. The great law-giver Moses had spoken with God and was blessed with a partial view of God; he could hardly contain himself as a result.

His face radiated the divine presence. No other ordinary human could ever survive such an experience. It would be overwhelming, burning in intensity.

But Isaiah is allowed to remain in God's presence. His lips are cleansed by a burning coal, and he is purified. The image recalls the purifying effects of fire, which burns away impurities from metal or clay. But let there be no mistake: Fire on human flesh is painful. Being made worthy to serve God is not an easy process.

When Isaiah's sins have been removed and he is cleansed, he is able to respond to the Lord's call. God requires a messenger; Isaiah volunteers eagerly. One senses that there was never any unwillingness on Isaiah's part, only a profound recognition of his own sinfulness. That is no longer an obstacle.

What a joyful, challenging and reassuring passage you share today! May we all join with Isaiah in humility before God and in eagerness to proclaim God's word. Describe with awe the heavenly scene, and let your voice be filled with remorse and anxiety as

**FEBRUARY 4, 2001** ■ 5TH SUNDAY IN ORDINARY TIME

Then I heard the *voice* of the *Lord* saying,
"*Whom* shall I *send*, and *who* will *go* for us?"
And I said, "*Here* am *I*; send *me*!"

> Read these final words slowly and with eagerness.

---

### READING II    1 Corinthians 15:1–11

**A reading from the first letter of Paul to the Corinthians**

> Paul is reminding the Corinthians of things they already know.

I would *remind* you, brothers and sisters,
of the *good news* that I *proclaimed* to you,
which you in turn *received*, in which also you *stand*.
This is the *good news* through which also you are being *saved*,
if you hold *firmly* to the message that I *proclaimed* to you—
unless you have come to *believe* in *vain*.

> Paul tries to encourage the community to remain faithful; speak supportively.

> Lower your voice and proceed solemnly.

For I handed *on* to you as of first *importance*
what *I* in *turn* had *received*:
that Christ *died* for our sins in *accordance* with the *scriptures*,
and that he was *buried*,
and that he was *raised* on the third *day*
in accordance with the *scriptures*,
and that he appeared to *Cephas*, then to the *twelve*.

> Lift your voice a little as you speak of Christ's resurrection.

> Cephas = SEE-fuhs
> "Peter" means "rock" in Greek. *Cephas* is the Aramaic word for "rock."

Then Christ appeared to more than five *hundred*
    brothers and sisters at one *time*,
*most* of whom are still *alive*, though *some* have *died*.

Then he appeared to *James*, then to *all* the apostles.
*Last* of all, as to one untimely *born*,
    *Christ* appeared also to *me*.

> Pause before proclaiming humbly Paul's own experience.

---

you speak Isaiah's self-effacing words. But concentrate especially on the eagerness of his response to God's call, so that each member of your community might be inspired to respond similarly.

**READING II** The passage you proclaim today provides a valuable insight into the earliest preaching of the Christian community. Paul's writings are the oldest Christian documents we have, and here he identifies traditions that were passed on to him, which he shares with the Corinthians. This passage contains the central teaching of Christianity: Jesus died for our sins, was buried, and rose again. This is the gospel in a nutshell, to which we assent every time we offer our "Amen" in the eucharistic assembly. Proclaim it solemnly and with certainty.

The details of Paul's account of Jesus' appearances are not the same as those recorded elsewhere. There are many stories of post-resurrection appearances, and various people are included among those present. The main point of the stories is that the early church experienced Jesus as having conquered death and that many witnessed his presence.

But Paul's theme is his own insignificance in comparison with the others. He, too, had an experience of the risen Lord, but he is the "least of the apostles." Like Isaiah in the first reading, he is aware of his own sinfulness and is especially sorrowful about his role in persecuting Christians before his encounter with the risen Christ. But part of his humility is in being able to accept, as

**5TH SUNDAY IN ORDINARY TIME** ■ FEBRUARY 4, 2001

**Speak with fervent trust. Read "I am what I am" especially slowly so that it will not sound trite.**

For *I* am the *least* of the apostles,
*unfit* to be *called* an apostle,
because I *persecuted* the church of *God*.
But by the *grace* of God I *am* what I *am*,
and his *grace* toward me has not been in *vain*.
On the *contrary*, I worked harder than *any* of the apostles—
though it was not *I*, but the grace of *God* that is *with* me.

Whether then it was *I* or *they*,
so we *proclaim* and so *you* have come to *believe*.

*[Shorter: 1 Corinthians 15:3–8, 11]*

---

**GOSPEL** Luke 5:1–11

**Gennesaret = geh-NES-uh-ret**

**A reading from the holy gospel according to Luke**

While Jesus was *standing* beside the lake of *Gennesaret*,
and the crowd was pressing *in* on him to hear the *word* of *God*,
he saw two *boats* there at the *shore* of the *lake*;
the *fishermen* had gone *out* of them and were washing their *nets*.

Jesus got into *one* of the boats, the one belonging to *Simon*,
and *asked* him to put out a little *way* from the *shore*.
Then he sat *down* and taught the *crowds* from the *boat*.
When he had finished *speaking*, he said to *Simon*,
"*Put* out into the *deep* water
and let down your *nets* for a *catch*."
Simon answered,
"*Master*, we have worked *all* night *long* but have caught *nothing*.
Yet if you *say* so, I will let down the *nets*."

**Pause briefly after these introductory verses.**

**Does Jesus speak as one with knowledge of what is to come? Or is his suggestion innocent? Phrase your proclamation according to your answer.**

**Peter is tired but trusting.**

---

Isaiah did, the reality of being cleansed by God. He is not going to argue with God's choices. And in spite of his worthiness, he has worked harder than anyone to spread the gospel.

As proclaimer of God's word, you are in much the same position as Paul. You have received these traditions and are passing them on to your own community. It is an awesome responsibility. Respond with Paul in humility and recognition of your own faults but also with certainty that God has chosen you. If you are truly able to make this message your own, you will effectively proclaim

it to others. Speak with pride and confidence, but without boasting.

**GOSPEL** Peter is one of the heroes of the gospel of Luke and the Acts of the Apostles, which together comprise a two-volume account of salvation history by the same author. Here the author of the gospel presents Peter sympathetically, and Jesus' call of Peter is reminiscent of Isaiah's call in the first reading and Paul's in

the second. The key theme is unworthiness in the face of the greatness of God. But Peter is called just as surely as the prophets and the other apostles.

The passage opens matter-of-factly, describing Jesus preaching from a boat. But the point of the story is not Jesus' preaching but the person of Simon (Peter). When Jesus tells Simon to put his fishing net into the water again, he is initially reluctant. He had been fishing for hours without success, but he quickly agrees to try.

**FEBRUARY 4, 2001 ■ 5TH SUNDAY IN ORDINARY TIME**

**Present this account with excitement. Surely those fishing must have been overjoyed.**

When they had *done* this,
they caught *so* many *fish* that their *nets* were beginning to *break*.
So they signalled their partners in the *other* boat
to come and *help* them.
And they *came* and filled *both* boats,
so that they began to *sink*.

**Speak Peter's words with humility and awe.**

But when Simon Peter *saw* it,
he fell down at Jesus' *knees*, saying,
"Go *away* from me, Lord, for I am a *sinful man!*"

For Simon *Peter* and all who were *with* him were *amazed*
at the catch of *fish* that they had taken;
and so *also* were *James* and *John*, sons of *Zebedee*,
who were *partners* with Simon.
Then Jesus said to Simon,

**Jesus speaks words of comfort.**

"Do *not* be *afraid*;
from *now on* you will be catching *people.*"

**Pause briefly after "everything" in order to stress the magnitude of what they were leaving behind.**

When they had brought their boats to *shore*,
they left *everything* and followed *Jesus*.

---

The success of Peter's fishing indicates several things. First, it points to Jesus' special relationship to God, revealed in his otherworldly knowledge or his miraculous abilities (the passage doesn't say which). The superior catch also provides Peter with the opportunity to express his awe in Jesus' presence and his knowledge of his own unworthiness. But Jesus assures him that he

need not be afraid, and soon he and his companions become disciples of Jesus. Finally, the record-breaking catch of fish indicates the success the gospel will enjoy when preached by Peter and the other apostles.

We are all called to lives of discipleship. Following Jesus requires recognizing our own sinfulness, but it also involves trusting in God's goodness and ability to use us as instruments of divine action. The gospel of Luke, read throughout Ordinary Time in this liturgical year, makes clear that discipleship

is costly and difficult. But the knowledge of Jesus' magnificence makes it not only worthwhile but almost impossible to resist.

Proclaim this gospel with enthusiasm, and give plenty of expression to the words of Jesus and Peter. Offer it to your community as a commentary on what it means to know Jesus and to respond to God's call to proclaim the good news to all.

## FEBRUARY 11, 2001

# 6TH SUNDAY IN ORDINARY TIME

*Lectionary #78*

### READING I    Jeremiah 17:5–8

**A reading from the book of the prophet Jeremiah**

*Thus* says the *Lord*:
"*Cursed* are those who trust in mere *mortals*
and make mere *flesh* their *strength*,
whose *hearts* turn away from the *Lord*.
They shall be like a *shrub* in the *desert*,
and shall not *see* when *relief* comes.
They shall live in the *parched* places of the *wilderness*,
in an uninhabited *salt* land.

"*Blessed* are those who *trust* in the *Lord*,
whose *trust* is the *Lord*.
They shall be like a *tree* planted by *water*,
sending out its *roots* by the *stream*.
This tree shall not *fear* when *heat* comes,
and its *leaves* shall stay *green*;
in the year of *drought* it is not *anxious*,
and it does not *cease* to bear *fruit*."

---

*These are strong statements. Speak boldly, even with a hint of anger.*

*Pause, then lighten your voice so that the contrast with what is above will be apparent.*

*Let your voice sound gentle and refreshing.*

---

READING I  Jeremiah's strong words make clear the importance of trusting in God rather than human beings. Jeremiah spent his entire career making just that claim. Against those prophets who tried to assure the kings that they were right and that Judah should assert itself with military power, Jeremiah preached the necessity of accepting limitations. Against those

who saw only impending doom, Jeremiah preached hope. He did so by practicing what he preaches here, by seeking God's favor rather than human favor.

The message is expressed in two sections, one chastising those who place human judgment above God's and one praising those who trust in God. The outcome of the former is devastation, but the one who turns to God in faith will prosper.

Stress the contrasts between the two figures you describe. Without overemphasizing, speak darkly of the fate of the former figure. Then raise your voice in hope as you reflect on the life-giving qualities available to those who hope in God.

FEBRUARY 11, 2001 ■ 6TH SUNDAY IN ORDINARY TIME

## READING II  1 Corinthians 15:12, 16–20

**A reading from the first letter of Paul to the Corinthians**

*Paul can hardly believe that anyone would say this. Speak with astonishment.*

If *Christ* is proclaimed as *raised* from the *dead,*
how can *some* of you say there is no *resurrection* of the *dead?*

*Read slowly and clearly, so that Paul's argument will be apparent.*

For if the *dead* are not *raised,*
then *Christ* has not been *raised.*
If *Christ* has not been *raised,*
your faith is *futile* and you are still in your *sins.*
Then those also who have *died* in Christ have *perished.*

*Lift your voice in hope and confidence.*

If for *this* life *only* we have *hoped* in Christ,
we are of *all* people *most* to be *pitied.*
But in *fact* Christ *has* been *raised* from the *dead,*
the *first fruits* of those who have *died.*

## GOSPEL  Luke 6:17, 20–26

**A reading from the holy gospel according to Luke**

*Tyre = tīr*
*Sidon = SĪ-duhn*

*Read each beatitude slowly and brightly. Begin by proclaiming the unexpected recipient of the blessing with assurance, then lower your voice a bit as you conclude each line.*

Jesus came down with the *twelve* and stood on a level *place,*
with a great *crowd* of his *disciples*
     and a great *multitude* of *people*
from all *Judea, Jerusalem,* and the coast of *Tyre* and *Sidon.*

Then Jesus looked up at his *disciples* and said:
"*Blessed* are you who are *poor,*
for *yours* is the kingdom of *God.*

---

READING II  As is so often true in Paul's correspondence with the Corinthian community, Paul here responds to an apparent misunderstanding on the part of some members of the community. Some people were denying the resurrection of the dead, perhaps reflecting on the fate of members of the community who had died before Christ's return. Since they expected Christ to reveal himself in glory during their own lifetimes, many thought that any Christian who had died would not be able to enjoy the splendor of that day.

The idea of the resurrection of the dead was a point of contention for Jews of the time, and perhaps this discussion affected the Gentile Corinthian community. Whatever the source of the conflict, Paul cuts to the heart of the debate. To deny the resurrection of the dead is to deny the resurrection of Christ; the entire faith of Christians rests on belief in Christ's resurrection. Just as Jesus has been raised, so also will those Christians who have died before his return rise again. Christ is the "first fruits," the first offering to God of those who have died.

Although the immediate issue of this passage might not affect your community directly, Paul presents a wonderful opportunity to proclaim with certitude our belief that Christ has conquered death. Speak slowly so that the argument can be followed. But proclaim with vigor the final line, asserting its truth with confident faith.

GOSPEL  The "sermon on the plain" in the gospel of Luke is similar in many ways to the "sermon on the mount" in the gospel of Matthew. But it is

**6TH SUNDAY IN ORDINARY TIME ■ FEBRUARY 11, 2001**

---

*These are amazing words. Sound reassuring in the face of all this opposition.*

*Blessed* are you who are *hungry* now,
for you will be *filled*.
*Blessed* are you who *weep* now,
for you will *laugh*.
*Blessed* are you when people *hate* you,
and when they *exclude* you, *revile* you, and *defame* you
on account of the Son of *Man*.

*Speak with sincere joy, then proceed calmly.*

"*Rejoice* in that day and *leap* for *joy*,
for surely your *reward* is great in *heaven*;
for *that* is what their *ancestors* did to the *prophets*.

*Let an ominous tone fill your voice. Grow slightly more forceful as you proceed through the woes.*

"But *woe* to you who are *rich*,
for you have *received* your *consolation*.
*Woe* to you who are *full* now,
for you will be *hungry*.
*Woe* to you who are *laughing* now,
for you will *mourn* and *weep*.
*Woe* to you when all speak *well* of you,

*Emphasize this final line, especially the term "false."*

for *that* is what their *ancestors* did to the *false* prophets."

---

also significantly different. While the Matthean account spiritualizes the sufferings of the blessed ("Blessed are those who hunger and thirst *for righteousness*"), the author of this passage speaks of the truly destitute. There is no reflection on spiritual longing, but a reference to the need for physical sustenance. In keeping with a theme we shall see repeated throughout the gospel of Luke, the emphasis is on the downtrodden, the outcasts, those who struggle just to survive. Justice will be theirs.

Accepting Jesus' words is dangerous business. Those who do will be ostracized, hated and persecuted. But this should be cause for great rejoicing. Reflect on a time when you have stuck to your position even when all others disagreed. Does this description fit your experience? It is never easy to take an unpopular stand, but the author seems to say that true discipleship will not be popular.

Only in Luke's gospel are the beatitudes balanced by corresponding woes. Those who have everything that the others

lack will lose it, while the poor, hungry and mourning will gain. Everything is turned upside down.

Stress the contrasts, speaking with encouragement at the beginning and challenging your listeners with the woes. And speak assuredly that those who are challenged for their faith are in good company.

# FEBRUARY 18, 2001

# 7TH SUNDAY IN ORDINARY TIME

*Lectionary #81*

## READING I    1 Samuel 26:2, 7–9, 12–13, 22–25

**A reading from the first book of Samuel**

**Ziph = zif**

Having *heard* that David was hiding out in the *desert*,
Saul *rose* and went down to the *Wilderness* of *Ziph*,
with three thousand *chosen* men of *Israel*,
to seek *David* in the Wilderness of *Ziph*.

**Abishai = uh-BĪ-shī**

*David* and *Abishai* went into Saul's *army* by *night*;
there Saul *lay* sleeping within the *encampment*,
with his *spear* stuck in the ground at his *head*;
and *Abner* and the *army* lay *around* him.
Abishai said to *David*,

**Speak softly (but not so softly that you cannot be heard), as in a conspiratorial tone.**

"*God* has given your enemy into your *hand* today;
now therefore let me *pin* him to the *ground*
with *one* stroke of the *spear*;
I will *not* strike him *twice*."
But David said to *Abishai*,

**Speak David's words more forcefully.**

"Do *not* destroy him;
for who can raise his *hand* against the Lord's *anointed*,
and be *guiltless*?"

So David took the *spear* that was at Saul's *head* and the *water* jar,
and they went *away*.
No one *saw* it, or *knew* it, nor did anyone *awake*;
for they were all *asleep*,

**Pause before proceeding.**

because a *deep sleep* from the *Lord* had fallen *upon* them.

---

READING I  The relationship between Saul, the first king of Israel, and David, the second and greatest of all the kings of Israel, was marked by tension caused by Saul's mistrust of David. David distinguished himself as a youth and became close to the royal family. He was deeply devoted to Saul's son and even married Saul's daughter. But Saul saw him as a threat. David was well-liked and talented, and handpicked by God. Saul, by contrast, disobeyed God and increasingly fell into disfavor. Out of spite, he pursued David relentlessly and unjustly.

Today's reading is a story of one of the encounters between the two men. Saul is pursuing David, intent on destroying him, but David gains the upper hand by entering the king's camp at night. Yet David resists the temptation to kill his enemy. Instead he chooses to prove his loyalty to the king God had anointed. Despite Saul's hatred for him and attempts to kill him, David still respects the divinely appointed ruler. He proves that Saul has nothing to fear from him.

David had already been anointed as the future ruler of Israel when this event occurred. Saul's death would not have left the people without a king. Surely he could have claimed that he was acting in self-defense or was following the rules of war in doing away with his pursuer. Yet more than once David rejected the opportunity to harm Saul, guided by a force greater than the human desire for retribution or safety. Here he acts with great magnanimity. Because David was not consumed with the desire for revenge, he was able to become a great and beloved ruler.

**7TH SUNDAY IN ORDINARY TIME ▪ FEBRUARY 18, 2001**

> *This is spoken over a great distance. Without shouting, raise your voice to convey this.*

Then David went over to the other *side*,
and stood on top of a *hill* far *away*,
with a great *distance between* them.
David called aloud to *Saul*,
"*Here* is the *spear*, O king!
Let one of the young men come *over* and *get* it.

> *This line is delivered solemnly and with conviction.*

The Lord *rewards* everyone for his *righteousness*
and his *faithfulness*;
for the Lord gave you into my *hand* today,
but I would *not* raise my *hand* against the Lord's *anointed*.

As your life was *precious* today in my *sight*,
so may *my* life be *precious* in the *sight* of the *Lord*,
and may he *rescue* me from all *tribulation*."

Then Saul said to David, "*Blessed* be *you*, my son *David*!
You will do many *things* and will *succeed* in them."

So David went *his* way, and Saul returned to his *place*.

---

### READING II    1 Corinthians 15:45–50

**A reading from the first letter of Paul to the Corinthians**

It is written:
"The *first* man, *Adam*, became a living *being*";
the *last* Adam became a life-giving *spirit*.

> *Speak slowly in order to make Paul's argument clear. Stress "spiritual."*

But it is not the *spiritual* that is first,
but the *physical*, and *then* the spiritual.

> *This is a key line. Read clearly and slowly.*

The *first* was from the *earth*, made of *dust*;
the *second* is from *heaven*.

---

This story of compassion and forgiveness by one who has been wronged is inspiring even today. Read with intensity in order to convey the suspense of the story. Stress David's words of respect for Saul. Most of all, proclaim this remarkable story in such a way that your listeners will know that forgiveness is possible, no matter how serious the wrong.

READING II In today's second reading Paul continues his discussion of the question of death and resurrection. Some of the Corinthians had denied the resurrection of those in their community who had died. They expected Jesus to return soon and thought only those Christians living when he came would be able to share in the life he promised.

Paul had earlier argued that the resurrection of Jesus confirms the resurrection of the dead; denying the resurrection of those already dead means denying that Jesus has

truly conquered death. The discussion then turns to the nature of the resurrected body. It is not simply a physical body with all the imperfections that bodies on earth have; it is a powerful spiritual vessel.

The two creation stories from Genesis provide a means for understanding this contrast. In the Jewish philosophical speculation of the time, the "first Adam" (Genesis 1) was a spiritual being, made in God's image, while the "second Adam" (Genesis 2) was an earthly creation, a "living soul." In today's

FEBRUARY 18, 2001 ■ 7TH SUNDAY IN ORDINARY TIME

**Speak solemnly and with assurance of what awaits us.**

As was the one of *dust*, so are those who are *of* the dust;
and as is the one of *heaven*, so are those who are *of* heaven.

Just as we have borne the *image* of the one of *dust*,
we will also bear the *image* of the one of *heaven*.

What I am *saying*, brothers and sisters, is *this*:
*flesh* and *blood* cannot *inherit* the kingdom of *God*,
nor does the *perishable* inherit the *imperishable*.

---

## GOSPEL   Luke 6:27–38

**A reading from the holy gospel according to Luke**

**Pause before "love," then let the full force of this surprising statement come through strongly. Perhaps a bit of astonishment in your voice can convey your own reaction to Jesus' words.**

**Do not rush through these instructions, but give each its due emphasis.**

Jesus addressed a great crowd of his *disciples*,
together with the *multitude*
        from *Judea*, *Jerusalem*, *Tyre* and *Sidon*.
"I say to you that *listen*:
*Love* your *enemies*, do *good* to those who *hate* you,
*bless* those who *curse* you,
*pray* for those who *abuse* you.
If anyone *strikes* you on the *cheek*, offer the *other* also;
and from anyone who takes away your *coat*
do not *withhold* even your *shirt*.
*Give* to everyone who *begs* from you;
and if anyone takes away your *goods*,
do not *ask* for them *again*.
*Do* to *others* as you would have *them* do to *you*."

**The "golden rule" is a traditional teaching found in many cultures. Pause before changing to a questioning tone.**

"If you *love* those who love *you*,
what *credit* is that to you?

---

reading, Paul corrects the order and insists that it is Jesus who is the second, heavenly Adam. He is the spiritual one.

The end of this short section draws us back to the issue of resurrection. Although we share the perishable body of the earthly Adam, we hope that we will someday bear the image of Christ, the heavenly one. In the final resurrection, our bodies will rise, as did Jesus' body, but they will not be the same. Just as Jesus walked and talked and shared meals, so also we will have real bodies. But Jesus also entered locked rooms and was not always recognizable to his

friends. Our frail bodies, too, will be transformed into glorious risen ones.

Proclaim this difficult passage slowly in order to allow your listeners to follow the argument as closely as possible. They will not have the same background you now have, so your task is to clarify the reading through your proclamation as much as possible. Stress the distinction between the first and the second Adams. Close with conviction; the final verses make Paul's point.

GOSPEL   Continuing the Lukan theme of reversal (see the commentary on last week's gospel passage), today's gospel challenges us to do precisely the opposite of what comes naturally. The first words of Jesus cut to the heart of the matter: Love your enemies; bless those who curse you. This is not easy! But it is what discipleship requires.

The exhortations that open the passage become clearer as Jesus continues. Almost everyone responds favorably when loved; real merit lies in going beyond reciprocal goodness. If it is too easy, it is not enough.

**7TH SUNDAY IN ORDINARY TIME** ▪ FEBRUARY 18, 2001

**This line is intentionally insulting.**

For even *sinners* love those who love *them*.
If you do *good* to those who do good to *you*,
what credit is *that* to you?
For even *sinners* do the *same*.
If you *lend* to those from whom you hope to *receive*,
what *credit* is that to you?
Even *sinners* lend to *sinners*, to *receive* as much *again*.

**Again, speak with solemnity, urging your listeners to respond by doing more than what seems reasonable.**

But *love* your *enemies*,
do *good*, and *lend*, expecting nothing in *return*.
Your *reward* will be *great*, and you will be
*children* of the Most *High*;
for he is *kind* to the *ungrateful* and the *wicked*.

**This is an important line. Pause before and after it, and proclaim it with both compassion and urging in your voice.**

Be *merciful*, just as your *Father* is *merciful*."

"Do not *judge*, and you will not be *judged*;
do not *condemn*, and you will not be *condemned*.
*Forgive*, and you will be *forgiven*;
*give*, and it will be *given* to you.

**Express your astonishment at the greatness of God's love.**

A good *measure*, pressed *down*, shaken *together*, running *over*,
will be put into your *lap*;
for the measure you *give* will be the measure you get *back*."

---

But Jesus' words do not make good sense! What business could run without expecting payment? Who could survive in a world in which thieves not only escape punishment but are given more goods? Jesus does not explain; he simply instructs.

Even as we want to argue, something deep inside recognizes that those who generously provide for others will not go for long in need. And the thief who is treated kindly just might decide to act kindly toward others. But it is frightening; the risk is almost more than we can bear.

The closing paragraph illustrates the results of following the illogical instructions of the passage. We shall receive what we have given others. When we act with mercy and compassion, God will act similarly toward us. Going beyond what is required will inspire God to be equally generous. It is almost as though human actions determine those of God. Perhaps the point is that humans are simply unable to comprehend the lavish generosity of God. But when we learn to offer compassion and forgiveness to others, we will learn to trust what God is offering to us.

This passage offers an immense challenge to all who hear it. Proclaim it boldly, without softening its message. Close with a passionate rendering of the generous measure of love and forgiveness God bestows on all.

FEBRUARY 25, 2001

# 8TH SUNDAY IN ORDINARY TIME

*Lectionary #84*

## READING I  Sirach 27:4–7

**A reading from the book of Sirach**

sieve = siv, refuse = REF-yoos

**Pause after the first line of each sentence, then lower your voice solemnly as you continue.**

When a sieve is *shaken*, the *refuse* appears;
so do a person's *faults* when one *speaks*.
The *kiln* tests the potter's *vessels*;
so the test of a *person* is in *conversation*.

Its *fruit* discloses the cultivation of a *tree*;
so a person's *speech* discloses the cultivation of the *mind*.
Do not *praise* people before they *speak*,
for *this* is the way people are *tested*.

**Slow down a bit for the last line.**

## READING II  1 Corinthians 15:54–58

**A reading from the first letter of Paul to the Corinthians**

**Read slowly in order to make the point clear. Pause after each line.**

When this *perishable* body puts on *imperishability*,
and this *mortal* body puts on *immortality*,
then the saying that is written will be *fulfilled*:
"*Death* has been swallowed up in *victory*."
"*Where*, O *death*, is your *victory*?
*Where*, O *death*, is your *sting*?"

**Allow your voice to ring out as you proclaim Christ's victory over death.**

The *sting* of death is *sin*,
and the *power* of sin is the *law*.

**Speak solemnly but briefly.**

READING I  The book of Sirach provides some reflections on how to act wisely. Today's passage offers a brief collection of maxims, all pointing to the importance of testing someone in order to learn that person's true character. Its message is similar to "you can't judge a book by its cover." Here, a person's speech reveals his or her true character.

To illustrate, the author draws examples from everyday life. The first two images point out how stress can often bring out someone's true nature. It is easy to speak kindly and act rightly when things are going well; the real test is when things go wrong. When a sieve is shaken, all the good grain falls through; what is left are useless husks. The fire of the kiln reveals all imperfections. Stress and difficulty do the same to people, revealing their hidden faults.

Proclaim the wisdom of this short passage simply but sincerely.

READING II  Paul's discussion here continues a line of argument that has been part of the second readings for the past two Sundays (see those commentaries). It might be helpful to look back at those earlier readings in order to understand this one better.

Paul responds to a discussion among the Corinthian Christians regarding the resurrection of the dead by asserting that indeed the dead will rise, just as Christ has. Here he closes the argument with a beautiful meditation on incorruptibility, ending with an exhortation to engage in the work of the Lord.

**8TH SUNDAY IN ORDINARY TIME ■ FEBRUARY 25, 2001**

*Again, raise your voice, this time with gratitude.*

*End on a quiet, encouraging note.*

But *thanks* be to *God*,
who gives us the *victory* through our *Lord* Jesus *Christ*.

*Therefore*, my beloved,
be *steadfast, immovable*,
always *excelling* in the *work* of the *Lord*,
because you know that in the *Lord* your *labour* is not in *vain*.

---

### GOSPEL   Luke 6:39–45

**A reading from the holy gospel according to Luke**

*Pause before moving on to the next example. Although the guide and the teacher clearly refer to the same type of person, the images are distinct.*

*Pause again before continuing, then speak with incredulity and perhaps some indignation.*

Jesus told his disciples a *parable*:
"Can a *blind* person guide a *blind* person?
Will not *both* fall into a *pit*?
A *disciple* is not above the *teacher*,
but everyone who is fully *qualified* will be *like* the *teacher*.

"Why do you see the *speck* in your *neighbour's* eye,
but do not notice the *log* in your *own* eye?
Or how can you *say* to your *neighbour*,
'Friend, let me take out the *speck* in your *eye*,'
when you *yourself* do not see the *log* in your *own* eye?

*This is a strong condemnation. Do not try to soften it.*

You *hypocrite*, *first* take the *log* out of your *own* eye,
and *then* you will see *clearly*
to take the *speck* out of your *neighbour's* eye.

*Observe a lengthy pause before continuing in a bit softer tone.*

"No *good* tree bears *bad* fruit,
nor again does a *bad* tree bear *good* fruit;
for *each* tree is known by its *own* fruit.

---

Just as Jesus conquered death by rising from the dead, so also each person will share in what Jesus has achieved. Resurrection means "incorruptibility" and "immortality." In other words, the human body will no longer decay, nor will death ever threaten us again. The words of the prophets are fulfilled in Jesus. Death has been vanquished, its power overcome by a far greater one.

Paul then briefly alludes to a teaching he makes elsewhere, linking sin and death. For Paul, faith in Jesus is the only thing that can lead to righteousness and life.

Proclaim Paul's message boldly. Speak comfortingly the prophetic words, and conclude with a call to action. Carefully proclaim Paul's various statements, offering assurance, comfort and challenge by your tone of voice.

GOSPEL  Jesus' teaching resonates with that found in the first reading. What is in one's heart reveals itself in one's actions, just as a tree shows its nature by its fruit. The earlier part of the reading provides lessons on discipleship and making judgments.

In a parable about the relationship between teachers and students, Jesus declares that the blind cannot lead the blind. Neither will reach the destination but will

FEBRUARY 25, 2001 ■ 8TH SUNDAY IN ORDINARY TIME

*Figs* are not gathered from *thorns*,
nor are *grapes* picked from a *bramble* bush.

**Speak encouragingly the words about the good person.**

"Out of the *good treasure* of the *heart*,
the *good* person produces *good*,
and out of *evil* treasure,
the *evil* person produces *evil*;
for it is out of the abundance of the *heart* that the *mouth* speaks."

stumble on the way. Jesus highlights the importance of having clear vision and knowing the path to follow, especially for the leaders of a community. Leaders do not need to have all the answers, but they must know the basic direction to follow. Otherwise they are simply blind guides.

The same is true of leaders today. Are the people we admire visionaries? Or do they go through life with blinders on? It is important to choose our mentors wisely, for their example influences how we live and the choices we make.

Jesus' harsh words about the hypocrisy of attempting to remove the splinter in another's eye despite the log in one's own can really hit home. Although the image is humorous, the message is not. It is often much easier to recognize what changes someone else needs to make than to address our own faults and failings. Today's gospel provides a needed reminder that reform begins at home.

**Proclaim this teaching of Jesus with vigor. Offer it as a challenge to yourself and to your community to concentrate on personal reform in order to produce good fruit.**

FEBRUARY 28, 2001

# ASH WEDNESDAY

*Lectionary #220*

### READING I    Joel 2:12–18

**A reading from the book of the prophet Joel**

*Draw attention to the present need for repentance; stress "now." Then speak slowly and sincerely.*

"Even *now*," says the Lord,
"*return* to me with all your *heart*,
with *fasting*, with *weeping*, and with *mourning*;
rend your *hearts* and not your *clothing*.

*Let the majestic nature of God's love shine through these words.*

"*Return* to the Lord, your *God*,
for he is *gracious* and *merciful*,
*slow* to *anger*, and *abounding* in steadfast *love*,
and relents from *punishing*."

*Speak with hope and awe.*

Who *knows* whether the Lord will not turn and *relent*,
and leave a *blessing* behind him:
a *grain* offering and a *drink* offering
to be presented to the Lord, your *God*?

*Read these short phrases forcefully. Be careful not to sacrifice clarity or to become sing-song.*

Blow the *trumpet* in *Zion*;
sanctify a *fast*;
call a *solemn assembly*;
*gather* the *people*.
*Sanctify* the congregation;
*assemble* the aged;
gather the *children*, even infants at the *breast*.
Let the *bridegroom* leave his *room*,
and the *bride* her *canopy*.

---

READING I  We begin our annual season of repentance, prayer and renewal with a stark reminder of our need to turn our hearts and minds to God. The first reading, from the prophet Joel, calls us to a heartfelt conversion, a return to the presence of a God who is compassionate and loving. But this God is also powerful, able to bring judgment to an erring people, using any means available to draw them back into a loving embrace.

Joel wrote during a time of crisis in Israel. The political situation was peaceful, but Israel faced a severe locust plague and drought. Joel understands these conditions to be indicative of the Day of the Lord, the judgment of God. He believes that the people of Israel and the cultic leaders have become complacent, relying too much on rituals without the accompanying sincerity of heart that God desires. As a result, the locusts were sent as a sign of God's judgment.

But just when utter destruction seems inevitable and the end appears to be imminent, God extends the invitation that we

read today. It is still possible to return to God, to weep before the Lord, to fast and pray. Joel offers the hope that the Day of the Lord will not only be a day of judgment but one of promise and vindication as well.

We gather today to acknowledge our own complacency before God, our own tendency to wander away from our home in the bosom of God, our own need to return to God with all our hearts. We too adopt the practices that Joel recommends: We fast and

FEBRUARY 28, 2001 ■ ASH WEDNESDAY

**Proclaim this with sadness but also with dignity.**

Between the *vestibule* and the *altar*
let the *priests*, the ministers of the Lord, *weep.*
Let them say, "*Spare* your people, O Lord,
and do not make your *heritage* a *mockery*,
a byword among the *nations.*
Why should it be said among the peoples,
'*Where* is their *God*?'"

**Pause, then let your voice ring with conviction as you proclaim God's compassionate response.**

Then the Lord became *jealous* for his *land*,
and had *pity* on his *people.*

---

### READING II    2 Corinthians 5:20—6:2

**A reading from the second letter of Paul to the Corinthians**

**Plead for reconciliation.**

We are *ambassadors* for *Christ*,
since God is making his *appeal* through *us*;
we *entreat* you on behalf of *Christ*,
be *reconciled* to *God.*

**Proclaim with wonder this willingness of Christ to take on responsibility for human sin.**

For *our* sake God made Christ to be *sin* who knew *no* sin,
so that in *Christ* we might become the *righteousness* of *God.*
As we work *together* with him,
we urge you also not to accept the *grace* of God in *vain.*
For the Lord says,
"At an acceptable *time* I have *listened* to you,
and on a day of *salvation* I have *helped* you."

**You proclaim hope in God's promises, as well as the demand to put into practice the appeal for reconciliation. Speak with force and urgency.**

See, *now* is the acceptable *time*;
see, *now* is the day of *salvation!*

---

weep and repent, standing before God mindful of our sinfulness and trusting in God's mercy and love.

Your task today is to proclaim, clearly and decisively, God's call to personal and communal conversion, and the urgency of leaving all else behind in order to respond. You have an awesome responsibility today. Let the solemnity of the occasion resonate in your words.

READING II  The apostle Paul implores the Corinthians to turn to God and recognize that salvation has been

won in Christ. It is a fitting address to us as well, alerting us to our urgent need for reconciliation with God as we begin our journey through Lent.

Paul's relationship with the Corinthian church was a stormy one. The community was prone to factionalism. Sometimes Paul needed to be severe in his rebukes, resulting in strained relations with the Corinthians. Paul writes this letter after sending a delegate to the community to convey his message. He expresses in this letter his gratitude for their positive response.

Paul's appeal in this passage is urgent. Yet he does not clarify here what precipitates his message. This makes it especially available to us, living in a different time and place. The thrust of the appeal—"Be reconciled to God!"—applies to us just as to the Corinthians. But Paul also asserts that we are not engaged in this process on our own. In fact, the opportunity for holiness, for being united with God, is offered because of the salvific action of Christ. He has taken on our sinfulness, that tendency to stray from God, so that we might be brought back into an intimate relationship with God. Quoting from

**ASH WEDNESDAY ■ FEBRUARY 28, 2001**

**GOSPEL** Matthew 6:1–6, 16–18

**A reading from the holy gospel according to Matthew**

Introduce the gospel by reading these lines with solemn sincerity.

Jesus said to the disciples,
"*Beware* of practising your piety before *others*
in order to be *seen* by them;
for then you have *no reward* from your Father in *heaven*.

"So whenever you give *alms*,
do *not* sound a *trumpet* before you,
as the *hypocrites* do in the *synagogues* and in the *streets*,
so that they may be *praised* by *others*.
Truly I tell you, they have *received* their reward.
But when *you* give alms,
do not let your *left* hand know what your *right* hand is doing,
so that your *alms* may be done in *secret*;
and your *Father* who *sees* in secret will *reward* you.

"And whenever you *pray*,
do not be like the *hypocrites*;
for they *love* to stand and pray
in the *synagogues* and at the *street* corners,
so that they may be *seen* by *others*.
Truly I tell you, they have *received* their reward.
But whenever *you* pray,
go into your *room* and shut the *door*
and pray to your *Father* who is in *secret*;
and your Father who *sees* in secret will *reward* you.

hypocrites = HIP-uh-krits
synagogues = SIN-uh-gogz
Emphasize the contrast between what the hypocrites do and what is admonished here. Raise your voice at the beginning of each practice—almsgiving, praying, fasting—and stress "Truly I tell you."

---

the book of Isaiah regarding the servant of God, Paul indicates that divine aid is available to all those who serve God.

Paul says that he and his companions in ministry are ambassadors for Christ, as well as "fellow workers" with the members of the community. This is also an apt description of the role of the minister of the word, one who is part of the community but also entrusted with a noble task. You share with Paul the responsibility and the dignity

inherent in proclaiming God's message. You too announce that the time for reconciliation, for acceptance of the salvation offered in Christ, for turning to God, is now.

GOSPEL The gospel of Matthew was written for a community of Jews who believed in the saving action accomplished in Jesus' death and resurrection. This community of Jewish Christians found itself at odds with the larger Jewish community. The entire gospel reflects a tension with the synagogue and its leaders,

while preserving traditional Jewish practices and beliefs. Today's gospel passage adopts the hyperbole found in much of the gospel regarding the proper ways to act in contrast to the deeds of the "hypocrites."

Prayer, fasting and almsgiving—the pillars of Lenten observance—were time-honored practices of the Jewish people. The author upholds them, suggesting that they are central to the Christian life as well. But what is most striking is the author's insistence that all is to be done in secret.

FEBRUARY 28, 2001 ■ ASH WEDNESDAY

*In reading this reversal of ordinary behavior, allow some amazement to enter your voice.*

*Slowly and warmly proclaim this promise.*

"And whenever you *fast*,
do not look *dismal*, like the *hypocrites*,
for they *disfigure* their *faces*
so as to show *others* that they are *fasting*.
Truly I tell you, they have *received* their reward.
But when *you* fast,
put *oil* on your head and wash your *face*,
so that your fasting may be seen *not* by *others*
but by your *Father* who is in *secret*;
and your Father who *sees* in secret will *reward* you."

These words challenge us as we solemnly begin a season in which we adopt practices of austerity and denial by marking our foreheads with ashes. We are called today to reflect on why we engage in these customs. Are we truly repenting, turning ourselves back to God with sincerity of heart? Or do we take pride in proclaiming to others what we are doing? Today's gospel insists that our duty is not so much to be examples for others, but rather to repent without drawing attention to ourselves: to care for the needs of others without recompense, to pray without being noticed, to fast and yet keep up our spirits.

The emphasis on private acts of piety comes at a time when we gather as community to begin our journey of 40 days. We know that we need one another. We come together to acknowledge our failings; we resolve, in the presence of others, to turn back to the path of righteousness. We also go forth from today's gathering to put into practice the exhortations of this gospel. Your task in proclaiming the gospel is to place God's invitation and demands before the community. Then step back and allow God to work in people's lives.

MARCH 4, 2001

# 1ST SUNDAY OF LENT

*Lectionary #24*

## READING I    Deuteronomy 26:4–10

**A reading from the book of Deuteronomy**

*Moses* spoke to the *people,* saying:
"When the priest takes the *basket* from your *hand*
and sets it *down* before the *altar* of the Lord your *God,*
you shall make this *response* before the *Lord* your *God:*

"'A wandering *Aramean* was my *ancestor;*
he went down into *Egypt*
        and lived there as an *alien, few* in number,
and *there* he became a great *nation, mighty* and *populous.*
When the Egyptians treated us *harshly* and *afflicted* us,
by imposing hard *labour* on us,
we *cried* to the *Lord,* the God of our *ancestors;*
the Lord *heard* our voice
and saw our *affliction,* our *toil,* and our *oppression.*

"'The *Lord* brought us *out* of *Egypt*
with a mighty *hand* and an outstretched *arm,*
with a terrifying display of *power,* and with *signs* and *wonders;*
and he brought us into *this* place and gave us this *land,*
a land *flowing* with *milk* and *honey.*
So now I bring the *first* of the fruit of the *ground*
that *you,* O Lord, have *given* me.'"

And Moses continued,
"You shall set it *down* before the Lord your *God*
and *bow* down before the *Lord* your *God.*"

*Aramean = ayr-uh-MEE-uhn*

**Speak forcefully as you recount God's wondrous deeds.**

**Pause before concluding Moses' instructions regarding the offering.**

READING I  **The book of Deuteronomy (or "second law") purports to be the teachings of Moses given during Israel's wandering in the desert between the exodus from Egypt and the entrance into the Promised Land. Today's instructions regard how the people are to conduct themselves after they enter the land of Canaan. Moses instructs the Israelites to offer the first fruits of the land as a thanksgiving to God. The offering of first fruits, long a part of ancient Hebrew tradition, is to continue every spring as a ritual for remembering God as the source of all blessings.**

**The agricultural festival of first fruits eventually became connected with the celebration of God's deliverance of Israel from the oppression of the Egyptians. This festival of Passover recalls God's liberation of the chosen people. Today's reading establishes the liturgical requirements of the feast and has been used in Passover celebrations for thousands of years. Jews continue to recount the exodus from Egypt as a sign of God's saving actions in their lives.**

**The "wandering Aramean" is Jacob, also called Israel, whose name was adopted to identify the entire people. Jacob and his family went to Egypt during a famine in the land of Canaan. The Israelites were enslaved there, but God delivered them and brought them home once again.**

**Notice that the passage does not recount only what God has done for Israel's distant ancestors. On the feast of Passover, each Jewish household recalls how God "has brought *us* out of Egypt." The entire Jewish people identifies with both the plight of their ancestors in Egypt and the experience of the loving kindness of God, who delivers "with signs and wonders."**

MARCH 4, 2001 ■ 1ST SUNDAY OF LENT

## READING II    Romans 10:8–13

### A reading from the letter of Paul to the Romans

Brothers and sisters,
what does *scripture* say?

"The *word* is *near* you,
on your *lips* and in your *heart*"
(that is, the word of *faith* that we *proclaim*);
because if you *confess* with your lips that *Jesus* is *Lord*
and *believe* in your *heart* that God *raised* him from the dead,
you will be *saved*.

For one *believes* with the *heart* and so is *justified*,
and one *confesses* with the *mouth* and so is *saved*.

The scripture says,
"No one who *believes* in him will be put to *shame*."
For there is no *distinction* between *Jew* and *Greek*;
the same *Lord* is Lord of *all*
and is *generous* to *all* who *call* on him.
For, "Everyone who calls on the *name* of the *Lord* shall be *saved*."

## GOSPEL    Luke 4:1–13

### A reading from the gospel according to Luke

Jesus, *full* of the Holy *Spirit*, returned from the *Jordan*
and was *led* by the Spirit in the *wilderness*,
where for forty *days* he was *tempted* by the *devil*.

---

**Emphasize these two aspects of faith, explained more fully below.**

**Speak slowly and assuredly this central claim.**

**The Christian faith is inclusive. It does not judge some to be less worthy than others.**

**Emphasize the role of the Spirit, who guides Jesus.**

---

Proclaim this passage with great solemnity, especially as you recount the words that form the core of the Passover celebration. Change your voice appropriately as you recount the abuses of the Egyptians, the cry of Israel and God's gracious response, and, finally, the wondrous deeds of God.

READING II  Paul wrote the letter to the Romans in large part to address the question of the relationship between the new faith in Jesus and its religious ancestor, Judaism. In today's passage, he discusses the relationship between inner faith and its outward expression.

Lest anyone emphasize one aspect of the faith over another, Paul makes clear that both inner belief and a confession of faith are required. Outward expression alone is not enough; there must be a genuine inner trust that God has conquered death in Jesus. But the belief must also be verbalized. An unwillingness to voice one's faith that Jesus is Lord belies a weak faith indeed.

The confession "Jesus is Lord" was an early Christian liturgical proclamation. The term "Lord" was used to translate the divine name in the Greek translation of the Hebrew scriptures. Applying it to Jesus, then, is a way of claiming divine status for him. This confession of Jesus' divinity set Christianity apart from other religions in antiquity, and later persecutors would use it against the Christians. During periods of persecution, anyone who assented to belief in Jesus' divinity risked being tortured or even killed.

Paul closes with a declaration that anyone—Jew or Gentile—can benefit from the saving actions of God in Jesus.

# 74
## 1ST SUNDAY OF LENT ■ MARCH 4, 2001

**Jesus responds to the devil with strength and conviction. Offer his words accordingly.**

**Again, speak Jesus' words firmly. He recognizes that only God deserves homage.**

**pinnacle = PIN-uh-k\*l**

**Is Jesus angry, impatient or weary? Do not be afraid to express forcefully the emotion that you think best expresses Jesus' feelings.**

He ate nothing at *all* during those days,
and when they were *over*, he was *famished*.

The devil said to him,
"If you are the *Son* of *God*,
command this *stone* to become a loaf of *bread*."
Jesus answered him,
"It is *written*, 'One does not *live* by bread *alone*.'"

Then the devil led him up
and showed him in an *instant* all the *kingdoms* of the *world*.
And the devil said to him,
"To *you* I will give their *glory* and all this *authority*;
for it has been given over to *me*,
and *I* give it to anyone I *please*.
If *you*, then, will *worship* me, it will all be *yours*."
Jesus answered him,
"It is *written*,
'*Worship* the Lord your *God*, and serve only *him*.'"

Then the devil took him to *Jerusalem*,
and placed him on the *pinnacle* of the *temple*, saying to him,
"If you are the *Son* of *God*, throw yourself *down* from here,
for it is written,
'He will command his *angels* concerning you, to *protect* you,'
and 'On their *hands* they will *bear* you *up*,
so that you will not dash your *foot* against a *stone*.'"
Jesus answered him, "It is said,
'Do *not* put the *Lord* your *God* to the *test*.'"

When the devil had *finished* every *test*,
he *departed* from him until an opportune *time*.

---

| GOSPEL | The story of Jesus' temptation in the desert affirms his full humanity. After his baptism, but before he began his ministry, he was tempted just as we are. But in the end, Jesus prevailed.

The setting of the temptation story recalls the experiences of the Israelites as they wandered in the desert. Like his Hebrew ancestors, Jesus went into the wilderness, and his 40-day period of fasting and temptation recalls Israel's 40 years of wandering after the escape from Egypt. All of Jesus' responses come from the book of Deuteronomy, which summarizes the law

God gave to Moses during Israel's wandering in the desert. Unlike the Israelites, however, Jesus resisted the temptation to rebel or take the easy way out.

The three temptations Jesus faced are familiar to us as well. We often desire comfort for ourselves, and a life free of effort in meeting our basic human needs. We also are tempted by the promise of power and sometimes sacrifice our values to pursue it. Finally, we sometimes desire to test God, thinking we can determine how God should communicate with us.

Jesus rejected all of these temptations, whether personal, political or religious. Although he could have had whatever he wanted, he chose to identify with the poor by being hungry, with the oppressed by rejecting displays of power, and with the unpretentious by refusing to demand that God save him.

The conflict in this passage makes it an especially exciting one to proclaim. Allow your voice to be filled with suspense. Speak the words of the devil with cunning but those of Jesus with conviction and strength.

MARCH 11, 2001

# 2ND SUNDAY OF LENT

*Lectionary #27*

### READING I  Genesis 15:5–12, 17–18

**A reading from the book of Genesis**

Abram = AY-br*m

Proclaim this as a solemn promise.

The Lord brought Abram *outside* and said,
"Look toward *heaven* and count the *stars*,
if you are *able* to count them."
Then the Lord said to him,
"*So* shall your *descendants* be."
And Abram *believed* the *Lord*;
and the Lord reckoned it to him as *righteousness*.

Then the Lord said to Abram,
"I am the *Lord* who brought you from *Ur* of the *Chaldeans*,
to give you this *land* to *possess*."

But Abram said,
"O Lord *God*, how am I to *know* that I shall *possess* it?"

This section, the account of the sacrifice, can be read more quickly.

The Lord said to him,
"Bring me a *heifer* three years *old*, a female *goat* three years *old*,
a *ram* three years *old*, a *turtledove*, and a young *pigeon*."
Abram *brought* the Lord all *these* and cut them in *two*,
laying each half over *against* the *other*;
but he did not cut the *birds* in *two*.
And when birds of prey came *down* on the *carcasses*,
Abram drove them *away*.

This signifies that God accepts the sacrifice. Allow some awe to enter your voice.

As the *sun* was going *down*, a deep *sleep* fell upon Abram,
and a deep and terrifying *darkness* descended *upon* him.

---

READING I  In the covenant between God and Abram, God promises descendants and land. Abram (later called Abraham) and his wife were old and childless, but God vows to provide offspring. We know the great significance of this promise, aware that the life of Isaac, Abraham's son, was almost extinguished. We also know that the land possessed by Abraham and passed on to the Hebrew people has been ruled by many different nations and continues to be a source of dispute. The sincerity of the promises and the depth of Abraham's faith are even more striking

when we reflect on our knowledge of what comes later.

In a time when few believed in an afterlife, having descendants promised immortality. This is why children were of such great importance in ancient Hebrew thought. Children carried on the traditions and name of the family, and could inherit the land and possessions of their parents.

God's promise to Abram included both descendants and land. Ancient covenants often involved the bestowal of land. Dwelling in the land given by God became both a blessing and a divinely assured right. In

today's passage, God also reminds Abraham how he was brought to a new region and blessed with the gift of the land. God's generosity is not isolated but constant throughout the life of Abraham.

The covenant made between God and Abraham reflects an ancient treaty between a powerful figure and a servant. The parties make promises and ratify the covenant with a sacrifice. In this case, however, God does all the promising. Abraham's response is faith in God's goodness and reliability.

Throughout the ages, the promises God made to Abraham have given hope to the

**2ND SUNDAY OF LENT ■ MARCH 11, 2001**

When the *sun* had gone down and it was *dark*,
a smoking *fire* pot and a flaming *torch*
      passed *between* these pieces.
On that *day* the Lord made a *covenant* with Abram, saying,
"To your *descendants* I give this *land*,
from the river of *Egypt* to the *great* river, the river *Euphrates*."

**This again is a solemn vow.**
**Euphrates = yoo-FRAY-teez**

---

### READING II    Philippians 3:17—4:1

**A reading from the letter of Paul to the Philippians**

Brothers and sisters,
join in *imitating* me,
and *observe* those who live
      according to the *example* you have in *us*.
For many live as *enemies* of the *cross* of *Christ*;
I have often *told* you of them,
and *now* I tell you even with *tears*.
Their end is *destruction*; their god is the *belly*;
and their *glory* is in their *shame*;
their minds are set on *earthly* things.

But *our* citizenship is in *heaven*,
and it is from *there* that we are expecting a *Saviour*,
the *Lord* Jesus *Christ*.
He will *transform* the *body* of our *humiliation*
that it may be *conformed* to the *body* of his *glory*,
by the *power* that also enables him
to make *all* things *subject* to *himself*.

**Lower your voice and speak with sorrow.**

**Let a bit of anger enter your voice here.**

**Our human bodies are holy, but they will be changed and glorified.**

---

Hebrew people. God chose a man, who responded with trust and obedience. God then promised that Abraham's descendants would be as numerous as the stars. Jews, Christians and Muslims alike consider themselves children of Abraham, heirs to the favor given him by God.

Today's passage is both a joy and a challenge to read. Concentrate your efforts on God's promises to Abraham, in order to express God's love and graciousness toward Abraham and all his descendants. Although the story of Abraham's sacrifice is less intriguing, read it as an account of the

reciprocal nature of the covenant relationship. God acts independently and decisively, but the human response is important. In this regard, Abraham can serve as a model for us in his willingness to respond to God in trust and faith.

READING II Paul's missionary churches were dear to his heart, and the Philippian community was especially beloved. Paul writes to the Philippians with joy and gratitude, but also out of concern because of the false teachings they were

receiving from some independent missionaries and perhaps even from members of their own community. In today's passage, Paul contrasts his teachings and reputation with those of the "enemies of the cross of Christ."

Paul exhorts the Philippians to look to the example of one person they know they can trust: Paul himself. Paul offers his life as an example because he knows that the Philippians need a model for proper behavior. He and his companions in ministry can be contrasted with those who are currently

MARCH 11, 2001 ■ 2ND SUNDAY OF LENT

**Speak with tenderness and joy.**

*Therefore*, my brothers and sisters,
whom I *love* and *long* for,
my *joy* and *crown*,
stand *firm*, my beloved, in the *Lord* in this *way*.

[Shorter: Philippians 3:20—4:1]

---

**GOSPEL**    Luke 9:28b–36

**A reading from the gospel according to Luke**

Jesus took with him *Peter* and *John* and *James*,
and went up on the *mountain* to *pray*.
And while he was *praying*,
the appearance of his *face changed*,
and his *clothes* became dazzling *white*.

**Emphasize the wonder of this sight.**

*Suddenly* they saw two *men*, *Moses* and *Elijah*, *talking* to Jesus.
They appeared in *glory* and were speaking of his *departure*,
which he was about to *accomplish* at *Jerusalem*.

Now *Peter* and his *companions* were weighed down with *sleep*;
but since they had stayed *awake*,
they saw his *glory* and the two men who stood *with* him.

Just as Moses and Elijah were *leaving* Jesus, Peter *said* to him,
"*Master*, it is *good* for us to *be* here;
let us make three *tents*,
one for *you*, one for *Moses*, and one for *Elijah*."
Peter did not *know* what he was saying.

**Peter's comment is impulsive and illustrates that he does not entirely understand what Jesus has been telling him. Allow his words to sound eager and perhaps a bit confused. Pause after them before continuing.**

---

trying to influence the community. These latter missionaries are concerned more with personal comfort than with the higher good.

Paul reminds his readers that their true home is in heaven and that this reality should be reflected in their conduct. From that heavenly abode will come Jesus, who will transform all people and bring everything under his authority. Originally, Paul expected the return of Christ to occur during his own lifetime, but this passage presents only the hope that Christ will reign decisively at some point in the future. Paul closes the

passage with his characteristic love and joy for the church in Philippi.

You may feel uncomfortable advising your listeners to imitate you, but know that it is not self-aggrandizement. Remember that you are speaking for Paul, or think of someone who serves as a model for you, so that you can offer the passage as encouragement to your listeners. Offer it also as a challenge to look toward our future hope rather than rely only on the satisfaction of present, "earthly things." Finally, as you read Paul's closing words, allow your voice to be filled with satisfaction and joy.

GOSPEL  The transfiguration is an awe-inspiring indication of the resplendent glory that belongs to Jesus as God's unique Son. It also points forward to Jesus' role as judge of all people.

The two figures who appear with the transfigured Jesus, Moses and Elijah, represent the Jewish law and the prophets. There was hope that Elijah and, later, Moses as well, would return, and there may be reference to the expected return of Jesus. What is clear, however, is that Jesus shares equal status with these historic figures. In fact,

## 2ND SUNDAY OF LENT ■ MARCH 11, 2001

**Clouds often signal encounters with God.**

**Speak God's words lovingly.**

While Peter was *saying* this,
a *cloud* came and *overshadowed* them;
and they were *terrified* as they entered the cloud.
Then from the *cloud* came a *voice* that said,
"This is my *Son*, my *Chosen*; *listen* to him!"
When the voice had *spoken*, Jesus was found *alone*.

And the disciples kept *silent*
and in *those* days told *no* one any of the things they had *seen*.

his authority exceeds even theirs, as the voice from heaven makes clear: Jesus is the beloved Son of God, to whom all are to listen.

What Moses and Elijah discuss with Jesus is his death, an event that would take place in Jerusalem. Both Moses and Elijah received glory without having to suffer an ignominious death, although both experienced resistance, even rejection, during their lives. In contrast, Jesus received glory only through suffering and dying.

This story of the glorification of Jesus follows Peter's declaration of faith in Jesus as the Messiah and Jesus' first teaching about his suffering and death. Here Peter anticipates only a glorious reign for Jesus, as his impetuous comment about erecting tents (places to commune with God) suggests. But the author does not allow the community to linger at the mountaintop. Instead, the disciples keep silent and Jesus' ministry continues. But now the tenor of Jesus' teaching has changed. Increasingly, there is discussion about the suffering and

death that awaits Jesus, which all who follow in his footsteps must be willing to undergo. From this point on in the gospel, Jesus moves steadily toward his death.

Your task today is to announce the splendor of the transfiguration to your community, to proclaim the uniqueness of the one we call "Lord." At the same time, do not lose sight of the broader message of the gospel: One who follows Jesus must be willing to do what he did, renouncing glory in exchange for suffering.

MARCH 18, 2001

# 3RD SUNDAY OF LENT

*Lectionary #30*

| READING I | Exodus 3:1–8a, 13–15 |

**A reading from the book of Exodus**

Midian = MID-ee-uhn

Horeb = HOHR-eb

*Moses* was keeping the flock of his father-in-law *Jethro,*
the priest of *Midian;*
he led his *flock* beyond the *wilderness,*
and came to *Horeb,* the mountain of *God.*
There the *angel* of the Lord *appeared* to him
in a flame of *fire* out of a *bush;*
Moses *looked,* and the bush was *blazing,*
yet it was not *consumed.*

Then Moses said,
"I must turn aside and *look* at this great *sight,*
and see why the *bush* is not burned *up.*"

**Speak God's words forcefully. Moses responds to God with sincerity.**

When the *Lord* saw that Moses had turned *aside* to *see,*
God *called* to him out of the *bush,* "*Moses, Moses!*"
And Moses said, "*Here* I am."
Then God said, "Come no *closer!*
*Remove* the sandals from your *feet,*
for the place on which you are *standing* is *holy* ground."

**No one was able to see God directly and live. Strive to convey the awe Moses must have felt.**

God said further, "I am the *God* of your *father,*
the God of *Abraham,* the God of *Isaac,* and the God of *Jacob.*"
And Moses *hid* his *face,* for he was afraid to *look* at God.

---

| READING I | After he was accused of killing an Egyptian, Moses fled Egypt and lived in the wilderness of the Sinai peninsula. While living there, he encountered God, as today's passage recounts, who called on Moses to lead the people of Israel out of bondage in Egypt and into the land God promised Abraham and his descendents.

Moses experiences the presence of God on a mountaintop. Mountains often serve as locations for encounters with the divine. This mountain, Horeb, is sometimes identified with Mount Sinai, the place where

Moses will later receive the divine commandments while leading the Israelites through the wilderness.

God's presence is made known in great spectacle. A bush is aflame but does not burn up, and from it comes a voice calling to Moses. God tells Moses to remove his sandals out of respect for the holiness of the place. Moses hides his face, a sign of the awesome nature of the encounter.

The conversation between Moses and God is intriguing. Although God does most of the speaking, Moses is not afraid to question God and seek clarification. God is

revealed first and foremost as a God of relationship, the one known in the past to the ancestors of Israel. God is not a distant concept or an otherworldly being but one who has spoken to and guided the patriarchs. Twice in this passage, God affirms that the covenant relationship with Israel's ancestors sums up the divine identity. God spoke to Abraham, promising descendants and giving him the land. God cared for Isaac, Jacob and their children. And God remains active in the life of Israel, promising to relieve the suffering of the people and once again bring them into the land designated for them.

## 3RD SUNDAY OF LENT ■ MARCH 18, 2001

God speaks compassionately of the plight of Israel and forcefully about the deliverance in store for the people.

Then the Lord said,
"I have *observed* the *misery* of my people who are in *Egypt*;
I have *heard* their *cry* on account of their *taskmasters*.
*Indeed*, I know their *sufferings*,
and I have come down to *deliver* them from the *Egyptians*,
and to bring them *up* out of that *land*
to a *good* and *broad* land,
a land *flowing* with *milk* and *honey*."
But Moses said to God,
"If I *come* to the Israelites and *say* to them,
'The God of your ancestors has sent me to you,'
and they *ask* me, 'What is his *name*?'
what shall I *say* to them?"

Moses shows boldness in daring to speak and must have been troubled about how to help the people believe his words.

Slow down your delivery and speak God's name with dignity.

God said to Moses, "*I AM* WHO I *AM*.'
He said further,
"*Thus* you shall say to the *Israelites*,
'*I AM* has sent me to you.'"

God *also* said to Moses,
"*Thus* you shall say to the *Israelites*,
'The *Lord*, the God of your *ancestors*,
the God of *Abraham*, the God of *Isaac*, and the God of *Jacob*,
has *sent* me to you.'
*This* is my name *forever*,
and *this* my *title* for all *generations*."

This is not a new god but one known to have acted before.

---

Although the original meaning of the four Hebrew letters that make up the divine name has been debated, there is no question about what the author understands it to mean: "I am who I am." No further explanation is necessary or even possible. The name, then, evokes awe; it stresses the majesty and mystery of the divine. It also emphasizes God's ability to act freely, to grant favor and compassion on those chosen.

The key to proclaiming this passage well is to read slowly and deliberately, always aware of the great mystery you are communicating. Emphasize the majesty of

God as well as Moses' awe as he realizes who is speaking to him. At the same time, speak with compassion as you relate God's promise to act on behalf of the persecuted Israelites, pledging to bring them out of misery and into peace and prosperity.

READING II Paul writes to the church at Corinth concerning the actions of some members of the community. The Corinthians, in their enthusiasm as new Christians, often needed reminders and further instruction from Paul. They had a tendency to take Paul's teachings to extremes,

and Paul needed to communicate continually his ethical concerns as a corrective to their emphasis on freedom. In this passage, Paul appeals to the exodus story to remind his readers not to make the same mistakes that the Israelites made on their desert journey.

Paul understands the Israelites' passage through the Red Sea at the beginning of the exodus as a type of baptism. Just as the Israelites passed through the water of the Red Sea and were baptized into Moses, so Christians are baptized into Christ. But, despite Israel's experience of deliverance and "initiation" into the divine mysteries,

MARCH 18, 2001 ■ 3RD SUNDAY OF LENT

## READING II   1 Corinthians 10:1–6, 10–12

**A reading from the first letter of Paul to the Corinthians**

I do not want you to be *unaware*, brothers and sisters,
that our *ancestors* were all under the *cloud*;
all passed through the *sea*;
all were *baptized* into *Moses* in the *cloud* and in the *sea*;
all *ate* the same spiritual *food*,
and all *drank* the same spiritual *drink*.
For they *drank* from the spiritual *rock* that *followed* them,
and the *rock* was *Christ*.

Nevertheless, God was not *pleased* with most of our *ancestors*,
and they were struck *down* in the *wilderness*.

Now these things occurred as *examples* for us,
so that we might not desire *evil* as *they* did.
And do not *complain* as some of *them* did,
and were *destroyed* by the *destroyer*.

These things happened to our *ancestors* to serve as an *example*,
and they were written *down* to *instruct us*,
on whom the *ends* of the *ages* have *come*.
So if you think you are *standing*,
watch *out* that you do not *fall*.

---

*Paul refers here to the experience of the exodus, when a pillar of fire and cloud accompanied the people on their journey.*

*Moses procured water for the Israelites by striking a rock at God's command. Later tradition had the rock following the people. Change your tone to convey God's displeasure.*

*Stress how your listeners can learn from the example of others.*

*This is a solemn warning.*

---

the people grumbled and complained as they continued their journey.

This, Paul asserts, is not to be the way Christians act. Baptism is the first significant encounter between God and the new Christian, an experience of divine favor and human commitment, but it is simply the first step on a long journey. It is essential to reaffirm the commitment and to avoid the pitfalls into which the Israelites fell. Their experience can be an example to the Christian, a warning of what to avoid.

During Lent we concentrate intently on our Christian journey. We also struggle and

sometimes grumble. But if we take Paul's words to heart, learning from the mistakes of others, we can look forward to our Easter celebration, when we will renew our baptismal promises and welcome new members into our community.

Paul's unusual style of interpretation makes this passage a bit difficult to read. Reflect on the exodus story, and offer this selection as a warning to your listeners. In the second paragraph, emphasize especially the example intended by referring to this story from long ago. It is not simply a rebuke but an attempt to turn people—whether

the original readers of the letter or your assembly—back to the right path.

GOSPEL  A common belief in ancient Hebrew thought was that blessings or misfortunes were the result of one's actions. Jesus does not question such an attitude in today's gospel, although he qualifies it. The parable, however, attests to God's tremendous patience, even with those who fail to bear fruit.

The terrible tragedies alluded to in today's selection are not corroborated by other sources, but they are easy to imagine.

# 3RD SUNDAY OF LENT ■ MARCH 18, 2001

## GOSPEL    Luke 13:1–9

**A reading from the gospel according to Luke**

Pilate had the Galileans killed when they came to Jerusalem to offer sacrifice.

Jesus was teaching the *crowds*;
some of those *present* told Jesus about the *Galileans*
whose *blood* Pilate had mingled with their *sacrifices*.

Jesus asked them,
"Do you *think* that because these Galileans *suffered* in this way
they were worse *sinners* than all *other* Galileans?

Speak emphatically Jesus' disagreement with the idea that they were worse sinners, as well as his warning to repent.

*No*, I tell you;
but unless you *repent*, you will all *perish* as *they* did.
Or those *eighteen* who were *killed*
when the *tower* of Siloam *fell* on them—
do you think that they were *worse* offenders
than all the *others* living in *Jerusalem*?
*No*, I tell you;
but unless you *repent*, you will all *perish* just as *they* did."

Again, speak strongly. Then pause before beginning the parable.

Then Jesus told this *parable*:
"A man had a *fig* tree planted in his *vineyard*;
and he came looking for *fruit* on it and found *none*.
So he said to the gardener, 'See *here*!
For three *years* I have come looking for *fruit* on this *fig* tree,
and still I find *none*.
Cut it *down*!
*Why* should it be wasting the *soil*?'

Offer the gardener's words with sincerity and hope.

The gardener replied, 'Sir, let it alone for *one* more *year*,
until I dig *around* it and put *manure* on it.
If it bears fruit *next* year, well and *good*;
but if *not*, you can cut it *down*.'"

---

Pilate was known for his cruelty and often directed it at the Galileans. And it is certainly possible that a tower could fall, whether as the result of shoddy construction or during an earthquake.

What is noteworthy in Jesus' treatment of these subjects is his placement of all the participants in the story on the same level. Far from being greater sinners and thus worthy of their tragic fates, those who died in the two incidents were much the same as Jesus' listeners. They did not bear greater guilt than others but neither were they completely innocent, as Jesus' address to his

listeners implies. The same fate could befall any who fail to repent and conform their lives to God's commands.

The value of repentance and God's forgiveness are the themes of the parable. Although the fig tree failed to produce fruit for three full years, it is given another chance. In the same way, we too can turn away from our fruitless lives and resolve to lead productive, beneficial ones. Just as the tree's fruit reveals its value, so also the worthiness of our lives is known through our actions. But God is patient, forgiving even years of inactivity, if only we repent and change our lives.

In the end, the entire gospel reading affirms that a judgment is coming. It is not enough simply to say that one is no more sinful than another, or to hope in God's loving forgiveness. Before another tragedy occurs, before the tree is chopped down, action must be taken. The time to repent is now.

Proclaim this passage as encouragement to your listeners but also with a sense of urgency, offering a lenten wake-up call for a people who are sometimes complacent.

MARCH 18, 2001

# 3RD SUNDAY OF LENT, YEAR A

*Lectionary #28*

## READING I    Exodus 17:3–7

**A reading from the book of Exodus**

In the *wilderness* the people thirsted for *water*;
and the people *complained* against *Moses* and *said*,
"*Why* did you bring us out of *Egypt*,
to kill *us* and our *children* and *livestock* with *thirst*?"
So Moses cried out to the Lord,
"What shall I *do* with this people?
They are almost ready to *stone* me."

The Lord said to Moses
"Go on *ahead* of the *people*,
and take some of the *elders* of Israel *with* you;
take in your hand the *staff* with which you struck the *Nile*,
        and *go*.
I will be *standing* there in *front* of you on the *rock* at *Horeb*.
*Strike* the rock, and water will come *out* of it,
so that the people may *drink*."
Moses *did* so, in the sight of the *elders* of *Israel*.

He called the place *Massah* and *Meribah*,
because the Israelites *quarrelled* and *tested* the Lord,
saying, "Is the Lord *among* us or *not*?"

---

**The people are upset, almost ready to revolt. Let their exasperation be heard in your words.**

**Moses is desperate.**

**Speak God's words calmly and firmly.**

**Massah = MAS-ah**
**Meribah = MAYR-ih-bah**
**Massah means "testing" and Meribah means "quarreling."**

---

READING I  Life-giving water figures prominently in today's readings, as we prepare to welcome new members into the community through the waters of baptism on Easter.

Despite God's continual intervention on behalf of the Israelites wandering in the desert, the Pentateuch records their constant grumbling against the Lord whenever they meet with adversity. At times they even plan to return to Egypt; freedom, with its attendant struggles, can be even more threatening than slavery. This might seem to be the case for us too as we journey through the

lenten wilderness. We would prefer to turn back rather than continue wandering with parched lips, longing for home. So today we are given refreshment to strengthen us on the way.

Although they have just been fed with quail and manna, the Israelites find the absence of water in the desert too much to bear. Although Moses rightly fears that he, as God's mouthpiece, is in danger of losing his life to the mob, the Israelites' revolt is really against God. As so often before, God instructs Moses to take symbolic action, and the result is a physical benefit for the

Israelites. Here their thirst is met with water in abundance, but their rebellious actions are recorded forever in the names given to the places where they questioned God.

There is plenty of drama in this passage to make for an interesting presentation. Let the people's words sound defiant, and express Moses' fear, but make God's control throughout the situation evident. Challenge your listeners also to reflect on their own times of rebellion. Do we really believe that God will provide everything that we need? Through the waters of baptism we have

**84**

3RD SUNDAY OF LENT, YEAR A ■ MARCH 18, 2001

Begin strongly but with a genuine peacefulness in your voice.

The word translated "boast" here is related to words meaning "rejoice" or "exult." Paul has been contrasting the presumptuous boasting of one who is overconfident with the certainty of one who genuinely trusts in God.

Stress words such as "rarely," "righteous" and "perhaps" in order to emphasize how unusual it would be for someone to die for another—even for one who is good.

Pause briefly after "that." This reality is truly amazing; let your voice be filled with joy and awe.

Sychar = SĪK-ahr

## READING II   Romans 5:1–2, 5–8

### A reading from the letter of Paul to the Romans

Since we are *justified* by *faith*,
we have *peace* with God through our *Lord* Jesus *Christ*,
through whom we have obtained *access*
    to this *grace* in which we *stand*;
and we *boast* in our hope of sharing the *glory* of *God*.

And *hope* does not *disappoint* us,
because God's *love* has been poured into our *hearts*
through the Holy *Spirit* that has been *given* to us.
For while we were still *weak*,
at the right *time* Christ *died* for the *ungodly*.
Indeed, *rarely* will anyone die for a *righteous* person,
though *perhaps* for a *good* person
someone might actually *dare* to die.
But God proves his *love* for us
in that while we still were *sinners* Christ *died* for us.

## GOSPEL   John 4:5–42

### A reading from the holy gospel according to John

Jesus came to a *Samaritan* city called *Sychar*,
near the plot of *ground* that *Jacob* had given to his son *Joseph*.
Jacob's *well* was there,
and *Jesus*, tired out by his *journey*, was *sitting* by the *well*.

become part of a community that commits itself to God, even as we know that God is completely committed to our welfare. Offer this reading to your assembly as a challenge to trust that God is indeed on our side.

READING II   This passage from Paul's letter to the Romans is filled with assurances about the great love of God. It spells out Paul's belief in the initiative taken by God for our sake, seen in the actions of Christ.

Paul begins this section by affirming one of his most cherished principles: We are made right ("justified") before God, brought back into relationship with God, not through anything we ourselves have done but through God's own gracious love. Because of this we can be at peace. Even in times of trial ("stand" in Paul's writings always means firmness in the face of adversity), we can turn to God in faith, knowing that God's glory will be revealed.

Our hope is not a false one. We can be confident because we know that God's love for us has been demonstrated in Jesus'

death. And that love has been poured out in abundance, filling our hearts to overflowing. It is through the Holy Spirit, given in baptism, that the overwhelming love of God for us is confirmed.

Jesus' actions demonstrate God's overflowing grace as well. Paul points out how rare it is for one person to die for another. We can think of instances when this happens, but usually it is a brave soul who saves a loved one or friend. It is much harder to imagine someone dying for the sake of an enemy. Yet that is what Jesus has done,

MARCH 18, 2001 ■ 3RD SUNDAY OF LENT, YEAR A

**Jesus' statement sounds rude and demanding. The woman does not understand it to be so. Phrase it in such a way that it sounds like a request rather than a demand.**

**In the gospel of John, the term "Jew" is usually applied to the religious leaders of the Jews. It is used of Jesus only here in this gospel.**

It was about *noon*.
A *Samaritan woman* came to draw *water*,
and Jesus said to her, "*Give* me a *drink*."
(His *disciples* had gone to the city to buy *food*.)

The Samaritan woman said to him,
"How is it that *you*, a *Jew*,
ask a drink of *me*, a *woman* of *Samaria*?"
(*Jews* do not share things in common with *Samaritans*.)
Jesus answered her,
"If you knew the *gift* of *God*,
and who it *is* that is *saying* to you, 'Give me a *drink*,'
you would have *asked* him,
and he would have given you *living* water."

**The woman is being practical and reasonable. In Greek the terms seem to refer to actual water.**

**Speak here with a bit of indignation and surprise at the notion.**

**Jesus' words are solemn and carry deep meaning. Let them build so that the words sound like the bubbling water they describe.**

**Convey the woman's eagerness, although she still does not understand.**

The woman said to him,
"*Sir*, you have no *bucket*, and the well is *deep*.
*Where* do you get that *living water*?
Are you *greater* than our ancestor *Jacob*, who *gave* us the well,
and with his *children* and his *flocks drank* from it?"
Jesus said to her,
"Everyone who drinks of *this* water will be thirsty *again*,
but those who drink of the water that *I* will give them
will *never* be thirsty.
The water that *I* will give will *become* in them a *spring* of water
gushing *up* to *eternal life*."
The woman said to him, "Sir, *give* me this water,
so that I may never be *thirsty*
or have to keep *coming* here to *draw* water."

Jesus said to her,
"*Go*, call your *husband*, and come *back*."

dying for us while we were caught in sin, having made ourselves enemies of God.

This is a solemn proclamation, yet the message is cause for great joy. Though we have done nothing to deserve it, God has given us the greatest gift of love. Inspire the members of your assembly to reflect on God's deep commitment and the tremendous love God offers us through Jesus. Encourage your listeners to stand firm in their faith in this season of Lent and always, knowing that God is always with us. In this there is truly a message of peace.

GOSPEL The story of the encounter between Jesus and the Samaritan woman at the well centers on the question of living water and the related significance of Jesus' identity. As always in the gospel of John, Jesus has full knowledge of his mission and identity, but his companions (here, primarily the woman, but also the disciples) have ordinary human knowledge, inadequate for fully comprehending what Jesus is saying. Here also, ordinary water— so important for sustaining life and for refreshment—gives way to living water, the kind of water necessary for eternal life.

As we prepare to approach the waters of baptism on Easter, whether to renew our baptismal commitment or to receive the life-giving waters, we are reminded of the source of our sustenance. It is through Jesus that we receive the water of life, essential for our thirsty souls.

Although Jesus could have avoided traveling through Samaria on his way to Galilee from Jerusalem, he finds himself in the heart of Samaritan territory. Samaritans and Jews, despite common roots, had long felt great animosity toward one another. Jews were convinced that "salvation is from

## 3RD SUNDAY OF LENT, YEAR A ■ MARCH 18, 2001

The woman answered him, "I *have* no *husband.*"
Jesus said to her, "You are *right* in saying, 'I *have* no *husband*';
for you have had *five* husbands,
and the one you have *now* is *not* your husband.
What you have said is *true!*"

The woman said to him, "Sir, I *see* that you are a *prophet.*
Our *ancestors* worshipped on this *mountain,*
but *you* say that the place where people must worship
is in *Jerusalem.*"

Jesus said to her,
"Woman, *believe* me, the hour is *coming*
when you will *worship* the *Father*
neither on *this* mountain nor in *Jerusalem.*
*You* worship what you do not *know;*
*we* worship what we *know,*
for *salvation* is from the *Jews.*
But the hour is *coming,* and is now *here,*
when the *true* worshippers will worship the Father
in *spirit* and *truth,*
for the Father *seeks such* as these to *worship* him.
*God* is *spirit,*
and those who *worship* him must worship in *spirit* and *truth.*"

The woman said to him, "I *know* that the Messiah is *coming*"
(who is called the *Christ*).
"When he *comes,* he will proclaim all *things* to us."
Jesus said to her, "*I* am *he,*
the one who is *speaking* to you."

Just *then* his *disciples* came.
They were *astonished* that he was speaking with a *woman,*
but no one said, "What do you *want?*"

---

the Jews," and Samaritans held fast to the Pentateuch and viewed later traditions—such as worship in Jerusalem—as accretions to the true faith. For a Jewish teacher to speak at length (or at all!) with a Samaritan was unheard of.

For a Jewish teacher to speak in public with a woman—even a Jewish woman—was also unknown. The disciples' surprise when they returned and saw Jesus conversing with the Samaritan woman is to be expected. Jesus was defying the tradition that kept strict social barriers in place between those of different nationalities,

religious traditions and sexes. Jesus reached out to the woman and offered her what she did not even realize she needed.

The story begins simply; in one of the few instances in John's gospel in which he displays human weakness, Jesus is tired and thirsty after a morning of travel. When he requests a drink of the woman, she immediately hides behind the barriers she has always known. Jesus' response does not address her issues, but rather turns the conversation to the question of water.

The term for "living" water can also mean "flowing," referring to water that is

not stagnant but fresh and pure. The woman misunderstands and is skeptical of Jesus' claims. Although she recognizes him as a teacher, she is convinced that he could not possibly be greater than Jacob, whose well they are using. The reader anticipates what is coming: Jesus is, of course, far greater. However, Jesus again does not reply directly but allows her to draw her own conclusions.

Jesus reveals that he has water for eternal life; the woman is intrigued. But she becomes convinced that he is no ordinary person when he has insight into her life and her character. Jesus brings her to fuller

MARCH 18, 2001 ■ 3RD SUNDAY OF LENT, YEAR A

**Express the woman's excitement.**

or, "*Why* are you *speaking* with her?"
Then the woman left her *water* jar and went back to the *city*.
She said to the *people*,
"*Come* and see a man who told me *everything* I have ever *done!*
He cannot be the *Messiah, can* he?"
They *left* the city and were on their *way* to him.
*Meanwhile* the disciples were *urging* him,
"*Rabbi, eat* something."
But he said to them,
"I have *food* to eat that you do not *know* about."
So the disciples said to one another,
"Surely no one has *brought* him something to *eat?*"

**The disciples, like the woman, do not initially understand. This provides Jesus with an opportunity to teach them.**

Jesus said to them,
"My *food* is to do the *will* of him who *sent* me
and to *complete* his *work*.
Do you not say, '*Four* months *more*, then comes the *harvest*'?
But I *tell* you, look *around* you,
and see how the fields are *ripe* for *harvesting*.
The *reaper* is already receiving *wages*
and is gathering *fruit* for *eternal life*,
so that *sower* and *reaper* may rejoice *together*.
For *here* the saying holds *true*, '*One sows* and another *reaps*.'
I sent you to *reap* that for which you did not *labour*.
*Others* have *laboured*, and *you* have entered into their *labour*."

Many *Samaritans* from that city *believed* in Jesus
because of the woman's *testimony*,
"He told me *everything* I have ever *done*."
So when the Samaritans *came* to him,
they asked him to *stay* with them;
and he stayed there two *days*.

understanding of his identity by establishing a relationship with her.

It is especially appropriate to contemplate the "living water" offered by Jesus on this day when catechumens undergo their first scrutiny in preparation for Easter baptism. Recall that, as with the Samaritan woman, the life-giving water is something that is offered only through personal contact; one comes to know Jesus by encountering those who trust in him.

Just when it seems that their religious differences are irrelevant, Jesus affirms that

"salvation is from the Jews." Here the gospel of John reveals itself as a document from a Jewish-Christian community. But, Jesus claims, the time soon approaches when true worship of God will be "in spirit and truth," rather than the rituals familiar to the Samaritans or the Jews. The evangelist is clearly alluding to Christian worship of the God who is revealed in Jesus. Jesus is truth, as the Johannine prologue asserts, and baptizes with the Holy Spirit. Although the old ways may have been valid in the past, the author leaves no doubt that a new way of living and worshiping is available in Jesus.

The woman's belief in a Messiah seems odd coming from a Samaritan. In fact, it is probably the Jewish expectation for a Davidic Messiah that is expressed, allowing Jesus to reveal himself as the fulfillment of that expectation.

The conversation is interrupted by the return of the disciples. Jesus continues his enigmatic claims by asserting that he has food of which his disciples are not aware. He then launches into a discussion of ministry under the metaphor of harvest. As is so

# 3RD SUNDAY OF LENT, YEAR A ■ MARCH 18, 2001

**Close with an emphasis on the personal nature of faith and on the title given Jesus.**

And many *more* believed because of *his* word.
They said to the woman,
"It is no *longer* because of what *you* said that we believe,
for we have heard for *ourselves*,
and we *know* that this is *truly* the *Saviour* of the *world*."

[Shorter: John 4:5–15, 19–26, 39, 40–42]

often true in agriculture and in life, the minister knows that it takes time for a seed to take root. The one who begins the work of evangelizing and nurturing faith is not always the one who sees that work come to fruition. We must recognize that no one individual or group can claim credit for success, precisely because we claim to be a community. One may plant the seed of faith, another may water it, and still another enjoy the fragrant blossoms of mature belief.

The Samaritan woman is sometimes remembered as the first evangelist. She ran to the town to tell others of her encounter with Jesus. Her neighbors came to believe, however, based on their own experience. Although others can introduce one to faith, each person must have his or her own encounter with Jesus.

This is an interesting and exciting story of faith. Allow the woman's sincerity and eagerness to be heard. Although Jesus' responses can be exasperating and elusive,

use them as the teaching tools they are, drawing your listeners to a deeper level of understanding. Challenge your community of faith to reflect on its ministry and the necessity of coordinating efforts in order to witness the greatest gains. Finally, remember that it is often in quiet darkness that the seeds of faith are first sown. Trust that God is working even when all evidence seems to indicate otherwise.

MARCH 25, 2001

# 4TH SUNDAY OF LENT

*Lectionary #33*

## READING I  Joshua 5:9a, 10–12

**A reading from the book of Joshua**

After the *Israelites* had crossed over the Jordan *river,*
and *entered* the promised *land,*
the *Lord* said to *Joshua,*
*"Today* I have rolled away from you the *disgrace* of *Egypt."*

While the *Israelites* were camped in *Gilgal*
they kept the *Passover*
in the *evening* on the fourteenth day of the *month*
in the plains of *Jericho.*

On the day *after* the Passover, on that very *day,*
they *ate* the *produce* of the *land,*
unleavened *cakes* and parched *grain.*
The manna *ceased* on the day they ate the *produce* of the *land,*
and the Israelites no *longer* had *manna;*
they ate the *crops* of the land of *Canaan* that year.

> Read this as the solemn vow that it is before continuing with the story.
> Gilgal = GIL-gahl
>
> Passover is always held on the fourteenth of the spring month of Nisan.

## READING II  2 Corinthians 5:17–21

**A reading from the second letter of Paul to the Corinthians**

If anyone is *in Christ,* there is a *new creation*:
everything *old* has passed *away;*
*see,* everything has become *new!*

> Speak with excitement in your voice.

---

**READING I** After God delivered Israel from slavery in Egypt, Moses led the Israelites through the desert, but he died before entering the land of Canaan. In today's reading, Joshua has taken on Moses' role as the leader of Israel.

On this day, God declares that the experience of slavery in Egypt is finally over. It has been years since the Israelites were under the rule of the Pharaoh, but only now do they finally return home. While in the desert, they had been a nomadic people, without land or organized government. They had been rebellious, proving themselves still enslaved to idol worship and unwilling to trust in God's supreme goodness and care for them. But all that ends on this day, when they enter into the land God has designated for them. God and Israel renew their commitment to one another.

The exodus had begun with a celebration of Passover, and it ends with the same feast. Immediately after celebrating this Passover, the manna that God had provided to feed the Israelites on their journey ceases. They now have a rich land, a land "flowing with milk and honey," to provide for them. God no longer needs to supply their daily sustenance, but gives them the resources to provide for themselves.

Today's passage reminds us of the graciousness of God, who provides for our every need. Offer it to your assembly as a simple story of God's goodness and love.

**READING II** Paul is convinced of the radical newness of all of life because of Jesus Christ. Today's reading expresses beautifully the new life available to the Christian and the promise of a new relationship with God effected in Christ.

**90**

4TH SUNDAY OF LENT ■ MARCH 25, 2001

> **Proceed slowly through this section, giving due emphasis to the repeated words referring to reconciliation.**

All *this* is from *God*,
who *reconciled* us to himself through *Christ*,
and has given us the *ministry* of *reconciliation*;
that is, in *Christ*, God was *reconciling* the world to *himself*,
*not* counting their trespasses *against* them,
and entrusting the *message* of *reconciliation* to *us*.

> **Speak as though you are begging your own community to set themselves on the right course.**

So we are *ambassadors* for *Christ*,
since God is making his *appeal* through *us*;
we *entreat* you on behalf of *Christ*,
be *reconciled* to *God*.
For *our* sake God made *Christ* to be *sin* who knew *no* sin,
so that *in* Christ *we* might become the *righteousness* of *God*.

---

## GOSPEL   Luke 15:1–3, 11–32

**A reading from the gospel according to Luke**

All the *tax* collectors and *sinners* were coming near
to *listen* to Jesus.
And the *Pharisees* and the *scribes* were *grumbling* and saying,
"*This* fellow welcomes *sinners* and *eats* with them."

> **Give plenty of emphasis to this central accusation: Jesus is keeping bad company and the religious leaders judge him negatively.**

So he told them a *parable*:
"There was a *man* who had two *sons*.
The *younger* of them said to his father,
'*Father*, give me the *share* of the *property*
that will *belong* to me.'
So the father divided his property *between* them.
A few days *later* the *younger* son gathered all he *had*
and travelled to a distant *country*,
and there he *squandered* his property in dissolute *living*.

---

For the person who abides in Christ, who is in Christ, everything is new. A principal characteristic of this new life is a new relationship with God. Through Christ the world is reconciled to God.

The reconciliation of humankind and God is made possible not by anything we have done but by Christ. Indeed, Paul says that God chooses not to count our transgressions against us, as we deserve. Instead Jesus, who was sinless, takes on the responsibility for our sins. By placing our faith in him, we are made right with God.

Paul recognizes that the gift of reconciliation is freely given but also knows that his readers have the responsibility to accept that gift and make it real. He thus implores the Corinthians to be reconciled to God. Although new life is fully available through Christ, Paul asserts that we must actively seek to be in right relationship with God.

Paul declares himself and his companions to be "ambassadors for Christ." He sees himself speaking for God, enticing the members of his communities into an intimate relationship with God. In much the same way, you are an ambassador for Christ. You

are entrusted with conveying God's message to the members of your assembly. Speak Paul's words as if addressed directly to your listeners, so that they too may embrace the new life offered in Christ and strive to be reconciled completely with God.

GOSPEL   The story of the prodigal son (or, rather, the parable of the loving father) is a familiar one and will require a skilled storyteller to convey it in a fresh manner. We know the main points of the story well: One of two brothers asks for

MARCH 25, 2001 ■ 4TH SUNDAY OF LENT

"When he had spent *everything*,
a severe *famine* took place *throughout* that country,
and he began to be in *need*.
So he went and *hired* himself *out*
to one of the *citizens* of that country,
who sent him to his *fields* to feed the *pigs*.
The young man would *gladly* have filled himself
with the *pods* that the *pigs* were eating;
and no one gave him *anything*.

**Allow the young man's plight to color your reading. Let your voice be filled with sadness, frustration and longing.**

"But when he came to *himself* he said,
'How many of my father's hired *hands*
      have bread *enough* and to *spare*,
but here *I* am *dying* of *hunger*!
I will get *up* and go to my *father*, and I will *say* to him,
"*Father*, I have sinned against *heaven* and before *you*;
I am no longer *worthy* to be called your *son*;
treat *me* like one of your hired *hands*."'

"So he set *off* and went to his *father*.
But while he was still far *off*,
his father *saw* him and was filled with *compassion*;
he *ran* and put his *arms* around him and *kissed* him.

**Express the joy of this encounter.**

"Then the son said to him,
'*Father*, I have sinned against *heaven* and before *you*;
I am no longer *worthy* to be called your *son*.'
But the father said to his *slaves*,
'*Quickly*, bring out a *robe*—the *best* one—and put it *on* him;
put a *ring* on his finger and *sandals* on his feet.

**Speak humbly and sincerely. The younger son is not presupposing any favor from the father.**

**The father's exuberance continues. He has barely heard his son's apology.**

his inheritance, wastes it, and then returns home to his father, who greets him with joy and forgiveness. Such outpouring of love offends the other son, who has remained with the father. The story is simultaneously one of penitence, of God's love and forgiveness, and of the dangers of a judgmental attitude.

When understood as a story of penitence, the focus is on the younger son. The son was arrogant in demanding his share of his father's wealth, foolish in squandering it away, and deserving of his fate. Every Jew listening to the tale would have known that the younger son had indeed hit bottom,

reduced to feeding pigs, the most unclean of animals. Finally, he recognizes his folly and humbly returns to his father, asking only to be treated as a servant.

The father in today's story rejoices to find the son who was lost. Clearly a metaphor for divine forgiveness and acceptance, this aspect of the tale leaves no doubt that the son's errant ways have been dismissed if not forgotten. The reader is left with the confidence that we, too, are forgiven completely whenever we sincerely leave behind our past life and turn in trust and humility to a God who loves us completely.

But the opening verses of today's passage suggest that the question of judgment of others is the real point of the story. The Pharisees and the scribes question Jesus' friendship with known sinners. Accusingly, they point out that Jesus actually shares meals with such delinquents, a sure sign that he shares in their sinfulness. It's as if they say, "You're known by the company you keep." Jesus not only challenges the assumptions made about him but turns the tables and demonstrates the dangers of their attitude in his parable. The older son is unable to forgive and rejoice. Although he

**4TH SUNDAY OF LENT ■ MARCH 25, 2001**

And get the fatted *calf* and *kill* it,
and let us *eat* and *celebrate*;
for this *son* of mine was *dead* and is *alive* again;
he was *lost* and is *found!*'
And they began to *celebrate*.

"Now his *elder* son was in the *field*;
and when he *came* and approached the *house*,
he heard *music* and *dancing*.
He called one of the *slaves* and asked what was going *on*.
The slave replied, 'Your *brother* has *come*,
and your *father* has killed the fatted *calf*,
because he has got him back *safe* and *sound*.'

**The mood darkens as the older son becomes resentful.**

"Then the elder son became *angry* and *refused* to go *in*.
His *father* came out and began to *plead* with him.
But he answered his father,
'*Listen!* For all these *years*
I have been working like a *slave* for you,
and I have *never* disobeyed your *command*;
yet you have never given me even a young *goat*
so that I might celebrate with my *friends*.
But when *this* son of yours came back,
who has *devoured* your property with *prostitutes*,
you killed the fatted *calf* for him!'

**Speak with loving reassurance.**

"Then the father said to him,
'*Son*, you are *always* with me,
and all that is *mine* is *yours*.
But we had to *celebrate* and *rejoice*,
because this *brother* of yours was *dead*
and has come to *life*;
he was *lost* and has been *found*.'"

---

has always done what is right, his heart is in the wrong place. The same could be said about the religious leaders who reject not only the well-known sinners in their midst but anyone who reaches out to such people in love.

For many of us who sincerely strive to lead upright lives, the story of the older son hits home. It simply isn't fair that someone who has wronged another should be welcomed with such lavish generosity, something never offered the upright son in the story. We too are tempted to feel "holier than

thou" when we encounter others who do not strive as hard as we do to live the moral life. But Jesus' message is clear: It is those who are tempted to look down on the sinners in their midst who have the most to learn. God accepts all people.

We are never told if the older son finally accepts his father's explanation and joins in the celebration. Each one of us is left to identify with him and decide for ourselves. The party is the heavenly banquet, and our attendance requires only that we accept all who seek forgiveness. The story is most of all about the fate of the "righteous" and

is addressed to us as much as it was to Jesus' listeners.

Read this exciting story with new eyes, and strive to convey that freshness to your community. Pretend that you are reading it for the first time, giving full expression to the different characters in the story, so that your listeners might hear it anew, taking its message to heart.

MARCH 25, 2001

# 4TH SUNDAY OF LENT, YEAR A

*Lectionary #31*

## READING I  1 Samuel 16:1b, 6–7, 10–13a

**A reading from the first book of Samuel**

The Lord said to *Samuel*,
"*Fill* your horn with *oil* and set *out*;
I will send you to *Jesse* of *Bethlehem*,
for I have provided for myself a *king* among his *sons*."

When the sons of Jesse *came*,
Samuel looked on *Eliab* and thought,
"*Surely* the Lord's *anointed* is now *before* the Lord."
But the Lord said to Samuel,
"Do *not* look on his *appearance*
or on the height of his *stature*,
because I have *rejected* him;
for the *Lord* does not see as *mortals* see;
they look on the *outward* appearance,
but the *Lord* looks on the *heart*."

Jesse made *seven* of his sons *pass* before Samuel,
and Samuel said to Jesse,
"The Lord has *not* chosen *any* of these."
Samuel said to Jesse, "Are *all* your sons here?"
And he said, "There remains yet the *youngest*,
but he is keeping the *sheep*."
And Samuel said to Jesse,
"*Send* and *bring* him;
for we will not sit *down* until he *comes* here."

*Speak with confidence; Samuel is sure that this is God's chosen one.*

*Express Samuel's disappointment and confusion, then the exasperation in his next question.*

*Speak Jesse's words with an uncertain tone; he too must not have expected his youngest to be chosen over the others.*

*Samuel is firm.*

READING I Saul, the first king of Israel, was chosen by the people against the advice of the prophet Samuel. But Samuel agreed to anoint him and supported him during his tenure as king, even while reprimanding him when he disobeyed God. But it was Saul's unwillingness to obey God in everything, and his inability to provide true leadership for the people, that led to his eventual downfall. In today's story, Samuel is sent to choose a successor for Saul, although the choice is kept secret and Saul remains in office until his death.

God sent Samuel to the insignificant town of Bethlehem to anoint the future king of Israel. Told that one of the sons of Jesse would be chosen by God to govern Israel, Samuel assumes that he should anoint the first and tallest son. When God rejects that one, Samuel examines six others, but none is God's choice for king. Only when the youngest is brought in from the fields is Samuel convinced that he has found the one to anoint.

This reading introduces the reader to the greatest king of Israel, David. God promises everlasting favor to David and his descendants, and under David the kingdom prospers. But the blessings that await David are only hinted at here. In this passage, it is the importance of sight that dominates the discussion.

4TH SUNDAY OF LENT, YEAR A ■ MARCH 25, 2001

**Speak with fondness; David was much loved.**

**Speak slowly and emphasize this line.**

**David was anointed with God's spirit as well as with oil. Speak with excitement in your voice and emphasize David's name.**

Jesse *sent* and brought *David* in.
Now he was *ruddy*, and had beautiful *eyes*, and was *handsome*.
The Lord said,
"*Rise* and *anoint* him; for *this* is the *one.*"

Then Samuel took the horn of *oil*,
and *anointed* him in the presence of his *brothers*;
and the *spirit* of the *Lord* came *mightily* upon *David*
from that day *forward*.

---

### READING II    Ephesians 5:8–14

**A reading from the letter of Paul to the Ephesians**

*Once* you were *darkness*,
        but *now* in the *Lord* you are *light*.
Live as *children* of light—
for the *fruit* of the light is found
in *all* that is *good* and *right* and *true*.

**Speak encouragingly.**

Try to find out what is *pleasing* to the *Lord*.
Take *no part* in the *unfruitful* works of *darkness*,
but instead *expose* them.
For it is *shameful* even to *mention* what such people do *secretly*;
but everything *exposed* by the light becomes *visible*,
for everything that becomes *visible* is *light*.
Therefore it is said,
"*Sleeper, awake!*

**Offer this quote as an exciting promise.**

*Rise* from the *dead*, and Christ will *shine* on you."

---

Just as the gospel reading will contrast the physical ability to see with genuine insight, so also this reading contrasts outward appearance with the qualities desired by God, qualities only God is able to see. For God does not see as humans do, but is able to look into the very heart of a person. The qualities within David's heart were those that made him a great leader.

Read this captivating story from the point of view of Samuel. Express Samuel's certainty when he sees Eliab, his confusion when none of the seven is chosen, and his conviction when he sees David. Stress also the words of God.

READING II Having discussed the fate of those who are disobedient, the author of Ephesians turns to discuss a positive way of life. Adopting the contrast of light and darkness found in Jewish writings and other Middle Eastern materials, the author encourages Christians to live in the light, to walk uprightly.

A contrast is made as well between the present life of the Christians at Ephesus and their former lives as pagans. In the past, the recipients of the letter did not see the proper way to behave. Now, living in the light of Christ, they can act rightly. Formerly,

MARCH 25, 2001 ■ 4TH SUNDAY OF LENT, YEAR A

## GOSPEL   John 9:1–41

**A reading from the holy gospel according to John**

As Jesus walked *along*, he saw a man *blind* from *birth.*
His disciples asked him,
"*Rabbi*, who *sinned*, *this* man or his *parents*,
that he was born *blind*?"

Jesus answered,
"Neither *this* man *nor* his parents sinned;
he was born *blind* so that God's *works* might be *revealed* in him.
We must work the *works* of him who *sent* me while it is *day*;
*night* is coming when *no* one can *work.*
As long as I am in the *world*, I am the *light* of the *world.*"
When he had said this, he *spat* on the *ground*
and made *mud* with the *saliva*
        and spread the mud on the man's *eyes,*
saying to him, "Go, *wash* in the pool of *Siloam*"
(which means *Sent*).

> This was not a typical healing but the actual giving of light to one who had never seen it. Express the amazement of the man's neighbors. Their question implies not only that the man now had sight, but also that his former behavior of begging had been changed as well.

Then the man who was *blind* went and *washed,*
        and came back able to *see.*
The *neighbours* and those who had seen him *before* as a *beggar*
began to ask, "Is *this* not the man who used to *sit* and *beg*?"
Some were saying, "It is *he.*"
*Others* were saying, "*No*, but it is someone *like* him."
He kept saying, "*I* am the *man.*"
But they kept asking him, "Then how were your eyes *opened*?"
He answered, "The man called *Jesus* made *mud*,
        spread it on my *eyes,*
and said to me, 'Go to *Siloam* and *wash.*'
Then I *went* and *washed* and received my *sight.*"

they had embraced the darkness of the world around them, so that they could be said to be darkness; as Christians, the author says, they are bearers of the light. Their former deeds are to be exposed—perhaps there is a reference to some type of public or private confession of sinfulness—so that they might be made light.

The final quotation from an unknown source is a vigorous call to live in the light of Christ. Mixing metaphors (as is done elsewhere in this passage), the author combines

the idea that the former life was death as well as darkness. The quotation may come from a hymn or Christian prayer, or some other unknown document; it would have been especially appropriate for use in the celebration of baptism.

This reading applies to all of us as we strive to live lives that are pleasing to God. When we allow the brightness of Christ's love to shine in our hearts, we are able to

see more clearly how to act justly and properly. Challenge your listeners to be fully alert in their Christian vocation, hiding nothing in darkness, but walking boldly in the light of day for all to see.

Offer this reading also for those who are preparing for initiation at Easter. We sometimes refer to initiation as "illumination," and we pray that those seeking baptism will always find a well-lit path on which to travel. Proclaim this message as an encouragement, in the hope that those

## 4TH SUNDAY OF LENT, YEAR A ■ MARCH 25, 2001

They said to him, "Where *is* he?"
He said, "I do not *know.*"

They brought to the *Pharisees*
      the man who had formerly been *blind.*
Now it was a *sabbath* day
      when Jesus made the *mud* and opened his *eyes.*
Then the Pharisees *also* began to ask him
*how* he had *received* his *sight.*
He said to them, "He put *mud* on my *eyes.*
Then I *washed,* and now I *see.*"
Some of the Pharisees said,
"This man is *not* from *God,*
      for he does not observe the *sabbath.*"
But *others* said,
      "How can a man who is a *sinner* perform such *signs?*"
And they were *divided.*
So they said *again* to the blind man,
"What do *you* say about him? It was *your* eyes he *opened.*"
He said, "He is a *prophet.*"

They did not *believe* that he had been *blind*
and had received his *sight*
until they called the *parents*
      of the man who had received his *sight*
and asked them, "Is *this* your *son,* who you say was born *blind?*
*How* then does he now *see?*"
His parents answered, "We *know* that this is our *son,*
and that he was born *blind;*
but we do *not* know how it is that now he *sees,*
nor do we know *who* opened his *eyes.*
Ask *him;* he is of *age.*
He will speak for *himself.*"

**The blind man has an insight that is lost on the others: Jesus is a prophet because he performs signs.**

**Suspecting a fabrication, they try to investigate all possibilities.**

---

preparing for initiation will receive enlightenment. Charge them also to meet the challenge to practice deeds that can be exposed to the light rather than hidden away in shame.

GOSPEL | The giving of sight to the man born blind affirms one of the favorite truths of this gospel: Jesus is the light and brings the ability to see with the eyes of faith to all who trust in him. It is this gift of insight that we desire for those

who approach initiation at Easter. We pray that their eyes, and the eyes of all the faithful, will be opened more fully to appreciate the brightness of God's love and the glory of God revealed in Jesus.

Although the healing itself is told only briefly, great interest is shown in the question of Jesus' disciples. Traditional belief held that a person was punished in this life for sins and rewarded with blessings for right behavior. In the absence of belief in an afterlife, affirmation of a just God required such belief. But, even before the development of hope in an afterlife, Jewish thought

had been questioning the accuracy of this simple system of reward and punishment.

Jesus does not question the justice of the assertion that the man was being punished, whether for his own sin or that of his parents, nor does he appeal to the idea of an afterlife. Instead, the occasion provides an opportunity for Jesus to demonstrate God's power. The affliction of the man allows the familiar Johannine themes of light and darkness to be played out literally for the blind

MARCH 25, 2001 ■ 4TH SUNDAY OF LENT, YEAR A

His parents said this because they were afraid
      of the Jewish *authorities,*
who had already *agreed*
that anyone who *confessed* Jesus to be the *Messiah*
would be put *out* of the *synagogue.*
Therefore his parents said, "*He* is of *age;* ask *him.*"

So for the *second* time they called the man who had been *blind,*
and they said to him, "Give *glory* to *God!*
We *know* that this man is a *sinner.*"
He answered, "I do not *know* whether he is a *sinner.*
One thing I *do* know, that though I was *blind,* now I *see.*"
They said to him, "What did he *do* to you?
How did he *open* your *eyes?*"
He answered them,
"I have told you *already,* and you would not *listen.*
*Why* do you want to hear it *again?*
Do *you* also want to become his *disciples?*"
Then they *reviled* him, saying,
"*You* are his *disciple,* but *we* are disciples of *Moses.*
We *know* that God has spoken to *Moses,*
but as for *this* man, we do *not* know where he *comes* from."

The man answered, "*Here* is an *astonishing* thing!
You do not *know* where he *comes* from,
      and yet he opened my *eyes.*
We *know* that God does not listen to *sinners,*
but he *does* listen to one who *worships* him and obeys his *will.*
*Never* since the world *began* has it been heard
that anyone *opened* the eyes of a person born *blind.*
If this man were *not* from *God,* he could do *nothing.*"

**The second questioning of the man is in a quasi-judicial hearing. The man speaks only of his own experience.**

**The man becomes sarcastic when they again ask questions he has already answered.**

**This is an accurate depiction of the Pharisees and a reason for them to be proud.**

**The man speaks with great strength and conviction here. Express his words forcefully.**

man. Surprisingly, those with both eyesight and knowledge, the Pharisees, are the ones who are "blind" to the light.

Not only is the man given sight for the first time, but his behavior is so changed that his neighbors do not even recognize him. He affirms that he is indeed the one who used to sit and beg, and recounts what has happened to him. He tells his story a second time, this time to the Pharisees. Although the Pharisees had no legal authority to declare

a person cured, they were apparently consulted because of their religious knowledge.

The fact that the miracle occurred on the Sabbath immediately arouses suspicion in some of the Pharisees. After ascertaining what has happened, they accuse the man of being Jesus' disciple. Although some are open to the possibility that Jesus performs signs as one sent from God (perhaps reflecting an openness to Jesus on the part of some Jewish leaders in the author's own day), the majority turn against the man. He unwaveringly states his belief that Jesus is

a prophet, one endowed with a divine ability to perform miraculous signs.

During the second questioning of the man, the atmosphere turns hostile. The Jewish leaders are harsh in their accusations, and the man responds with sarcasm and contempt. He can tell only what he knows—that he was blind but can now see—and the Pharisees cling to their belief that they alone are best able to interpret the law of Moses. Finally the man speaks a truth that they refuse to believe: God, who does

## 4TH SUNDAY OF LENT, YEAR A ■ MARCH 25, 2001

**The man's strength of character is threatening, and they rely on the old line that he must have been sinful to have been born blind.**

**The man is open to faith, although he does not yet understand the significance of what has happened to him.**

**Speak reverently and sincerely.**

**This summarizes the entire passage: Those who do not see can be healed; those who insist that they have not only working eyes but insight into God's will are in the end proven to be blind.**

They answered him, "*You* were born *entirely* in *sins*,
and are *you* trying to teach *us*?"
And they drove him *out*.

Jesus *heard* that they had driven him *out*,
and when he *found* him, he said,
"Do you *believe* in the Son of *Man*?"
He answered, "And who *is* he, sir?
*Tell* me, so that I may *believe* in him."
Jesus said to him, "You have *seen* him,
and the one *speaking* with you is *he*."
He said, "Lord, I *believe*."
And he *worshipped* him.

Jesus said, "I came into this *world* for *judgment*
so that those who do *not* see may *see*,
and those who *do* see may become *blind*."
Some of the *Pharisees* near him *heard* this and said to him,
"Surely *we* are not blind, *are* we?"
Jesus said to them,
"If you were *blind*, you would have no *sin*.
But *now* that you say, 'We *see*,' your sin *remains*."

*[Shorter: John 9:1, 6–9, 13–17, 34–38]*

not listen to sinners, has acted decisively through Jesus. Far from being a sinner, Jesus must be a man of God. The one who was blind has real insight into Jesus' heavenly origin, while those who supposedly have the light of God's favor are in fact blind.

Rather than assist those less fortunate, the religious leaders would prefer to follow blindly the dictates of the law. Experts in the law, they refuse to help others understand what God asks of them, choosing instead to leave others in the dark. Although they think of themselves as enlightened leaders, they

are seen in the end to be stumbling in darkness, and those they accuse of being filled with sin hold the lantern to guide them, if they would only open their eyes to see its brilliance.

This is an especially appropriate reading for us as we struggle through the dark days of Lent. We know that the light is available for us, if we but acknowledge it. With the catechumens, who are gradually being illuminated through their prayer and study, we pray that we will all grow in our ability to see Christ. Read this passage as a challenge to your community to proclaim Christ

as the source of light for the world. Offer it also as encouragement to trust in the one who offers insight and enlightenment, even if those in power refuse to accept it. Finally, read this as a preparation for the baptismal promises of Easter, whether spoken for the first time by the newly initiated or renewed by the assembly.

APRIL 1, 2001

# 5TH SUNDAY OF LENT

Lectionary #36

**READING I** Isaiah 43:16–21

**A reading from the book of the prophet Isaiah**

The first section recalls God's actions during the exodus from Egypt.

*Thus* says the *Lord,*
who makes a *way* in the *sea,*
a *path* in the mighty *waters,*
who brings out *chariot* and *horse, army* and *warrior;*
they lie *down,* they cannot *rise,*
they are *extinguished,* quenched like a *wick*:
Do not remember the *former* things,
or consider the things of *old.*

These are the words of God, introduced by the earlier "Thus says the Lord."

I am about to do a *new* thing;
*now* it springs *forth,* do you not *perceive* it?
I will make a *way* in the *wilderness*
and *rivers* in the *desert.*

This is the central proclamation of the passage. Speak as though you are letting your listeners in on a wonderful surprise.

The wild *animals* will *honour* me,
the *jackals* and the *ostriches;*
for I give *water* in the *wilderness, rivers* in the *desert,*
to give *drink* to my chosen *people,*
the people whom I *formed* for *myself*
so that they might *declare* my *praise.*

Close with a strong assent to the idea of giving praise to God.

READING I The section of the book of Isaiah starting with chapter 40 and including the passage used today is called Second Isaiah. Written centuries after the historical prophet Isaiah was active, it celebrates the end of the Babylonian exile. In the early part of the sixth century BCE the leaders of the kingdom of Judah were deported to Babylon; the city of Jerusalem lay in ruins. But by the year 540 BCE, it was clear that the Babylonian empire would be defeated and the anonymous prophet of this section believed that the exile would come

to an end. It is a time of hope and joy, and of renewed commitment to God.

The exile in Babylon was a painful experience for Israel. The people longed to return to their homeland. Both the period of slavery in Egypt and the exodus had long influenced Israel's self-identity, but it must have become especially meaningful during the period of exile. Israel knew that it had been enslaved before but that God had brought the people out of bondage and into the Promised Land. Longing to return to that land, the prophets of this time saw the period of exile as a punishment for unfaithfulness.

But today the prophet has a new message and recalls God's actions on behalf of Israel. God made a way for the Israelites to pass through the waters of the Red Sea but brought destruction upon the Egyptian army. Yet that is no longer to be seen as the defining moment in God's dealings with Israel. God is inaugurating a new day and once again providing for this beloved people. The desert through which the exiles will return will no longer be parched but will be filled with rivers. Wild animals will see the might

**5TH SUNDAY OF LENT ■ APRIL 1, 2001**

---

### READING II    Philippians 3:8–14

**A reading from the letter of Paul to the Philippians**

Begin strongly, then pause briefly after "loss," lowering your voice a bit for the words that follow.

I regard everything as *loss*
because of the surpassing *value* of knowing Christ *Jesus* my *Lord*.
For *his* sake I have suffered the *loss* of all *things*,
and I regard them as *rubbish*,
in order that I may gain *Christ* and be found in *him*,

Throughout, speak slowly and clearly. Emphasize the idea that all righteousness comes from faith in Christ.

not having a righteousness of my *own* that comes from the *law*,
but one that comes through *faith* in *Christ*,
the *righteousness* from *God* based on *faith*.

Build to this line.

I want to *know* Christ
and the *power* of his *resurrection*
and the *sharing* of his *sufferings* by becoming like him
in his *death*,
if somehow I may attain the *resurrection* from the *dead*.

Paul clarifies that resurrection is not a present reality but an object of hope.

Not that I have *already* obtained this
or have already *reached* the *goal*;
but I press *on* to make it my *own*,
because Christ *Jesus* has made *me* his *own*.

*Beloved*, I do not consider that I *have* made it my *own*;
but this *one* thing I *do*:

Lift your voice again, expressing eagerness and the effort required to reach the goal.

*forgetting* what lies *behind* and straining *forward*
to what lies *ahead*,
I press *on* toward the *goal*
for the *prize* of the heavenly *call* of God in Christ *Jesus*.

---

of God and bow down in homage. All creation will honor God.

Praise for God will be the result of Israel's deliverance; Israel itself will sing praise. No longer will the people cry and mourn; they will instead shout out the glory of God.

Proclaiming this passage well requires a sensitivity to the actions of God in the past and an exuberant recounting of God's new creation. Begin with conviction, building as you proceed, until you announce with joy the closing lines. Speak lovingly of God's

choice of this people, and close strongly in a tone of praise.

READING II | The community of Christians in Philippi was one of Paul's favorite churches. He writes its members with love and longing, but he is not afraid to rebuke them when necessary. In today's passage, he stirringly sums up the depth of his commitment to Christ.

Nothing else means anything compared with the opportunity to know Jesus Christ. Paul goes so far as to call everything

else "rubbish," not because of its inherent lack of value but because in comparison with the righteousness made possible in Christ all else is worthless. Emphasizing a characteristic theme in his writings, Paul contrasts the Jewish law with faith in Christ and concludes that justification comes only by faith. God freely chooses to make people righteous; we are not saved by our own actions. Such a gift can only be accepted in faith.

APRIL 1, 2001 ■ 5TH SUNDAY OF LENT

## GOSPEL John 8:1–11

### A reading from the gospel according to John

Jesus went to the Mount of *Olives*.
Early in the *morning* he came again to the *temple*.
All the people *came* to him
and he sat down and began to *teach* them.

The *scribes* and the *Pharisees* brought a *woman*
who had been caught in *adultery*;
and making her *stand* before the *people*,
they said to Jesus,
"*Teacher*, this woman was caught
in the very *act* of committing *adultery*.
In the *law*, Moses commanded us to *stone* such women.
Now what do *you* say?"
They said this to *test* Jesus,
so that they might have some charge to bring *against* him.

Jesus bent *down*
and wrote with his *finger* on the *ground*.
When the scribes and Pharisees kept on *questioning* him,
Jesus straightened *up* and said to them,
"Let *anyone* among you who is without *sin*
be the *first* to throw a *stone* at her."
And once *again* Jesus bent down and wrote on the *ground*.

When the scribes and Pharisees *heard* what Jesus had said,
they went *away*, one by *one*, beginning with the *elders*;
and Jesus was left *alone* with the woman standing *before* him.

---

**Here the drama really begins. Think about how the woman must have felt.**

**These are strong words. Speak in an angry, perhaps mocking, tone.**

**Jesus' words are solemn and bear a gentle forcefulness.**

---

But faith is not simply assent to a principle or set of beliefs. Through it the Christian not only comes to know the power of Jesus' resurrection but also participates in Jesus' suffering. Faith in Christ means being willing to travel the same path Christ did. Paul hopes that the end of this journey will be the same for the Christian as it was for Christ: resurrection.

Against those who must have claimed that they were already living a heavenly life in company with the angels, Paul asserts that resurrected life remains a future reality.

Resurrected life is Paul's great hope, but one he still awaits. He sees himself as a runner striving to complete a race, pressing ever forward with his goal—the resurrected life—in mind.

Proclaim this powerful passage with full attention to Paul's strong language. Begin in a somewhat subdued voice, reaching a crescendo with the phrase "the power of his resurrection." Lower your voice again before building to the end, then stress the wondrous prize that awaits the Christian, who with Paul holds nothing dearer than knowing Christ Jesus.

GOSPEL Today's gospel story of the woman caught in adultery was not originally part of John's gospel (the earliest manuscripts do not contain it). It was probably added during a period of controversy about forgiveness of serious sins committed after baptism.

The dramatic story about the woman's fate is a challenging story for people of any era. Its message is stark: No one has the right to condemn another, for we are all guilty of sin. Yet Jesus does not condone

## 102
5TH SUNDAY OF LENT ■ APRIL 1, 2001

**Proceed especially slowly now. Jesus speaks with compassion, the woman with trust. Close firmly.**

Jesus straightened *up* and said to her,
"*Woman*, where *are* they?
Has no one *condemned* you?"
She said, "*No* one, sir."
And Jesus said, "Neither do *I* condemn you.
Go your *way*, and from now *on* do not sin *again*."

what the woman does. In fact, he knows that her actions were wrong and encourages her to leave behind her sinful ways.

The religious leaders were trying to trap Jesus, apparently by bringing before him a situation that had no easy legal resolution. The passion scene in the gospel of John makes it clear that the Roman occupiers forbid the Jews to put anyone to death. Since the Mosaic law advised stoning an adulterous woman, posing the question to

Jesus placed him in a difficult position. He could neither deny the authority of the Jewish law, nor could he blatantly defy the Roman government.

Jesus' response to this challenge is inspiring. Instead of taking a stand on either side of the question, he seeks a change of heart, telling the woman not to sin again. But even more profound is the change demanded of the lynch mob that had brought the woman to him. Jesus' challenge to them—"Let anyone among you who is without sin be the

first to throw a stone at her"—forces them to look deep inside their own hearts.

Proclaim this moving tale with compassion and conviction. Allow the drama of the story to be heard in your voice, and give special weight to the words of Jesus.

APRIL 1, 2001

# 5TH SUNDAY OF LENT, YEAR A

*Lectionary #34*

---

### READING I    Ezekiel 37:12–14

**A reading from the book of the prophet Ezekiel**

This is a message of comfort and love; speak with encouragement in your voice.

The exiles longed for their homeland.

*Thus* says the Lord *God:*
"I am going to *open* your *graves,*
and bring you *up* from your graves, O my *people;*
and I will bring you *back* to the land of *Israel.*
And you shall *know* that *I* am the *Lord,*
when I *open* your *graves,*
and bring you *up* from your graves, O my *people.*

This promise is especially inspiring; lift your voice and speak slowly and with conviction from here until the end.

"I will put my spirit *within* you, and you shall *live,*
and I will *place* you on your own *soil;*
then you shall *know*
that *I,* the *Lord,* have *spoken* and will *act,*"
says the Lord.

---

### READING II    Romans 8:8–11

**A reading from the letter of Paul to the Romans**

Pause slightly after the first line in order to provide a contrast with those (believers) who are not in the flesh.

Those who are in the *flesh* cannot *please* God.
But *you* are *not* in the flesh;
you are in the *Spirit,*
since the Spirit of *God dwells* in you.

---

READING I  The prophet Ezekiel writes during the bleak years of Judah's exile in Babylon. Ezekiel's message is largely one of hope: God is with this people, wherever they are, and will one day restore them to their own land.

Coming right after Ezekiel's vision of dry bones, today's passage speaks of the new life that God will give to the people. Both the vision and this selection picture a people coming to life again after having been dead, a people filled with God's spirit. The message is one of hope: God will restore

the nation and symbolically bring it back to life. The sad period of exile will end.

Although it was several hundred years before the belief in an actual resurrection of the dead developed, this passage certainly sounds as though it promises such. In fact, the graves are symbolic of the nation's current state, and the promise is that the people will once again live in their own land. But it has also inspired many who hope for an

afterlife, and this is the reason it is used in our liturgy today. The picture of graves opening and living people emerging fittingly introduces the gospel story of the raising of Lazarus from the tomb.

Offer this reading to your listeners on several levels. For those who are struggling, it is a message of hope that God will take care of them. Read it compassionately as a firm promise. For many of us, the passage can affirm our belief that this life is not final; we have hope in something greater. Finally, encourage the catechumens to reflect on the new life they are receiving in their Easter

5TH SUNDAY OF LENT, YEAR A ■ APRIL 1, 2001

Anyone who does *not* have the Spirit of *Christ*
does not *belong* to him.

But if Christ is *in* you,
though the body is *dead* because of *sin*,
the *Spirit* is *life* because of *righteousness*.

**Pause briefly after "dead."**
**Proclaim this with hope and confidence.**

If the Spirit of *God* who *raised* Jesus from the *dead dwells* in you,
he who raised *Christ* from the *dead*
will give *life* to your mortal bodies *also*
through his *Spirit* that dwells *in* you.

---

**GOSPEL**   John 11:1–45

**A reading from the holy gospel according to John**

Now a certain man, *Lazarus*, was *ill.*
He was from *Bethany*, the village of *Mary* and her sister *Martha.*
*Mary* was the one who *anointed* the Lord with *perfume*
and wiped his *feet* with her *hair*;
her brother *Lazarus* was *ill.*

**Mary is said to have anointed Jesus with costly oil, although the event has not yet been told in this gospel.**

So the sisters sent a *message* to Jesus,
"*Lord*, he whom you *love* is *ill.*"
But when Jesus *heard* this, he said,
"This *illness* does not lead to *death*;
rather it is for God's *glory*,
so that the Son of *God* may be glorified *through* it."
*Accordingly*, though Jesus *loved* Martha
        and her sister and Lazarus,

**Emphasize the love Jesus had for Lazarus here and wherever it occurs.**

**What Jesus says of Lazarus here is much the same as his attitude toward his own death as presented in this gospel.**

---

profession of faith. Allow God's promise of life in the Spirit to be addressed especially to them.

READING II Paul writes to the community in Rome, whose members he had never met, in a theoretical rather than a personal tone. Here he contrasts the new life available in Christ with life in the "flesh."

When Paul speaks here of living in the flesh, he is talking about a mindset and a lifestyle. He contrasts living according to the dictates of the world with living as one who belongs to God. His addressees, he knows, are those who are committed to God, who are in the Spirit. The presence of the Spirit confirms whether one is Christian.

But Paul also recognizes that resurrected life remains in the future. We live in an age that is still under the rule of sin and death, but the Christian is also infused with the Spirit of life. We live in two worlds in a sense, the world of death and the world of

life in Christ. Obviously Paul's audience is not actually dead, but was still dwelling in a world under the sway of death. Yet the Romans could have hope, not only while in this life, but also after death, when they would be raised as Christ was. The hope is for an actual afterlife, although the life of the Spirit begins before death for the Christian.

This passage offers the same hope in the indwelling of God's Spirit as the first reading, together with the same genuine belief in life after death evidenced in the

APRIL 1, 2001 ■ 5TH SUNDAY OF LENT, YEAR A

after having *heard* that Lazarus was *ill*,
he stayed *two* days *longer* in the place where he *was*.

Then after *this* Jesus said to the disciples,
"Let us *go* to *Judea* again."
The disciples said to him,
"*Rabbi*, the people there were just *now* trying to *stone* you,
and are you going there *again*?"
Jesus answered,
"Are there not *twelve* hours of *daylight*?
Those who walk during the *day* do not *stumble*,
because they see the *light* of this *world*.
But those who walk at *night stumble*,
because the *light* is not *in* them."

After *saying* this, he told them,
"Our friend *Lazarus* has fallen *asleep*,
but I am *going* there to *awaken* him."
The disciples said to him,
"*Lord*, if he has fallen *asleep*, he will be all *right*."
*Jesus*, however, had been speaking about his *death*,
but *they* thought that he was referring merely to *sleep*.
Then Jesus told them plainly,
"*Lazarus* is *dead*.
For *your* sake I am glad I was *not* there,
so that you may *believe*.
But let us *go* to him."
*Thomas*, who was called the *Twin*,
said to his fellow disciples,
"Let us *also* go, that we may *die* with him."

When Jesus *arrived*,
he found that Lazarus had already been in the *tomb* four *days*.

**The disciples must have been afraid for themselves and for Jesus; express their dismay effectively.**

**This author often plays on the contrast between light and darkness. This obscure statement is apparently Jesus' claim that he will not be swayed by the powers of darkness.**

**Although the euphemism "to fall asleep" is a common one, the disciples, as usual, misunderstand.**

**Pause briefly after "days."**

gospel. Offer it to your community as an encouragement to recognize the life of the Spirit within. It is an especially poignant promise to those who will be initiated into the community on Easter. But the new life offered is not contrasted only with the life prior to conversion or initiation, although it begins at initiation. We can all be more fully open to the Spirit of God in our hearts. Encourage your listeners to live more completely in Christ, with lives determined not by the values of the world around them, but by the Holy Spirit.

GOSPEL | The story of the raising of Lazarus is inspiring and touching, and, most of all, it reveals Jesus' power over death. It is a precursor to Jesus' own death and resurrection, and inspires the characters within the story, as well as the reader of it, to accept the message that the opportunity for life is offered in Jesus. We also use this passage to indicate the life that will be available to the newly initiated this Easter, as well as a promise of life after death.

The story, which appears only in the gospel of John, begins with an introduction of the sick man, Lazarus, later identified as especially beloved of Jesus, and his two sisters, Martha and Mary. Throughout, the author repeatedly insists on Jesus' profound love for Lazarus, Martha and Mary.

When Jesus learns of the illness of Lazarus, he responds with an enigmatic statement about giving glory to God. Oddly, he takes his time responding to the urgent message. The protests of the disciples when

**106**

5TH SUNDAY OF LENT, YEAR A ■ APRIL 1, 2001

Now Bethany was *near Jerusalem*,
some *two* miles *away*,
and many *Jews* had come to Martha and Mary
to *console* them about their *brother*.
When *Martha* heard that Jesus was *coming*,
    she went and *met* him,
while *Mary* stayed at *home*.
Martha said to Jesus,
"*Lord*, if you had *been* here, my brother would not have *died*.
But even *now* I know
    that God will *give* you whatever you *ask* of him."
Jesus said to her, "Your *brother* will *rise* again."
Martha said to him,
"I *know* that he will rise again
    in the *resurrection* on the last *day*."

**This is the central teaching of today's gospel. Read slowly and forcefully in order to give it due emphasis.**

Jesus said to her, "*I* am the resurrection and the *life*.
Those who *believe* in me,
even though they *die*, will *live*,
and everyone who *lives* and believes in me will *never* die.
Do you *believe* this?"
She said to him,

**Speak Martha's declaration of faith with quiet but firm assurance.**

"*Yes*, Lord, I *believe* that *you* are the *Messiah*,
the Son of *God*, the one coming into the *world*."

When she had *said* this,
    she went back and called her sister *Mary*,
and told her *privately*,
"The *Teacher* is here and is *calling* for you."
And when Mary *heard* it, she got up *quickly* and *went* to him.
Now Jesus had not yet come to the *village*,
but was still at the place where Martha had *met* him.

---

**Jesus announces his decision to return to Judea make the reader aware of the perils inherent in the decision. The danger is underscored by Thomas' blustery remark, which indicates his willingness to die with Jesus.**

    **As always in this gospel, Jesus speaks on a level deeper than that of his companions, and even his closest disciples misunderstand what he is saying. Jesus must finally spell out the situation, claiming that the entire event will be for their sake.**

**Throughout this story, Jesus acts in order to instruct others, to inspire faith in the characters of the story and in the reader.**

    **Both Martha and Mary seem to reproach Jesus for his delay, saying that Lazarus would not have died had he been present. But the statements may in fact be claims of faith; Martha's encounter with Jesus is especially telling. She immediately affirms that God will grant whatever Jesus asks, and the two discuss the resurrection of the dead, which leads to Martha's confession of faith in Jesus.**

**Whenever Jesus speaks, he offers fuller insight into his identity. Here he declares that he is the resurrection and the life. This is not simply a promise of a future resurrection of the dead, which Martha already accepts, but is a declaration of a present reality for the believer. Resurrected life begins now in faith, says the evangelist. Martha's response indicates a partial understanding; she recognizes that, in Jesus, the future hope has**

APRIL 1, 2001 ■ 5TH SUNDAY OF LENT, YEAR A

The *Jews* who were *with* her in the house, *consoling* her,
*saw* Mary get up quickly and go *out.*
They *followed* her because they thought
that she was going to the *tomb* to weep *there.*

When Mary came where *Jesus* was and *saw* him,
she *knelt* at his feet and *said* to him,
"*Lord*, if you had *been* here, my *brother* would not have *died.*"
When Jesus saw her *weeping*,
and the Jews who came *with* her *also* weeping,
he was greatly *disturbed* in *spirit* and deeply *moved.*
Jesus said, "Where have you *laid* him?"
They said to him, "*Lord*, come and *see.*"
Jesus began to *weep.*
So the Jews said, "*See* how he *loved* him!"
But some of them said,
"Could not *he* who *opened* the eyes of the *blind* man
have kept *this* man from *dying*?"

Then *Jesus*, again greatly *disturbed*, came to the *tomb.*
It was a *cave*, and a stone was lying *against* it.
Jesus said, "Take away the *stone.*"
*Martha*, the sister of the *dead* man, said to him,
"*Lord*, already there is a *stench*
because he has been dead *four days.*"
Jesus said to her,
"Did I not *tell* you that if you *believed*,
you would see the glory of *God*?"
So they took away the *stone.*
And Jesus looked upward and said,
"*Father*, I *thank* you for having *heard* me.

**Be sure to convey the great sorrow Jesus felt.**

**Pause after "weep." Jesus' love for Lazarus, and for Martha and Mary, ran deep. Let it sink in for your listeners.**

**This is probably a wistful expression rather than criticism.**

become present. Jesus is the Messiah for whom Israel has been waiting.

In a rare instance of human emotion in this gospel, Jesus is moved to tears when he sees the profound sadness of Mary. The reader, just like the Jewish visitors who were mourning with the family, is struck by the depth of Jesus' love for the dead man. The mourners are not hostile to Jesus, which is evident in their expression of belief in his healing of the blind man.

The reality of Lazarus' death is affirmed once again through the words of Martha as Jesus approaches the tomb. As is typical in this gospel, Jesus' prayer is not for himself but for his listeners. He thanks God in advance for hearing him and responding in the raising of Lazarus.

When the dead man emerges from the tomb against all human expectations, those present respond with faith. The giving of life, an activity reserved for God, leads directly to the plot against Jesus in the verses that follow today's reading. The revelation of Jesus'

person and mission, indeed the affirmation of his declaration to Martha that he is the resurrection and the life, is too threatening to the religious leaders in this gospel. The raising of Lazarus was accomplished for the glory of God. Jesus' death will also serve as the supreme moment of his revelation, when he is raised up in glory for all to see.

# 5TH SUNDAY OF LENT, YEAR A ■ APRIL 1, 2001

**Speak this command firmly and with authority.**

I knew that you *always* hear me,
but I have *said* this for the sake of the *crowd* standing here,
so that they may *believe* that you *sent* me."

When he had *said* this, he cried with a loud voice,
"*Lazarus*, come *out!*"
The dead man came *out*,
his hands and feet *bound* with strips of *cloth*,
and his *face* wrapped in a *cloth*.
Jesus said to them, "*Unbind* him, and let him *go*."

**The story is meant to inspire us with more profound faith.**

Many of the *Jews* therefore, who had come with *Mary*
and had *seen* what Jesus did, *believed* in him.

*[Shorter: John 11:3–7, 17, 20–27, 33b–45]*

The superhuman knowledge of Jesus in this story—indeed, throughout this gospel—often makes it difficult to employ the best storytelling techniques to Jesus' words and deeds. But in this passage you are offered the words of others as well, and an indication that Jesus was deeply moved after his friend's death. Capitalize on these comments and proclaim the story with all its drama and emotion. Read Jesus' declarations regarding his person as statements intended to elicit faith, as they are intended.

## APRIL 8, 2001

# PALM SUNDAY OF THE LORD'S PASSION

*Lectionary #37*

## GOSPEL AT THE PROCESSION   Luke 19:28–40

**A reading from the holy gospel according to Luke**

Jesus went on *ahead*, going up to *Jerusalem*.
When he had come near *Bethphage* and *Bethany*,
at the place called the Mount of *Olives*,
he sent *two* of the *disciples*, saying,
"*Go* into the village *ahead* of you,
and as you *enter* it you will find *tied* there
a *colt* that has never been *ridden*.
*Untie* it and bring it *here*.
If anyone *asks* you, 'Why are you *untying* it?'
just say this, 'The Lord *needs* it.'"

So those who were sent *departed*
and found it as Jesus had *told* them.
As they were *untying* the *colt*, its owners *asked* them,
"*Why* are you *untying* the colt?"
They said, "The Lord *needs* it."

Then they brought the colt to *Jesus*;
and after throwing their *cloaks* on the colt,
they set Jesus *on* it.

As he rode *along*,
people kept spreading their *cloaks* on the *road*.
As he was now approaching the path
     *down* from the Mount of *Olives*,
the whole *multitude* of the disciples began to *praise* God *joyfully*,

**Bethphage = BETH-fayj**
**Bethany = BETH-uh-nee**

**Jesus knows what will happen; he is in control.**

**Everything occurs just as Jesus had said.**

**Let your voice gradually build as you describe the processional scene.**

---

**PROCESSION GOSPEL** Jesus' entrance into Jerusalem honors him as the awaited Messiah and indicates the favor accorded him by the crowds. In language recalling the nativity story in the gospel of Luke, Jesus' arrival is greeted by multitudes singing praise to God. Indeed, the entire cosmos joins in the praise: If his followers did not rejoice, the stones themselves would cry out.

The Mount of Olives was traditionally associated with the Messiah, the foremost "Anointed One" of God; the oil pressed from olives grown there was used to anoint

Israel's rulers. Jesus' arrival in Jerusalem from the Mount of Olives is accompanied by shouts of blessings for one who "comes in the name of the Lord" (Psalm 118:26). He is both Messiah and king, fulfilling the words of Zechariah 9:9 ("Behold, your king comes to you; triumphant and victorious is he, humble and riding on a donkey, on a colt, the foal of a donkey"). The image fits well with the Lukan theme of reversal. The holy one of God, the one most deserving of honor and glory, arrives on a humble colt.

The story about the colt, which occupies so much of this selection, demonstrates

Jesus' foreknowledge and provides a prophetic link. But it is the procession that is most dramatic.

Read the story of the colt as a straightforward narrative of events. Hold nothing back, however, when you recount the procession itself. Lift your voice as you tell of the reaction of the crowds to Jesus, and close with a triumphant tone.

**READING I** The servant songs from the book of Isaiah have long been understood to refer to Jesus' humility

PALM SUNDAY ■ APRIL 8, 2001

**Sing out in joy.**

and with a loud *voice*,
for all the deeds of *power* that they had *seen*, saying,
"*Blessed* is the *king* who comes in the *name* of the *Lord!*
*Peace* in *heaven*,
and *glory* in the *highest* heaven!"

Some of the *Pharisees* in the crowd said to him,
"*Teacher*, order your disciples to *stop*."

Jesus answered, "I *tell* you,
if *these* were silent, the *stones* would shout out."

*Lectionary #38*

## READING I    Isaiah 50:4–7

**A reading from the book of the prophet Isaiah**

**Read this with certainty and an eagerness to speak God's word.**

The servant of the Lord said:
"The Lord *God* has given me the tongue of a *teacher*,
that I may know how to *sustain* the *weary* with a *word*.
*Morning* by *morning* he *wakens*—
wakens my *ear* to *listen* as those who are *taught*.

The Lord God has *opened* my *ear*,
and I was not *rebellious*,
I did not turn *backward*.

**Pause, then proceed in a tone of drama, emphasizing the torments experienced by the servant.**

"I gave my *back* to those who *struck* me,
and my *cheeks* to those who pulled out the *beard*;
I did not *hide* my *face*
from *insult* and *spitting*.

and willingness to endure pain and humiliation. This passage is especially poignant, followed in our liturgy by the reading of the passion narrative.

The servant sees himself as one who learns and then shares his knowledge with others. His task is to teach despite opposition. He knows that the people are exhausted, that they continue to be in pain, but his own pain cannot silence him. He listens attentively to God, then instructs those who fear the God of Israel.

The gospel accounts of Jesus' passion echo the description of the servant's sufferings. Jesus, like the servant, is struck, abused and insulted. Yet he does not give up but knows that he will ultimately be vindicated.

Your task is similar to that of the servant: You are entrusted with God's word and asked to present it to your assembly, teaching and encouraging, continuing at all costs. Offer this reading to the members of your assembly with an eye to the sufferings of Jesus. Speak of the suffering in a dark tone of pain, and close with an air of conviction and courage.

READING II  The hymn quoted here by Paul was inserted into a passage of ethical instruction. Paul offers encouragement to the Philippians to be humble and obedient, just as Christ was. As a demonstration of Christ's humility, Paul quotes this hymn, celebrating the willingness of Christ to give up his rightful exalted state and be humiliated.

The hymn in Philippians is one of the earliest Christian passages that refers to the preexistence of Christ. Rather than laying claim to the exaltation of heaven, he humbled himself by becoming human and by

APRIL 8, 2001 ■ PALM SUNDAY

**Pause before reading this line, then continue with a peaceful, trusting tone.**

"The Lord God *helps* me;
therefore I have *not* been *disgraced*;
therefore I have set my *face* like *flint*,
and I know that I shall *not* be put to *shame*."

---

### READING II    Philippians 2:6–11

**A reading from the letter of Paul to the Philippians**

Let the *same* mind be in *you* that was in Christ *Jesus*,
*who*, though he was in the *form* of *God*,
did not regard *equality* with God
as something to be *exploited*,
but *emptied* himself,
taking the form of a *slave*,
being born in human *likeness*.
And being found in human *form*,
he *humbled* himself
and became *obedient* to the point of *death*,
even *death* on a *cross*.

*Therefore* God highly *exalted* him
and gave him the *name* that is above *every* name,
so that at the name of *Jesus* every *knee* should *bend*,
in *heaven* and on *earth* and *under* the earth,
and every tongue should *confess* that *Jesus Christ* is *Lord*,
to the *glory* of God the *Father*.

**Stress the contrast of these lines with what has gone before.**

**Pause after this line, then change your tone to a lighter one.**

**Slow down and emphasize every phrase, allowing your voice to grow in intensity and wonder until you practically shout "Jesus Christ is Lord!" The final line is a bit more subdued but still emphasized; be careful not to rush.**

---

being willing to die on the cross, only then to be glorified with God.

What is most exciting in this hymn is the name accorded Jesus. At the mention of his name, all honor will be given him, and everyone will proclaim that "Jesus Christ is Lord." The Greek word for "Lord" is the word that is used to translate the divine name from the Hebrew scriptures. Jesus can be addressed with the same title given to the creator of the world, the God who saved the Israelites from their oppressors in Egypt, who was revealed at Sinai, who spoke

through the prophets and restored the people after the exile in Babylon. The same God who acted on behalf of the Jewish people has now acted decisively for all the world.

Begin your reading, as does Paul, with an exhortation to proper behavior. Then recount solemnly the "emptying" of Jesus, giving special weight to the reference to his death. Speak triumphantly of his exaltation, allowing your voice to reach a crescendo with the proclamation that Jesus is Lord. Inspire your listeners to give the same praise and honor to Jesus that was offered by the early Christians.

PASSION The mood quickly darkens as we turn to the passion narrative from the gospel of Luke. After a joyous procession into Jerusalem, after the servant's expression of trust in God despite opposition, and, finally, after the proclamation of praise that closes the second reading, we now turn to the darkest hour of Jesus' life.

The passion account in Luke displays some characteristic themes of the gospel. Prominent are the themes of reversal and of the exaltation of the lowly. All expectations are turned upside down. The wealthy and

PALM SUNDAY ■ APRIL 8, 2001

**PASSION** Luke 22:14—23:56

## The Passion of our Lord Jesus Christ according to Luke

The reading of the passion begins without the customary introduction and responses.

(1) When the *hour* came,
Jesus took his place at the *table*, and the apostles *with* him.
He said to them,
"I have eagerly *desired*
        to eat this *Passover* with you before I *suffer*;
for I *tell* you, I will not *eat* it
until it is *fulfilled* in the kingdom of *God*."

Speak Jesus' words with solemnity.

Then he took a *cup*,
and after giving *thanks* he said,
"*Take* this and *divide* it among *yourselves*;
for I tell you that from now *on*
I will not *drink* of the fruit of the *vine*
        until the kingdom of God *comes*."

Then Jesus took a loaf of *bread*,
and when he had given *thanks*,
he *broke* it and *gave* it to them, saying,
"This is my *body*, which is given for *you*.
*Do* this in *remembrance* of me."
And he did the *same* with the *cup* after supper, saying,
"This *cup* that is poured *out* for you
        is the new *covenant* in my *blood*.

There is an ominous tone to these words. Speak accordingly.

(2) But *see*, the one who *betrays* me is *with* me,
and his *hand* is on the *table*.
For the Son of Man is *going* as it has been *determined*,
but *woe* to that one by whom he is *betrayed!*"
Then they began to *ask* one another,
which *one* of them it could *be* who would *do* this.

powerful of the world are brought low while the poor and disenfranchised are honored. The theme of discipleship is emphasized as well: The Last Supper becomes an occasion for Jesus to teach about what it means to be his follower. Finally, at the climax of his life, Jesus displays the compassion characteristic of him in this gospel right to the end, comforting the mourning women and even granting forgiveness from the cross.

We are so accustomed to seeing depictions of the passion and speaking of the cross of Christ that we sometimes forget

how offensive to Judaism the idea of a suffering and dying Messiah was. The cross was an instrument of torture, a symbol of degradation and humiliation. Even more, however, it was a sign of being cursed by God. For the Jew awaiting a Messiah who would overthrow the occupying forces, or a Messiah who would demonstrate God's victory and righteousness, or a Messiah who would bring about peace and justice, the cross represented failure. Rather than acting decisively, God seemed to be silent. Rather than celebrating victory, the Messiah suffered helplessly. For the people of Jesus'

time, the idea of a suffering Messiah was a contradiction in terms.

Although today's selection ends without an account of the resurrection, the passion narrative still proclaims the victory of Jesus. During the meal, he declares that his followers will share in his heavenly dominion. At his trial before the religious leaders he anticipates being seated at the right hand of God. After Jesus' death, the centurion proclaims his innocence. We know, as does the author, that the ugly events recounted here are not the last word. There is more yet to come.

APRIL 8, 2001 ■ PALM SUNDAY

(3) A *dispute* also arose among them
as to which *one* of them was to be regarded as the *greatest*.

But Jesus said to them,
"The *kings* of the *Gentiles* lord it *over* them;
and those in *authority* over them are called *benefactors*.

But not so with *you*;
rather the *greatest* among you must become like the *youngest*,
and the *leader* like one who *serves*.
For who is *greater*,
the one who is at the *table* or the one who *serves*?

**Pause slightly, then speak solemnly.**

Is it not the one at the *table*?
But *I* am among you as one who *serves*.

"*You* are those who have stood by me in my *trials*;
and I *confer* on you,
just as my *Father* has conferred on *me*, a *kingdom*,
so that you may *eat* and *drink* at my *table* in my *kingdom*,

**There is an abrupt change in subject after this verse. Pause, then speak in a tone of warning.**

and you will sit on *thrones* judging the twelve *tribes* of *Israel*.

(4) "*Simon, Simon, listen!*
*Satan* has demanded to *sift* all of you like *wheat*,
but I have *prayed* for you that your *own* faith may not *fail*;
and *you*, when once you have turned *back*,
*strengthen* your *brothers*."
And Peter said to Jesus,
"*Lord*, I am ready to go *with* you to *prison* and to *death!*"
Jesus said, "I *tell* you, Peter,
    the *cock* will not *crow* this day,
until you have *denied* three *times* that you *know* me."

(5) Jesus said to them,

**The mood lightens a bit.**

"When I sent you *out* without a *purse*, *bag*, or *sandals*,
did you *lack* anything?"

---

The method of reading the passion varies from parish to parish. Your parish may choose to have one well-prepared reader proclaim the entire passion, or a group of readers may proclaim the reading in parts. A group may choose to divide the reading by sections, or each individual might take a role. Sometimes the congregation is involved, although this unfortunately requires the entire assembly to read along throughout the passage rather than listen attentively.

Perhaps a congregational antiphon will follow each section, indicating shifts in the narrative. However your community proclaims the passion, proper preparation is essential.

If several participants share the responsibility of reading, they should be chosen for their ability to make the reading come alive for their listeners. This involves reading the entire passion alone or in a group, discussing it and praying about it, allowing the tension and drama to sink into your very bones. Remember that in sharing this important reading with the rest of the assembly, you are helping your entire community to

participate in the events described, making them present today.

All of the readers should have strong voices and clear diction. Although Jesus' words are few and his tone sometimes subdued, his speech is central; whoever reads them should have an especially strong voice. Determine in advance who will read what sections and practice together. Make sure each reader is comfortable with the difficult words and understands the significance of the action. Finally, practice in the place of worship. Know when you will move and

**114**

PALM SUNDAY ■ APRIL 8, 2001

The apostles said, "*No*, not a *thing*."
Jesus said to them,
"But *now*, the one who has a purse must *take* it,
    and likewise a *bag*.
And the one who has no *sword*
    must sell his *cloak* and *buy* one.
For I *tell* you, this *scripture* must be *fulfilled* in me,
'And he was *counted* among the *lawless*';
and indeed what is *written* about me is being *fulfilled*."

The apostles said, "Lord, *look*, here are two *swords*."
Jesus replied, "It is *enough*."

**Jesus speaks with exasperation. Pause before beginning a new scene.**

(6) Jesus came out and *went*, as was his *custom*,
    to the Mount of *Olives*;
and the disciples *followed* him.
When he *reached* the place, he said to his disciples,
"*Pray* that you may not come into the time of *trial*."

Then Jesus *withdrew* from them about a stone's *throw*,
knelt down, and *prayed*,

**Jesus prays sincerely but not in anguish.**

"*Father*, if you are *willing*, *remove* this cup from me;
yet, not *my* will but *yours* be done."

Then an angel from heaven *appeared* to Jesus
    and gave him *strength*.
In his *anguish* he prayed more *earnestly*,
and his *sweat* became like great drops of *blood*
    falling down on the *ground*.
When Jesus got *up* from prayer,
he *came* to the disciples
    and found them *sleeping* because of *grief*,
and he said to them, "*Why* are you *sleeping*?
Get up and *pray* that you may not come into the time of *trial*."

where you will stand; be comfortable with the text and with the microphone. If there is to be music, practice with the musicians, so that you will all be familiar with the flow of proclamation and song. At least one person who is not reading or involved with music should be present to listen from various parts of the church to offer feedback regarding clarity and volume. When the details are settled in advance, all involved will be able to concentrate on the important ministry of proclaiming these central events of our salvation history.

(1) Jesus' passion, death and resurrection occurred at the time of the Jewish celebration of Passover, the commemoration of the Israelites' flight from Egypt. Passover is a celebration of new life, a proclamation of hope. It recalls God's action in preserving the lives of the Israelite children on the night of the last plague against Egypt, the death of the firstborn, and of bringing the people out of slavery and leading them to the land of promise. We recall the events of Jesus' passion, death and resurrection as offering rebirth, liberating us from lives held captive by sin.

The "hour" in this passage refers to the time when the Passover meal was celebrated. But it also designates the time when decisive events take place in Jesus' life. By sharing this meal with his disciples, Jesus transforms it into a reflection on the significance of his impending death, and commands his followers to continue sharing the meal, remembering him as they do so. He establishes a new covenant, similar to the covenants between God and the Hebrew people, especially the covenant established in the first Passover, when God led the people out of Egypt.

**APRIL 8, 2001 ■ PALM SUNDAY**

**Allow tension to enter your voice.**

(7) While Jesus was still *speaking*, suddenly a *crowd* came,
and the one called *Judas*, one of the *twelve*, was *leading* them.
He approached Jesus to *kiss* him;
but Jesus said to him,
"*Judas*, is it with a *kiss* that you are betraying the Son of *Man*?"

When those who were *around* Jesus
saw what was *coming*, they asked,
"*Lord*, should we strike with the *sword*?"
Then *one* of the disciples struck the *slave* of the high priest
and cut off his right *ear*.
But Jesus said, "No *more* of this!"
And Jesus *touched* the slave's ear and *healed* him.

**Jesus is frustrated and angry. Pause slightly and change your tone as you proceed.**

Then Jesus said to the chief *priests*,
the officers of the temple *police*,
and the *elders* who had *come* for him,
"Have you come out with *swords* and *clubs* as if I were a *bandit*?
When I was *with* you *day* after *day* in the *temple*,
you did not lay *hands* on me.
But *this* is your *hour*, and the power of *darkness*!"

(8) Then they *seized* Jesus and led him *away*,
bringing him into the high priest's *house*.
But *Peter* was following at a *distance*.

When they had kindled a *fire* in the middle of the *courtyard*
and sat down *together*, Peter sat *among* them.
Then a *servant* girl, seeing him in the *firelight*,
*stared* at him and said, "*This* man *also* was with him."

But Peter *denied* it, saying,
"Woman, I do not *know* him."
A little later someone *else*, on seeing him, said,
"You *also* are one of them."

During this "hour" and until his death, the forces of evil are active. Satan has already entered Judas Iscariot. Later, vicious hatred will be so strong that it will, paradoxically, unite former enemies and alienate Jesus' friends. But evil and hatred do not prevail. Jesus will be vindicated in the end. Even during his time of helplessness, he acts as one in control, offering love and forgiveness to those in need of it.

The Passover meal has a forward-looking meaning. Jesus will not again share it with his friends on earth. But his words over the bread look forward to his passion

and death, equating the bread with his body on the cross. In verses that are perhaps from another ancient tradition but have been added here, Jesus takes up a second cup and establishes the new covenant, again looking forward to his passion with reference to his blood. Yet he asks his disciples to continue the celebration of this special meal, looking back and remembering him.

(2) In Luke's gospel (unlike those of Matthew and Mark), Judas partakes of the bread and wine with the other disciples before he is revealed as Jesus' betrayer. This emphasizes the blame that he must

bear as one who was not only a disciple of Jesus but one who has shared in the covenant meal. Even this gospel of forgiveness proclaims "woe to that one" who turns against the Lord.

(3) The other disciples begin to wonder who among them could perform such a horrendous deed. But even in their shock at the possibility of betrayal, they cannot refrain from competing for greatness. Jesus reverses the usual expectations regarding greatness. The greatest ones are not those who exercise authority or enjoy leisure but those who serve others. Jesus provides the supreme

**116**

PALM SUNDAY ■ APRIL 8, 2001

---

**Speak the accusations with increasing force, and express Peter's denials with vigor.**

**Slow your reading and let your voice be filled with sadness.**

**Pause in sorrow.**

**prophesy = PROF-uh-sī**

**Jesus speaks with authority.**

But Peter said, "Man, I am *not!*"
Then about an hour *later* still *another* kept insisting,
"Surely *this* man *also* was with him; for he is a *Galilean.*"
But Peter said, "Man, I do not *know* what you are *talking* about!"
At *that* moment, while he was still *speaking,* the *cock* crowed.
The Lord turned and *looked* at Peter.
Then Peter *remembered* the word of the *Lord,*
    how he had said to him,
"*Before* the cock *crows* today,
you will *deny* me three *times.*"
And Peter went *out* and wept *bitterly.*

(9) Now the men who were *holding* Jesus
    began to *mock* him and *beat* him;
they also *blindfolded* him and kept *asking* him,
"*Prophesy!*
Who is it that *struck* you?"
They kept heaping many other *insults* on him.

(10) When *day* came, the assembly of the *elders* of the people,
both *chief priests* and *scribes,* gathered *together,*
and they brought *Jesus* to their *council.*
They said, "If you are the *Messiah, tell* us."
Jesus replied, "If I *tell* you, you will not *believe;*
and if I *question* you, you will not *answer.*
But from now *on*
the Son of Man will be *seated*
        at the right *hand* of the power of *God.*"
All of them asked, "Are *you,* then, the Son of *God?*"
Jesus said to them, "*You* say that I am."
Then they said, "What further *testimony* do we *need?*
We have heard it *ourselves* from his own *lips!*"

---

example of one who serves, and those who stand by him will, in yet another reversal, be granted positions of authority in heaven, even judging the twelve tribes of Israel.

(4) Peter does not draw special attention to himself in this gospel but is singled out by Jesus. Satan is back in force, having been temporarily restrained after Jesus' temptation in the desert. During the events of the passion, Satan seems to prevail but in the end is vanquished. Peter rashly proclaims his willingness to die with Jesus, but the reader knows that Jesus' prediction of denial will prove to be true.

(5) In chapter 10 of Luke's gospel, Jesus sends his followers out on the road with no provisions. They return overjoyed, declaring that even the demons submitted to them in Jesus' name. In these verses in the passion narrative, found only in Luke, they acknowledge that they had lacked nothing on that journey. Now, in this dark hour, the opposition is fierce. Jesus says that his followers must equip themselves for battle, even with swords. They will need all the strength they can get.

Jesus is speaking metaphorically of bags and swords, as is evident in his decisive

response to their procurement of weapons: "Enough!" Violence is not what Jesus advocates but preparedness. Jesus' disciples must be ready for the opposition they will face. But, as they so often do, Jesus' disciples misunderstand him, unable to comprehend the nature of the battle they will face.

(6) The scene shifts as Jesus, followed by his disciples, goes to the Mount of Olives. In this gospel, prayer has marked every step of Jesus' ministry, and now, at the decisive moment, Jesus again turns to God in prayer.

The reference to the angel strengthening Jesus and his sweat like drops of blood

APRIL 8, 2001 ■ PALM SUNDAY

**Pilate is curious. He appears as a somewhat sympathetic figure in this gospel.**

**Galilean = gal-ih-LEE-uhn**
**Jesus' ministry had been centered in Galilee, where Herod was in charge.**

**Allow your tone to darken.**

(11) Then the assembly rose as a *body*
  and brought Jesus before *Pilate*.
They began to *accuse* him, saying,
"We found this man *perverting* our *nation*,
*forbidding* us to pay *taxes* to the *emperor*,
and saying that he *himself* is the *Messiah*, a *king*."

Then Pilate asked Jesus, "Are *you* the king of the *Jews?*"
He answered, "*You* say so."
Then Pilate said to the chief *priests* and the *crowds*,
"I find no *basis* for an *accusation* against this man."
But they were *insistent* and said,
"He stirs up the *people* by teaching throughout all *Judea*,
from *Galilee* where he *began* even to *this* place."
(12) When Pilate *heard* this,
  he asked whether the man was a *Galilean*.
And when he learned that he was under *Herod's* jurisdiction,
he sent him off to *Herod*,
who was *himself* in Jerusalem at that time.

When Herod saw *Jesus*, he was very *glad*,
for he had been *wanting* to see him for a long *time*,
because he had *heard* about him
and was hoping to *see* Jesus perform some *sign*.
Herod *questioned* him at some *length*,
but Jesus gave him no *answer*.
The chief *priests* and the *scribes* stood *by*,
vehemently *accusing* him.
Even *Herod* with his *soldiers* treated him with *contempt*
  and *mocked* him;
then he put an elegant *robe* on him,
and sent him back to *Pilate*.

---

are not found in the earliest manuscripts of this gospel and were probably added later. As it is, they emphasize Jesus' anguish in the face of death. But when they are removed, Jesus does not appear to be in great distress. He turns to God in trust, praying only once, not multiple times as in other gospels. He does not throw himself on the ground but kneels. Prayer gives Jesus all the strength he needs.

The disciples are portrayed in a more positive light in this gospel than in the others. Jesus rebukes them only once for sleeping, and their slumber is caused not by fatigue

but by grief. Peter, James and John are not separated out from the others, but all the disciples are told to pray. The author claims that all followers of Jesus need to gain strength, as he did, from prayer.

(7) Events move quickly now. The sleeping disciples awaken to see a crowd. Judas indicates who Jesus is with an embrace; his act of treason is made even more bitter by his audacious use of a gesture of friendship. But Jesus retains his dignity and challenges Judas' deceit. The violent confrontation turns bloody when someone cuts off the ear of the high priest's servant. Jesus harshly

rejects his followers' violence and even sets matters right by healing the severed ear, a miracle recounted only in this gospel.

Jesus addresses with anger the religious leaders who pursue him. He was not an armed robber, and he had never hidden from the authorities, yet they treat him as a common criminal. They have aligned themselves with the powers of darkness. Now is Satan's hour of triumph.

(8) We are not told what happens to the other disciples when Jesus is taken to the high priest's house. Only Peter follows. As Jesus had foretold, Peter turns his back

**PALM SUNDAY ▪ APRIL 8, 2001**

*Speak with wonder at such an ill-favored friendship.*

That same *day* Herod and Pilate became *friends* with each other;
*before* this they had been *enemies*.

(13) Pilate then called together the chief *priests*,
    the *leaders*, and the *people*,
and said to them,
"You *brought* me this man as one who was *perverting* the *people*;
and here I have *examined* him in your *presence*
and have *not* found this man *guilty*
    of any of your charges *against* him.
Neither has *Herod*, for he sent him *back* to us.
Indeed, he has done *nothing* to deserve *death*.
I will therefore have him *flogged* and *release* him."

*The assembly becomes ugly.*
*Barabbas = buh-RAB-uhs*
*The name, ironically, means "son of the father."*

Now Pilate was *obliged*
    to *release* someone for them at the *festival*.
Then they all shouted out *together*,
"*Away* with this fellow! Release *Barabbas* for us."
(*This* was a man who had been put in *prison*
for an *insurrection* that had taken place in the *city*,
    and for *murder*.)
*Pilate*, wanting to *release* Jesus, addressed them *again*;

*The tension mounts. Raise your voice in bloodthirsty rage.*

but they kept shouting, "*Crucify, crucify* him!"
A *third* time he said to them, "*Why*, what *evil* has he done?
I have found in him no *ground* for the sentence of *death*;
I will therefore have him *flogged* and then *release* him."

But they kept urgently *demanding* with loud *shouts*
that he should be *crucified*;
and their voices *prevailed*.
So Pilate gave his *verdict* that their demand should be *granted*.

---

on his friend and three times denies him. But Peter does not curse and swear, as in other gospels. Instead, the scene becomes painfully poignant when Jesus makes eye contact with him, thus reminding Peter of Jesus' earlier prediction.

(9) Immediately after his prediction regarding Peter is fulfilled, Jesus' accusers revile him and call on him to prophesy. The guards mock him, but Jesus meets the abuse with silence.

(10) The account of the trial of Jesus before the supreme Jewish council, the Sanhedrin, is brief. There are no witnesses

and no question about destroying the temple. Instead, the focus is on Jesus' identity: Is he indeed the awaited Messiah? But Jesus' response to their question is not limited to whether he is the Messiah. Jesus seems to affirm his identity as the Messiah, but he raises the stakes by declaring his heavenly status. Jesus combines Psalm 110:2 ("Sit at my right hand") with the exalted figure in Daniel 7 to acknowledge that he will act as heavenly judge, receiving dominion and glory.

Jesus' response to the next question posed by the council solidifies the forces of

opposition arrayed against him. Although Jesus does not affirm that he is the Son of God, the way the question is asked seems to presume a positive response. The Jewish leaders themselves become responsible for the claim and the resulting decision to condemn him. It is ironic that, while completely powerless, Jesus responds with claims of total power; clearly his authority is not the kind we are accustomed to. The author presents Jesus as one wrongly charged and convicted, maltreated and subsequently executed as a criminal by the Romans. He is

APRIL 8, 2001 ■ PALM SUNDAY

He *released* the man they asked for,
the one who had been put in prison
⠀⠀⠀⠀for *insurrection* and *murder*,
and he handed *Jesus* over as they *wished*.

(14) As they led Jesus *away*, they seized a *man*, Simon of *Cyrene*,
who was coming from the *country*,
and they laid the *cross* on him,
and made him *carry* it behind *Jesus*.

A great *number* of the people *followed* him,
and among them were *women*
who were beating their *breasts* and *wailing* for him.

But Jesus *turned* to them and said,
"Daughters of *Jerusalem*, do not *weep* for *me*,
but weep for *yourselves* and for your *children*.
For the days are surely *coming* when they will say,
'Blessed are the *barren*, and the *wombs* that never *bore*,
and the *breasts* that never *nursed*.'
Then they will begin to say to the *mountains*, '*Fall* on us,'
and to the *hills*, '*Cover* us.'
For if they do this when the wood is *green*,
what will happen when it is *dry*?"

(15) Two others *also*, who were *criminals*,
were led *away* to be put to *death* with *Jesus*.
When they came to the place that is called The *Skull*,
they *crucified* Jesus there with the *criminals*,
one on his *right* and one on his *left*.

Then Jesus said, "*Father*, *forgive* them;
for they do not *know* what they are *doing*."
And they cast *lots* to divide his *clothing*.

---

**Speak with sad resignation, then pause as the scene shifts.**
**Cyrene = sĭ-REE-nee**

**Jesus addresses the women tenderly, even as he warns of impending danger.**

---

alone, stripped of dignity, yet he claims ultimate power.

(11) When Jesus is brought before the local Roman authority, Pilate, he resumes his silence, responding only with an ambiguous answer to Pilate's query. The Jewish leaders have altered the charge from one regarding Jesus' identity to political subversion: He opposes the payment of taxes and has made himself king. Indeed, the manner of Jesus' execution—by crucifixion, a Roman form of capital punishment—indicates that he was convicted of being an enemy of the

state. The gospel portrays Pilate as reluctant to crucify Jesus, although his cruelty and hatred for the Jewish people are well documented. Jesus gives Pilate the same response he gave the Jewish assembly, but Pilate understands it to indicate his innocence while the Jewish leaders concluded from it that he was guilty.

(12) Jesus' appearance before Herod Antipas (not the Herod of the infancy narrative) is told only in this gospel. The story takes some of the responsibility for Jesus' conviction away from Pilate. Jesus refuses to answer Herod's questions, whereupon

Herod mocks him, attempting to ridicule Jesus' claim of royalty and heavenly status. But this gospel turns upside down the usual claims to power and authority. The one who is abused is truly the king of Israel.

(13) The practice of releasing a prisoner during the feast is unknown outside the gospels, as is the insurrection, although the Jews were often rebellious under Roman rule. Perhaps the crowd was disappointed that Jesus did not take up arms against the Romans and preferred one whose defiance of Rome had been demonstrated. But it is hard to imagine why the Roman governor

PALM SUNDAY ■ APRIL 8, 2001

**The tone is one of mocking and derision.**

And the people stood *by, watching;*
but the leaders *scoffed* at him, saying,
"He saved *others;*
let him save *himself*
if he is the *Messiah* of *God,* his *chosen* one!"

The soldiers *also* mocked Jesus,
coming up and offering him sour *wine,*
and saying, "If *you* are the King of the *Jews,* save *yourself!"*
There was also an *inscription* over him,
"*This* is the King of the *Jews."*

(16) One of the *criminals* who were *hanged* there
kept *deriding* him and saying,
"Are you *not* the *Messiah?*
*Save* yourself and *us!"*
But the *other* criminal *rebuked* the first, saying,
"Do you not fear *God,*
since you are under the same *sentence* of *condemnation?*
And *we* indeed have been condemned *justly,*
for we are getting what we *deserve* for our *deeds,*
but *this* man has done nothing *wrong."*

**Contrast with your voice the jeering of the first criminal with the sincere contrition of the second.**

Then he said,
"*Jesus, remember* me when you come into your *kingdom."*
Jesus replied,
"Truly I *tell* you, *today* you will be with me in *Paradise."*

**Proclaim Jesus' words with force, then quietly conclude the scene. Observe a lengthy pause for meditation.**

(17) It was now about *noon,*
and *darkness* came over the whole *land*
until three in the *afternoon,*
while the sun's light *failed;*
and the *curtain* of the *temple* was torn in *two.*

---

would agree with them and release a dangerous rebel.

(14) In this gospel, Jesus makes his way to the place of crucifixion alone. Although Simon of Cyrene is mentioned in other gospels, here he becomes a true disciple of Jesus, following behind him as he bears some of the burden of the cross. A large crowd of women also follows, grieving and lamenting. Women are often noticeable figures in this gospel and here courageously accompany Jesus on his path to death, providing an opportunity for Jesus to extend his compassion to them despite his own burden.

(15) Although Jesus' forgiveness of his persecutors is missing from some authorities, it does fit well with the tenor of this gospel. Even on the cross, Jesus looks with compassion on those around him and extends forgiveness to the guilty.

Given the title "King of the Jews," Jesus receives abuse from the leaders. They attempt to undermine the claim of royalty accorded Jesus, insulting and taunting him. What they do not realize is that the gospel inverts all claims to power and authority. Ironically, Jesus' vindication by God will

demonstrate that all of the titles accorded him as derision are true.

(16) Although the crucifixion of two others with Jesus is recorded in all four gospels, only Luke contains the story of the penitent criminal. One of the criminals joins with the executioners and others who are mocking Jesus, but the other recognizes Jesus' innocence and his own guilt. In addition, he acknowledges Jesus' ability to lay claim to otherworldly authority by appealing to be remembered in Jesus' "kingdom." Jesus replies with characteristic forgiveness and

APRIL 8, 2001 ■ PALM SUNDAY

Then *Jesus*, crying with a loud *voice*, said,
"*Father*, into *your* hands I commend my *spirit*."

Having *said* this, he breathed his *last*.

*[All may kneel for a period of silence.]*

centurion = sen-TYOOR-ee-uhn

Speak with conviction.

(18) When the *centurion* saw what had taken *place*,
he *praised* God and said,
    "*Certainly* this man was *innocent*."
And when all the *crowds*
        who had gathered there for this *spectacle*
saw what had taken place,
they returned *home*, beating their *breasts*.

But all his *acquaintances*,
including the *women* who had followed him from *Galilee*,
stood at a *distance*, *watching* these things. *

Arimathea = ayr-ih-muh-THEE-uh

(19) Now there was a *good* and righteous *man* named *Joseph*,
*who*, though a member of the *council*,
had not *agreed* to their plan and *action*.
He came from the Jewish town of *Arimathea*,
and he was waiting *expectantly* for the kingdom of *God*.
*This* man went to *Pilate* and asked for the *body* of Jesus.
Then he took it *down*, *wrapped* it in a linen *cloth*,
and laid it in a rock-hewn *tomb* where no one had ever been *laid*.

It was the day of *Preparation*, and the *sabbath* was beginning.
The *women* who had come with Jesus from *Galilee followed*,
and they saw the *tomb* and how his body was *laid*.
Then they *returned*, and prepared *spices* and *ointments*.
On the *sabbath* these women *rested*
        according to the *commandment*.

*[Shorter: Luke 22:66—23:49]*

the promise that the criminal will join him in paradise.

(17) The momentous nature of Jesus' crucifixion is evident in the supernatural phenomena that accompany it: At the sun's highest point, the sky is darkened, and when Jesus dies, the temple curtain is torn. This event is not simply an execution; it is a fulfillment of divine intent, a sign of the presence of God. The darkness indicates that the final Day of the Lord has arrived.

Although Jesus has kept his dignity throughout the story of the passion in the gospel of Luke, the account of his death still

drains us of all energy when we hear it. Jesus' final words can be spoken with confidence, but lower your voice in respect as you read of his death. A period of silent meditation customarily follows the death.

(18) The centurion is the Roman military official overseeing the crucifixion and thus is emblematic of the Gentile occupiers of Judea. For both Jewish and Gentile worlds, the cosmic nature of Jesus' death becomes evident. The centurion glorifies God and confesses the innocence of Jesus, drawing the reader to confess it as well.

(19) The story of Joseph of Arimathea requesting the body of Jesus serves several purposes. It provides for the burial of Jesus before sundown, in accord with Jewish tradition, although it was not uncommon for victims of crucifixion to rot on the cross. The story also indicates that there were religious leaders of the Jews who were receptive to Jesus' message, despite the actions of some to have him executed. Finally, the stage is set for the visit of the women to the empty tomb on Easter morning, to hear the news that Jesus had risen.

## APRIL 12, 2001

# HOLY THURSDAY: MASS OF THE LORD'S SUPPER

*Lectionary #39*

### READING I    Exodus 12:1–8, 11–14

**A reading from the book of Exodus**

The *Lord* said to *Moses* and *Aaron* in the land of *Egypt:*
*This* month shall mark for you the *beginning* of months;
it shall be the *first* month of the *year* for you.
Tell the whole congregation of *Israel*
that on the *tenth* of this month
they are to take a *lamb* for each *family,*
a *lamb* for each *household.*
If a household is too *small* for a *whole* lamb,
it shall join its closest *neighbour* in *obtaining* one;
the *lamb* shall be *divided*
in proportion to the number of *people* who *eat* of it.

Your *lamb* shall be without *blemish,* a year-old *male;*
you may take it from the *sheep* or from the *goats.*
You shall keep it until the *fourteenth* day of this *month;*
then the *whole* assembled congregation of *Israel*
shall *slaughter* it at *twilight.*
They shall take *some* of the blood
and put it on the two *doorposts* and the *lintel*
of the houses in which they *eat* it.
They shall *eat* the lamb that *same* night;
they shall eat it *roasted* over the *fire*
with unleavened *bread* and bitter *herbs.*

---

Nisan, in the spring, is the first month of the Hebrew calendar.

Passover has long been celebrated as a feast of hospitality.

The prescriptions concerning the sacrifice ensure that the animal is healthy and is consumed immediately after slaughter.

The foods recall the exodus from Egypt. Unleavened bread was used by the Israelites because they did not have time to allow the dough to rise; bitter herbs recall the bitterness of slavery.

---

**READING I** Because the synoptic gospels of Matthew, Mark and Luke recall Jesus' last meal with his friends as a Passover meal, we also remember the origins of Passover on this night before we commemorate Jesus' death.

The passage from the book of Exodus tells of the instructions God gave the Israelites in Egypt before visiting the final and most severe plague, the death of the firstborn child, on the Egyptians. Adopting ancient rituals and reinterpreting them in light of the Exodus, the account recalls the preparations for the Passover meal, as well as the fulfillment of God's promises in freeing the Israelites from their oppressors.

The blood of an animal on the door of a dwelling was long understood as a means of warding off evil and protecting a household. In this case, it serves to keep the Israelite houses safe from the devastating plague brought by God. Blood is a sign of life; here it becomes a symbol of death being thwarted and of the "new" life now available.

The Hebrew people were instructed to remember this event always and to celebrate it faithfully. Indeed, Jews today continue to tell this story of their deliverance from tyranny. The events of long ago become present in the retelling and ritual sharing of the Passover meal.

Christians too recall Jesus' words at his last meal and celebrate them in a similar fashion, participating again at every eucharist in the meal Jesus shared with his friends.

APRIL 12, 2001 ■ HOLY THURSDAY

Stress the urgency of the situation; this is a people escaping by night.

This is how you shall *eat* it:
your loins *girded*, your *sandals* on your *feet*,
and your *staff* in your *hand*;
and you shall eat it *hurriedly*.
It is the *Passover* of the *Lord*.

For I will pass *through* the land of Egypt that *night*,
and I will strike *down* every *firstborn* in the land of *Egypt*,
both human *beings* and *animals*;
on all the *gods* of Egypt I will execute *judgments*:
I am the *Lord*.

The blood, a sign of life, ensures that those in the houses marked by it will be allowed to live.

The blood shall be a *sign* for you on the *houses* where you *live*:
when I see the *blood*, I will pass *over* you,
and no *plague* shall *destroy* you
when I *strike* the land of *Egypt*.

Pause, then conclude in a strong voice; these words have proven true for the Jewish people of every generation.

This *day* shall be a day of *remembrance* for you.
You shall *celebrate* it as a *festival* to the *Lord*;
*throughout* your *generations*
you shall *observe* it as a perpetual *ordinance*.

---

**READING II**   1 Corinthians 11:23–26

**A reading from the first letter of Paul to the Corinthians**

Beloved:
I *received* from the Lord what I also handed *on* to *you*,
that the Lord *Jesus* on the night when he was *betrayed*
took a loaf of *bread*,
and when he had given *thanks*,

Pause after "you," then continue slowly and clearly.

And just as the blood of the Passover lamb promised life for those protected by it, so also we celebrate the life available to us who share in the eucharistic meal of the Lamb of God, who died for our sake.

Take care to give this passage the attention it deserves. Make the urgency and significance of the Passover story apparent. Speak with forcefulness God's promise not to destroy the Israelites. Close with confidence in a God who keeps that promise.

READING II  Paul, quoting here from traditional material, gives us the earliest account of the eucharistic words of Jesus The passage looks back to the death of Jesus, but also looks forward to his coming again. Just as the Hebrew people celebrating Passover make present events of long ago, so also we participate in the ancient ritual of eucharist that becomes new every time we celebrate it. We too tell a story of freedom, a story that recalls the shedding of the blood of the Lamb for the safety and well-being of others, a story of God's love for this people.

Central to Paul's proclamation, here and elsewhere, is the death of Christ. An embarrassment, a source of confusion and ridicule, it is Jesus' death that is paradoxically the source of life for the world. It cannot be ignored or glossed over; it is to be proclaimed at every eucharist. As the Passover lamb was slaughtered and the bread broken, so too was Jesus' body broken on the cross. As the covenants of old were ratified in the blood of animals, the new covenant in Christ was ratified in his blood.

HOLY THURSDAY ■ APRIL 12, 2001

**Pause briefly after "me."**

he *broke* it and said,
"*This* is my *body* that is for *you*.
Do this in *remembrance* of me."

In the *same* way he took the *cup* also, after *supper*, saying,
"This *cup* is the *new* covenant in *my* blood.
*Do* this, as often as you *drink* it, in *remembrance* of me."

**Take a breath before continuing with the last sentence. Speak it as though it was written for your assembly.**

For as often as you *eat* this bread and *drink* the cup,
you proclaim the Lord's *death* until he *comes*.

---

GOSPEL    John 13:1–15

**A reading from the holy gospel according to John**

Now before the festival of the *Passover*,
Jesus *knew* that his hour had *come*
to *depart* from this *world* and go to the *Father*.
Having loved his *own* who were in the world,
he *loved* them to the *end*.

**Iscariot = is-KAYR-ee-uht**

The devil had already put it into the heart of *Judas*,
        son of Simon *Iscariot*,
to *betray* him.
And during *supper*
*Jesus*, knowing that the Father had given *all* things
        into his *hands*,
and that he had *come* from God and was *going* to God,

**For a Passover meal, the group would have been reclining on couches. Although the Passover comes later in the gospel of John, this also was no ordinary meal.**

got *up* from the *table*,
took off his outer *robe*,
and tied a *towel* around *himself*.

---

This is an extremely important selection and should be read with all solemnity. The beginning and ending lines are less familiar than the rest and should be emphasized. Speak Jesus' words quietly and forcefully, but without exaggeration. To you is given the task of reminding the members of your assembly of the importance of what we do in every eucharist, when we gather to remember Jesus' death.

GOSPEL Washing the feet clean of the dust of the road when entering a home was common in Jesus' day. Usually one washed one's own feet, although another might wash the feet of a revered teacher. Jesus, acknowledging his role as teacher, reverses the custom and thus honors his disciples.

The account of Jesus washing his disciples' feet is found only in the gospel of John. It is placed in a setting in which Jesus' death is imminent, a death that gives Jesus the opportunity to show his love for "his own."

There are two interpretations of the footwashing within the passage. One emphasizes the importance of sharing in Jesus' life and especially in his death. Peter goes from refusing to permit Jesus to wash his feet to enthusiastic and excessive acceptance. The second section of the story stresses Jesus' revered status and his humility in serving the disciples in this manner. Jesus calls on the disciples to join in the action; he has set the example.

APRIL 12, 2001 ■ HOLY THURSDAY

Then he poured *water* into a *basin*
and began to *wash* the disciples' *feet*
and to *wipe* them with the *towel* that was tied *around* him.

He came to Simon *Peter*, who said to him,
"*Lord*, are you going to *wash* my *feet*?"
Jesus answered,
"You do not know *now* what I am doing,
but *later* you will understand."
Peter said to him, "You will *never* wash *my* feet."
Jesus answered,
"Unless I *wash* you, you have no *share* with me."
Simon Peter said to him,
"*Lord*, not my feet *only* but also my *hands* and my *head!*"
Jesus said to him,
"One who has *bathed* does not *need* to wash,
except for the *feet*, but is entirely *clean*.
And *you* are clean, though not *all* of you."
For he knew who was to *betray* him;
for *this* reason he said,
"Not *all* of you are *clean*."

After he had *washed* their feet, put on his *robe*,
and returned to the *table*,
Jesus said to them,
"Do you *know* what I have *done* to you?
You call me *Teacher* and *Lord*—
and you are *right*, for that is what I *am*.
So if *I*, your *Lord* and *Teacher*,
have washed *your* feet,
*you also* ought to wash one *another's* feet.
For I have set you an *example*,
that you *also* should do as I have done to *you*."

**Read Peter's words with a sense of both surprise and objection to the proposed action.**

**Jesus explains the meaning later in the narrative.**

**Continue speaking Peter's words with enthusiasm.**

**The author here interprets Jesus' words about cleanliness in terms of the presence of his betrayer within the community of disciples.**

**Stress the parallel between what Jesus does and what those who follow him are expected to do. Close with solemnity.**

The footwashing then has two meanings: It is both a sign of sharing in Jesus' fate and one of humble service to another. The second is usually emphasized in modern celebrations of the rite, but the use of this selection on the day preceding our commemoration of Jesus' passion and death suggests that we are asked to share in Jesus' death as well. Just as Paul insists on proudly proclaiming Jesus' death, so also does participation in the footwashing rite lead us directly into the darkness of Good Friday.

There is an ominous tone throughout the first part of the selection, but the words of Peter provide comic relief. Stress Peter's enthusiastic embrace of anything that brings him close to Jesus. Close with an exhortation to your own community to be willing to stoop before even the most lowly in whatever act of humble service is required.

In many parishes, the celebration of the footwashing ritual sometimes gives the impression that these words are directed only to the ordained or to liturgical ministers. They are not; they are for all Christians.

APRIL 13, 2001

# GOOD FRIDAY: CELEBRATION OF THE LORD'S PASSION

*Lectionary #40*

### READING I    Isaiah 52:13—53:12

**A reading from the book of the prophet Isaiah**

**God is speaking here.**

*See*, my *servant* shall *prosper*;
he shall be *exalted* and lifted *up*,
and shall be very *high*.

Just as there were *many* who were *astonished* at him
—so *marred* was his appearance, beyond human *semblance*,
and his *form* beyond that of *mortals*—
so he shall startle many *nations*;
*kings* shall shut their *mouths* because of him;
for that which had not been *told* them they shall *see*,
and that which they had not *heard* they shall *contemplate*.

**The people speak now.**

*Who* has *believed* what we have *heard*?
And to *whom* has the *arm* of the *Lord* been *revealed*?

For he grew *up* before the Lord like a young *plant*,
and like a *root* out of dry *ground*;
he had no *form* or *majesty* that we should *look* at him,
nothing in his *appearance* that we should *desire* him.

**The tone becomes very serious. Because the servant was not attractive in appearance, people treated him poorly.**

He was *despised* and *rejected* by *others*;
a man of *suffering* and acquainted with *infirmity*;
and as one from whom others *hide* their *faces*
he was *despised*,
and we held him of *no account*.

READING I One of the suffering servant songs of Second Isaiah, this passage depicts first God and then the people of Israel discussing one who served God so faithfully, despite ridicule and punishment, that others were able to benefit from it. The death does not appear to have been a physical one, but represents the pain and anguish of the Babylonian exile, when the rulers and elite of the kingdom of Judah were deported to Babylon. The servant accepted the exile, obediently experiencing it as just punishment for Israel's former sins. Others tried to flee

the exile or settled in Babylon, but the servant, representing all of Israel, knew that it was a punishment for wrongdoing. The servant's actions allow the nation to continue to exist and eventually to return to Palestine. In the end, the servant is vindicated.

This passage has long been understood to foreshadow the work of the servant of God *par excellence:* Jesus. It is especially appropriate to read today, when we also hear the account of Jesus' passion from the gospel

of John. There Jesus suffers, but he is exalted through his suffering, just as God claims of the servant in this reading. The words of the people describing the servant can easily be applied to Jesus. He was lowly in appearance yet was esteemed by God. He was rejected; he wrongly suffered; he died. But he did so in order that others might benefit. He silently offered his life for the sin of others. His punishment brought healing; it fulfilled God's will. In the end, God rewarded him.

On this solemn occasion, offer this selection to your assembly as a meditation on the consequences that await one who

APRIL 13, 2001 ■ GOOD FRIDAY

**Speak now with some hope but also regret for how the servant was regarded. Emphasize the strong verbs in this section.**

*Surely* he has borne our *infirmities* and carried our *diseases*;
yet we accounted him *stricken*,
struck *down* by God, and *afflicted*.
But he was *wounded* for our *transgressions*,
*crushed* for our *iniquities*;
upon *him* was the punishment that made us *whole*,
and by his *bruises we* are *healed*.

All we like *sheep* have gone *astray*;
we have all *turned* to our own *way*,
and the Lord has laid on *him*
the iniquity of us *all*.
He was *oppressed*, and he was *afflicted*,
yet he did not *open* his *mouth*;
like a *lamb* that is led to the *slaughter*,
and like a *sheep* that before its shearers is *silent*,
so he did *not* open his *mouth*.

**One who accepts mistreatment without objecting can be inspiring; such a one certainly catches people's attention.**

**This perhaps refers to the exile and the plight of the servant, and all of Israel, separated from their homeland.**

By a perversion of *justice* he was taken *away*.
Who could have *imagined* his *future*?
For he was cut *off* from the land of the *living*,
*stricken* for the *transgression* of my *people*.
They made his *grave* with the *wicked*
and his *tomb* with the *rich*,
although he had done no *violence*,
and there was no *deceit* in his *mouth*.

**Pause before beginning this line. It is God who is again speaking.**

Yet it was the will of the *Lord* to *crush* him with *pain*.
When you make his *life* an offering for *sin*,
he shall see his *offspring*, and shall prolong his *days*;
through *him* the will of the Lord shall *prosper*.
Out of his *anguish* he shall see *light*;
he shall find *satisfaction* through his *knowledge*.

truly serves God. Speak clearly and forcefully, inspiring your listeners to think especially of Jesus, but also to reflect on their own roles as God's servants.

READING II  Jesus, as the great high priest, did what every high priest of the temple did: He offered a sacrifice in expiation for the people's sin. Yet he is enthroned in heaven, not as one unable to understand our human frailties but as one who knows our weaknesses, who himself suffered and turned to God in prayer. It was

through his suffering that he was perfected and because of it that he can offer salvation to all.

It is appropriate to reflect on this passage today. Jesus' passion was not without purpose. Read this as a reminder to your assembly of the fact that Jesus understands pain and can identify with the struggles of your community.

PASSION  The gospel of John presents a distinctive portrait of Jesus, a portrait that reaches a climax in the passion narrative. In this gospel, Jesus does not hesitate to reveal himself, to speak of his mission and his relationship with God.

This gospel diverges from the others in recounting Jesus' ministry, but is more in line with them regarding the details of his passion and death. The accounts of the passion in the gospels show greater agreement than accounts of other events in Jesus'

## GOOD FRIDAY ■ APRIL 13, 2001

**Speak triumphantly; the servant is vindicated, even honored.**

The *righteous* one, my *servant*, shall make many *righteous*,
and he shall bear their *iniquities*.

Therefore I will allot him a *portion* with the *great*,
and he shall divide the *spoil* with the *strong*;
because he *poured out* himself to *death*,
and was *numbered* with the *transgressors*;
yet he bore the *sin* of *many*,
and made *intercession* for the *transgressors*.

---

### READING II   Hebrews 4:14–16; 5:7–9

**A reading from the letter to the Hebrews**

Since we have a great *high priest*
who has passed through the *heavens*,
*Jesus*, the Son of *God*,
let us hold *fast* to our *confession*.

**Though heavenly high priest, Jesus was fully human and underwent trials and temptations.**

For we do not have a *high priest*
who is *unable* to sympathize with our *weaknesses*,
but we have one who in every respect has been *tested* as *we* are,
yet without *sin*.

**Speak confidently, with a sure voice.**

Let us therefore *approach* the throne of *grace* with *boldness*,
so that we may receive *mercy*
and find *grace* to help in time of *need*.

In the *days* of his *flesh*,
Jesus offered up *prayers* and *supplications*,
with loud *cries* and *tears*,

**Jesus prayed to God with trust and sincerity, just as we can.**

to the one who was able to *save* him from *death*,
and he was *heard* because of his reverent *submission*.

---

life. Jesus' suffering, death and resurrection formed the earliest core of the Jesus story. But the meaning of the events is told here in the distinctive style and with the particular interpretation and theological outlook of the fourth evangelist.

Throughout the gospel, Jesus hints at his own passion. He will be "lifted up"—in glory, on the cross. He lays down his life freely; he is not an abused victim but in control of events, the ruler of all. The cross provides the opportunity for Jesus to be revealed as king; it is his exaltation, his throne.

The suffering of Jesus is not denied but is his to embrace. The silent, pained Jesus of the other gospels is gone. The Jesus of the gospel of John boldly approaches the soldiers, heals while being arrested, and discusses his fate and his person with the religious and civil authorities. He is sure of himself, advancing to the cross as a victorious king marches to the triumphant shouts of throngs of admiring subjects.

John's gospel is marked by artful composition; the scenes of the arrest and trial are intertwined, and the crucifixion and death follow quickly. Peter's denial does not appear as a discrete unit but is embedded in the trial. The trial itself presents Pilate moving back and forth between the unruly crowd outside and the peaceful, composed figure of Jesus within the praetorium. The contrast is further heightened by the ugly demands of the religious leaders and the controlled discussion of Pilate and Jesus regarding kingship and truth.

**The idea of obedience is central to this passage; stress it here and in the last line.**

Although he was a *Son*,
he learned *obedience* through what he *suffered*;
and having been made *perfect*,
he became the source of eternal *salvation*
for all who *obey* him.

---

**PASSION**   John 18:1—19:42

**The Passion of our Lord Jesus Christ according to John**

**Kidron = KID-ruhn**

(1) After they had eaten the *supper*,
Jesus went out with his *disciples* across the Kidron *valley*
to a place where there was a *garden*,
which he and his disciples *entered*.
Now *Judas*, who *betrayed* him, *also* knew the place,
because Jesus often *met* there with his *disciples*.
So Judas brought a detachment of *soldiers*
together with *police* from the chief *priests* and the *Pharisees*,
and they came there with *lanterns* and *torches* and *weapons*.

**Jesus is calm and in control, as he is throughout the passion narrative.**

**Nazareth = NAZ-uh-reth**

Then *Jesus*, knowing all that was to *happen* to him,
came forward and asked them,
"*Whom* are you *looking* for?"
They answered, "Jesus of *Nazareth*."
Jesus replied, "*I* am *he*."
*Judas*, who *betrayed* him, was standing *with* them.
When Jesus said to them, "*I* am *he*,"
they stepped *back* and *fell* to the *ground*.
Again he asked them, "*Whom* are you *looking* for?"
And they said, "Jesus of *Nazareth*."
Jesus answered, "I *told* you that *I* am *he*.

**From the outset of this story, Jesus' power is evident. Rather than being dragged off by these armed guards, he controls their behavior.**

Jesus is identified early in the gospel of John as the Lamb of God, and the image is especially apparent in the passion account. Jesus does not celebrate Passover with his disciples as in the other three gospels, but dies on the day of preparation for the feast. As a result, Jesus is crucified at the same time as the Passover lambs are being sacrificed in the temple. He is presented as the true Lamb whose blood offers life for those who believe. The evangelist even quotes from the regulations regarding the paschal lamb, noting that Jesus' legs were not broken, as were those of the criminals crucified with him.

The assertion that Jesus is the Passover lamb is combined with the image of the scapegoat from Leviticus. On the Day of Atonement, the scapegoat bore the sins of the Jewish people, cleansing them. The high priest's suggestion that Jesus die for the people is significant. As the one who presided over the Day of Atonement rituals, Caiaphas symbolically sent Jesus into the wilderness, bearing the sins of the people, just as he sent the scapegoat on Yom Kippur.

Although all the gospels suggest complicity between the Jewish religious authorities and the Roman governor in Jesus' execution, this gospel insists that the Jewish

## GOOD FRIDAY ■ APRIL 13, 2001

So if you are looking for *me*, let *these* men *go*."
This was to fulfill the *word* that he had *spoken*,
"I did not lose a single *one* of those whom you *gave* me."

Then Simon *Peter*, who had a *sword*,
*drew* it, struck the high priest's *slave*,
and cut off his right *ear*.
The slave's name was *Malchus*.
Jesus said to Peter,
"Put your sword *back* into its *sheath*.
Am I not to drink the *cup* that the Father has *given* me?"

(2) So the *soldiers*, their *officer*, and the Jewish *police*
*arrested* Jesus and *bound* him.
First they took him to *Annas*,
who was the father-in-law of *Caiaphas*,
the *high priest* that year.
*Caiaphas* was the one who had advised the Jewish *leaders*
that it was better to have *one* person die for the *people*.

(3) Simon *Peter* and *another* disciple *followed* Jesus.
Since *that* disciple was *known* to the *high priest*,
he went *with* Jesus into the *courtyard* of the high priest,
but *Peter* was standing outside at the *gate*.
So the *other* disciple, who was *known* to the high priest,
went *out*, spoke to the woman who *guarded* the gate,
and brought Peter *in*.
The woman said to Peter,
"You are not *also* one of this man's disciples, *are* you?"
He said, "I am *not*."
Now the *slaves* and the *police* had made a charcoal *fire*
because it was *cold*,
and they were standing *around* it and *warming* themselves.
Peter *also* was standing with them and *warming* himself.

---

**Malchus = MAL-kuhs**

**The tribune was the chief officer of the cohort.**

**Annas = AN-uhs**
**Caiaphas = KĪ-uh-fuhs**

**Caiaphas said this after the raising of Lazarus; see John 11:49–50.**
**Pause briefly.**

---

leaders are actually responsible; Pilate is presented as a pawn in their hands. This can be misleading.

All four gospels attest to the conflict between Jesus and the Jewish religious leaders. Indeed, the party of the Sadducees, in power at the time, may have been frightened by Jesus' popularity. The Sadducees were surely offended by his preaching about the resurrection of the dead, which they did not accept. But the fact remains that Jesus

was crucified by the Romans for political reasons, as the placard on the cross indicates, rather than stoned as a blasphemer by the Jewish authorities. In addition, although Pilate is known from other sources as having been particularly cruel to and contemptuous of the Jews, each gospel portrays Pilate somewhat sympathetically. This is particularly true of John's gospel, although it is unlikely that Pilate acted solely at the request of the Jewish leaders. Jesus may indeed have been delivered to Pilate by the Jewish

authorities, but all the evidence points to a Roman execution of an insurgent.

The negative portrait of "the Jews" in the gospel of John must also be qualified by the situation in the community of the evangelist. The Johannine Christians were Jews who proclaimed their belief in Jesus. At some point, the Jewish religious leaders had expelled these Jewish Christians from the synagogue for their unorthodox beliefs. The polemic against "the Jews" in this gospel,

APRIL 13, 2001 ■ GOOD FRIDAY

**Pause before continuing, to indicate a change in scene.**

**The high priest does not bring charges to be refuted, illustrating once again the total ineffectiveness of the Jewish authorities in this passion account. Instead, Jesus challenges them as to why he is being questioned at all.**

(4) Then the high priest *questioned* Jesus
about his *disciples* and about his *teaching.*
Jesus answered, "I have spoken *openly* to the *world;*
I have always taught in *synagogues* and in the *temple,*
where all the Jews come *together.*
I have said *nothing* in *secret.*
Why do you ask *me?*
Ask those who *heard* what I *said* to them;
*they* know what I said."

**Jesus does not flinch but responds in a calm, composed manner.**

When he had *said* this,
one of the police standing nearby *struck* Jesus on the *face,* saying,
"Is *that* how you answer the *high priest?*"
Jesus answered, "If I have spoken *wrongly,*
*testify* to the wrong.
But if I have spoken *rightly,*
why do you *strike* me?"

**Although Annas had influence, Caiaphas held the office of high priest at the time. Pause briefly.**

Then *Annas* sent him bound to *Caiaphas* the *high priest.*

(5) Now Simon *Peter* was standing and *warming* himself.
They asked him,
"You are not *also* one of his disciples, *are* you?"
He *denied* it and said, "I am *not.*"
One of the *slaves* of the high priest,
a *relative* of the man whose *ear* Peter had cut *off,*

**A connection is drawn between the encounter in the garden and this incident.**

asked, "Did I not see you in the *garden* with him?"
*Again* Peter denied it,
and at that *moment* the cock *crowed.*

**Observe a lengthier pause here.**

(6) Then they took Jesus from *Caiaphas* to Pilate's *headquarters.*
It was early in the *morning.*
They *themselves* did not enter the *headquarters,*
so as to avoid ritual *defilement*
and to be able to eat the *Passover.*

and against the Jewish leaders in particular, must be read in light of this conflict.

Reading the passion effectively is a challenging task. Take your time in order to do justice to the message you present. Allow a bit of wonder to enter your voice at the power and authority demonstrated by Jesus. Remember that Jesus is always in control, and attempt to convey that in your manner of speaking. Even on this dark day, when the vicious cries of the crowd attempt to drown out any seeds of compassion, this reading is triumphant.

**(1)** The meal Jesus had shared with his disciples is not a Passover meal in the gospel of John. This allows the evangelist to present Jesus as the paschal lamb *par excellence.* There is also no agony in Gethsemane. The garden is simply a familiar meeting place for Jesus and the disciples. Jesus is in command in this scene; his self-assurance and power are visible.

Judas brings Roman soldiers and temple police with him to arrest Jesus. Simply

by speaking, Jesus causes them all to fall to the ground in awe or fear. His enemies are powerless in his presence. He does not avoid arrest, but neither does he resign himself to it. In this gospel, Jesus offers himself for arrest. His only concern is for his companions; their safety is preserved, not because they flee but in order to fulfill Jesus' own words.

The violent encounter between one of Jesus' followers and the slave of the high priest is given more detail in this gospel

# GOOD FRIDAY ■ APRIL 13, 2001

So Pilate went *out* to them and said,
"What *accusation* do you bring against this *man*?"
They answered, "If this man were not a *criminal*,
we would not have handed him *over* to you."
Pilate said to them,
"Take him *yourselves* and judge him according to *your* law."
They replied, "We are not *permitted* to put anyone to *death*."
(This was to *fulfill* what Jesus had *said*
when he indicated the kind of *death* he was to *die*.)

(7) Then Pilate entered the headquarters *again*,
*summoned* Jesus, and asked him,
"Are you the *King* of the *Jews*?"

Jesus answered, "Do you ask this on your *own*,
or did *others* tell you about me?"
Pilate replied, "*I* am not a *Jew*, *am* I?
Your own *nation* and the chief *priests* have handed you *over* to me.
What have you *done*?"
Jesus answered, "My *kingdom* is not from this *world*.
If my kingdom *were* from this world,
my *followers* would be fighting
to *keep* me from being handed *over* to the Jewish *authorities*.
But as it *is*, my kingdom is not from *here*."
Pilate asked him, "So you *are* a king?"
Jesus answered, "*You* say that I am a *king*.
For *this* I was born,
and for *this* I came into the *world*,
to *testify* to the *truth*.
Everyone who *belongs* to the truth *listens* to my *voice*."
Pilate asked him, "What is *truth*?"

---

**In this gospel, Pilate is sincerely trying to get information. The title "king" has not been suggested yet in the narrative, but it is the charge for which Jesus is crucified.**

**It is not clear if Pilate is speaking contemptuously or simply indicating his distance from the accusation.**

**This question could be spoken either by raising the voice at the end (indicating a genuine query) or by lowering it at the end (suggesting that the questioner knows that the answer is affirmative).**

**Pilate demonstrates that he is not one of those who knows the truth or he would listen to Jesus. Pause briefly.**

---

than elsewhere. The combatants are identified: Peter strikes the slave, whose name is Malchus. But Jesus rejects any attempts to deny him his opportunity for glory.

(2) There is no trial of Jesus before the Sanhedrin in the gospel of John. Jesus is instead taken to the home of the former high priest, Annas. In addition to being the father-in-law of the current high priest, Annas also had five sons who served in the high priestly office. Therefore, he was still an influential figure in the management of the temple.

Caiaphas' proposal that one person die on behalf of the people ironically makes him suggest that Jesus fulfills the role of the scapegoat on Yom Kippur, the Day of Atonement. On that feast, the high priest symbolically placed the sins of the people on the back of a goat that was sent into the wilderness to die. Caiaphas continues to perform his high priestly function, but does

so not with a goat but with Jesus. Jesus dies bearing the sins of the people.

(3) Although Peter is unknown to the high priest, the fourth evangelist provides a means to get him into the high priest's courtyard. The unnamed disciple is probably the same as the "one whom Jesus loved," and apparently represents John, son of Zebedee, who was revered by the community that produced this gospel. The scene is set for the first of Peter's three denials of Jesus.

APRIL 13, 2001 ■ GOOD FRIDAY

(8) After he had *said* this,
Pilate went out to the Jewish leaders *again* and told them,
"I find no case *against* him.

But you have a *custom* that I *release* someone for you
     at the *Passover*.
Do you want me to *release* for you the *King* of the *Jews*?"
They shouted in reply,
"Not *this* man, but *Barabbas!*"
Now *Barabbas* was a *bandit*.

**Pilate is probably mocking the crowd with this question.**
**Barabbas = buh-RAB-uhs**

(9) Then Pilate took *Jesus* and had him *flogged*.
And the soldiers wove a *crown* of *thorns*
and put it on his *head*,
and they *dressed* him in a purple *robe*.
They kept coming *up* to him, saying,
"*Hail, King* of the *Jews!*"
and they *struck* him on the *face*.

**The abuse of the soldiers lacks the bite of what is recorded in the other gospels. Jesus' response to it is not detailed.**

(10) Pilate went out *again* and said to them,
"*Look*, I am bringing him *out* to you
to let you *know* that I find no case *against* him."
So Jesus came out,
wearing the crown of *thorns* and the purple *robe*.
Pilate said to them,
"*Here* is the *man!*"

When the chief priests and the police *saw* him, they shouted,
"*Crucify* him! *Crucify* him!"
Pilate said to them,
"Take him *yourselves* and *crucify* him;
I find no case *against* him."
They answered him, "We have a *law*,
and *according* to that *law* he ought to *die*
because he has *claimed* to be the Son of *God*."

**Again, Pilate is probably mocking. His statement seems to be, "Look at this guy! How could he be dangerous?"**

(4) In this gospel, no witnesses are brought against Jesus; there is no charge of blasphemy or questions regarding Jesus' messianic status. Annas asks about his disciples and his teaching. Jesus responds somewhat harshly but truthfully, suggesting that the high priest consult those who have heard him preach. Jesus does not challenge the secretive nature of the arrest, as in the other three gospel accounts, but challenges the questioning itself.

(5) Peter denies that he knows Jesus two more times. The cock then begins to crow, confirming Jesus' words. The denial is not as forceful here as in the other gospels, but the threefold rejection is underscored after Jesus' resurrection, when Jesus asks Peter three times, "Do you love me?" Thus Peter is given the opportunity to right his wrong.

(6) During Jesus' trial, Pilate moves between the inner court and the public space, between dialogue with Jesus and discussion with the Jewish officials eager to see the captive die. There are no charges

brought against Jesus (implying that none were valid), only the weak claim that he must be a criminal or they would not have brought him to Pilate. The claim that they could not put anyone to death does not fit the evidence from other periods but might have been true during Roman occupation.

(7) Pilate asks Jesus if he is the king of the Jews. The evangelist understands the ministry of Jesus in entirely nonrevolutionary terms: He is king, but not of an earthly

# GOOD FRIDAY ■ APRIL 13, 2001

**Pilate's question was apparently suggested by the statement that Jesus claimed to be God's Son.**

(11) Now when Pilate heard *this*, he was more afraid than *ever*.
He entered his headquarters *again* and asked Jesus,
"*Where* are you *from*?"
But Jesus gave him no *answer*.
Pilate therefore said to him,
"Do you refuse to *speak* to me?
Do you not *know* that I have power to *release* you,
and power to *crucify* you?"
Jesus answered him,
"You would have *no* power *over* me
unless it had been *given* you from *above*;
therefore the one who handed me *over* to you
is guilty of a *greater* sin."
(12) From *then* on Pilate tried to *release* him,
but the Jewish leaders cried out,
"If you *release* this man, you are no *friend* of the *emperor*.
Everyone who claims to be a *king*
sets himself *against* the emperor."
When Pilate heard *these* words,
he brought Jesus *outside* and sat on the *judge's* bench
at a place called "The Stone *Pavement*,"
or in Hebrew "*Gabbatha*."

**Gabbatha = GAB-uh-thuh**

Now it was the day of *Preparation* for the *Passover*;
and it was about *noon*.
Pilate said to the Jewish leaders,
"*Here* is your *King!*"

**Now Pilate mocks the crowd.**

They cried out,
"*Away* with him! *Away* with him! *Crucify* him!"
Pilate asked them, "Shall I *crucify* your *King*?"
The chief priests answered,

**At the time of Jesus' death, there was no local king. The statement attributed to the chief priest is theological (denying Jesus' kingship). Pause before continuing.**

"We have *no* king but the *emperor*."

---

realm. Anyone who recognizes the truth will recognize that Jesus bears witness to the truth. Pilate refuses to acknowledge the truth.

(8) Pilate appears as one who wants to save Jesus' life, offering to release Jesus. He mentions a custom known only to the gospels of releasing a prisoner at Passover. But the crowd demands the release of Barabbas. They choose a fighter over one who has just rejected violence.

(9) The abuse received by Jesus is told with less detail here than in the other gospels. Never is Jesus a spectacle for pity or revulsion. The royal fixtures—crown, royal robe and homage—are given to one whose kingdom lies elsewhere.

(10) Pilate repeatedly tries to free Jesus, but becomes fearful at the crowd's vehemence and its claim that Jesus made himself God's Son. Responsibility for Jesus' death is placed squarely on the shoulders of his Jewish accusers. In the gospels Jesus is

executed for religious reasons rather than political ones.

(11) Pilate questions Jesus once again in an attempt to ascertain his origin, perhaps afraid that Jesus was a divine figure appearing as a human. Trying to assert his authority, Pilate is met with Jesus' calm discussion of power; there is no real power on earth, but all comes from God. It is evident that Jesus is the one endowed with divine

**APRIL 13, 2001 ■ GOOD FRIDAY**

**Golgotha = GOL-guh-thuh**

(13) *Then* Pilate handed Jesus *over* to them to be *crucified*.

So they took *Jesus*;
and carrying the cross by *himself*,
he went out to what is called The *Place* of the *Skull*,
which in Hebrew is called *Golgotha*.
There they *crucified* him,
and with him two *others*, one on either *side*,
with Jesus *between* them.

Pilate also had an *inscription* written and put on the *cross*.
It read, "*Jesus* of *Nazareth*, the *King* of the *Jews*."
*Many* of the people read this *inscription*,
because the place where Jesus was *crucified* was near the *city*;
and it was written in *Hebrew*, in *Latin*, and in *Greek*.
Then the chief *priests* of the Jews said to *Pilate*,
"Do *not* write, 'The *King* of the *Jews*,'
but, 'This man *said*, I am *King* of the *Jews*.' "
Pilate answered, "What I have *written* I have *written*."

**For once, Pilate refuses to give in to the demands of the Jewish leaders.**

(14) When the soldiers had *crucified* Jesus,
they took his *clothes* and divided them into four *parts*,
*one* for each *soldier*.
They also took his *tunic*;
now the tunic was *seamless*, woven in one *piece* from the *top*.
So they said to one another,
"Let us not *tear* it,
but cast *lots* for it to see who will *get* it."
This was to fulfill what the *scripture* says,
"They *divided* my clothes *among* themselves,
and for my *clothing* they cast *lots*."
And *that* is what the soldiers *did*.

**The fulfillment of Scripture is made explicit in this gospel; the passage quoted is Psalm 22:18.**

---

authority, and from his lips comes a statement placing blame for his fate not on Pilate but on the Jewish authorities.

(12) This makes Pilate even more eager to free Jesus, but he is compelled to give in to the crowd according to this author. They no longer bring religious charges against Jesus but appeal to Pilate's political vulnerability; if he frees this "king" he is aligning himself with an opponent of Caesar. Although

Pilate taunts the crowd, he eventually consents to their wishes. The Jewish authorities profess their allegiance to Caesar, the ruler of the forces occupying their land and the chief obstacle to Jewish political, social and religious freedom. Indeed, there were Jewish leaders who were friendly with Rome. The Romans had originally been welcomed into the region to settle disputes.

(13) Jesus remains in control even on his path to crucifixion. He carries his own cross. Nothing is said about taunts directed

at him or abuse from the other criminals. Only the chief priests raise their voices, but this is in opposition to the title "King of the Jews" placed above the cross. Once again, Pilate dismisses them.

The crucifixion is recounted without great detail. Far from being a pathetic figure, Jesus is accorded honor. The religious leaders and, to a lesser extent, Pilate, are the characters to be pitied in this gospel.

**136**

GOOD FRIDAY ■ APRIL 13, 2001

Clopas = KLOH-puhs
Magdalene = MAG-duh-luhn
There are four women here; adjust your phrasing so there is no mistake that Mary the wife of Clopas is not identified with the sister of Jesus' mother.

In this gospel, Jesus often addresses his mother as "Woman." Here it is spoken with tenderness.

Pause again.

hyssop = HIS-uhp
The use of the small hyssop plant for this is odd but connects the events with Passover. Hyssop was used to apply the lamb's blood to the doorposts of the Hebrews' houses before the exodus from Egypt.

Jesus died on a Friday and the Sabbath began that evening. This Sabbath, according to the gospel of John, was also the feast of Passover.

Breaking the legs of the crucified hastened death; they could no longer support their bodies but hung in exhaustion.

(15) *Meanwhile*, standing *near* the cross of *Jesus* were his *mother*,
and his mother's *sister*, *Mary* the wife of *Clopas*,
and Mary *Magdalene*.

When Jesus saw his *mother*
and the *disciple* whom he loved standing *beside* her,
he said to his mother,
"*Woman*, *here* is your *son*."
Then he said to the disciple,
"*Here* is your *mother*."
And from that *hour* the disciple *took* her into his own *home*.

(16) After *this*, when Jesus *knew* that all was now *finished*,
he said (in order to *fulfil* the *scripture*),
"I am *thirsty*."
A *jar* full of sour *wine* was standing there.
So they put a *sponge* full of the *wine* on a branch of *hyssop*
and held it to his *mouth*.
When Jesus had *received* the wine, he said,
"It is *finished*."
Then he bowed his *head* and gave up his *spirit*.

*[All may kneel for a period of silence.]*

(17) Since it was the day of *Preparation*,
the Jewish *leaders* did not want the *bodies* left on the *cross*
during the *sabbath*,
especially because *that* sabbath was a day of great *solemnity*.
So they asked *Pilate*
to have the *legs* of the crucified men *broken*
and the bodies *removed*.

Then the *soldiers* came
and broke the legs of the *first* and of the *other*
who had been *crucified* with him.

(14) Only the gospel of John mentions a seamless garment in the story of the soldiers dividing Jesus' clothing. Roman soldiers were allowed to confiscate the possessions (including the clothes) of those they executed; here, the action is seen as a fulfillment of Psalm 22:18, alluded to in the other passion accounts.

(15) The words of Jesus to his mother and the unnamed disciple make a statement about the church. The Acts of the Apostles indicates that Mary was present with the disciples in the early days of the Christian community. Jesus' words can be understood literally—that the disciple is to take Jesus' place and care for Jesus' mother—and figuratively. The disciple thus becomes the individual believer, while Mary represents the Christian church as a whole. Both interpretations have been a part of Christian tradition.

Although the other disciples are absent, Jesus is not alone. The women do not watch from afar but are close enough to speak with Jesus. In this gospel the disciple whom Jesus loved does not abandon Jesus but faithfully stands with the women.

(16) Even to his death, Jesus is in command of events. He determines that his time to die has come; he ensures that scripture is fulfilled. There is no cry of abandonment or pain. The author does not deny the reality of Jesus' death, but it remains a glorification rather than an ignominious fate.

**APRIL 13, 2001 ■ GOOD FRIDAY**

But when they came to *Jesus*
and saw that he was already *dead*,
they did *not* break his legs.
*Instead*, one of the soldiers *pierced* his side with a *spear*,
and at once *blood* and *water* came *out*.

He who *saw* this has testified so that you *also* may *believe*.
His testimony is *true*,
and he *knows* that he tells the *truth*.

These things *occurred* so that the *scripture* might be *fulfilled*,
"*None* of his *bones* shall be *broken*."
And again *another* passage of scripture says,
"They will *look* on the one whom they have *pierced*."

Arimathea = ayr-ih-muh-THEE-uh

(18) After these things, *Joseph* of *Arimathea*,
who was a *disciple* of Jesus,
though a *secret* one because of his fear of the Jewish *authorities*,
*asked* Pilate to let him take *away* the body of Jesus.
Pilate gave him *permission*;
so he *came* and removed his *body*.

Nicodemus = nik-oh-DEE-muhs
aloes = AL-ohz

*Nicodemus*, who had at *first* come to Jesus by *night*,
*also* came, bringing a mixture of *myrrh* and *aloes*,
weighing about three hundred *grams*.
They took the *body* of Jesus
and *wrapped* it with the *spices* in linen *cloths*,
according to the *burial* custom of the *Jews*.
Now there was a *garden* in the place where he was *crucified*,
and in the *garden* there was a new *tomb*
in which *no* one had ever been *buried*.
And so, because it was the Jewish day of *Preparation*,
and the tomb was *nearby*,
they *laid* Jesus there.

Only this gospel indicates that the tomb was near the place of crucifixion.

Traditionally, a moment of reverent silence accompanied by bowing or kneeling follows at this point.

(17) In Jewish practice, a dead body was buried before sunset. The Romans had no such sensibilities; crucified corpses could be left on crosses to rot. Breaking the legs of the crucified was a merciful act, designed to hasten death. Jesus' legs were not broken because he was already dead, and this fact allows the author to apply to him the words spoken of the Passover lamb. The lamb was to be unblemished, with no broken bones. Once again the Jewish authorities are responsible. Pilate acts at their request.

The blood and water that flowed from Jesus' side have long been understood to refer to Christian eucharist and baptism, rituals connected with the saving death of Jesus. The author insists that a reliable witness observed the occurrence so that the reader might recognize its truth. The witness is probably the beloved disciple.

(18) The other gospels also attest to Joseph of Arimathea's role in burying the body of Jesus. Here he becomes a full-fledged follower of Jesus. Joining him in honoring the body is Nicodemus, whose nocturnal visit to Jesus is told only in this gospel. He anoints the body here, an act of tribute the women in the other gospels intended to do on Sunday morning. The stage is set for Mary Magdalene to arrive and find the empty tomb.

APRIL 14 – 15, 2001

# EASTER VIGIL

*Lectionary #41*

## READING I   Genesis 1:1— 2:2

### A reading from the book of Genesis

In the *beginning*
when God created the *heavens* and the *earth*,
the *earth* was a formless *void*
and *darkness* covered the face of the *deep*,
while the spirit of God *swept* over the face of the *waters*.
*Then* God said,
"Let there be *light*";
and there was *light*.
And God saw that the light was *good*;
and God *separated* the *light* from the *darkness*.
God called the *light* "*Day*,"
and the *darkness* he called "*Night*."
And there was *evening* and there was *morning*, the *first* day.

And *God* said,
"Let there be a *dome* in the midst of the *waters*,
and let it separate the *waters* from the *waters*."
So God made the *dome*
and separated the waters that were *under* the dome
from the waters that were *above* the dome.
And it was *so*.
God called the *dome* "*Sky*."
And there was *evening* and there was *morning*, the *second* day.

**Make "swept" sound like what it means.**

**Speak God's words in a strong, commanding tone.**

**This is spoken with sincerity and satisfaction; stress the word "good."**

**Pause slightly between "light" and "day."**

**Lower your voice in a concluding, satisfied tone.**

**Declare the success of God's command slowly and decisively. Pause slightly after "dome."**

**Practice this line with a microphone until you are able to speak "second day" without swallowing any letters.**

READING I **When you proclaim the creation story to your community, you set the mood for the readings and prayers that follow. You tell the story of primeval beauty and the plan of God in forming the earth. Read it with wonder and awe, inspiring your listeners to accept their role in protecting the earth, preserving it unblemished and reflecting its original goodness.**

**Convey God's power over everything in being able to bring about such a wondrous creation, a universe twirling in a cosmic dance, carefully balanced, reflecting the greatness and goodness of its maker.**

**The story of the creation is poetic. It is similar to creation myths from other traditions, but unique as well. It establishes a six-day "work week," with a day devoted to rest. For the human the day of rest is appropriately devoted to marveling at the beauties of creation and giving praise to God for them and for all God's deeds.**

**In the creation story recounted here, God reigns supreme from beginning to end. There is no cosmic struggle for control, as in other creation accounts. The world begins in chaos, but God's spoken word brings order and beauty. As Christians we proclaim that God most fully communicates through the Son, the incarnate Word, through whom the world was made.**

APRIL 14–15, 2001 ■ EASTER VIGIL

And *God* said,
"Let the *waters* under the sky be gathered *together* into one *place,*
and let the dry *land* appear."
And it was *so.*

**Pause slightly after "land."**

God called the *dry land "Earth,"*
and the *waters* that were gathered *together* he called *"Seas."*
And God saw that it was *good.*

Then God said,
"Let the earth put forth *vegetation:*
*plants* yielding *seed,*
and *fruit* trees of every *kind* on earth
that bear *fruit* with the *seed* in it."
And it was *so.*
The *earth* brought forth *vegetation:*
*plants* yielding *seed* of every *kind,*
and *trees* of every kind bearing *fruit* with the *seed* in it.

**Speak sincerely and with satisfaction.**
**Take care not to swallow the "d" in "third."**

And God saw that it was *good.*
And there was *evening* and there was *morning,* the *third* day.

And God said,
"Let there be *lights* in the dome of the *sky*
to separate the *day* from the *night;*
and let them be for *signs* and for *seasons*
and for *days* and *years,*
and let them be *lights* in the dome of the *sky*
to give *light* upon the *earth."*
And it was *so.*

God made the *two* great *lights*—
the *greater* light to rule the *day*
and the *lesser* light to rule the *night*—
and the *stars.*
God *set* them in the dome of the *sky*

This story of creation announces the origin of the world from a dark void. God forms the world, beginning in the broadest possible way, by making light and darkness. From here, God proceeds to refine the work, making it ever more specific and detailed until finally reaching the creation of humanity. Human beings are the crown of creation because God declares them made in the divine image. This is both a declaration and a promise. We must fulfill God's word and reflect the divine in our words and actions.

Begin your proclamation by imagining the sound of a rushing wind, and try to convey that image as you read the introductory verses of this selection. Throughout the description of creation, speak as slowly and clearly as you can, careful always not to swallow any words or phrases. Never rush the repetition in the passage but draw attention to it. Emphasize the words describing the elements of creation: light, waters, earth, plants, fruit, birds, animals, and so on. Give special emphasis to the creation of humans. Close with a quiet, satisfied voice.

There is a natural rhythm to this passage. Allow it to guide your proclamation, but try not to sound sing-song or too formal.

# EASTER VIGIL ■ APRIL 14–15, 2001

to give *light* upon the *earth*,
to rule over the *day* and over the *night*,
and to separate the *light* from the *darkness*.
And God saw that it was *good*.
And there was *evening* and there was *morning*, the *fourth* day.

And God said,
"Let the waters bring forth *swarms* of living *creatures*,
and let *birds* fly above the *earth* across the *dome* of the *sky*."
So God created the great *sea* monsters
and *every* living creature that *moves*, of every *kind*,
with which the waters *swarm*,
and every winged *bird* of every *kind*.
And God saw that it was *good*.
God *blessed* them, saying,
"Be *fruitful* and *multiply* and *fill* the waters in the *seas*,
and let birds *multiply* on the *earth*."
And there was *evening* and there was *morning*, the *fifth* day.

And *God* said,
"Let the earth bring *forth* living *creatures* of every *kind*:
*cattle* and *creeping* things
and wild *animals* of the *earth* of every *kind*."
And it was *so*.
God made the wild *animals* of the *earth* of every *kind*,
and the *cattle* of every *kind*,
and everything that creeps upon the *ground* of every *kind*.
And God saw that it was *good*.

Then God said,
"Let us make human *beings* in our *image*,
　　according to our *likeness*;
and let them have *dominion* over the *fish* of the sea,
and over the *birds* of the air,

**Once again, speak sincerely and with satisfaction.**

**Draw out "swarms" in order to convey how many there were, then lift your voice and sound a bit excited as you describe the birds.**

**Practice this sentence until the phrasing is clear.**

**Say "blessed" in a confident tone and with the same satisfaction that you display when declaring the goodness of God's creation.**

**All of creation is made by God and is good, even those creatures we consider less than noble.**
**Pause before beginning this important proclamation, then lift your voice anew as you describe the creation of humanity.**

Speak in a strong voice, and lift it a bit as you speak the words of God. Declare with warmth in your voice how good each aspect of creation is. Each "and it was so" should be spoken after a slight pause and in a voice that expresses confidence rather than surprise. Pause slightly before and after the announcement of the day of the week ("evening" and "morning," the first day, and so on). Read slowly, but with a tone of finality and satisfaction. Be sure to enunciate each word. Then pause before beginning the account of the succeeding day.

Your community might have the practice of beginning this reading in partial darkness, or the reading may be accompanied by a choral refrain or visual presentation. Be sure you understand what your liturgy committee or director has planned, and practice until you are confident that you can proceed smoothly, giving your entire attention to proclaiming the word of God. You are given the task of announcing that the light has dawned, a message that will also be imparted through song and ritual. Pray about the passage. After

APRIL 14–15, 2001 ■ EASTER VIGIL

**Stress "God."**
**Men and women are both made in God's image.**

and over the *cattle*,
and over all the wild *animals* of the *earth*,
and over every *creeping* thing that creeps upon the *earth*."
So God created human *beings* in his *image*,
in the image of *God* he created them;
*male* and *female* he *created* them.

God *blessed* them, and God said to them,
"Be *fruitful* and *multiply*, and *fill* the earth and *subdue* it;
and have *dominion* over the fish of the *sea*
and over the *birds* of the air
and over every *living* thing that moves upon the *earth*."

**There is a purpose for everything, and all creation is in harmony.**

*God* said,
"*See*, I have given you every *plant* yielding *seed*
that is upon the face of *all* the *earth*,
and every *tree* with seed in its *fruit*;
you shall *have* them for *food*.

"And to every *beast* of the earth, and to every *bird* of the air,
and to everything that *creeps* on the earth,
everything that has the *breath* of *life*,
I have given every green *plant* for *food*."
And it was *so*.

**Slow down as you read this, and stress the great goodness of creation.**

God saw everything that he had *made*,
and *indeed*, it was very *good*.
And there was *evening* and there was *morning*, the *sixth* day.

**Conclude the passage by reading slowly and with finality.**

Thus the *heavens* and the *earth* were *finished*,
and all their *multitude*.
And on the *seventh* day God *finished* the work that he had *done*,
and he *rested* on the *seventh* day from all the *work*
that he had *done*.

*[Shorter: Genesis 1:1, 26–31a]*

you have reflected on the beauty of God's creation, you will be better able to convey your wonder and awe to your listeners.

READING II During our celebration of the Triduum, we reflect on the new covenant established in Jesus. It is appropriate, then, to learn about the covenant God first established with the patriarch Abraham. Today's passage follows the fulfillment of God's promise to Abraham and

Sarah that they would have a child even though they were beyond childbearing years. Abraham's part of the covenant was to institute circumcision, while God promised to bless Abraham and his descendants. In today's passage, the breadth of God's promise is evident: Abraham and Sarah will have descendants as numerous as the stars of the sky and the sands of the seashore.

Before that promise is reiterated, however, Abraham must demonstrate his faith in God by being willing to follow God's commands, even when they seem to contradict God's promises. The chilling story of the binding of Isaac shows just how far Abraham is willing to go. There is no doubt that Abraham loves his son; God's words make that clear. Yet he responds in faith, and it is for that faith that he is rewarded with the promise of many descendants.

# 142
EASTER VIGIL ■ APRIL 14–15, 2001

**READING II**   Genesis 22:1–18

### A reading from the book of Genesis

Speak Abraham's name as if someone is calling him, then pause before giving his response.

God *tested* Abraham.
He said to him, "*Abraham!*"
And Abraham said, "*Here* I am."
God said,

Speak slowly and stress "only" and "love" in order to emphasize what a great gift this child was to Abraham and Sarah.

Moriah = moh-RĪ-uh

"Take your *son*, your *only* son *Isaac*, whom you *love*,
and go to the *land* of *Moriah*,
and *offer* him there as a burnt *offering*
on one of the *mountains* that I shall *show* you."

So Abraham rose *early* in the morning, saddled his *donkey*,
and took *two* of his young men *with* him, and his son *Isaac*;
he cut the *wood* for the burnt *offering*,
and set *out* and went to the place in the *distance*
that God had *shown* him.

The tension begins to mount as Abraham and Isaac approach the mountain.

On the *third* day Abraham looked *up* and saw the place far *away*.
Then Abraham said to his young men,
"Stay *here* with the *donkey*;
the *boy* and I will go over *there*;
we will *worship*, and then we will come *back* to you."
Abraham took the *wood* of the burnt *offering*

Isaac carries the wood just as Jesus will carry his cross.

and laid it on his son *Isaac*,
and he *himself* carried the *fire* and the *knife*.
So the *two* of them walked on *together*.
Isaac said to his father Abraham, "*Father!*"
And Abraham said,

Although Isaac's words can be spoken lightly, allow some sadness to fill Abraham's responses.

"*Here* I am, my *son*."
Isaac said, "The *fire* and the *wood* are here,
but where is the *lamb* for a burnt *offering*?"

Written before a belief in an afterlife developed, this is the closest the text can come to speaking of immortality.

Although the idea of a father sacrificing his son to God is horrifying, the purpose of the story is actually to assert that the God of Abraham does not require such an action. The gods of neighboring peoples accepted human sacrifice, but this God does not. God wants a demonstration of faith but rejects the violence practiced by the nations.

Read this dramatic account with a tone of tension and horror just below the surface. Although it begins matter-of-factly, the story quickly threatens our sensibilities and causes us anxiety. Be aware of the discomfort that may be present in your assembly, but do not attempt to soften the message. When reading the dialogue, speak Isaac's words innocently, but allow some sorrow as

well as nervousness to enter your voice as you read Abraham's words. Let the suspense build until the angel intervenes. Allow your voice to reflect relief when Abraham finds the ram, but continue to speak God's promise in a strong yet comforting tone.

READING III   The book of Exodus is the story of the plight of the Israelites in Egypt and their escape from the army of Pharaoh as it chased them into the

APRIL 14–15, 2001 ■ EASTER VIGIL

Abraham said,
"God *himself* will provide the *lamb* for a burnt *offering*, my *son.*"
So the *two* of them walked on *together.*

When Abraham and Isaac came to the place
    that God had *shown* him,
Abraham built an *altar* there and laid the *wood* in order.
He *bound* his son *Isaac,*
and laid him on the altar, on top of the wood.

Then Abraham *reached* out his *hand*
and took the *knife* to *kill* his son.

But the *angel* of the Lord *called* to him from *heaven,* and said,
"*Abraham, Abraham!*"
And he said, "*Here* I am."
The angel said,
"Do *not* lay your hand on the *boy* or do *anything* to him;
for now I *know* that you *fear* God,
since you have not withheld your *son,* your *only* son, from *me.*"
And Abraham looked *up* and saw a *ram,*
caught in a *thicket* by its *horns.*
Abraham went and *took* the ram
and offered it *up* as a burnt *offering* instead of his *son.*

So Abraham *called* that place "The *Lord* will *provide*";
as it is said to this *day,*
"On the *mount* of the *Lord* it shall be *provided.*"

The *angel* of the Lord called to Abraham
    a *second* time from heaven,
and said, "By *myself* I have *sworn,* says the Lord:
Because you have *done* this,
and have not *withheld* your *son,* your *only* son,
I will indeed *bless* you,

**This is not to be spoken matter-of-factly. Let your voice display some tightness in order to indicate what is coming.**

**Read these three lines slowly, and allow tension to fill your voice.**

**Speak very slowly and deliberately, with a tone of subdued horror. Then pause at length. When you begin again, speak with urgency and pick up your pace.**

**Although these are solemn words, you may speak with relief.**

**The tension continues to subside.**

**This is a solemn promise, spoken with great sincerity.**

desert. Today's passage begins shortly after the journey has begun, just as Pharaoh's army is approaching the Israelite procession. As they would do so many times on this journey to their Promised Land, the Israelites turn against Moses and lose heart. They regret the decision to flee Egypt, preferring to live in slavery than to die in the wilderness. The current selection follows immediately after Moses tries to reassure the people.

The Israelites know that Pharaoh's army is near, but God seems far away. But the divine presence is manifested when the two camps approach the sea. The presence of God in the angel and in the pillar of cloud separates the Egyptians from the Israelites and protects them, then strikes the Egyptians and frightens them. When Moses follows God's instructions, the waters of the sea open for the Israelites but close again over the army of Pharaoh.

The spectacular account of God's intervention during the flight from Egypt ends with a song of praise to God. (The account of Miriam leading the women in the song is included in the reading; the song follows immediately and the usual conclusion to the reading is omitted.) It is appropriate for us to join our voices with those of the Israelites today, for God's promise to care for and protect the Israelites gives glory to God and

**144** EASTER VIGIL ■ APRIL 14–15, 2001

and I will make your *offspring* as *numerous*
     as the *stars* of *heaven*
and as the *sand* that is on the *seashore.*
And your *offspring* shall possess the *gate* of their *enemies,*
and *by* your offspring
shall all the *nations* of the *earth* gain *blessing* for *themselves,*
because you have *obeyed* my *voice."*

*[Shorter: Genesis 22:1–2, 9–13, 15–18]*

**Speak the final line slowly and with emphasis.**

---

### READING III  Exodus 14:15–31; 15:20, 1

**A reading from the book of Exodus**

The *Lord* said to *Moses,* "Why do you cry *out* to me?
Tell the *Israelites* to go *forward.*
But *you,* lift up your *staff,*
and *stretch* out your hand over the *sea* and *divide* it,
that the Israelites may go *into* the sea on dry *ground.*
Then I will *harden* the *hearts* of the *Egyptians*
so that they will go in *after* them;
and so I will gain *glory* for *myself* over *Pharaoh* and all his *army,*
his *chariots,* and his chariot *drivers.*
And the *Egyptians* shall *know* that *I* am the *Lord,*
when I have gained *glory* for *myself* over *Pharaoh,*
his *chariots,* and his chariot *drivers."*

The angel of *God* who was going *before* the Israelite army
*moved* and went *behind* them;
and the pillar of *cloud* moved from in *front* of them
and took its place *behind* them.
It came *between* the army of *Egypt* and the army of *Israel.*
And so the *cloud* was there with the *darkness,*

**It is for God's glory that these events have been recorded. That is also the reason we recall them today.**

**The angel and the pillar of cloud had signified God's presence, leading the Israelites on the journey. Now they separate the Israelites from the Egyptians, offering protection and assistance.**

---

brings favor to the Israelites. In addition to giving God glory, the exodus event provides salvation for the Hebrew people and convinces them of the great power of God.

Christians understand this key reading to be especially important on this holy night, when we proclaim that Jesus has passed through death to life. In addition, the

Israelites' crossing of the sea is understood as an image of baptism, when the Christian passes through the waters to new life. Paul's understanding of baptism in his letter to the Romans, which follows shortly, speaks of dying in baptism with the promise of new life. Paul uses the exodus event to explain Christian baptism. For the Israelites and for Christians, going through the waters and leaving the former life acknowledges the salvation offered by God.

There is a great deal of excitement in the story about the Israelites' flight from Egypt. Begin by speaking God's words forcefully; emphasize the glory that rightfully belongs to God. Let your voice reflect some of the anxiety that must have accompanied the Israelites as they passed through the sea, and allow it to grow in intensity until

APRIL 14–15, 2001 ■ EASTER VIGIL

**Raise your voice and speak majestically of God's intervention.**

and it lit up the *night*;
one did not come *near* the other all *night*.
Then Moses *stretched* out his *hand* over the *sea*.
The Lord *drove* the sea back by a strong east *wind* all *night*,
and turned the *sea* into dry *land*;
and the waters were *divided*.
The Israelites went into the *sea* on dry *ground*,
the waters forming a *wall* for them on their *right* and on their *left*.

**Pick up the pace a bit, as the Egyptians follow in hot pursuit.**

**This line can be tricky; prepare your phrasing well.**

The Egyptians *pursued*, and went into the sea *after* them,
all of Pharaoh's *horses*, *chariots*, and chariot *drivers*.
At the morning *watch*,
the *Lord* in the pillar of *fire* and *cloud*
looked *down* upon the Egyptian *army*,
and threw the Egyptian army into *panic*.
He *clogged* their chariot *wheels*
      so that they turned with *difficulty*.
The Egyptians said,
"Let us *flee* from the *Israelites*,
for the Lord is *fighting* for them against *Egypt*."

**Two explanations are given for Pharaoh's defeat. Here the wheels of the chariots became clogged and the Egyptians retreat, but in the next paragraph the Egyptians drown when the waters return.**

Then the *Lord* said to *Moses*,
"*Stretch* out your *hand* over the *sea*,
so that the water may come *back* upon the *Egyptians*,
upon their *chariots* and chariot *drivers*."
So Moses *stretched* out his hand over the *sea*,
and at *dawn* the sea *returned* to its normal *depth*.
As the Egyptians fled *before* it,
the Lord *tossed* the Egyptians into the *sea*.
The waters *returned*
and covered the *chariots* and the chariot *drivers*,
the *entire* army of *Pharaoh* that had *followed* them into the *sea*;
not *one* of them *remained*.

**Increase your speed here.**

**This is spoken with satisfaction. The danger has passed.**

the Egyptians are finally vanquished. Speak triumphantly of the safety of the Israelites, and proclaim joyfully the victory song of the people.

The key theme of this reading is God's constant presence and care for the people, despite their grumbling. Offer it to your assembly as a commentary on God's continual care and the necessity of passing through tribulations, even death, on the path to true life.

READING IV Chapters 40–55 of Isaiah are often called Second Isaiah because they were written centuries after the prophet Isaiah was active. The prophet Isaiah had counseled the king of Judah when Jerusalem was threatened by the Assyrians. Second Isaiah comes from a time near the end of the Babylonian exile, when the people were eagerly waiting to return to their homeland. Jerusalem had been destroyed and its inhabitants led away, but they kept alive the hope that they would one day return. As the political events of the day indicated that the time was drawing near, a prophet wrote these reassuring words. God speaks of the exile as a time of punishment that is drawing to a close. God also eagerly awaits the return of the chosen people to Jerusalem, to the holy mountain of Zion.

**146**
EASTER VIGIL ■ APRIL 14–15, 2001

As will so often happen on this journey, Israel is in awe of God's tremendous deeds.
Speak this with great joy, giving glory to God.

But the *Israelites* walked on dry *ground* through the *sea*,
the waters forming a *wall* for them on their *right* and on their *left*.
Thus the Lord *saved* Israel that day from the *Egyptians*;
and Israel saw the Egyptians *dead* on the *seashore*.
Israel saw the great *work* that the Lord did against the *Egyptians*.
So the people *feared* the Lord and *believed* in the Lord
and in his servant *Moses*.

The prophet *Miriam*, Aaron's *sister*,
took a *tambourine* in her hand;
and all the *women* went out after her with *tambourines*
and with *dancing*.
*Moses* and the *Israelites* sang this *song* to the *Lord*:

*[The canticle is sung immediately after the reading. The usual conclusion to the reading, "The word of the Lord," is omitted.]*

---

## READING IV     Isaiah 54:5–14

**A reading from the book of the prophet Isaiah**

Thus says the *Lord*, the God of *hosts*.

Convey the intimacy of this relationship between God and Israel.

Your *Maker* is your *husband*,
the *Lord* of *hosts* is his name;
the Holy One of *Israel* is your *Redeemer*,
the *God* of the whole *earth* he is called.
For the Lord has *called* you

There is hope here, but sadness in the following lines.

like a wife *forsaken* and grieved in *spirit*,
like the wife of a man's *youth* when she is cast *off*,
says your God.

---

God speaks throughout today's reading, first as a husband filled with love for a wife he had abandoned. Brimming with compassion, he calls her back. God was angry, but the moment of anger was brief and has passed. The image of Israel as a bride of God is expressed most poignantly in another prophet, Hosea; there God is faithful always, despite Israel's waywardness. Here God

regrets the momentary anger, although elsewhere the exile is seen as a necessary period of instruction and testing.

God's word is forceful in the next section of the passage, as the author recalls the story of the flood in the days of Noah. At that time God also spoke, declaring never again to destroy the earth. Now the prophet proclaims that nothing can interfere with God's tremendous love for this people. Even if the mountains move and the hills quake, God will remember the covenant with Israel.

Finally, God addresses the city of Jerusalem directly. The city is lying in waste after the defeat by the Babylonians, and God promises to renew its splendor, decorating it with precious stones. Israel thought of the city of Zion as the one place that could not be defeated by the enemies of God. Even with Jerusalem in ruins, that hope is renewed here, for God will care for the city.

APRIL 14–15, 2001 ■ EASTER VIGIL

**Speak with regret.**

For a brief *moment* I *abandoned* you,
but with great *compassion* I will *gather* you.
In overflowing *wrath* for a *moment*
I hid my *face* from you,
but with everlasting *love* I will have *compassion* on you,
says the *Lord*, your *Redeemer*.

**Convey the tender love of God in a warm but firm voice.**

**A new idea begins here. Lift your voice as though starting afresh.**

*This* is like the days of *Noah* to me:
Just as I *swore* that the *waters* of Noah
would *never again* go over the *earth*,
so I have *sworn* that I will not be *angry* with you
and will not *rebuke* you.

**Speak this as a solemn oath.**

For the *mountains* may *depart*
and the *hills* be *removed*,
but my steadfast *love* shall not *depart* from you,
and my covenant of *peace* shall not be *removed*,
says the *Lord*, who has *compassion* on you.

**God speaks tenderly to Jerusalem.**

**Let your voice grow in intensity as you describe the majesty of Jerusalem.**

O *afflicted* one, *storm*-tossed, and not *comforted*,
I am about to set your *stones* in *antimony*,
and lay your *foundations* with *sapphires*.
I will make your *pinnacles* of *rubies*,
your *gates* of *jewels*,
and all your *walls* of precious *stones*.

**Speak these final lines in a sure, commanding voice. They are a promise of peace and justice.**

All your *children* shall be taught by the *Lord*,
and *great* shall be the *prosperity* of your *children*.
In *righteousness* you shall be *established*;
you shall be *far* from *oppression*, for you shall not *fear*;
and from *terror*, for it shall not come *near* you.

---

The people will also be renewed, taught by God and established in righteousness. In everything, God will offer protection and love.

Speak quietly but joyfully as you read these reassuring promises. Address this beautiful statement of God's commitment directly to the members of your assembly. Offer it as an assurance that God always wants to live in intimacy and love with this people. Remind them that times when God may seem distant are temporary, but God's love is eternal.

READING V This passage from Isaiah follows almost immediately after the verses of the fourth reading. It is an invitation to eat and drink and be satisfied. It is offered to all, even to those who cannot afford to purchase the food necessary to prepare the feast. This food is available to anyone because it is not food for physical sustenance but nourishment for the spirit. Just as we often gather together to celebrate momentous occasions by sharing in a

banquet, so also the banquet is spread here in order to invite people to consume the food of wisdom.

In fact, the invitation to come and eat sounds very much like the invitation of Wisdom in the book of Proverbs. There, Lady Wisdom entices her listeners, inviting them to share a meal with her and drawing them especially to embrace her and act always in accordance with her instruction.

In today's passage, God invites a people living in exile to feast. The author recognizes that the end of the exile is near and the

148

EASTER VIGIL ■ APRIL 14–15, 2001

## READING V    Isaiah 55:1–11

**A reading from the book of the prophet Isaiah**

Speak this invitation quietly but clearly. Stress "come" throughout the reading in a way that sounds like you are eager for the guests to arrive.

Everyone who *thirsts*,
*come* to the *waters*;
and you that have no *money*,
*come*, *buy* and *eat!*

Sound eager and encouraging. It is free!

*Come*, buy *wine* and *milk*
without *money* and without *price*.
*Why* do you spend your *money* for that which is not *bread*,
and your *labour* for that which does not *satisfy*?

These are reassuring words. Continue to sound inviting, but in a firmer tone.

Listen *carefully* to me, and eat what is *good*,
and *delight* yourselves in rich *food*.
*Incline* your ear, and *come* to me;
*listen*, so that you may *live*.

Speak these words with great promise.

I will *make* with you an everlasting *covenant*,
my *steadfast*, sure *love* for *David*.

See, I made him a *witness* to the *peoples*,
a *leader* and commander for the *peoples*.
See, *you* shall call *nations* that you do not *know*,
and *nations* that do not *know* you shall *run* to you,
because of the *Lord* your *God*, the *Holy* One of *Israel*,
for he has *glorified* you.

Pause before beginning this line, and lower your voice again, gently urging your listeners to seek God.
This is meant to be encouraging, not disdainful. Do not give undue emphasis to "wicked."

*Seek* the Lord while he may be *found*,
*call* upon him while he is *near*;
let the wicked *forsake* their way,
and the unrighteous their *thoughts*;
let them *return* to the Lord, that he may have *mercy* on them,
and to our *God*, for he will abundantly *pardon*.

---

people will soon be restored to their homeland. The covenant that God established with David is still valid despite the exile; it will be renewed as an everlasting covenant. Israel will once again be a light to all the nations of the world.

One of the lessons of the exile was the necessity to repent for wrongdoing. God again invites the wicked to forsake their deeds, to turn to God and learn. All of Israel needs to hear this (as do we), and to recognize that God's ways are fundamentally different from the ways of humans. But those

who listen to God's word will recognize this, for like the rain and the snow that cause the earth to produce vegetation, God's word is effective and brings forth new life.

We accept God's call today to come to the waters. We come not for physical refreshment, but to reaffirm our commitment to the one who provides life-giving water. For those in your community who are approaching the waters of baptism, as well as for those renewing their baptismal commitment, offer this selection as an invitation to approach

with confidence and trust, knowing that God will teach them and work through them. God has also spread a feast in the eucharist that we will soon share. Invite your community to partake of the sustenance that satisfies more than physical hunger. Read with a welcoming tone and a reassuring voice as you become the vessel through whom God's word is sown.

READING VI The book of Baruch, like Second Isaiah, was written in connection with Israel's exile in Babylon and expresses a hope for return to

APRIL 14–15, 2001 ■ EASTER VIGIL

**Pause before this line, then speak with majesty.**

For *my* thoughts are not *your* thoughts,
nor are *your* ways *my* ways, says the Lord.
For as the heavens are *higher* than the *earth*,
so are *my* ways *higher* than *your* ways
and my *thoughts* than *your* thoughts.

**This final section is a promise. It is one long complex sentence and will have to be carefully prepared. Read it slowly, knowing when you will pause for breath.**

**With "so shall" you begin the fulfillment of the promise. Pause before this line and speak it and what follows slowly and forcefully.**

For as the *rain* and the *snow* come down from *heaven*,
and do not *return* there until they have *watered* the *earth*,
making it bring *forth* and *sprout*,
giving *seed* to the *sower* and *bread* to the *eater*,
so shall my *word* be that goes out from my *mouth*;
it shall not return to me *empty*,
but it shall *accomplish* that which I *purpose*,
and *succeed* in the thing for which I *sent* it.

---

**READING VI**     Baruch 3:9–15, 32—4:4

**A reading from the book of the prophet Baruch**

**Baruch = buh-ROOK**

**Speak as though a herald, calling from the rooftops.**

*Hear* the commandments of *life*, O Israel;
give *ear*, and learn *wisdom!*
Why *is* it, O Israel,
why *is* it that you are in the *land* of your *enemies*,
that you are growing *old* in a foreign *country*,
that you are *defiled* with the *dead*,
that you are *counted* among those in *Hades*?
You have *forsaken* the fountain of *wisdom*.
If you had *walked* in the way of *God*,
you would be living in *peace forever*.

**Do not end this long question by raising your voice at the end. It is rhetorical; God knows how and why the people went into exile.**

**Here is the answer to the question. Speak it forcefully.**

**Lower your voice a bit and speak encouragingly.**

Learn where there is *wisdom*,
where there is *strength*,
where there is *understanding*,

---

the Promised Land. The present section is a poem in honor of wisdom, a pastiche of quotes from the Hebrew scriptures designed to draw the reader to recognize that wisdom is found in living according to the commandments of God.

The author begins by declaring that Israel's exile is a punishment for disobeying God's commands. Living in exile is such a humiliation that it can be compared with dwelling among the dead. Such is the destiny of those who abandon wisdom.

Wherever there is wisdom, there is strength and understanding, but also a long

and happy life. Wisdom is a grammatically feminine term and is elsewhere personified as a woman. Yet wisdom is not easy to find. Fortunately for Israel, God has found her and given her as a gift to this chosen people.

Hebrew wisdom literature speaks of Lady Wisdom as the joint creator of the universe with God. Although that specific teaching is not present in this passage, it does recall the creation account in Genesis. The one who created the universe knows Wisdom and bestowed her upon Israel. Through this people she has dwelt on earth.

In a move that is somewhat surprising (developed to an even greater extent in the book of Sirach), Lady Wisdom is now identified with the Torah, the law given to Moses. The gift of wisdom is the same as the gift of the law. To keep the commandments of the law is to hold on to wisdom and to have life. Israel can rejoice in having received the law. Through it Israel knows how to please God.

Christians have long understood the reference to Lady Wisdom living on earth among humans to refer to the incarnate Son of God, Jesus. He is truly Wisdom, from whom we learn about God and ourselves.

**150**

EASTER VIGIL ■ APRIL 14–15, 2001

**Wisdom is hard to find.**

**What follows is a brief recapitulation of the Genesis creation account. As in Genesis, God is the one in control of everything.**

**The stars speak eagerly and joyfully.**

**Pause before beginning this section, then read with great conviction.**

**Israel believes that wisdom resides in the law.**

**Slow your pace and speak tenderly, joyfully and encouragingly from here to the end.**

so that you may at the *same* time *discern*
where there is length of *days*, and *life*,
where there is *light* for the eyes, and *peace*.
Who has *found* her *place*?
And who has entered her *storehouses*?

But the one who knows *all* things knows *her*,
he *found* her by his *understanding*.
The one who prepared the *earth* for all *time*
*filled* it with four-footed *creatures*;
the one who sends *forth* the light, and it *goes*;
he *called* it, and it *obeyed* him, *trembling*;
the *stars* shone in their *watches*, and were *glad*;
he *called* them, and they said, *"Here* we *are!"*
They shone with *gladness* for him who *made* them.

*This* is our *God*;
no *other* can be *compared* to him.
He found the *whole* way to *knowledge*,
and *gave* her to his servant *Jacob*
and to *Israel*, whom he *loved*.
*Afterward* she appeared on *earth*
and lived with *humanity*.

She is the *book* of the *commandments* of *God*,
the *law* that endures *forever*.
All who hold her *fast* will *live*,
and those who *forsake* her will *die*.

*Turn*, O Jacob, and *take* her;
walk toward the *shining* of her *light*.
Do not give your *glory* to *another*,
or your *advantages* to an alien *people*.

Happy are *we*, O Israel,
for we *know* what is *pleasing* to God.

We embrace the gift God has given us in Jesus and pledge our commitment to hold fast to him, so that we might live.

This is both an invitation and a bold challenge to the members of your community. Speak in encouraging tones as you coax them ever closer to the source of all life and knowledge.

READING VII Ezekiel was a prophet during the Babylonian exile. He rebukes Israel for its unfaithfulness to God, which resulted in the destruction of

Jerusalem and the deportation of its leaders to a foreign land. Yet his is also a strong voice of hope that the exile would soon end and Israel would be restored.

The present passage is written entirely in God's words. God details the sins for which the punishment of the exile occurred. A new claim is added: The people in exile have profaned God's name simply by the fact that they are living in exile. God gave them a land, but the exile made it appear that God was unable to care for the chosen people as promised. As a result, God pledges to return them to their homeland regardless of their

worthiness. Israel's God acts to protect the divine name, to display holiness for all the nations to see.

The passage closes with a beautiful promise that God will not only restore the people to the land but will also make them worthy, cleansing them and removing idols from among them. God vows to place within the people a new heart, a heart of flesh to replace their stone-cold heart. God will also put God's own spirit in them, instructing them in the correct ways to live.

APRIL 14–15, 2001 ■ EASTER VIGIL

## READING VII    Ezekiel 36:16–17a, 18–28

**A reading from the book of the prophet Ezekiel**

The *word* of the *Lord* came to me:
*Mortal*, when the house of *Israel* lived on their own *soil*,
they *defiled* it with their *ways* and their *deeds*;
their *conduct* in my sight was *unclean*.
So I poured *out* my wrath *upon* them
for the *blood* that they had shed upon the *land*,
and for the *idols* with which they had *defiled* it.
I *scattered* them among the *nations*,
and they were *dispersed* through the *countries*;
in accordance with their *conduct* and their *deeds* I *judged* them.

But when they came to the *nations*,
wherever they *came*, they *profaned* my holy *name*,
in that it was said of them,
"*These* are the people of the *Lord*,
and yet they had to go *out* of his *land*."

But I had *concern* for my holy *name*,
which the house of *Israel* had *profaned*
among the *nations* to which they *came*.
Therefore *say* to the house of *Israel*,
*Thus* says the Lord *God*:
It is not for *your* sake, O house of Israel, that I am about to *act*,
but for the sake of my holy *name*,
which you have *profaned* among the *nations* to which you *came*.

I will *sanctify* my great *name*,
which has been *profaned* among the *nations*,
and which you have *profaned among* them;
and the *nations* shall know that *I* am the *Lord*,

---

**Lower your voice and let anger enter into it as you express God's wrath.**

**Let "scattered" sound like what it means.**

**Give emphasis to the statement about profaning God's name. As if their lawless deeds were not enough, the exile itself sullied God's name.**

**Pause before this line and then speak calmly and reassuringly.**

**Speak forcefully, increasing your volume.**

**This is a solemn promise.**

---

See this selection both as a historical lesson and as a challenge to your listeners to recognize God's greatness and to pledge to live as God's people. Raise your voice to read the final fifteen or so lines—the promise of God to reestablish the people. Inspire your community to open its heart to God, to rejoice in its homecoming, and to be willing to live according to the statutes of God.

EPISTLE    In keeping with his emphasis on the cross of Christ, Paul's classic treatment of baptism also emphasizes the death of Christ and the

believer's share in that death. In baptism, the old self is left behind, indeed crucified, in order to embrace the promise of a new life. And the resurrection is, for Paul, always a future hope, something to be sought.

On this night, we begin our celebration in the darkness of death. But we are expectant and hopeful, knowing that our Lord is risen. Tonight we welcome into our community new members who have long been preparing for this day. We recall as well our own baptism and renew our baptismal promises. It is fitting that we be reminded of

Paul's understanding of baptism and reflect on its significance in our lives.

It is your task tonight to remind the members of your community of their baptismal pledge to leave sin behind. Urge them also to look forward, as does Paul, to the promise of being united with Christ in his resurrection. Proclaiming that Christ is risen allows us also to acknowledge that we shall rise with him.

This passage is not easy to proclaim and will require careful preparation. Stress the central concepts and terms: death, life, resurrection, freedom from sin. Close by

EASTER VIGIL ■ APRIL 14–15, 2001

says the Lord God,
when through *you* I display my *holiness* before their *eyes*.

**The emphasis returns to what God will do for Israel. Speak with comfort.**

I will *take* you from the *nations*,
and *gather* you from all the *countries*,
and *bring* you into your *own* land.

**The sprinkling of water symbolizes purity. It reminds Christians of baptism.**

I will sprinkle clean *water upon* you,
and you shall be *clean* from all your *uncleanness*,
and from all your *idols* I will *cleanse* you.

**Speak tenderly and encouragingly.**

A new *heart* I will *give* you,
and a new *spirit* I will put *within* you;
and I will *remove* from your body the heart of *stone*
and give you a heart of *flesh*.
I will put my spirit *within* you,
and make you follow my *statutes*
and be careful to *observe* my *ordinances*.

**Close with a tone of solemn satisfaction.**

Then you shall *live* in the land that I gave to your *ancestors*;
and *you* shall be my *people*, and *I* will be your *God*.

---

**EPISTLE ⬝ Romans 6:3–11**

**A reading from the letter of Paul to the Romans**

**This is a rhetorical question and can be read either with or without raising your voice at the end.**

Do you not *know*
that all of us who have been *baptized* into Christ *Jesus*
were *baptized* into his *death*?
Therefore we have been *buried* with him
        by *baptism* into *death*,
so that, just as Christ was *raised* from the *dead*

**This is the hope that Paul has; lighten your voice and read with an expectant expression.**

by the *glory* of the *Father*,
so we *too* might walk in *newness* of *life*.

---

offering Paul's exhortation to the Romans to be alive in Christ Jesus as a direct appeal to your own community.

GOSPEL  The gospel of Luke (together with its sequel, the Acts of the Apostles) has a unique approach to the significance of Jesus and the events of his life. Instead of being understood simply as an itinerant Jewish preacher in Roman Palestine, the author of Luke sees Jesus as a person with a message of significance for

the entire world. Although he was born and lived in a particular place and time, his life and death change all of history. Although sent to the Jewish people, the chosen race, he offers life to members of every nation. At the same time, the author of the gospel proclaims the centrality of the promises of God to the Jews and the importance of the holy city of Jerusalem. From this people and this place comes the promise of salvation and life for all people.

The story of Christ's triumph over death—the defining moment in salvation history—is told also from this unique perspective in the gospel of Luke. All of the appearances of Jesus in the gospel of Luke occur in or near Jerusalem. Before his ascension (as described at the beginning of the Acts of the Apostles), Jesus commissions the community of disciples to be his witnesses first in Jerusalem and then to the ends of the earth. Jerusalem is the center of the earth, the source of the message of everlasting significance. And Easter is the dawn of a new age.

APRIL 14–15, 2001 ■ EASTER VIGIL

For if we have been *united* with him in a *death* like his,
we will certainly be *united* with him
    in a *resurrection* like his.

**Paul begins with what is past and moves on to the hope of sharing life with Christ. Stress the contrasts.**

We know that our *old* self was *crucified* with him
so that the body of *sin* might be *destroyed*,
and we might no *longer* be *enslaved* to *sin*.
For whoever has *died* is *freed* from sin.
But if we have *died* with Christ,
we believe that we will also *live* with him.

**Speak with firm conviction.**

We know that *Christ*, being *raised* from the dead,
will never die *again*;
*death* no longer has *dominion* over him.

**Make all of the contrasts clear.**

The *death* he *died*, he died to sin, *once* for *all*;
but the life he *lives*, he lives to *God*.
So you *also* must consider yourselves *dead* to *sin*
and *alive* to *God* in Christ *Jesus*.

---

### GOSPEL   Luke 24:1–12

**A reading from the holy gospel according to Luke**

**Let your voice express astonishment and awe.**

On the *first* day of the *week*, at early *dawn*,
the *women* who had accompanied Jesus from *Galilee*
    came to the *tomb*,
taking the *spices* that they had *prepared*.
They found the *stone* rolled *away* from the tomb,
but when they went *in*, they did not find the *body*.

**Pause before this line. Then read slowly and forcefully.**

While they were *perplexed* about this,
*suddenly* two *men* in dazzling *clothes* stood *beside* them.

---

The proclamation of Jesus' resurrection and the story of the empty tomb, told in today's gospel passage, together with the story of Jesus' ascension, are the chief means by which the author conveys the central Christian belief that Jesus has conquered death and is glorified with God. The humiliation and agony of the passion give way to the glory of the resurrection. An intense light dispels all darkness, and Jesus' followers are able to see once again.

This was not all immediately clear to Jesus' friends, however, as the confusion of the women and the disbelief of the male

apostles makes clear. In the accounts of Jesus' appearances to his friends, he must explain to them the necessity for his death before they are able to acknowledge that he is risen. He is changed beyond their ability to recognize him. But he is also the same person they once knew, and he reveals himself in the familiar ritual of sharing a meal.

Today's selection opens with the story of the female disciples from Galilee who had been with Jesus until the end and had seen where his body was laid. They arrive to perform a burial ritual in order to honor

their friend. To their amazement, they are able to enter the tomb with ease, but do not see Jesus' body. They apparently recognize the men in dazzling garments as angelic messengers because they bow in homage and understandable astonishment. The messengers offer the central proclamation that stirs our hearts on this day: The living one has no place among the dead. Death has been conquered, and its companion—sin— has been vanquished. Evil has been overcome by the forces of good, embodied in the broken flesh of this man from Galilee. God is triumphant.

## 154
EASTER VIGIL ■ APRIL 14–15, 2001

The women were *terrified*
and bowed their *faces* to the *ground*,
but the men said to them,
"Why do you look for the *living* among the *dead*?
He is not *here*, but has *risen*.
Remember how he *told* you, while he was still in *Galilee*,
that the Son of *Man* must be handed over to *sinners*,
and be *crucified*, and on the *third* day *rise* again."

Then the women *remembered* Jesus' *words*,
and *returning* from the tomb,
they told *all* this to the *eleven* and to all the *rest*.
Now it was Mary *Magdalene*, *Joanna*,
Mary the mother of *James*,
and the *other* women *with* them
     who *told* this to the apostles.

These *words* seemed to the apostles an idle *tale*,
and they did not *believe* the women.
But *Peter* got up and ran to the *tomb*;
stooping and looking *in*,
he saw the linen cloths by *themselves*;
then he went *home*, *amazed* at what had *happened*.

**The number of women present is unclear. There were several more than those named.**

**Read this line with awe.**

The messengers remind the women that Jesus had spoken of the necessity of his suffering, but had foreseen that his humiliation would not be the final word. In their excitement, they run to tell the others, but the news is too much. The others must see for themselves. Peter sees the empty tomb himself; others will observe Jesus' wounds and talk with him. From this point forward, all is changed.

The task of proclaiming this gospel passage is both joyful and awesome. In this liturgy, we listen to the stories of God's action throughout history. We reflect on the significance of our own initiation into the mysteries and will soon welcome new members. And most of all we proclaim that God acts most fully in the person of Jesus, offering life and wholeness to a broken world. Today, after the deafening silence of recent weeks, the gospel proclamation is preceded by the return of the "Alleluia" in all its joy-filled splendor. In majestic procession, the gospel is brought before the assembly, which awaits the word with eager anticipation.

Approach this text with the recognition that it is the climactic proclamation of the liturgical year. Prepare carefully, so that you will be able to offer it with power and enthusiasm. God is speaking through you a message of victory. Proclaim it forcefully, so that you might be able to draw your entire assembly into praise for God's goodness and glory.

APRIL 15, 2001

# EASTER SUNDAY

*Lectionary #42*

## READING I   Acts 10:34a, 36–43

**A reading from the Acts of the Apostles**

Peter began to *speak* to those *assembled*
        in the house of Cornelius.
*"You know* the message God sent to the people of *Israel*,
preaching *peace* by Jesus *Christ*—
he is *Lord* of *all*.
That *message* spread throughout *Judea*,
beginning in *Galilee* after the baptism that *John* announced:
how God *anointed* Jesus of *Nazareth*
with the *Holy Spirit* and with *power;*
how he went about doing *good*
and *healing* all who were oppressed by the *devil*,
for God was *with* him.

*"We* are *witnesses* to all that he *did*
both in *Judea* and in *Jerusalem*.
They put him to *death* by hanging him on a *tree;*
but God *raised* him on the third *day*
and allowed him to *appear*,
not to *all* the people
but to *us* who were chosen by God as *witnesses*,
and who *ate* and *drank* with him after
he *rose* from the *dead*.

---

Cornelius = kohr-NEEL-yuhs

**Peter's speech begins here. Lift your voice and speak slowly, especially at the beginning, in order to make this sound like a speech.**

**Pause.**

**Here is the core of the Christian faith. Emphasize it, especially stressing "raised."**

---

READING I   The speech of Peter to the household of Cornelius, the first Gentiles to be included among the followers of Christ, contains in a nutshell the truths of the Christian faith. Peter speaks about the ministry of Jesus on earth, as well as the core of Christian faith—Jesus' death and resurrection and his appearances to the disciples—and closes with a statement of belief in Christ as the heavenly judge, in whom sins are forgiven. It is appropriate to proclaim this message on this central feast of our liturgical year.

Peter's speech follows his realization that the salvation offered in Christ is available to all people, Jews and Gentiles alike. He also claims to be a witness to Jesus' ministry, as well as to Jesus' death, and claims to have experienced the risen Jesus. The author makes it clear that Peter's testimony is reliable.

The command to preach about Jesus paves the way for the readings at our liturgies during the Easter season. In the coming weeks, we will hear about the early growth of the new community of believers and will be challenged to share the message of the risen Christ with those we meet.

Read this speech as a direct proclamation to your assembly. It provides you with a chance to remind your listeners of the core of their faith, a faith based on the testimony of prophets, apostles and "everyone who believes in him."

EASTER SUNDAY ■ APRIL 15, 2001

**Everyone who believes—both Jew and Gentile—will receive the salvation wrought by Jesus.**

"He *commanded* us to *preach* to the people
and to *testify* that *he* is the one *ordained* by *God*
as *judge* of the *living* and the *dead*.
All the *prophets* testify about him
that *everyone* who *believes* in him
receives *forgiveness* of sins through his *name*."

---

### READING II   Colossians 3:1–4

**A reading from the letter of Paul to the Colossians**

**Challenge your listeners to set their sights on heavenly goals.**

If you have been *raised* with Christ,
seek the things that are *above*,
where *Christ* is, seated at the *right hand* of God.
Set your minds on things that are *above*,
*not* on things that are on *earth*,
for you have *died*,
and your life is *hidden* with Christ in *God*.
When *Christ* who is your life is *revealed*,
then you *also* will be revealed with him in *glory*.

**Or:**

---

There is a choice of second readings today. Speak with the liturgy coordinator or pastor to find out which reading will be used.

READING II   **COLOSSIANS. For Paul, resurrection is always in the future. But here, in an apparent reference to the experience of baptism, the author (an admirer of Paul who wrote in his name) claims that the Christian has already been raised with Christ. "You have died"— probably in the waters of baptism, but surely**

to a past sinful life—and must therefore live as one who is already sharing in the heavenly life of Christ enthroned with God. The splendor of resurrected life is not yet revealed to all but will be when Christ appears in glory.

Offer this exhortation to your community as it was first offered to the Colossians: Encourage your listeners to strive for high goals in their behavior, remembering always that they have a share in the life available in Christ.

**1 CORINTHIANS.** Paul exhorts the Corinthians to live new, pure lives by referring to the feast of Passover and using the metaphor of leavened and unleavened bread. Even Gentiles would understand the domestic metaphor, although they probably did not understand leaven to be impure as the Jews did.

Paul assumes that his readers understand the way yeast or leaven is used: A small amount of leavened dough is saved and used to start a new loaf, providing the agent that will make the new dough rise. If left too long, the dough will ferment too much

APRIL 15, 2001 ■ EASTER SUNDAY

---

**READING II**   1 Corinthians 5:6b – 8

**A reading from the first letter of Paul to the Corinthians**

Do you not *know* that a *little* yeast
leavens the *whole* batch of *dough*?
*Clean* out the *old* yeast so that you may be a *new* batch,
as you really are *unleavened*.
For our paschal *lamb*, *Christ*, has been *sacrificed*.
Therefore, let us *celebrate* the *festival*,
not with the *old* yeast, the yeast of *malice* and *evil*,
but with the *unleavened* bread of *sincerity* and *truth*.

The ideas progress quickly here. Pause before continuing.

Pause again.

Speak with enthusiasm.

---

**GOSPEL**   John 20:1–18

**A reading from the holy gospel according to John**

Early on the *first* day of the *week*,
while it was still *dark*,
Mary *Magdalene* came to the *tomb*
and saw that the *stone* had been *removed* from the tomb.
So she *ran* and went to Simon *Peter* and the *other* disciple,
the one whom Jesus *loved*, and *said* to them,
"They have taken the *Lord* out of the *tomb*,
and we do not know *where* they have *laid* him."

Then *Peter* and the *other* disciple set out
and *went* toward the *tomb*.
The two were running *together*,
but the *other* disciple *outran* Peter
and reached the tomb *first*.

Magdalene = MAG-duh-luhn

The passage began quietly, but the pace picks up with this line. Increase your speed slightly and allow your voice to indicate amazement.

Mary is a bit distraught; reflect this in your voice.

---

and begin to smell. Unleavened bread, in contrast, is a flat bread whose dough does not rise. Every Passover, Jews discard all yeast products from their homes and prepare unleavened bread, just as the Israelites did before fleeing Egypt.

Paul suggests that the moral life of the Christian is like the dough used to make bread. Wicked thoughts and actions can mushroom, negatively affecting a person or an entire community. Paul encourages the Corinthians to be like unleavened bread, free of any undesirable qualities. The mention of unleavened bread reminds him of the

feast of Passover, when Jesus was crucified and became the "paschal lamb," the one who brought freedom through his death.

Encourage your community to purify itself this Easter season and to recognize the new life available to it. We too are celebrating the feast on which our paschal lamb gave us life; let us live in a manner worthy of our calling.

The gospel from the Easter Vigil may be read at any Mass on Easter Sunday, at any time of the day. The gospel for the Third Sunday of Easter, Year A, may be used at an afternoon or evening Mass (see lectionary #46).

GOSPEL   The gospel of John recounts several appearances of the risen Jesus to his followers. Only one is included here, but it, together with the witness of the empty tomb, provides touching,

**158**

EASTER SUNDAY ■ APRIL 15, 2001

He bent *down* to look *in*
and saw the linen wrappings *lying* there,
but he did *not* go *in*.

Then Simon *Peter* came, *following* him, and went *into* the tomb.
He saw the linen wrappings *lying* there,
and the *cloth* that had been on Jesus' *head*,
*not* lying with the linen *wrappings*
but rolled up in a place by *itself*.
Then the *other* disciple, who reached the tomb *first*, *also* went in,

**Emphasize this line; read slowly and forcefully.**

and he *saw* and *believed*;
for as *yet* they did not *understand* the scripture,
that he must *rise* from the *dead*.

Then the disciples *returned* to their homes.
But Mary *Magdalene* stood *weeping* outside the *tomb*.
As she *wept*, she bent over to look *into* the tomb;
and she saw two *angels* in *white*,
sitting where the body of *Jesus* had been *lying*,
one at the *head* and the other at the *feet*.
They said to her,

**The angels speak kindly.**

"Woman, *why* are you *weeping*?"
She said to them,

**Mary remains upset and confused.**

"They have *taken* away my *Lord*,
and I do not *know* where they have *laid* him."

When she had said this,
she turned *around* and saw *Jesus* standing there,
but she did not *know* that it was Jesus.
Jesus said to her,

**Speak Jesus' words gently and lovingly.**

"Woman, *why* are you *weeping*?
Whom are you *looking* for?"
Supposing him to be the *gardener*, she said to him,
"Sir, if you have *carried* him *away*,

powerful testimony to our Easter proclamation: Jesus is risen. Alleluia!

Mary Magdalene, remembered in many sources as an especially close friend of Jesus and the first to encounter the risen Christ in the gospel of John, approaches the tomb but runs away when she sees that the stone has been removed. Understandably, she believes that the body has been stolen. Peter and the beloved disciple (probably John), the most prominent of the Twelve in

this gospel, follow. Although the author indicates that the beloved disciple "saw and believed," the statement that the disciples did not yet understand that Jesus was to rise from the dead, as well as the witness of the other gospels, suggests that the women—in this gospel, Mary Magdalene—were the first to encounter both the empty tomb and the risen Lord.

The story of Peter and the beloved disciple racing to the tomb is exciting; the account of Mary meeting Jesus is touching and telling. Mary continued to grieve, first for the death of Jesus and now for the theft of his body. Although she does not at first recognize him when she sees him, suggesting that the risen Jesus had been transformed, she comes to know who it is when he calls her name. The personal encounter

APRIL 15, 2001 ■ EASTER SUNDAY

**Mary's words now carry an edge of accusation, as well as sorrow.**

**Speak warmly.**

**Mary is surprised and excited.**

*tell* me where you have *laid* him,
and I will *take* him *away*."

Jesus said to her, "*Mary!*"
She turned and said to him in Hebrew,
"*Rabbouni!*" which means *Teacher*.
Jesus said to her,
"Do not hold *on* to me,
because I have not yet *ascended* to the *Father*.
But go to my *brothers* and *say* to them,
'I am *ascending* to *my* Father and *your* Father,
to my God and *your* God.'"

**Speak these words with great excitement. Mary is the first evangelist of the risen Lord.**

Mary Magdalene went and *announced* to the *disciples*,
"*I* have *seen* the *Lord*,"
and she *told* them that he had said these *things* to her.

[*Shorter: John 20:1–9*]

*Lectionary #46*

### AFTERNOON GOSPEL   Luke 24:13–35

**A reading from the holy gospel according to Luke**

On the *first* day of the *week*,
*two* of the disciples were going to a *village* called *Emmaus*,
about *eleven* kilometres from *Jerusalem*,
and *talking* with each other about *all* these things
      that had *happened*.
While they were *talking* and *discussing*,
Jesus *himself* came near and *went* with them,
but their *eyes* were kept from *recognizing* him.

**Emmaus = eh-MAY-uhs**

**All the resurrection appearances of Jesus indicate that he had been transformed; he was no longer easily recognizable.**

and the use of a name brings recognition and joy. The gospel hints that Mary tried to embrace Jesus, for he must tell her not to touch him because he must ascend to the Father. Finally, Mary becomes the first evangelist of the risen Jesus, announcing to the disciples what she experienced.

This gospel passage moves quickly, with much to catch the assembly's attention. Read it as though for the first time, and make the story come alive with your telling. This

reading provides not only a testimony of faith to the resurrection of Jesus but most of all shows the tender love shared by Jesus and his followers.

AFTERNOON GOSPEL The beautiful story of the encounter between Jesus and two of his disciples on the road to Emmaus is touching, inspiring and revealing. It recounts the disciples' sadness and confusion in the beginning, their joy at recognizing Jesus, and their

need to understand what the prophets had said about him, as well their recognition of his presence in their lives. It is written for Christians of any age or era, and provides inspiration for embracing an Easter faith.

On the first Easter, two disciples discuss all they have experienced. The gospel writer suggests that the events of the crucifixion and death of Jesus were known to the residents of Jerusalem and to the pilgrims who had traveled there for the Passover festival.

## EASTER SUNDAY ▪ APRIL 15, 2001

*Jesus' question seems innocent, but the response is one of frustration and sorrow.*

*Cleopas = KLEE-oh-puhs*

And Jesus said to them,
"What are you *discussing* with each other while you walk *along*?"
They stood *still*, looking *sad*.
Then *one* of them, whose name was *Cleopas*, answered him,
"Are you the *only* stranger in *Jerusalem*
who does not *know* the things
that have taken *place* there in these *days*?"

Jesus asked them, "*What* things?"
They replied, "The things about *Jesus* of *Nazareth*,
who was a prophet *mighty* in *deed* and *word*
before *God* and all the *people*,
and how our *chief priests* and *leaders* handed him over
to be *condemned* to death and *crucified* him.
But we had *hoped* that *he* was the one to *redeem* Israel.
Yes, and *besides* all this,
it is now the *third* day since these things took *place*.
Moreover, some *women* of our group *astounded* us.
They were at the tomb *early* this *morning*,
and when they did not find his *body* there,
they came *back*
and told us that they had indeed seen a *vision* of *angels*
who said that Jesus was *alive*.
*Some* of those who were with us *went* to the tomb
and found it *just* as the women had said;
but they did *not* see *Jesus*."
Then Jesus said to them,
"Oh, how *foolish* you are,
and how *slow* of *heart*
to believe *all* that the prophets have *declared*!
Was it not *necessary* that the Messiah should *suffer* these things
and *then* enter into his *glory*?"

*They recognized him as a prophet and had hoped that he was the Messiah.*

*Women were clearly members of the group of Jesus' disciples and were the first to recognize that Jesus had risen.*

*Speak Jesus' words with tired sadness and a bit of frustration.*

*Although we know the answer, speak this as a real question.*

*The two proceed to tell Jesus about himself: his deeds in life, their belief in him as a prophet, and his death, which crushed their hopes that he was the Messiah. Even though they knew the story of the empty tomb and of angels saying that Jesus was alive, they did not understand its meaning. They were clearly pondering these matters as they walked along the road.*

When Jesus appears to them as a stranger and explains the scriptures to them, they experience their hearts "burning within" them. The disciples' need to have Jesus' mission explained to them suggests how important it is to comprehend the faith in order to believe truly. Education is imperative in order to have informed believers who really understand what they claim. But knowing that the prophets had predicted all that had

to happen to the Messiah is not enough for these disciples. It is only through a personal encounter with Jesus that their faith is able to come to life.

Although Jesus appears to be continuing through the village, the disciples reach out to him in hospitality, inviting him to join them for a meal. It is this meal encounter

APRIL 15, 2001 ■ EASTER SUNDAY

Then beginning with *Moses* and all the *prophets,*
Jesus *interpreted* to them
the things about *himself* in all the *scriptures.*
As they came *near* the village to which they were *going,*
Jesus walked *ahead* as if he were going *on.*
But they urged him *strongly,* saying,
"*Stay* with us, because it is almost *evening*
and the day is now nearly *over.*"
So Jesus went in to *stay* with them.

When he was at the *table* with them,
he took *bread, blessed* and *broke* it,
and *gave* it to them.
*Then* their eyes were *opened,* and they *recognized* Jesus;
and he *vanished* from their sight.

**Speak with amazement. It is through sharing food that the disciples come to know who their companion is.**

The *two* disciples said to each other,
"Were not our hearts *burning* within us
while he was talking to us on the *road,*
while he was *opening* the *scriptures* to us?"

That *same* hour they got up and returned to *Jerusalem;*
and they found the *eleven* and their companions
        gathered *together.*
*These* were saying,
"The *Lord* has risen *indeed,* and he has *appeared* to *Simon!*"

**There is great excitement in this announcement. Apparently the male disciples, previously unwilling to believe the women, now accept what Peter says.**

**End on a quiet note.**

Then the *two* disciples told what had *happened* on the *road,*
and how the *Lord* had been made *known* to them
in the *breaking* of the *bread.*

that finally opens their eyes. Sharing in something as ordinary as a meal provides a powerful opportunity for enlightenment to occur. It is for this reason that we gather to share the eucharist: to read the scriptures, to teach and understand, and finally to recognize Jesus in the breaking of the bread.

Your task today is made particularly enjoyable by the interesting, exciting story you are privileged to share with your community. Read it with plenty of expression, conveying the disciples' surprise that the stranger did not know about the events that

had recently ocurred. Express the disciples' disappointment and Jesus' exasperation at their lack of understanding, and finally the joy of the encounter and of the other disciples. Offer the story to your community as a loving challenge to recognize Jesus in its midst, especially in the eucharist and the assembly gathered to share it.

APRIL 22, 2001

# 2ND SUNDAY OF EASTER

*Lectionary #45*

## READING I    Acts 5:12–16

**A reading from the Acts of the Apostles**

Speak with awe.

Many *signs* and *wonders* were done among the people
through the *apostles*.
And the believers were *all together* in Solomon's *Portico*.
None of the rest dared to *join* them,
but the people held them in high *esteem*.

Emphasize the large numbers of new
converts.

Yet more than *ever* believers were added to the *Lord*,
great *numbers* of both men and women,
so that they even carried out the *sick* into the *streets*,
and laid them on *cots* and *mats*,
in order that Peter's *shadow* might fall on some of them
as he came by.
A great number of people would *also* gather
from the towns *around* Jerusalem,

Close with a note of triumph.

bringing the *sick* and those tormented by unclean *spirits*,
and they were all *cured*.

---

READING I  The author of the Acts of the Apostles characterizes the earliest days of the Christian community as a period of harmony and success in preaching the gospel. Continuing in the manner of Jesus, the believers are able to heal the sick and those possessed by demons. In addition, as faithful Jews, they continue to pray and gather in the area of the temple in Jerusalem, just as Jesus had.

Peter's prominence in the Acts of the Apostles is seen in this passage in his ability to heal without even touching the sick person. Peter becomes the mouthpiece for the author's message that Jesus is the fulfillment of God's promises to Israel and is the savior of the world.

Apparently because of their healing ministry, many people from Jerusalem and the surrounding area come to visit the followers of Jesus and become believers.

Although there are some tensions in this early community, the gospel is always triumphant and new believers in the risen Jesus abound. The Christian community is expanding, both in numbers and in space, extending into the towns around Jerusalem.

Speak triumphantly yet contentedly as you recount the success of the first followers of Jesus.

APRIL 22, 2001 ■ 2ND SUNDAY OF EASTER

## READING II  Revelation 1:9–11a, 12–13, 17–19

**"Revelation," not "Revelations."**

**Patmos = PAT-muhs**

**Speak with wonder at this vision.**

**The risen Christ offers words of comfort but also speaks with authority.**

### A reading from the book of Revelation

I, *John*, your *brother*
who share with you in Jesus
the *persecution* and the *kingdom* and the patient *endurance*,
was on the island called *Patmos*
because of the *word* of God and the *testimony* of *Jesus*.
I was in the *spirit* on the *Lord's* day,
and I heard behind me a loud *voice* like a *trumpet*
saying, "Write in a *book* what you *see*
and send it to the seven *churches*."

Then I turned to see whose *voice* it was that *spoke* to me,
and on *turning* I saw seven golden *lampstands*,
and in the *midst* of the lampstands
I saw one like the *Son* of *Man*,
clothed with a long *robe*
and with a golden *sash* across his *chest*.

When I *saw* him, I fell at his *feet* as though *dead*.
But he placed his right *hand* on me, saying,
"Do *not* be *afraid*;
I am the *first* and the *last*,
and the *living* one.
I was *dead*, but see, I am *alive forever* and *ever*;
and I have the keys of *Death* and of *Hades*.
Now *write* what you have *seen*,
what *is*, and what is to take place *after* this."

READING II John, the author of the book of Revelation, here recounts his ecstatic experience of being commissioned by God to proclaim individual messages to seven churches. They are messages of correction and instruction, as well as encouragement.

John writes to others who share his faith but who also know the reality of persecution. He was presumably exiled to the island of Patmos because of his faith in the "word" of God and the "testimony" of Jesus.

On the "Lord's day," Sunday, John has a vision in which he receives the command to write what he sees. He also encounters a glorified human figure who inspires great awe. John's description of the glorified person is reminiscent of the human figure from the book of Daniel who is given dominion over all the earth. Although John falls to the ground in awe, the glorified person encourages him. This person then describes himself as the "first" and the "last," one who was dead but now lives, and one who even controls the entrances to the regions of the dead. John depicts Christ as having all authority;

he is judge of the world and even wears clothes that designate him priest and king.

This exalted one instructs John to proclaim the present situation of the church—the reality of persecution, the faithfulness or the errors of each community—as well as its future. For the seven churches, what is coming immediately is a period of greater testing that carries with it the opportunity to "conquer." In the end, the entire book of Revelation speaks of the triumph of Christ and those who remain faithful.

**2ND SUNDAY OF EASTER** ■ APRIL 22, 2001

---

### GOSPEL   John 20:19–31

**A reading from the holy gospel according to John**

It was *evening* on the day Jesus *rose* from the *dead*,
the *first* day of the *week*,
and the *doors* of the house
where the disciples had *met* were *locked*
       for fear of the *authorities*.
*Jesus* came and stood *among* them and said,
"*Peace* be with *you*."
After he said this, he showed them his *hands* and his *side*.
Then the disciples *rejoiced* when they saw the *Lord*.
Jesus said to them again,
"*Peace* be with *you*.
As the *Father* has sent *me*, so *I* send *you*."

When he had said this, he *breathed* on them and *said* to them,
"*Receive* the Holy *Spirit*.
If you *forgive* the sins of *any*, they are *forgiven* them;
if you *retain* the sins of any, they are *retained*."

But *Thomas*, who was called the *Twin*, one of the *twelve*,
was not *with* them when Jesus *came*.
So the *other* disciples told him,
"We have *seen* the *Lord*."
But he said to them,
"Unless I see the mark of the *nails* in his *hands*,
and put my *finger* in the mark of the *nails*
and my *hand* in his *side*,
I will not *believe*."

*Speak Jesus' words with genuine peacefulness and tenderness in your voice.*

*The other disciples are ecstatic.*

*Thomas is hesitant; he does not want to be misled by idle tales.*

---

The book of Revelation, with its fantastic images and bizarre figures, inspires awe in its readers. Draw on that sense of wonder as you share this passage with your assembly. Read the words of the exalted figure with authority.

GOSPEL   The stories of the appearances of the risen Jesus in the gospel of John differ somewhat from those found elsewhere. In all the resurrection accounts, Jesus is changed and must make himself known, even to his intimate companions. In this scene, Jesus is able to walk through closed doors, a feature unknown to the other gospel writers, and he reveals himself not by sharing a meal with his followers but by showing the marks of his wounds and greeting his friends with a message of peace.

The hallmark of the presence of the risen Jesus is his gift of the Spirit to his disciples. After initially cowering in fear, the disciples are strengthened to preach the good news through the power of the Spirit.

Jesus commissions them to go forth, and they are given the authority to forgive or retain sins. This scene provides us with the Johannine vision of the origin of the Christian community, the body of believers in the risen Lord that is sent forth to preach and serve in the power of the Spirit.

The story of Thomas follows the initial account of Jesus' appearance to his followers. Thomas was absent when Jesus came to inspire (literally, "breathe into") his followers to belief in him. As a result, Thomas finds it hard to accept what the others tell him. He does not stubbornly refuse to believe

APRIL 22, 2001 ■ 2ND SUNDAY OF EASTER

**Again, offer Jesus' words with gentleness.**

A week *later* his disciples were *again* in the house,
and Thomas was *with* them.
Although the doors were *shut,*
*Jesus* came and stood *among* them and said,
*"Peace* be with *you."*
Then he said to *Thomas,*
"Put your finger *here* and see my *hands.*
Reach out your *hand* and put it in my *side.*
Do *not doubt* but *believe."*
Thomas answered him,

**Thomas is awestruck.**

"My *Lord* and my *God!"*

Jesus said to him,
"Have you *believed* because you have *seen* me?
*Blessed* are those who have *not* seen
and yet have come to *believe."*

**This is offered to your community.**

Now Jesus did many *other* signs in the presence of his *disciples,*
which are not *written* in this *book.*
But *these* are written so that you may come to *believe*
that *Jesus* is the *Messiah,* the *Son* of *God,*
and that through *believing* you may have *life* in his *name.*

---

the obvious but, like so many of us, does not want to be misled by easy answers or mere gossip. He tries to assess the validity of the claims being made and, because the disciples' story seems so unlikely, he needs to see for himself. Just as **Mary Magdalene** was told by Jesus at the empty tomb not to touch him, so also Thomas does not actually touch Jesus, although Jesus invites him to do so. In the end, what opens Thomas' eyes is not the proof he had said he needed but rather the entire encounter with the risen Lord.

Thomas' experience is much like our own; we want to believe but have never actually heard the risen Jesus speak or seen him in the flesh. In the story about Thomas, however, the author proclaims that even those who are removed from the events he describes and who have not personally known Jesus can still believe in him. Thomas' statement of confession ("My Lord and my God") vindicates him and erases his doubt; it is one of the strongest statements of the divinity of Jesus in the New Testament.

Read this exciting story with plenty of expression. Give Thomas a strong voice as

he first insists on empirical evidence and especially when he proclaims his faith. Allow Jesus to speak directly to your assembly the blessing on those who have not seen and yet believe.

APRIL 29, 2001

# 3RD SUNDAY OF EASTER

*Lectionary #48*

## READING I  Acts 5:27–32, 40b–41

### A reading from the Acts of the Apostles

The *captain* went with the temple *police*
and brought the *apostles*, who were *teaching* in the temple,
and had them stand before the *council*.
The high priest *questioned* the apostles, saying,
"We gave you strict *orders* not to teach in this *name*,
yet here you have *filled* Jerusalem with your teaching
and you are *determined* to bring this man's *blood* on *us*."

**Speak Peter's words with boldness and conviction.**

But Peter and the apostles answered,
"We must obey *God* rather than any *human* authority.
The God of our *ancestors* raised up *Jesus*,
whom you had *killed* by hanging him on a *tree*.
God *exalted* him at his right *hand*
as *Leader* and *Saviour*
that he might give *repentance* to *Israel*
and forgiveness of *sins*.
And we are *witnesses* to these things,
and so is the Holy *Spirit*
whom God has given to those who *obey* him."

**Draw attention to Jesus' name, which carries power and inspires faithfulness.**

Then the council *ordered* the apostles
        not to *speak* in the name of *Jesus*,
and let them *go*.

---

**READING I** The rosy picture of the early Christian community painted in the first part of the Acts of the Apostles begins to darken. Not all goes well for these first followers of Jesus, as they continue to teach and preach in the area of the temple in Jerusalem. They attract the ire of the temple leaders and are brought before the Sanhedrin, the Jewish legal council. The high priest understands their teaching to implicate the religious leaders in the death of Jesus.

Although several of the apostles are arrested, it is Peter, the hero of the first part of the Acts of the Apostles, who acts as their mouthpiece. Peter was also the one who spoke for the believers before the Sanhedrin when they were arrested the first time for preaching the resurrection of the dead. At that time, they were thrown into prison and ordered not to teach in the name of Jesus. They violated that order and so were arrested again.

In today's passage, Peter proclaims that Jesus was raised from the dead and exalted to the right hand of God. After a council member suggests adopting a wait-and-see attitude (in intervening verses not found in today's reading), the apostles are again released and rejoice to have suffered for the name of Jesus.

Jesus' name of has profound power; it is teaching in his name that gets the disciples into trouble in the first place. By speaking Jesus' name the apostles are able to heal the sick. Jesus' name has an authority

APRIL 29, 2001 ■ 3RD SUNDAY OF EASTER

As they *left* the council,
they *rejoiced* that they were considered *worthy*
to suffer *dishonour* for the sake of the *name.*

---

**READING II**   Revelation 5:11–14

**A reading from the book of Revelation**

I, *John, looked,*
and I heard the voice of many *angels* surrounding the *throne*
and the living *creatures* and the *elders;*
they numbered *myriads* of *myriads*
and *thousands* of *thousands,*
singing with full *voice,*
"*Worthy* is the *Lamb* that was *slaughtered*
to receive *power* and *wealth* and *wisdom* and *might*
and *honour* and *glory* and *blessing!*"

Then I heard every creature in *heaven* and on *earth*
and *under* the earth and in the *sea,*
and *all* that is *in* them, singing,
"To the one seated on the *throne* and to the *Lamb*
be *blessing* and *honour* and *glory* and *might*
*forever* and *ever!*"
And the four living creatures said, "*Amen!*"
And the *elders* fell down and *worshipped.*

"Revelation," not "Revelations."

Speak with wonder.

Declare this statement of praise slowly and with great conviction, giving emphasis to each element in the list.

Again, speak slowly as you weigh every word.

---

and power that goes beyond simply a memory of him; it is active and forceful. The Sanhedrin recognizes the power of the name and orders that it not be spoken.

Emphasize the importance of Jesus' name in the charges brought against the apostles and in their response. Proclaim Peter's speech with confidence.

READING II The seer John continues to describe his heavenly vision, a description that we will read throughout the season of Easter. Today's passage follows upon John's vision of the Lamb who has been slaughtered but found worthy to open the scroll of God. At first John had thought that no one could be worthy of such an honor, but he is told that the descendant of Judah has already conquered and is worthy. Opening the scroll will inaugurate an era of tribulation, but in the end the righteous will triumph.

When the Lamb takes the scroll, all creation breaks out in song. The passage reflects an ancient understanding of the division of the cosmos into three sections, with the earth sandwiched between heaven and the netherworld. The angels in heaven proclaim the Lamb's greatness, while all the creatures on the earth and under it sing the praises of the enthroned one and the Lamb.

3RD SUNDAY OF EASTER ■ APRIL 29, 2001

## GOSPEL   John 21:1–19

**A reading from the holy gospel according to John**

*Jesus* showed himself *again* to the disciples
by the Sea of *Tiberias*;
and he showed himself in *this* way.
Gathered there *together* were Simon *Peter*,
*Thomas* called the Twin, *Nathanael* of Cana in Galilee,
the sons of *Zebedee*, and two *others* of his disciples.
Simon Peter said to them, "I am going *fishing*."
They said to him, "We will go *with* you."
They went *out* and got into the *boat*,
but that night they caught *nothing*.

Just after *daybreak*, *Jesus* stood on the *beach*;
but the disciples did not *know* that it was Jesus.
Jesus said to them,
"*Children*, you have no *fish*, *have* you?"
They answered him, "*No*."
He said to them,
"Cast the net to the *right* side of the boat,
and you will *find* some."
So they *cast* it, and now they were not able to haul it *in*
because there were so many *fish*.

That disciple whom Jesus *loved* said to Peter,
"It is the *Lord!*"
When Simon Peter heard that it was the *Lord*,
he put on some *clothes*, for he was *naked*,
and *jumped* into the *sea*.

*Jesus' words are tender and kind.*

*Read this line with quiet excitement in your voice.*

*The image is humorous. Read the line as though you were telling a child. Speak in a low voice about Peter's nakedness, then raise your voice and emphasize "jumped."*

---

The language in the book of Revelation is highly symbolic. Clearly, the enthroned figure is God, judge and ruler of all. The Lamb who was slain is Jesus the Christ in his role as paschal lamb, slaughtered in order to give life to all. The four living creatures are beings near the throne of God and resemble animals, although one has human features as well. Twenty-four elders also surround God's throne, sitting in thrones of their own and probably representing the twelve tribes of Israel and the twelve apostles. Everyone who has breath proclaims the greatness of God and the righteousness of the Lamb, who was killed for the sake of the world.

Although the images in the book of Revelation are sometimes bizarre, the purpose of the work and especially of today's selection is to give glory and praise to God. Lift your voice with the angels and creatures as you too sing the praises recorded here. Speak with awe and reverence for the majesty of the Lamb.

GOSPEL   Jesus' appearances after his resurrection often have something to do with meals. In the ordinary but life-sustaining act of sharing food, Jesus' friends learn to recognize him. Today's story begins with the apostles going fishing. In fact, it is the miracle of the unexpected great catch of fish that leads Peter to recognize Jesus. As elsewhere, Jesus' appearance is changed; his friends do not immediately recognize him, yet they come to know that it is he.

APRIL 29, 2001 ■ 3RD SUNDAY OF EASTER

But the *other* disciples came in the *boat*,
     dragging the net full of *fish*,
for they were not *far* from the *land*,
only about *ninety* metres *off*.

When they had gone *ashore*, they saw a charcoal *fire* there,
with *fish* on it, and *bread*.
Jesus said to them,
"Bring some of the *fish* that you have just *caught*."
So Simon Peter went *aboard* and hauled the net *ashore*,
*full* of large *fish*, a hundred fifty-*three* of them;
and though there were so *many*, the net was not *torn*.
Jesus said to them, "*Come* and have *breakfast*."
Now *none* of the disciples dared to *ask* him,
"Who *are* you?"
because they *knew* it was the *Lord*.
Jesus *came* and took the *bread* and *gave* it to them,
and did the *same* with the *fish*.
This was now the *third* time that Jesus *appeared* to the disciples
after he was *raised* from the *dead*.

**Read this touching story with sincerity and compassion.**

When they had finished *breakfast*,
Jesus said to Simon Peter,
"*Simon* son of *John*, do you *love* me more than *these*?"
He said to him,
"*Yes*, Lord; you *know* that I love you."
Jesus said to him,
"*Feed* my *lambs*."

A *second* time he said to him,
"*Simon* son of *John*, do you *love* me?"
He said to him,
"*Yes*, Lord; you *know* that I *love* you."
Jesus said to him, "*Tend* my *sheep*."

**Peter is insistent, perhaps even a little impatient.**

The story itself is from a section of the gospel of John that might have been added later. It does not seem to recognize that Jesus had already revealed himself to his followers and breathed the Spirit into them. In addition, it takes place in Galilee rather than Jerusalem. Finally, it provides an opportunity to focus on a figure who was important among the early Christians, Peter.

The central story of the passage is the poignant conversation between Jesus and Peter. Just as Peter had three times denied Jesus before Jesus' death, so Peter is now asked to affirm his love for Jesus three times. Eagerly, Peter affirms his commitment to Jesus, but by the third question he is hurt and even more insistent. We are never told if Peter comes to recognize the hurt Jesus must have felt when Peter denied him or if Peter even connects the two experiences.

Each time Peter proclaims his love for Jesus, Jesus gives him a commission. Peter is to care for Jesus' "sheep," clearly members of the Christian community, those who themselves are committed to proclaiming the risen Lord. But Peter is also to "follow," for it is impossible for him to lead if he is not focused on Jesus.

**3RD** SUNDAY OF EASTER ■ APRIL 29, 2001

**Express Peter's hurt in your voice.**

He said to him the *third* time,
"*Simon* son of *John*, do you *love* me?"
Peter felt *hurt* because he said to him the *third* time,
"Do you *love* me?"
And he said to him,
"*Lord*, you know *everything*; you *know* that I *love* you."
Jesus said to him,
"*Feed* my *sheep*.

"Very truly, I *tell* you,
when you were *younger*,
you used to fasten your *own* belt
and go wherever you *wished*.
But when you grow *old*,
you will stretch out your *hands*,
and someone *else* will fasten a belt *around* you
and take you where you do *not* wish to *go*."
He said this to indicate the kind of *death*
by which he would glorify *God*.
After this he said to him,
"Follow *me*."

The final section of the passage alludes to the death of Peter. The tradition of Peter's death by martyrdom in Rome is never told in the New Testament, but this passage affirms that indeed Peter met his fate at the hands of others and died for the sake of his faith.

Read the two sections of this passage as discrete units. The recognition scene in the first half has elements of the miraculous, and the disciples are in awe at the presence of the risen Jesus in their midst. But there is

also humor, as Peter pulls on his clothes and jumps into the water to greet the Lord. The second half of the story turns serious. Let your voice be filled with compassion as you recount Jesus' questions and Peter's proclamation of the depth of his love. Conclude by addressing Jesus' command, "Follow me," to all the members of your assembly.

MAY 6, 2001

# 4TH SUNDAY OF EASTER

*Lectionary #51*

## READING I    Acts 13:14, 43–52

**A reading from the Acts of the Apostles**

Perga = PER-guh
Antioch = AN-tee-ahk
Pisidia = pih-SID-ee-uh

*Paul* and *Barnabas* went on from *Perga*
and came to *Antioch* in *Pisidia*.
On the *sabbath* day they went into the *synagogue* and sat *down*.

When the meeting of the synagogue broke *up*,
many *Jews* and devout *converts* to Judaism
        *followed* Paul and Barnabas,
who *spoke* to them and *urged* them
to *continue* in the grace of *God*.

**Emphasize the enormous size of the crowd that comes to hear Paul and Barnabas.**

The *next* sabbath almost the whole *city* gathered
to hear the *word* of the *Lord*.
But when the Jewish officials saw the *crowds*,
they were filled with *jealousy*;
and *blaspheming*, they *contradicted* what was spoken by Paul.

Then both *Paul* and *Barnabas* spoke out *boldly*, saying,
"It was *necessary* that the word of God
        should be spoken *first* to *you*.
Since you *reject* it
and judge *yourselves* to be *unworthy* of eternal *life*,
we are now turning to the *Gentiles*.
For so the Lord has *commanded* us, saying,
'I have set you to be a *light* for the *Gentiles*,
so that you may bring *salvation* to the ends of the *earth*.'"

READING I  The Acts of the Apostles consistently presents the gospel being preached first to Jews, at least some of whom subsequently reject it, and only then to Gentiles. Paul describes himself as the apostle to the Gentiles and gives no hint that he first tried to preach to Jews. But the author of Acts strongly affirms Jesus' role as the fulfillment of the promises made to Israel, as well as his cosmic role as savior of the world.

The story of the earliest Christian communities is one in which initial success is followed by failure, often because of the objections of powerful members of the larger Jewish community. Here, we are told that many Jews were interested in the message of Paul and Barnabas, but the Jewish leaders and other prominent Jews impeded the progress of the gospel. The final note, however, is one of triumph; God overcomes all opposition.

Christianity's success among Gentiles is well known. This passage depicts Paul and Barnabas quoting from one of the suffering servant songs of the prophet Isaiah, in which the promises to Israel are extended to all the nations. Like the servant, the Christian community is to reach out to all peoples in order to bring salvation. You share the servant's mission: to proclaim the faith to all so that everyone may proclaim Christ's universal reign.

Read this passage with the same boldness that Paul and Barnabas must have felt as they proclaimed the word of God. Do not shrink from the reality of opposition that they experienced, but at the same time emphasize the success of their mission and the ultimate victory of God.

**4TH SUNDAY OF EASTER ■ MAY 6, 2001**

When the *Gentiles* heard this,
they were *glad* and *praised* the word of the *Lord*;
and as many as had been destined for eternal *life*
	became *believers*.

Thus the *word* of the Lord *spread* throughout the *region*.
But the *officials* incited the devout *women* of high standing
and the leading *men* of the city,
and stirred up *persecution* against Paul and Barnabas,
and *drove* them out of their *region*.
So they shook the *dust* off their *feet* in protest *against* them,
and went to *Iconium*.
And the disciples were filled with *joy* and with the Holy *Spirit*.

---

**READING II**     Revelation 7:9, 14b–17

**"Revelation," not "Revelations."**

**A reading from the book of Revelation**

After this *I*, John, *looked*,
and there was a great *multitude* that no one could *count*,
from every *nation*, from all *tribes* and *peoples* and *languages*,
standing before the *throne* and before the *Lamb*,
robed in *white*, with *palm* branches in their hands.

And one of the *elders* then said to me,
"*These* are *they* who have come out of the great *ordeal*;
they have *washed* their *robes*
and made them *white* in the blood of the *Lamb*.

---

**READING II** John the seer continues to describe his visionary experience in today's reading, building upon the accounts we have been hearing throughout the Easter season. John witnesses the heavenly scene in which the righteous—purified and holy, including those martyrs who have been made victorious in death—stand before God (the throne) and Christ (the Lamb). Together with the heavenly host, they offer praise to God, who protects them.

There are two key concepts that deserve emphasis in this passage. The first is the universality of the righteous community. The righteous ones, as is made clear elsewhere in Revelation, include members from all the tribes of Israel but are not limited to the Jews. Instead, the redeemed are from every people and nation. Salvation is available to all who have "washed their robes" by trusting in the saving action of Jesus, the Lamb of God.

The second important aspect of the vision is the comfort and life-giving sustenance that Christ the shepherd provides for his sheep. They will have no want or discomfort but will be refreshed with the waters of life. The selection ends with the touching affirmation that there will no longer be pain or sorrow on that day.

In this Easter season, we celebrate the promise of John's vision and look forward to the day when all tears will be wiped away. Proclaim the beginning of this passage boldly, emphasizing the universality of salvation, and conclude with tenderness as you describe the joys of the eternal life.

MAY 6, 2001 ■ 4TH SUNDAY OF EASTER

**Speak this promise with hope and a sense of comfort. All will be well.**

For *this* reason they are before the throne of *God*,
and *worship* him day and night within his *temple*,
and the one who is *seated* on the *throne* will *shelter* them.
"They will *hunger* no more, and *thirst* no more;
the *sun* will not *strike* them, nor any scorching *heat*;
for the *Lamb* at the *centre* of the throne will be their *shepherd*,
and he will *guide* them to *springs* of the water of *life*,
and God will wipe away every *tear* from their *eyes*."

---

### GOSPEL    John 10:27–30

**A reading from the holy gospel according to John**

**Since the gospel is so short, read it slowly and with extra care.**

Jesus said:
"My *sheep* hear my *voice*.
I *know* them, and they *follow* me.
I give them eternal *life*, and they will never *perish*.
*No* one will snatch them out of my *hand*.
What my Father has *given* me is *greater* than all *else*,
and *no* one can snatch it out of the Father's *hand*.

**This statement suggests Jesus' lordship. Speak slowly and clearly.**

The *Father* and I are *one*."

---

GOSPEL   The gospel of John often uses the image of a sheepfold to explain the relationship between Jesus and his followers. The shepherd guides and cares for the sheep, and the sheep follow willingly. Just as the shepherd risks his life to care for the sheep, so also Jesus gives his life for his flock.

The larger context of this passage is the conflict between the Jewish leadership and Jesus. When the leaders ask Jesus if he is the Messiah, Jesus responds with the pastoral imagery that fills this passage. But

the thrust of his message is that those who question him do not belong to him and do not listen to his message. Those who belong to him know him and he knows them. He gives them life, a life that is eternal and cannot be taken from them.

In addition to the loving care Jesus provides for his followers and their devotion to him, Jesus here affirms his oneness with God. In a remarkably strong statement of the unity of Jesus and the Father, Jesus claims to bear God's power and authority. It is this claim—"The Father and I are one"—that will stir up animosity among his Jewish

adversaries. It is too much for them to take, and they will threaten to stone him.

Offer this short passage to your assembly as a statement of Christ's profound love and care for the church. Speak tenderly but with authority, just as Jesus does. Give yourself plenty of time so that your listeners can ponder every word.

MAY 13, 2001

# 5TH SUNDAY OF EASTER

*Lectionary #54*

### READING I    Acts 14:21b–27

**A reading from the Acts of the Apostles**

Lystra = LĪS-truh
Iconium = ī-KOH-nee-uhm
Antioch = AN-tee-ahk

*Paul* and *Barnabas* returned to *Lystra*,
then on to *Iconium* and *Antioch*.
There they *strengthened* the souls of the *disciples*
and encouraged them to *continue* in the *faith*, saying,
"It is through many *persecutions*
that we must enter the *kingdom* of *God.*"
And after they had appointed *elders* for them in each *church*,
with *prayer* and *fasting* they entrusted them to the *Lord*
in whom they had come to *believe*.

Pisidia = pih-SID-ee-uh
Pamphylia = pam-FIL-ee-uh
Perga = PER-guh
Attalia = uh-TAHL-ee-uh

Then they passed through *Pisidia* and came to *Pamphylia*.
When they had spoken the word in *Perga*,
they went down to *Attalia*.
From *there* they sailed back to *Antioch*,
where they had been *commended* to the grace of *God*
for the *work* that they had *completed*.

Stress the activity of God in their ministry.

When they *arrived*, they called the church *together*
and related *all* that God had *done* with them,
and how he had opened a *door* of *faith* for the *Gentiles*.

---

READING I Paul's first missionary journey ended with a return to Antioch in Syria, following stops in several of the cities he had visited earlier. Barnabas was Paul's faithful companion and coworker on that first journey, but they soon parted ways after an argument to pursue separate missionary careers.

The Acts of the Apostles presents Antioch as the community from which Paul began his missionary activity. Paul and Barnabas report back to the Christians in Antioch about their travels and their work among the Gentiles. The author also reports that Paul and Barnabas established church leadership in each of the communities they visited, a detail lacking in Paul's own letters. The author of Acts was writing several decades later than Paul did and may have depended on his own knowledge of contemporary church structure.

Given their own experience of rejection during their missionary work, it is not surprising that Paul and Barnabas find it necessary to encourage the newly-formed communities to withstand persecution. Their message that one enters the kingdom of God through persecution is strikingly similar to the message in Paul's letters that suffering is an essential component of the Christian life. Yet it is through suffering that Christians find deep joy.

This passage is a fairly straightforward account of the return of Paul and Barnabas to Antioch. Be sure to practice the place names until you are comfortable with them. Stress the message Paul and Barnabas convey to their churches and the fact that they are not working on their own. Rather, it is God who works through them.

MAY 13, 2001 ■ 5TH SUNDAY OF EASTER

## READING II    Revelation 21:1–5a

**A reading from the book of Revelation**

"Revelation," not "Revelations."

Then I, *John*, saw a new *heaven* and a new *earth*;
for the *first* heaven and the *first* earth had passed *away*,
and the *sea* was no *more*.

And I saw the holy *city*, the new *Jerusalem*,
coming *down* out of *heaven* from *God*,
prepared as a *bride* adorned for her *husband*.

Speak with authority.

And I heard a loud *voice* from the *throne* saying,
"*See*, the *home* of *God* is among *mortals*.
He will *dwell* with them as their *God*;
they will be his *peoples*,
and God *himself* will be *with* them;

Lower your voice and speak tenderly.

he will wipe every *tear* from their *eyes*.
*Death* will be no *more*;
*mourning* and *crying* and *pain* will be no *more*,
for the *first* things have passed *away*."
And the one who was seated on the *throne* said,

Close strongly, with a bright voice, as you relay God's promise.

"*See*, I am making *all* things *new*."

---

**READING II** As on previous Sundays during the Easter season, we again hear from the visionary John about his experience in the heavenly realm. Found near the end of the book of Revelation, the present passage describes the period of Christ's reign.

Christ's reign will usher in a new age, characterized by a new heaven and a new earth. In that coming age, a new Jerusalem, symbolic of the church, will be united with God, just as the earthly Jerusalem had once served as the center of God's activity on earth. God's union with the chosen people

will be complete and final. In that new era, God will no longer be distant, reigning only in heaven. God's home will be among humankind. It will be a time of joy and peace, a time when the sting of death will no longer be felt.

The promises of Revelation have yet to be completely realized. They were written to give hope to a persecuted people, and they continue to provide hope for us today. Proclaim this passage as God's promise to your community and to all Christians. Let your voice be filled with hope as you share this encouraging message.

**GOSPEL** The setting for this scene is Jesus' last meal with his disciples. The Passover is approaching, the time when Jesus' role as the paschal lamb will be evident. His love for his followers is apparent in all that he does, but especially in his willingness to die for them. The theme of love returns when Jesus' discusses the responsibility of his followers to love one another.

Jesus speaks of his own glorification which, in this gospel, always refers to his death on the cross. Far from an ignominious, shameful death, it is the means by which

# 5TH SUNDAY OF EASTER ■ MAY 13, 2001

## GOSPEL  John 13:1, 31–33a, 34–35

**A reading from the holy gospel according to John**

Before the *festival* of the *Passover*,
Jesus *knew* that his *hour* had come
to *depart* from this world and go to the *Father*.
Having loved his *own* who were in the world,
he *loved* them to the *end*.

**Speak slowly and solemnly.**

During the *supper*, when Judas had gone *out*, Jesus said,
"*Now* the Son of Man has been *glorified*,
and *God* has been glorified *in* him.
If God has been glorified *in* him,
God will also glorify *him* in *himself*
and will *glorify* him at *once*.

**Let your voice be filled with tenderness.**

"Little *children*, I am with you only a little *longer*.
I give you a *new* commandment,
that you *love* one *another*.
Just as *I* have loved *you*,
you *also* should love one *another*.

**Offer this directly to your community, as both encouragement and challenge.**

By *this* everyone will *know* that you are my *disciples*,
if you have *love* for one *another*."

---

Jesus is exalted and revealed as Lord of all. The author writes from the perspective of a believer in the risen Jesus, and Jesus speaks in this passage as the one who is already exalted. Everything is spoken in the context of his death and resurrection. He is already glorified and gives glory to God by being raised up—exalted—on the cross.

The new commandment to love is a theme throughout this gospel and, indeed, throughout the New Testament. Here, however, it has a very specific meaning. It is the members of the church, the followers of the risen Jesus, who are to love one another. There is no concern for the community beyond the church in this particular passage. This love stems from Jesus' own love for his followers and is a sign of their discipleship. Indeed, the early Christian community was characterized by its adherence to this command, and Christians were proud to

know that others said of them, "See how they love one another."

Since this reading is being used during the Easter season, Jesus' words that he will remain only a little while longer might be understood to refer to his time on earth before his ascension. It is not entirely necessary to concern your listeners with correct chronology. Emphasize instead the two themes of this short selection: Jesus' glorification and the command to love.

MAY 20, 2001

# 6TH SUNDAY OF EASTER

*Lectionary #57*

### READING I    Acts 15:1–2, 22–29

## A reading from the Acts of the Apostles

Certain *individuals* came down from *Judea*
and were teaching the brothers,
"Unless you are *circumcised* according to the custom of *Moses*,
you cannot be *saved*."
And after *Paul* and *Barnabas* had no small *dissension*
and *debate* with them,
*Paul* and *Barnabas* and some of the *others* were appointed
to go up to *Jerusalem* to *discuss* this question
with the *apostles* and the *elders*.

Then the *apostles* and the *elders*,
with the consent of the *whole* church,
decided to choose men from among their *members*
and to send them to *Antioch* with *Paul* and *Barnabas*.

They sent *Judas* called *Barsabbas*, and *Silas*,
	*leaders* among the brothers,
with the following *letter*:

"The *brothers*, both the *apostles* and the *elders*,
to the believers of Gentile *origin*
in *Antioch* and *Syria* and *Cilicia*, greetings.

---

**This was a very emotional issue. Try to convey some of the anguish of the debate in your voice.**

**Antioch = AN-tee-ahk**

**Barsabbas = bahr-SAH-buhs**
**Silas = SĪ-luhs**

**Cilicia = sih-LISH-ee-uh**

---

In the dioceses of Canada, the solemnity of the Ascension of the Lord is celebrated on Sunday, May 27, 2001. For this reason, the second reading and the gospel for the Seventh Sunday of Easter may be used today. Consult you liturgy coordinator or pastor to find out which readings will be used today.

READING I | The most pressing issue facing the young church in the first century was the question of whether

Gentiles were included in the salvation offered in Christ. Some people held that it was necessary to become Jewish in order to be Jesus' disciple, since Jesus himself said that he had come to save the lost sheep of Israel. Others, notably Paul, argued strongly for freedom in Christ and believed that the gospel was to be preached to everyone, Jews and non-Jews alike.

Today's reading describes this conflict and the compromise solution envisioned by the author of Acts. As always in Acts, the Jerusalem community is central and has decision-making power. The Jerusalem

Christians send delegates with a letter insisting that they had not been consulted about the Jewish-Christian claim that circumcision was necessary for followers of Christ. Instead, they reject such a requirement but affirm the importance of certain dietary restrictions and ethical demands.

We know from Paul's own letters that including all people in God's embrace was of paramount importance to him. Paul emphatically rejects the necessity of the Jewish

## 6TH SUNDAY OF EASTER ■ MAY 20, 2001

Since we have *heard* that certain *persons*
    who have gone *out* from us,
though with no *instructions* from *us*,
have said things to *disturb* you and have *unsettled* your *minds*,
we have decided *unanimously* to choose *representatives*
and *send* them to you,
along with our beloved *Barnabas* and *Paul*,
who have risked their *lives*
for the sake of our *Lord* Jesus *Christ*.
We have therefore sent *Judas* and *Silas*,
who *themselves* will tell you the *same* things by word of *mouth*.
"For it has seemed *good* to the Holy *Spirit* and to *us*
to *impose* on you no further *burden* than these *essentials*:
that you *abstain* from what has been sacrificed to *idols*,
and from *blood* and from what is *strangled*,
and from *fornication*.
If you *keep* yourselves from *these*, you will do *well*.
*Farewell*."

law, although he continues to uphold ethical demands for Christians. In addition, Paul views himself as an apostle directly called by Christ, not one sent from the community in Jerusalem or any other place.

The solution to the question of circumcision offered by the Jerusalem community is one with biblical precedent. The specified regulations are those that were required of Gentiles who were dwelling among Jews.

The author of Acts, therefore, upholds the importance of the Jewish law and the central claim that salvation is first for the Jews, while at the same time extending the possibility of salvation to all. By following the requirements to abstain from certain foods and from sexual immorality, the non-Jews

are, in a strict sense, keeping the law of Moses as far as it was intended for them.

The central message of this passage is the universality of the Christian message. Jesus came to save all nations, and all people are able to be his followers. Emphasize strongly this message of inclusion and acceptance of others.

MAY 20, 2001 ■ 6TH SUNDAY OF EASTER

**READING II** Revelation 21:10–14, 22–23

## A reading from the book of Revelation

In the *spirit* the angel carried me *away* to a great, high *mountain*
and showed me the holy city *Jerusalem*
coming *down* out of heaven from *God.*
It has the *glory* of *God* and a *radiance* like a very rare *jewel,*
like *jasper,* clear as *crystal.*

It has a *great,* high *wall* with twelve *gates,*
and at the *gates* twelve *angels,*
and *on* the gates are inscribed the *names*
of the twelve *tribes* of the *Israelites;*
on the *east* there were *three* gates,
on the *north* three gates,
on the *south* three gates,
and on the *west* three gates.

And the *wall* of the city has twelve *foundations,*
and on *them* are the twelve *names*
of the twelve *apostles* of the *Lamb.*

I saw *no temple* in the city,
for its *temple* is the Lord God the *Almighty* and the *Lamb.*
And the city has no need of *sun* or *moon* to *shine* on it,
for the *glory* of *God* is its *light,*
and its *lamp* is the *Lamb.*

"Revelation," not "Revelations."

Let your voice convey the beauty of the image.

Begin this sentence with a tone of surprise, then conclude with conviction.

READING II The seer John continues to describe his otherworldly vision, building on the images we have heard throughout the Easter season. In today's passage, he sees a vision of the heavenly Jerusalem. Jerusalem was regarded by the Jewish faithful and by Christians—Jewish and non-Jewish—as the spiritual center of the world. But it was destroyed by the Romans a few decades before John wrote Revelation. Jerusalem remains central to his

thought, however, but the city he envision is a new Jerusalem, resplendent and holy.

The new Jerusalem has twelve gates, each bearing the name of one of the twelve tribes of Israel, and twelve foundation stones with the names of the apostles. These features confirm that the new Jerusalem is in fact the Christian church, built on the foundation of the apostles and the heritage of

Israel. It is a priestly city, yet it has no need of a temple. In the temple's place is God and the Lamb who has been sacrificed. The city shines, bedecked in jewels and illuminated by the glory of God.

Meditate on this passage until you can proclaim with awe the splendor of God's people, imaged as the city of Jerusalem. Read the passage with wonder in your voice and also firm conviction of God's glory evident in the church.

6TH SUNDAY OF EASTER ■ MAY 20, 2001

## GOSPEL    John 14:23–29

**A reading from the holy gospel according to John**

Jesus said to his disciples:
"Those who *love* me will keep my *word*,
and my *Father* will love *them*,
and we will *come* to them
        and make our *home* with them.
Whoever does *not* love me does *not* keep my words;
and the word that you *hear* is not *mine*,
but is from the *Father* who *sent* me.

"I have *said* these things to you while I am still *with* you.
But the *Advocate*, the Holy *Spirit*,
whom the Father will *send* in my *name*,
will teach you *everything*,
and *remind* you of all that I have *said* to you.

"*Peace* I leave with you;
my *peace* I *give* to you.
I do not *give* to you as the *world* gives.
Do not let your hearts be *troubled*,
and do not let them be *afraid*.

"You heard me *say* to you,
'I am going *away*, and I am *coming* to you.'
If you *loved* me,
you would *rejoice* that I am going to the *Father*,
because the *Father* is *greater* than I.
And now I have *told* you this before it *occurs*,
so that when it *does* occur, you may *believe*."

---

**There is challenge in this message: Rejecting Jesus' word is to reject the Father who sent him.**

**Speak with warmth and comfort.**

---

GOSPEL    In the gospel of John, Jesus addresses his disciples in a farewell discourse prior to his arrest and crucifixion. It focuses on the centrality of love in the life of each of his followers and the unity in love of the Father and Jesus. Both of these aspects of the love command are found in today's gospel.

Loving Jesus has demands; it involves keeping his word, which is not simply his own but the word of the Father. But the primary feature of this word is precisely the importance of love. There are also rewards to keeping Jesus' command: God will come to dwell in those who adhere to his word. And when he is gone he will not leave his followers to struggle alone but will send the Spirit to teach and guide them.

In words that suggest he will soon depart, Jesus offers peace to his listeners. This peace is not simply the absence of conflict or lack of anxiety, but a deep, abiding peace. Although in the context of this passage Jesus' departure refers to his death (which, in this gospel, is identical with his glorification), your listeners might understand it to refer to his ascension, to be celebrated later this week. Jesus goes away to take his rightful place with the Father, and those who love him should rejoice.

Read this passage slowly and carefully as a word of comfort and challenge to your assembly. Jesus offers peace to those who trust in him but also demands that Christian communities be places of profound love.

# MAY 24, 2001

# ASCENSION OF THE LORD

*Lectionary #58*

## READING I   Acts 1:1–11

**A reading from the Acts of the Apostles**

Theophilus = thee-OF-uh-luhs
The name means "lover of God."

In the *first* book, *Theophilus*,
I wrote about *all* that Jesus *did* and *taught* from the *beginning*
until the *day* when he was taken up to *heaven*,
after giving *instructions* through the Holy *Spirit*
to the *apostles* whom he had *chosen*.
After his *suffering* he presented himself *alive* to them
by *many* convincing *proofs*,
*appearing* to them during *forty* days
and *speaking* about the *kingdom* of God.

While *staying* with them,
    he *ordered* them not to leave *Jerusalem*,
but to *wait* there for the *promise* of the *Father*.
"*This*," he said, "is what you have *heard* from *me*;
for *John* baptized with *water*,
but *you* will be baptized with the Holy *Spirit*
not many *days* from *now*."

Speak this sentence slowly and forcefully, addressing it to your assembly. The Acts of the Apostles is written as a fulfillment of this prediction.

So when they had come *together*, they asked him,
"*Lord*, is *this* the time
    when you will restore the *kingdom* to *Israel*?"
He replied, "It is *not* for you to *know* the *times* or *periods*
that the *Father* has *set* by his own *authority*.

---

In the dioceses of Canada, the solemnity of the Ascension of the Lord is celebrated on Sunday, May 27, 2001.

READING I The opening section of the Acts of the Apostles tells of Jesus' presence with the disciples after the resurrection and of his ascension into heaven. Because he is said to have appeared among them for 40 days, this feast has been fixed on the calendar 40 days after Easter.

In biblical terminology, 40 days indicates a considerable length of time; it is not to be taken at face value. In fact, this dating contradicts the gospel of Luke, to which the Acts of the Apostles is the sequel. In the gospel, Jesus ascends to heaven on the evening of Easter Sunday.

The events described in the opening chapters of the Acts of the Apostles (including the ascension and Pentecost) are not told as historical occurrences. Rather, the author is creatively making claims of faith about Jesus and his followers. The story of

the ascension conveys that Jesus is glorified, that his rightful home is with God in heaven. Similarly, the story of Pentecost describes the disciples' experience of the Spirit of God in their lives.

What is important is that the 50 days from Easter to Pentecost are all included in the Easter season. This is the time when we ritually celebrate for an extended period the victory of Christ over death, his vindication after being executed, his exaltation and his

**182**

ASCENSION OF THE LORD ■ MAY 24, 2001

But you will receive *power*
when the Holy *Spirit* has come *upon* you;
and *you* will be my *witnesses* in *Jerusalem*,
in all *Judea* and *Samaria*, and to the *ends* of the *earth*."

When he had *said* this, as they were *watching*,
he was lifted *up*, and a *cloud* took him out of their *sight*.
While he was *going* and they were gazing up toward *heaven*,
*suddenly* two men in white *robes* stood *by* them.
They said, "Men of *Galilee*,
*why* do you stand looking up toward *heaven*?
This *Jesus*, who has been taken *up* from you into *heaven*,
will *come* in the *same* way as you saw him *go* into *heaven*."

The expectation that Jesus would soon return on the clouds of heaven was active in the early years of Christianity.

---

**READING II**    Hebrews 9:24–28; 10:19–23

**A reading from the letter to the Hebrews**

*Christ* did not enter a sanctuary made by human *hands*,
a mere *copy* of the true one,
but he entered into heaven *itself*,
to appear in the presence of *God* on our *behalf*.
Nor was it to *offer* himself again and *again*,
as the high *priest* enters the Holy Place
year after *year* with *blood* that is not his *own*;
for *then* he would have had to *suffer* again and *again*
since the *foundation* of the *world*.
But as it *is*, he has *appeared* once for *all* at the end of the *age*
to remove *sin* by the *sacrifice* of *himself*.

Make clear the contrast between Christ's action and that of the temple high priest.

---

continued presence, through the working of the Holy Spirit, with his followers on earth. The Easter season is one extended feast, although we concentrate on different aspects of Christ's triumph at different times during the season.

Today's reading is an awe-inspiring account of Jesus' exaltation to his rightful place with God. As a good teacher, he instructs his followers right to the end and closes by giving them a commission to go

forth in his name. In a manner similar to the women's discovery of the empty tomb, two men (presumably angels) appear to the apostles and tell them where Jesus is. Because they have yet to receive the gift of the Holy Spirit, the disciples remain confused, even after all that they have seen and heard.

There are several "voices" to adopt in the reading of this selection. It opens on a historical note, summarizing the gospel; this can be read in a straightforward manner. Raise your voice to proclaim the words of Jesus to his followers. Their question to him

is asked innocently enough, ignorant though it may sound to us. Finally, the ascension itself is exciting, and the proclamation of the angels should be given due emphasis. Throughout, your goal is to make real to your listeners the great majesty of Jesus, now enthroned in heaven.

READING II  The letter to the Hebrews contrasts the true and perfect heavenly sacrifice made by Christ, the heavenly high priest, with the sacrifice of

MAY 24, 2001 ■ ASCENSION OF THE LORD

**Pause after "judgment," then raise your voice as if to start anew.**

Just as it is appointed for *mortals* to die *once*,
and *after* that comes the *judgment*,
so *Christ*, having been offered *once* to bear the sins of *many*,
will appear a *second* time,
not to deal with *sin*,
but to *save* those who are eagerly *waiting* for him.

**Speak warmly and confidently.**

*Therefore*, my friends,
since we have *confidence* to enter the *sanctuary*
by the *blood* of *Jesus*,
by the *new* and living *way* that he *opened* for us
through the *curtain*, that is, through his *flesh*,
and since we have a *great priest* over the house of *God*,
let us *approach* with a true *heart* in full *assurance* of *faith*,
with our *hearts* sprinkled *clean* from an evil *conscience*
and our bodies *washed* with pure *water*.
Let us hold *fast* to the confession of our *hope* without *wavering*,
for he who has *promised* is *faithful*.

the Jewish cult. Today's passage is an excellent summary of some of the main issues and claims.

Hebrews envisions a heavenly temple upon which the temple in Jerusalem was modeled. The Jerusalem temple was first and foremost a place of animal sacrifice, but it also contained within it an especially sacred area, the Holy of Holies. Once a year, on the feast of Yom Kippur, the high priest of the temple would enter into this holiest area of the building and emerge to pronounce the

divine name. A scapegoat was then sent into the desert to carry away the people's sins. Animal sacrifices were also performed on a daily basis in the temple for other purposes: in thanksgiving, to ask for forgiveness, and so on.

The principle contrast here between Christ's sacrifice and that of the Hebrew cult is the uniqueness of Jesus' action. He entered heaven itself to offer himself once for all. The Jewish cult operated in a copy of the true sanctuary, and its sacrifices had to be repeated over and over again. The high priest could only offer inadequate animal

sacrifices, but Jesus offered the perfect sacrifice of himself.

Jesus' entry into that heavenly sanctuary opens the way for all of his followers to enter as well. Because of what he has done, Christians can approach the gate of heaven in sincerity and trust, knowing that we have been forgiven.

Although the imagery may be foreign to your listeners, the message of forgiveness and confidence in approaching God is one that we all need to hear. Address the second

# ASCENSION OF THE LORD ■ MAY 24, 2001

---

## GOSPEL    Luke 24:44–53

**A reading from the holy gospel according to Luke**

Jesus said to the disciples,
"*These* are my words that I *spoke* to you
while I was still *with* you —
that everything *written* about me in the law of *Moses*,
the *prophets*, and the *psalms* must be *fulfilled*."

Then he *opened* their minds to understand the *scriptures*,
and he said to them,
"*Thus* it is *written*, that the *Messiah* is to *suffer*
and to *rise* from the *dead* on the third *day*,
and that *repentance* and forgiveness of *sins* is to be *proclaimed*
in his *name* to all *nations*, beginning from *Jerusalem*.
You are *witnesses* of these things.

"And *see*, I am sending upon you what my Father *promised*;
so stay here in the *city*
until you have been clothed with *power* from on *high*."

Then he led them *out* as far as *Bethany*,
and, lifting up his *hands*, he *blessed* them.
While he was *blessing* them,
he *withdrew* from them and was carried up into *heaven*.
And they *worshipped* him,
and *returned* to Jerusalem with great *joy*;
and they were continually in the *temple* blessing *God*.

---

*Pause and take a breath after "day."*

*Speak forcefully the promise of heavenly power.*

*Let your voice be filled with awe and peacefulness.*

---

section of the passage directly to the members of your assembly, in order to encourage them to approach God boldly, knowing that forgiveness is theirs.

**GOSPEL** Both the gospel of Luke and its companion volume, the Acts of the Apostles, contain accounts of the ascension of Jesus into heaven; we read both passages today. The gospel account is simpler than the one in Acts, but both affirm that Jesus is exalted at the right hand of God, where he is given dominion and glory.

The disciples who witness the ascension have already participated in the great events of salvation. They were crushed by the reality of Jesus' death but have experienced his victory over death. They have been preaching about him and his offer of forgiveness. Now they see him exalted, and soon they will be given the gift of power.

Jesus' departure is relatively uneventful in the gospel account. He blesses his friends and takes leave of them. But their response is telling: They worship him and rejoice, knowing that he has prevailed and that what he has promised will occur.

We too have participated in the anguish of Jesus' death and the joy of knowing that he has triumphed over death. We too are witnesses to his name. Proclaim this passage as a call to the members of your assembly to open their hearts continually to the activity of the Spirit in their lives and to join their voices in praise to God.

MAY 27, 2001

# 7TH SUNDAY OF EASTER

*Lectionary #61*

## READING I   Acts 7:55–60

**A reading from the Acts of the Apostles**

Standing before the high *priest* and the *council*,
*Stephen*, filled with the Holy *Spirit*,
gazed into *heaven* and saw the *glory* of *God*
and *Jesus* standing at the right *hand* of God.
"*Look*," he said, "I see the heavens *opened*
and the Son of *Man* standing at the right *hand* of *God!*"

But they covered their *ears*,
and with a loud *shout* all *rushed* together *against* him.
Then they *dragged* him out of the *city* and began to *stone* him;
and the *witnesses* laid their *coats*
at the *feet* of a young man named *Saul.*

While they were *stoning* Stephen, he prayed,
"Lord *Jesus*, receive my *spirit.*"
Then he knelt *down* and cried out in a loud *voice*,
"*Lord*, do not hold this sin *against* them."
When he had *said* this, he *died.*

**Speak Stephen's words with forcefulness and conviction. Then let your voice express the anger and hostility of the crowd.**

**Again, Stephen speaks with conviction and a sense of peacefulness.**

---

In the dioceses of Canada, the solemnity of the Ascension of the Lord is celebrated today.

READING I Stephen is the first Christian martyr, the first person to suffer death for his faith. His fate resembles that of Jesus: He is innocent, but his detractors are filled with animosity; he prays for forgiveness for those who are taking his life; and he asks Jesus to receive his spirit.

Although Stephen is already on trial as the scene opens, it is his description of a vision that apparently stirs the ire of his accusers. Not only does he claim that Jesus was no longer dead, but he also declares that Jesus is exalted with God. Such talk must have sounded like blasphemy to the religious leadership.

Stephen's hearers attack him in anger, viciously dragging him out of the city and stoning him. Ironically, the only member of the mob who is named is Saul (later renamed Paul), the person who will figure prominently in the Acts of the Apostles as the missionary to the Gentiles and who will repeatedly risk his life for the sake of the gospel. Indeed, Paul himself admits that he zealously persecuted the Christians prior to his own encounter with the risen Lord.

The drama in this passage makes it especially interesting to read. Proclaim the opening vision with a sense of awe, then increase the tension in your voice as you describe the fury of Stephen's attackers. Close with a declaration of Stephen's conviction and generous spirit.

**186**
7TH SUNDAY OF EASTER ▪ MAY 27, 2001

### READING II    Revelation 22:12–14, 16–17, 20

"Revelation," not "Revelations."

Alpha = AHL-fuh
Omega = oh-MAY-guh

Speak gently these words of comfort and promise.

Let each line stand on its own, and emphasize the word, "Come." Proclaim the final line of the reading as a fervent prayer of hope.

### A reading from the book of Revelation

I, *John*, heard a voice saying to me:
"*See*, I am coming *soon;*
my *reward* is *with* me,
to *repay* according to everyone's *work.*
I am the *Alpha* and the *Omega,*
the *first* and the *last,*
the *beginning* and the *end.*"

*Blessed* are those who *wash* their *robes,*
so that they will have the *right* to the *tree* of *life*
and may enter the *city* by the *gates.*

"It is I, *Jesus,* who sent my *angel* to you
with this *testimony* for the *churches.*
I am the *root* and the *descendant* of *David,*
the *bright* morning *star.*"

The *Spirit* and the *bride* say, "*Come.*"
And let everyone who *hears* say, "*Come.*"
And let everyone who is *thirsty* come.
Let anyone who *wishes* take the water of *life* as a *gift.*
The one who *testifies* to these things says,
"*Surely* I am coming *soon.*"
*Amen. Come,* Lord *Jesus!*

---

READING II John's vision concludes with Christ's promise to come again. The passages from the book of Revelation that have been read during the Easter season have described persecution and terror, victory and triumph. Now John conveys the eschatological hope that Jesus will return to bring to completion the work he has begun. He is the first and last, the sum of everything, beyond all human comprehension. He comes as judge to draw his

own into the heavenly abode so that they may eat of the fruit of immortality.

In response to Jesus' promise to come soon, the Spirit and the bride (the Christian church) proclaim, "Come." All who hear are welcome to join in the appeal to the risen Lord. The cry of hope rises to heaven: "Come, Lord Jesus." But, in a paradoxical move, believers are also invited to come to the water of life available in baptism. All Christian liturgy is an expression of the belief that there is yet more to come and that Jesus will return as righteous judge.

We know that Jesus did not return immediately, as the early Christians hoped and expected. Yet we too can join our voices with theirs in a fervent prayer that God's work will be brought to completion. Proclaim this text with joyful expectation in Jesus' return and the profound belief that the risen Jesus is indeed first and last, the one who offers life in full and promises to draw all to himself.

MAY 27, 2001 ▪ 7TH SUNDAY OF EASTER

## GOSPEL  John 17:20–26

**A reading from the holy gospel according to John**

Jesus looked up to *heaven* and *prayed*:
"Holy *Father*,
I ask not only on behalf of *these*,
but also on behalf of those
who will *believe* in me through their *word*,
that they may *all* be *one*.
As *you*, Father, are in *me* and *I* am in *you*,
may they *also* be in *us*,
so that the *world* may *believe* that you have *sent* me.
The *glory* that you have given *me* I have given *them*,
so that they may be *one*, as *we* are one,
*I* in *them* and *you* in *me*,
that they may become *completely one*,
so that the world may *know* that you have *sent* me
and have *loved* them even as you have loved *me*.

"Father,
I desire that those *also*, whom you have *given* me,
may be *with* me where I *am*,
to see my *glory*, which you have *given* me
because you *loved* me before the *foundation* of the *world*.

"Righteous *Father*,
the world does not *know* you, but *I* know you;
and *these* know that you have *sent* me.
I made your name *known* to them,
and I *will* make it *known*,
so that the *love* with which you have *loved* me
may be in *them*, and *I* in them."

Offer this prayer for the members of your assembly, who have come to believe through the word of others.

Speak slowly and deliberately, so that the progression of thought will be clear.

Stress the unity of Jesus and the Father, and the love they share with one another and with us.

---

GOSPEL  The prayer of Jesus at the Last Supper in the gospel of John speaks of his unity with the Father and his glorification. In this gospel, Jesus' glorification is always tied to his crucifixion. Jesus is exalted in glory precisely as he is raised up on the cross.

Jesus' prayer extends beyond his intimate followers to include all believers, especially those who come to believe without having experienced him directly. Jesus prays that they may be as intimately united

with one another and with his heavenly Father as he is. This unity will serve to proclaim to the world the truth of Jesus' role as messenger of God's love.

Just as Jesus' true realm is heavenly, so also is the destiny of his followers. He prays that they might witness his exaltation. Most of all, Jesus insists that the love that the Father has for him inspires and enlivens his followers. Because Jesus and the Father are one, knowing Jesus means knowing God, and knowing God means abiding in God's love.

Proclaim this rich passage as the prayer that it is. Reflect on the members of your own community, and offer it for their sake, sincerely desiring their unity in love. Speak solemnly, yet with the hope that your prayer will be answered positively.

JUNE 2, 2001

# PENTECOST VIGIL

Shinar = SHĪ-nahr

bitumen = bih-TYOO-m*n

The sin is threefold: building a tower to the sky, seeking a great reputation, and remaining in one place.

*Lectionary #62*

## READING I    Genesis 11:1–9

**A reading from the book of Genesis**

Now the *whole* earth had *one language* and the same *words*.
And as people *migrated* from the *east*,
they came upon a plain in the land of *Shinar* and *settled* there.
And they said to one another,
"*Come*, let us make *bricks*, and burn them *thoroughly*."
And they had *brick* for *stone*,
and *bitumen* for *mortar*.

Then they said,
"*Come*, let us build ourselves a *city*,
and a *tower* with its top in the *heavens*,
and let us make a *name* for ourselves;
*otherwise* we shall be scattered *abroad*
upon the face of the *whole* earth."

The *Lord* came down to *see* the *city* and the *tower*,
which mortals had *built*.
And the Lord said, "*Look*, they are *one* people,
and they have all one *language*;
and this is only the *beginning* of what they will *do*;
*nothing* that they propose to do will *now* be *impossible* for them.
*Come*, let us go *down*, and *confuse* their language there,
so that they will not *understand* one another's *speech*."

So the Lord *scattered* them abroad from there
over the face of *all* the *earth*,

There is a choice of first readings today. Speak with the liturgy cordinator or pastor to find out which reading will be used.

READING I GENESIS. The story of the Tower of Babel is about human sin and alienation from God. The writer recalls a time at the beginning of human history when human relations were not characterized by division and when there

was no enmity between the divine and the human realms. But the writer's own experience is one of a world inhabited by many peoples who cannot communicate with one another and who are scattered widely over the earth. Today's reading explains what caused the change to occur.

The story of the Tower of Babel follows the tale of Noah, who was saved from the waters of the flood with his family because of his devotion to God. But they were not without sin, as Genesis makes clear. Noah's descendants build a city and a tower for the

express purpose of "making a name" (that is, gaining fame) for themselves, and to remain together against the command of God. The result is disastrous and their hope for unity destroyed; God scatters them and they cease to speak the same language.

At the root of the crime committed by the people was a desire to exceed human limitations, to make themselves as great as God (the phrase "to make a name" is reserved for actions of a ruler or of God). We know also that Near Eastern cultures built

JUNE 2, 2001 ■ PENTECOST VIGIL

**Babel = BAB-*l**
There is a play on words here between the name of the city and the Hebrew word for "confuse." It is somewhat like the English play on the words "Babel" and "babble."

and they left off *building* the *city*.
Therefore it was called *Babel*,
because *there* the Lord *confused* the language of *all* the *earth*;
and from *there* the Lord *scattered* them abroad
over the face of *all* the *earth*.

**Or:**

---

**READING I**    Exodus 19:3–8a, 16–20

**A reading from the book of Exodus**

Speak these words solemnly.

Moses went up to God;
the Lord *called* to him from the *mountain*, saying,
"*Thus* you shall say to the house of *Jacob*,
and tell the *Israelites*:
You have *seen* what I did to the *Egyptians*,

Lighten your voice as you read this beautiful image of how God rescued the people.

and how I bore you on *eagles'* wings
        and *brought* you to *myself*.
*Now* therefore, if you *obey* my voice and *keep* my covenant,
you shall be my treasured *possession* out of all the *peoples*.
Indeed, the whole *earth* is mine,
but *you* shall be for me a priestly *kingdom* and a *holy* nation.
*These* are the words
        that you shall *speak* to the *Israelites*."

So Moses *came*, summoned the *elders* of the people,
and set *before* them *all* these *words*
that the Lord had *commanded* him.
The people *all* answered as *one*:
"*Everything* that the Lord has *spoken* we will *do*."

Proclaim this slowly, so that your listeners can join in silently in their hearts. Then pause.

---

towers to the heavens in order to enter the realm of the gods. God acts to punish the pride of the humans and to keep them in their proper realm. As a result, they resume moving into the land as God had commanded, but without the ability to communicate with each other. Division and lack of understanding result.

Pentecost provides a reversal of the Babel story. At Pentecost, the misunderstandings that occur because of language differences are nullified; the Spirit moves so that the hearers understand Jesus' disciples speaking in their own languages. Unity is restored, but it is a unity under God's rule, not one that threatens to usurp divine authority.

Proclaim the reading with expression, communicating the arrogance of the people and the determination of God to correct their waywardness. Inspire your own community to seek unity and open communication, always acting under divine guidance.

**EXODUS.** God's presence is sometimes revealed in spectacular ways, as the appearance of the Holy Spirit on Pentecost will demonstrate. In that story, there is a sound like rushing wind, and tongues as of fire appear over the believers' heads. In this reading God's direct presence is also signaled by fire and smoke, by a loud trumpet and by the mountain shaking. Although we know that God is always present, we can sometimes forget this reality. The dramatic signs described in these readings make

**PENTECOST VIGIL ■ JUNE 2, 2001**

**God's presence is announced unmistakably. Speak awe in your voice.**

On the morning of the *third* day
  there was *thunder* and *lightning,*
as well as a thick *cloud* on the *mountain,*
and a blast of a *trumpet* so *loud*
that all the *people* who were in the camp *trembled.*
Moses brought the people *out* of the camp to meet *God.*
They took their *stand* at the foot of the *mountain.*
Now Mount *Sinai* was wrapped in *smoke,*
because the *Lord* had descended upon it in *fire;*
the *smoke* went up like the *smoke* of a *kiln,*
while the whole *mountain* shook *violently.*
As the *blast* of the *trumpet* grew *louder* and *louder,*
Moses would *speak* and God would *answer* him in *thunder.*

**Close quietly, with a sense of finality.**

When the Lord *descended* upon Mount *Sinai,*
to the *top* of the *mountain,*
the Lord summoned *Moses* to the top of the *mountain,*
and Moses went *up.*

Or:

---

**READING I**   Ezekiel 37:1–14

**A reading from the book of the prophet Ezekiel**

**The image is striking: God picks up Ezekiel and moves him into the valley.**

The *hand* of the Lord came *upon* me,
and he brought me out by the *spirit* of the *Lord*
and set me *down* in the middle of a *valley;*

**Imagine a scene of utter destruction in the middle of the desert. Try to convey this image to your listeners.**

it was *full* of *bones.*

---

**God's presence unmistakable, both to those who experienced them and to us.**

The present passage details part of Israel's encounter with God at Sinai. Immediately following this passage is the giving of the Ten Commandments by God. It is especially appropriate to hear this story today, since the Jewish feast of Pentecost (or Shavuot, the feast of Weeks) celebrates the giving of the law at Sinai. For both Christians and Jews, Pentecost is a time to recall the establishment of a covenant with God. But the covenant also involves accepting responsibility. The Israelites were to obey God and keep the law, while the first Christians were to go forth under the guidance of the Spirit and preach to all the good news of salvation in Christ.

Israel is reminded of all that God has already done for it before being asked to keep God's covenant. The people respond with a statement of profound commitment: "All that the Lord has said, we will do." This is our inspiration today, as we renew our pledge of faith.

The passage you are reading contains plenty of drama. Summon up your skills to convey the great love of God for the people in choosing them, the positive response on the part of Israel, and the magnificence of God evident in the signs. Challenge your listeners as well to proclaim with Israel a willingness to obey and serve God in whatever is asked of them.

JUNE 2, 2001 ■ PENTECOST VIGIL

He led me all *around* them;
there were very *many* lying in the *valley*,
and they were very *dry*.
He said to me, *"Mortal*, can these bones *live?"*
I answered, *"O* Lord *God, you* know."

Then he said to me,
*"Prophesy* to these bones, and *say* to them:
O dry *bones, hear* the *word* of the *Lord.*
*Thus* says the Lord God to these *bones:*
I will cause *breath* to *enter* you, and you shall *live.*
I will lay *sinews* on you,
and will cause *flesh* to come *upon* you,
and *cover* you with *skin*, and put *breath* in you,
and you shall *live;*
and you shall *know* that *I* am the *Lord."*

So I *prophesied* as I had been *commanded;*
and *as* I *prophesied*, suddenly there was a *noise*, a *rattling,*
and the bones came *together, bone* to its *bone.*
I *looked*, and there were *sinews* on them,
and *flesh* had come *upon* them, and *skin* had *covered* them;
but there was no *breath* in them.

Then he said to me,
*"Prophesy* to the *breath, prophesy*, mortal,
and *say* to the *breath: Thus* says the Lord *God:*
*Come* from the four *winds,*
and *breathe* upon these *slain*, that they may *live."*
I *prophesied* as he *commanded* me,
and the *breath* came *into* them,
and they *lived*, and stood on their *feet*, a vast *multitude.*

---

prophesy = PROF-uh-sī

sinews = SIN-yooz

The purpose of the bones coming to life is to acknowledge God. This is our purpose too, just as it was for Israel.

Although the bones appear human, they have life only with the coming of God's spirit.

---

**EZEKIEL.** Ezekiel's vision of dry bones was also used on the Fifth Sunday of Lent, Year A (see that commentary). Ezekiel wrote during the Babylonian exile, when the leaders of the kingdom of Judah were separated from their beloved land and forced to live in exile. It was a time of near despair, when many lost hope that they would ever return or that they would again live freely as a people.

The vision of dry bones is fundamentally a vision of hope. Ezekiel sees a valley filled with dry, lifeless bones. When he speaks the word of the Lord, the bones come together and take on human form. But only

when Ezekiel calls upon the breath or spirit to breathe into them do they truly come to life. It is God's spirit that gives life.

The renewed life accorded the bones is a symbol of the life that will come to Israel. God promises in this vision that Israel will be reconstituted, that it will once again exist as a nation. God has not abandoned Israel, but will always take care of the chosen people.

The life of the church also begins when the Holy Spirit breathes into the disciples on

Pentecost. It is a powerful Spirit, one that can bring life where there is only death. Read this story as it was first offered to the people in exile, as a promise of new life under God's care. Inspire your readers to be renewed and filled with life and energy as they reflect on the power of the Holy Spirit in their lives.

**JOEL.** The prophet Joel believed that the people of Israel had become complacent and as a result deserved to experience the judgment of God on the "great and terrible" Day of the Lord. But God chose not to act in

**PENTECOST VIGIL** ■ JUNE 2, 2001

This is a message of great hope to Israel, which considered itself dead in a foreign land.

Then he said to me,
"*Mortal*, these *bones* are the whole house of *Israel*.
They say, 'Our *bones* are dried *up*, and our *hope* is *lost*;
we are cut off *completely*.'
Therefore *prophesy*, and *say* to them,
*Thus* says the Lord *God*:
I am going to *open* your *graves*,
and bring you *up* from your *graves*, O my *people*;
and I will bring you *back* to the land of *Israel*.
And you shall *know* that *I* am the *Lord*,
when I *open* your *graves*,
and bring you *up* from your *graves*, O my *people*.
I will put my spirit *within* you, and you shall *live*,
and I will place you on your *own soil*;
then you shall know that *I*, the *Lord*,
have *spoken* and will *act*," says the Lord.

Speak this solemn vow with firmness.

**Or:**

---

## READING I    Joel 2:28–32

**A reading from the book of the prophet Joel**

*Thus* says the *Lord*:
I will *pour out* my *spirit* on all *flesh*;
your *sons* and your *daughters* shall *prophesy*,
your *elders* shall dream *dreams*,
and your *young* people shall see *visions*.
Even on the male and female *slaves*,
in those days, I will *pour out* my *spirit*.

prophesy = PROF-uh-sī

---

wrath but to draw Israel close and give this promise: God's spirit will be given to all people, regardless of nationality, age, sex or social status. Then, when the Day of the Lord arrives, those who respond to God's spirit and are faithful will be saved. It is a promise of hope and a fitting introduction to the feast of Pentecost, when the Holy Spirit is poured out on believers.

Offer this reading as a great promise of God's love and the inspiration of the Spirit. It is to be spoken forcefully, as a pledge made by God. Even the section about the sun turning to darkness and the moon to blood is a

statement of God's sovereignty over all things, including nature. Inspire your listeners to respond to the Holy Spirit in their lives and to strive to be part of the faithful remnant.

READING II  For Paul, all creation awaits fulfillment in God. Despite any sufferings he currently experiences, he is convinced that there is a glorious future to be revealed. In the present, the "first

fruits" of the Spirit (like a first installment) have been given, but this is simply a promise of what lies ahead. "Adoption" is both a present reality and something not yet completed. Paul often claims that Christians have been adopted into the family of God that is Israel, but in this passage, he says we still await adoption. This isn't all there is!

But the belief that there is more to come is part of the hope that saves us. We await it with patience; in the meantime, the Spirit moves through us, helping us to pray and interceding for us before God. In the

JUNE 2, 2001 ■ PENTECOST VIGIL

**Those who are faithful have nothing to fear.**

I will show *portents* in the *heavens* and on the *earth*,
*blood* and *fire* and columns of *smoke*.
The *sun* shall be turned to *darkness*,
and the *moon* to *blood*,
before the *great* and terrible *day* of the Lord *comes*.
Then *everyone* who calls on the *name* of the *Lord*
shall be *saved*;
for in Mount *Zion* and in *Jerusalem*
there shall be those who *escape*, as the Lord has *said*,
and among the *survivors* shall be *those* whom the Lord *calls*.

---

### READING II    Romans 8:22–27

**A reading from the letter of Paul to the Romans**

*Beloved*,
we *know* that the *whole creation*
has been *groaning* in *labour* pains until *now*;
and not only the *creation*, but we *ourselves*,
who have the *first fruits* of the *Spirit*,
groan *inwardly* while we wait for *adoption*,
the *redemption* of our *bodies*.

For in *hope* we were *saved*.
Now *hope* that is *seen* is *not* hope.
For who *hopes* for what is *seen*?
But if we *hope* for what we do *not* see,
we *wait* for it with *patience*.

**The "first fruits" were the portions of a grain sacrifice that were harvested first and offered in the temple as a promise of what was to come.**

**The key word here is "hope."**

---

end, everything will work for the good, and we will share in the glory of God.

The reading is straightforward but filled with reassurances. It is a reflection on what is and what is to be. Paul intends it as a way to instill hope in his readers. Offer it to the members of your community in the same manner, drawing them into a vision for the future in which all creation is united and at peace.

GOSPEL  The festival in question in today's gospel is the feast of Tabernacles or Booths, an important pilgrimage feast in the first century. It was associated with the triumph of God on the Day of the Lord, but retained some of its agricultural origins as an occasion of prayer for rain. The importance of water was emphasized during the feast; each day, water was carried in procession from a spring to the temple, where it was poured out and flowed onto the ground.

The emphasis on water apparently inspired Jesus to announce a truth about himself. He describes himself as a fountain from which the believer can drink to receive refreshment. The image of drinking from a fountain is used often in connection with Lady Wisdom, who satisfies the thirst for knowledge and right action. The Jewish scriptures hold Wisdom in high esteem. With God she cocreates the world. Jesus

**PENTECOST VIGIL ■ JUNE 2, 2001**

**While we are waiting in hope, the Spirit inspires us and prays through us.**

*Likewise* the Spirit *helps* us in our *weakness;*
for we do not know *how* to pray as we *ought,*
but that very Spirit *intercedes* with sighs too *deep* for *words.*
And *God*, who searches the *heart,*
*knows* what is the mind of the *Spirit,*
because the Spirit *intercedes* for the *saints*
according to the *will* of *God.*

---

**GOSPEL**   John 7:37–39

**A reading from the holy gospel according to John**

**Lift your voice and speak invitingly.**

On the last day of the *festival*, the *great* day,
while Jesus was *standing* in the *temple*, he cried out,
"Let *anyone* who is *thirsty come* to me,
and let the one who *believes* in me *drink.*
As the scripture has said,
'Out of the believer's *heart* shall flow *rivers* of living *water.'"*

Now he *said* this about the *Spirit,*
which *believers* in him were to *receive;*
for as *yet* there *was* no Spirit,
because *Jesus* was not yet *glorified.*

**The Spirit was given after Jesus' resurrection.**

---

is the font of wisdom, or even Wisdom in the flesh.

It should be noted that there has long been discussion about the source of the flowing waters; the Greek is unclear. Either the believer is the source of the water, as here, or Jesus is, as implied by some translations. Either way, the waters represent wisdom, a wisdom given by Jesus to those who seek it.

Although the water is a symbol of the teaching of Jesus, it is also identified by the redactor of the gospel as a representation of the Spirit, which will be given by Jesus after his death and resurrection. We proclaim on the feast of Pentecost that the Spirit indeed fills our lives and inspires our actions.

Emphasize the words of Jesus in this short passage. Invite the members of the assembly to approach him in confidence and to learn from him, filled with the fervent hope and faith inspired by God's gift of the Spirit.

# JUNE 3, 2001

# PENTECOST

*Lectionary #63*

## READING I    Acts 2:1–11

### A reading from the Acts of the Apostles

When the day of *Pentecost* had *come*,
they were all *together* in one *place*.
And *suddenly* from *heaven* there came a *sound*
like the *rush* of a violent *wind*,
and it *filled* the entire *house* where they were *sitting*.
Divided *tongues*, as of *fire*, appeared *among* them,
and a *tongue* rested on *each* of them.
*All* of them were filled with the *Holy Spirit*
and began to speak in other *languages*,
as the *Spirit* gave them *ability*.

Now there were devout *Jews* from every nation under *heaven*
living in *Jerusalem*.
And at this *sound* the crowd *gathered* and was *bewildered*,
because *all* heard them speaking in their own *languages*.
*Amazed* and *astonished*, they asked,
"Are not all these who are speaking *Galileans*?
And how *is* it that we *hear*, *each* of us,
in our own *language*?
*Parthians*, *Medes*, *Elamites*, and residents of *Mesopotamia*,
*Judea* and *Cappadocia*, *Pontus* and *Asia*,
*Phrygia* and *Pamphylia*,
*Egypt* and the parts of *Libya* belonging to *Cyrene*,
and visitors from *Rome*, both *Jews* and *converts*,

---

Pentecost (which means "fifty") is Jewish in origin and developed into a celebration of the reception of the law at Sinai.

Proclaim this as though you are reading the most exciting part of a mystery novel.

Express their confusion in your voice.
Galileans = gal-ih-LEE-uhnz
Parthians = PAHR-thee-uhnz
Medes = meedz, Elamites = EE-luh-mīts
Pause after "Elamites." Then read "residents of" all the following regions:
Mesopotamia = mes-uh-poh-TAY-mee-uh
Judea = joo-DEE-uh
Cappadocia = kap-uh-DOH-shuh
Pontus = PON-tuhs
Phrygia = FRIJ-ee-uh
Pamphylia = pam-FIL-ee-uh
Libya = LIB-ee-uh, Cyrene = sī-REE-nee

---

**READING I** The presence of God at Pentecost is manifested in several ways. There is a roaring sound, tongues as of fire, and a distinct change in the disciples' ability to communicate. The description in Acts recalls the ancient predictions that God would pour out the Holy Spirit upon all people and that God would renew the people and give them hope. The dramatic symbols of God's presence (the tongues as of fire and the sound like wind)

remind one of similar events when the law was given at Sinai. Most significant, the divisions created by differences in communication, said to have begun after the building of the Tower of Babel, are reversed. All people are able to hear about and understand the wondrous deeds God has done in Jesus.

In the Pentecost account, people from many nations can understand the disciples' preaching. The differences between Jews and Gentiles are wiped out. This is important for us to recall as well: We Christians do not have ownership of God's Spirit. We need to

remember that God is much bigger than we are and is able to include all peoples in a loving embrace.

Share the excitement of this story with your listeners so that they might also experience the Holy Spirit in their lives. Read the first part of the reading a bit breathlessly, in order to convey the sweeping movement of the Spirit and the astonishment of the disciples. Slow down a bit in the second part, but continue to allow your voice to be filled with amazement. Stress in the final line the power

**196**

PENTECOST ■ JUNE 3, 2001

Cretans = KREE-tuhnz
Arabs = AYR-uhbz

**Slow down and emphasize the final line.**

*Cretans* and *Arabs*—
in our *own* languages we hear them *speaking*
about God's *deeds* of *power."*

---

**READING II**   Romans 8:8–17

**A reading from the letter of Paul to the Romans**

Those who are in the *flesh* cannot please *God.*
But *you* are *not* in the flesh;
*you* are in the *Spirit,*
since the Spirit of God *dwells* in you.
*Anyone* who does not have the Spirit of *Christ*
does not *belong* to him.

But if Christ is *in* you,
though the body is *dead* because of *sin,*
the *Spirit* is *life* because of *righteousness.*
If the Spirit of *God* who *raised* Jesus from the dead *dwells* in you,
he who raised *Christ* from the *dead*
will give *life* to *your* mortal bodies *also*
through his *Spirit* that *dwells* in you.

**Speak slowly and lift your voice in hopeful certitude.**

So then, brothers and sisters,
we are *debtors,* not to the *flesh,*
to live *according* to the flesh—
for if you live according to the *flesh,* you will *die;*
but if by the *Spirit* you put to *death* the deeds of the body,
you will *live.*

**This line interrupts the flow of the sentence. Speak it more quickly and in a low voice.**

For all who are led by the Spirit of *God* are *children* of God.
For you did not receive a spirit of *slavery*

---

of God. You are a vehicle through whom God's Spirit moves in your community on this day. Inspire your listeners to open their hearts to God and to work to break down barriers to communication in their own lives.

READING II   In this passage Paul contrasts a mindset that is not fixed on God (which he calls being "in the flesh") with the proper Christian mindset (one that is "in the Spirit"). The "flesh" and the "body" are hallmarks of the corruptible world, the world not yet freed from sin and

given the promise of life through Jesus. The Spirit is the one who dwells within and enlivens each believer.

It is this Spirit that makes each Christian an heir of God and a joint heir with Christ. The Christians of Rome already know this, says Paul, because of their experience of the Spirit in their prayer. It is the Spirit who inspires them to call out to God as Father, thus giving evidence of their status as adopted children of God. In a typical Pauline statement, the letter asserts that adoption as children of God is available to us through our willingness to suffer as Jesus did, but

the future holds out hope of being exalted with Christ.

Offer this meditation to your community with sincerity and conviction. Speak slowly, so that the progression of thought will not be lost on your listeners.

GOSPEL   Jesus' last discourse to his followers in the gospel of John lays out his primary teaching in this gospel: the command to love. If his followers truly love him, they will keep his commandments, and his commandment is precisely to

JUNE 3, 2001 ■ PENTECOST

**Begin afresh with this thought.**

to fall back into *fear*,
but you have received a spirit of *adoption*.
When we cry, "*Abba! Father!*"
it is that very *Spirit* bearing *witness*
with *our* spirit that we are *children* of *God*,
and if *children*, then *heirs*,
*heirs* of God and *joint* heirs with *Christ*—
if, in fact, we *suffer* with him
so that we may also be *glorified* with him.

---

**GOSPEL** John 14:15–16, 23b–26

---

**A reading from the holy gospel according to John**

Jesus spoke to the disciples:
"If you *love* me, you will keep my *commandments*.

**Proclaim this directly to your community.**

And I will ask the *Father*,
and he will give you *another* Advocate,
to be with you *forever*.

"Those who *love* me will keep my *word*,
and my *Father* will love *them*,
and we will *come* to them and make our *home* with them.
Whoever does *not* love me does not keep my *words*;

**There is challenge in this message. To reject Jesus' word is to reject the Father who sent him.**

and the word that you *hear* is not *mine*,
but is from the *Father* who *sent* me.

**Speak with warmth and comfort.**

"I have said these things to you while I am still *with* you.
But the *Advocate*, the Holy *Spirit*,
whom the Father will send in my *name*,
will teach you *everything*,
and *remind* you of all that I have *said* to you."

love one another. Loving Jesus and keeping his command to love results in the indwelling of God in the believer. Rejecting Jesus' words and failing to love is a rejection of the Father.

To strengthen and inspire his disciples, Jesus leaves the Holy Spirit to be with them after his return to the Father in glory. Although we celebrate this gift of the Spirit today, the gospel of John describes the experience differently than Luke does in Acts. In John, Jesus breathes his Spirit on his followers during an appearance to them, whereas Luke narrates a dramatic coming of the Spirit in

wind and fire. Each author is trying to provide an image to describe the tremendous outpouring of love and inspiration that the early Christians received after Jesus' departure from them. That same Spirit continues to work in each of us.

Proclaim this brief passage slowly and solemnly. Remind your listeners of God's great promise to send the Spirit and affirm that God's promises last forever.

JUNE 10, 2001

# HOLY TRINITY

*Lectionary #166*

## READING I    Proverbs 8:22–31

**A reading from the book of Proverbs**

*Thus* says the *wisdom* of *God*:
"The Lord *created* me at the *beginning* of his *work*,
the *first* of his acts of long *ago*.
*Ages* ago I was set up,
at the *first*, before the beginning of the *earth*.
When there were no *depths* I was brought *forth*,
when there were no *springs* abounding with *water*.

"Before the *mountains* had been *shaped*,
before the *hills*, *I* was brought *forth*—
when he had not yet made *earth* and *fields*,
or the world's first bits of *soil*.

"When he established the *heavens*, I was *there*,
when he drew a *circle* on the face of the *deep*,
when he made *firm* the skies *above*,
when he *established* the fountains of the *deep*,
when he assigned to the *sea* its *limit*,
so that the *waters* might not transgress his *command*,
when he marked *out* the foundations of the *earth*,
then I was *beside* him, like a master *worker*;
and I was daily his *delight*,
*rejoicing* before him *always*,
*rejoicing* in his inhabited *world*
and *delighting* in the human *race*."

**Stress the words that describe the antiquity of Wisdom.**

**Speak in lofty tones of Wisdom's presence throughout creation.**

**Pause briefly before the word "then"; proceed with a strong voice filled with exuberance.**

READING I    In a beautiful declaration of her greatness, Wisdom claims that God created the world through her. Wisdom was present from the beginning and worked with God in establishing the world and all that is in it.

Christians have long associated the figure of Wisdom with the person of Christ, using the wisdom tradition to understand the relationship of the Father and the Son. Just as Wisdom asserts her participation in creation, so also Christians hold that all things came into being through the divine Word, Jesus Christ. Christians believe that

Jesus, the Son of God, is the wisdom of God, which is why this passage is used for today's celebration of the Trinity.

Read this passage as though you are sharing exciting, breathtaking news. Close on a note of joy as you share God's delight in the beauty of Wisdom.

JUNE 10, 2001 ■ HOLY TRINITY

## READING II    Romans 5:1–5

**A reading from the letter of Paul to the Romans**

Since we are *justified* by *faith*,
we have *peace* with God through our Lord Jesus *Christ*,
through whom we have obtained
        *access* to this *grace* in which we *stand;*
and we *boast* in our *hope* of sharing the *glory* of *God*.

And not only *that*,
but we also boast in our *sufferings*,
knowing that *suffering* produces *endurance*,
and *endurance* produces *character*,
and *character* produces *hope*,
and *hope* does not *disappoint* us,
because God's *love* has been poured into our *hearts*
through the Holy *Spirit* that has been *given* to us.

---

*God's peace is the direct result of faith in Christ. Emphasize this concept.*

*Avoid a sing-song voice in these lines.*

---

READING II  In a warm declaration of the peace that comes through Jesus and the working of the Holy Spirit, Paul discusses the centrality of faith in the Christian life. It is by faith in Jesus' saving actions that Christians are justified before God, which gives us hope that we shall one day share in God's glory.

But lest that message be misunderstood, Paul immediately highlights the importance of suffering for the faith. He knew from his own experience that some early churches often emphasized glorification over the necessity of suffering. Paul acknowledges a future glorification but asserts that our present reality often involves pain and struggle. But such pain can build character, making the Christian stronger and eager to serve God. Stronger character generates greater hope, a hope that is not in vain because it is confirmed by the love of God and the action of the Holy Spirit.

We proclaim this reading today because of its reference to all three persons of the Trinity. It is not an exposition of trinitarian doctrine, however, which took several centuries to develop. As Paul intended it, it is a statement of encouragement to stand firm in the faith, trusting in God's goodness and love. Offer it as such to your assembly.

# HOLY TRINITY ■ JUNE 10, 2001

---

**GOSPEL**    John 16:12–15

**A reading from the holy gospel according to John**

Jesus said to his disciples:
"I still have many things to *say* to you,
but you cannot *bear* them *now*.
When the Spirit of *truth* comes,
he will *guide* you into all the *truth*;
for he will *not* speak on his *own*,
but will speak whatever he *hears*,
and he will *declare* to you the things that are to *come*.
He will glorify *me*,
because he will take what is *mine* and *declare* it to you.
All that the *Father* has is *mine*.
For *this* reason I said
that he will take what is *mine* and *declare* it to you."

**Begin in a straightforward manner. Pause deliberately at each punctuation mark in order to guide your hearers through the text.**

**Do not pause after "said" but read these last two lines as one complete thought.**

---

GOSPEL    In Jesus' farewell discourse in the gospel of John, Jesus tells the disciples what will happen to him and to them, and what they can expect when he is gone. Since the gospel was actually written many years after Jesus' death and resurrection, his words reflect the experience of the community that produced the gospel. In today's passage, it is the presence of the Spirit in the lives of Christians that gives rise to these promises of Jesus.

Jesus declares that there are many more things he wants to teach his followers, but it is the Spirit who will bring them greater understanding. The Spirit will guide Jesus' disciples—and Christians of all ages as well—and will instruct and comfort the faithful. But, as Jesus' words attest, the Spirit is always revealing and glorifying Jesus himself, and Jesus is so intimately united with the Father that he is able to claim in another passage, "The Father and I are one."

Emphasize the relationship of the Father, Son and Spirit, while remaining true to the thrust of the passage that the Spirit provides guidance for Christians in the time of Jesus' absence.

JUNE 17, 2001

# BODY AND BLOOD OF CHRIST

*Lectionary #169*

**READING I**   Genesis 14:18–20

**A reading from the book of Genesis**

When *Abram* heard that his nephew, *Lot*, had been taken *captive*,
he led forth his trained *men*, and *routed* the *abductors*.

After Abram's *return*
King *Melchizedek* of *Salem* brought out *bread* and *wine*;
he was *priest* of God Most *High*.
He *blessed* Abram and said,
"Blessed be *Abram* by God Most *High*,
maker of *heaven* and *earth*;
and blessed be *God* Most *High*,
who has delivered your *enemies* into your *hand!*"
And Abram gave him one *tenth* of *everything*.

**Speak slowly and clearly throughout this short passage, so that nothing will be lost on your listeners.**
**Melchizedek = mel-KEEZ-ih-dek**
**Salem = SAY-luhm**

**Proclaim this line of praise with enthusiasm.**

READING I   **The figure of Melchizedek appears only in this passage, in Psalm 110, and in the letter to the Hebrews, where he prefigures Jesus as priest and king. Here he appears out of nowhere and yet is given honor and authority. As priest, he presides over a liturgy involving bread and wine, suggestive of the Christian eucharist and the reason we proclaim this passage today, the solemnity of the Body and Blood of Christ. Abraham (here still called Abram) offers Melchizedek a tithe—one-tenth—of his possessions, just as one-tenth of a person's**

**resources were later offered to God at the temple in Jerusalem.**

**Melchizedek has the authority to bless Abram and offers a stirring praise of God. Abram was returning victorious from battle, winning despite all odds, and Melchizedek declares that it was God who had blessed Abram and given him victory.**

**Take your time in proclaiming this passage to your assembly, emphasizing the bread and wine offerings of Melchizedek and savoring every word of the blessings. Pause before you begin, so that you are assured**

**of your listeners' rapt attention. Then speak with dignity.**

READING II   **The first letter of Paul to the Corinthians contains the oldest known tradition about the eucharist. It is the one most familiar to us, since it is the model for the eucharistic prayers that we use each time we celebrate eucharist. It is not simply Paul's own understanding but something he received from the risen Lord, which he now passes on to the members of the Corinthian community. They, in turn, will**

# BODY AND BLOOD OF CHRIST ■ JUNE 17, 2001

**With Paul, you hand on this account of Jesus' words to your community.**

**Proclaim this solemnly.**

---

### READING II    1 Corinthians 11:23–26

**A reading from the first letter of to Paul to the Corinthians**

Beloved,
I *received* from the *Lord* what I also handed on to *you*,
that the Lord *Jesus* on the night when he was *betrayed*
took a loaf of *bread*,
and when he had given *thanks*,
he *broke* it and said,
"*This* is my *body* that is for *you*.
Do this in *remembrance* of *me*."

In the same way he took the cup *also*, after supper, saying,
"This *cup* is the *new covenant* in my *blood*.
*Do* this, as often as you *drink* it,
⁣        in *remembrance* of *me*."
For as often as you *eat* this *bread* and *drink* the *cup*,
you proclaim the Lord's *death* until he *comes*.

---

share it with those who come after them. Faith is a communal event.

Although the words are familiar, it is important to reflect on them and pray about them before proclaiming them. Jesus gives thanks for the bread and shares it with his disciples. The act of sharing is central; we join together to partake of the eucharist and become one body of Christ because of what we share. It is Christ's body, a body that is broken and battered on the cross. His words look forward to his passion as he tells his friends to remember him. Indeed, we look back in each eucharist to that time when

heaven broke through into human life, when eternity invaded our temporal existence, when God became one of us.

Jesus also recalls the covenants established between God and the chosen faithful of old, especially Abraham. Covenants were agreements between God and a person in which God promised protection and the human partner pledged loyalty. The covenant was ratified with the sacrifice of an animal. Here, Jesus looks forward to his death on the cross, declaring that his blood is sufficient for ratifying this new covenant. No other need die to fulfill this covenant.

In addition to remembering Jesus when sharing the bread and cup, Christians also look to a future time when Christ's reign will be complete. Far from shrinking from the reality of Jesus' passion and death, Paul proclaims it, but he also looks forward in hope to future glory. As we wait in hope, we proclaim Jesus' death, for it is precisely in that moment of brokenness and pain that true peace has entered the world. We remember it at every eucharist.

Proclaim this message to your listeners with great solemnity. Speak Jesus' words as though you are reading them for the first

JUNE 17, 2001 ■ BODY AND BLOOD OF CHRIST

## GOSPEL  Luke 9:11b–17

**A reading from the holy gospel according to Luke**

*Jesus* spoke to the crowds about the kingdom of *God*,
and *healed* those who needed to be *cured.*

The day was drawing to a *close,*
and the twelve *came* to him and said,
"Send the crowd *away,*
so that they may go
      into the surrounding *villages* and *countryside,*
to *lodge* and get *provisions;*
for we are here in a *deserted* place."
But Jesus said to them,
"*You* give them something to *eat.*"
They said, "We have no more than *five loaves* and *two fish*—
unless we are to go and *buy* food for all these people."
For there were about five *thousand* men.

And Jesus said to his disciples,
"Make the people sit *down* in groups of about *fifty* each."
They *did* so and made them all sit *down.*

And taking the five *loaves* and the two *fish,*
he looked up to *heaven,* and *blessed* and *broke* them,
and gave them to the *disciples* to set before the *crowd.*

And all *ate* and were *filled.*
What was left *over* was gathered *up,*
twelve *baskets* of broken *pieces.*

---

**Are the disciples concerned about their own well-being or that of the crowd? Let your response to this question dictate your tone of voice.**

**Jesus speaks with confidence, but his disciples begin to panic.**

**Jesus takes control. Proclaim this with dignity.**

---

time, so that the members of your assembly may hear them with fresh ears, especially on this day when we reflect on the centrality of the eucharist in our lives.

GOSPEL  The story of the loaves and fishes has long been a favorite of Christians. It speaks of sharing and of nourishment, of hospitality and of providing for others. Today's selection opens with Jesus providing for the crowds in several ways: by filling their spirits with teaching about God, and by healing their bodies of disease. But it concentrates on the way Jesus cares for the people by providing them with food.

The Twelve, the inner circle of Jesus' followers, see the mass of people and want to send them away. Perhaps they are concerned about the crowd, but they might also be overwhelmed by the mob. Jesus responds matter-of-factly: Feed them. When the Twelve are dismayed at the thought of having to share their meager supplies, Jesus takes action, blessing and sharing the food.

The text does not describe how the miracle occurs. (Did Jesus increase the food, or did he inspire generosity?) What it does teach is that we will find abundance when we include others in our embrace.

Give plenty of expression to the words of the Twelve, and speak Jesus' words with calm assurance. Close with conviction, drawing your hearers to see the eucharistic connotations of the closing paragraphs.

# JUNE 23, 2001

# BIRTH OF JOHN THE BAPTIST VIGIL

*Lectionary #586*

## READING I    Jeremiah 1:4–10

**A reading from the book of the prophet Jeremiah**

*Speak God's words with tenderness.*

The *word* of the Lord *came* to me saying,
"Before I formed you in the *womb* I *knew* you,
and before you were *born* I *consecrated* you;
I appointed you a *prophet* to the *nations.*"

*There is a bit of fear in Jeremiah's words.*

Then I said, "Ah, Lord *God*!
Truly I do *not* know how to *speak,*
for I am only a *boy.*"
But the Lord said to me,
"Do not *say,* 'I am only a *boy*';

*Let your voice grow in intensity as you read God's response.*

for you shall go to *all* to whom I *send* you,
and you shall *speak* whatever I *command* you,
Do not be *afraid* of them,
for I am *with* you to *deliver* you,
says the Lord."

Then the Lord put out his *hand* and touched my *mouth;*
and the Lord said to me,
"*Now* I have put my *words* in your *mouth.*

*Be careful not to become sing-song, but speak forcefully.*

See, *today* I *appoint* you over *nations* and over *kingdoms,*
to *pluck* up and to pull *down,*
to *destroy* and to *overthrow,*
to *build* and to *plant.*"

---

READING I  The prophet Jeremiah was active at the end of the seventh and beginning of the sixth centuries BCE, a time when Judah was threatened by a powerful nation from the north.

Jeremiah is often remembered as a prophet of doom, foretelling the defeat of the nation. But Jeremiah also spoke with tenderness and comfort in the face of Judah's impending defeat. He asserted that the exile would be temporary and that God intended it as a period of chastisement for the sake of teaching the people how to be truly faithful.

We read today from the account of Jeremiah's call to God's service as a prophet. The passage opens with the tender words of God, declaring God's knowledge and choice of this servant. Even before Jeremiah was born, indeed before he was even conceived, he was chosen to proclaim God's word.

Responding in humility and perhaps fear, Jeremiah argues with God. The prophets were often honest with God about their shortcomings, and they sometimes even tried to convince God to choose someone else. Jeremiah insists that he is too young and inexperienced, but God is not convinced.

God will provide both the words and the strength to speak; Jeremiah is compelled to go forth.

The lips of the prophet Isaiah were touched with a burning coal in order to purify his mouth for prophecy. In a similar gesture, God touches Jeremiah's mouth in order to infuse him with the word of God. He is given a mission, and much of the mission involves destruction. But in the end he will provide hope and encouragement.

Proclaim this reading as a direct call to the members of your community. Share the

JUNE 23, 2001 ■ BIRTH OF JOHN THE BAPTIST VIGIL

## READING II    1 Peter 1:3, 8–12

**A reading from the first letter of Peter**

Blessed be the *God* and *Father* of our Lord Jesus *Christ*!
By his great *mercy* he has given us
a new *birth* into a living *hope*
through the resurrection of Jesus *Christ* from the *dead*.

**Speak with certainty and encouragement.**

Although you have not *seen* Jesus Christ,
you *love* him;
and even though you do not see him *now*,
you *believe* in him
and *rejoice* with an *indescribable* and *glorious joy*,
for you are receiving the *outcome* of your *faith*,
the *salvation* of your *souls*.

**This is a long sentence; practice your phrasing carefully.**

The *prophets* who prophesied of the *grace*
that was to be *yours*
concerning this *salvation* made careful *search* and *inquiry*,
inquiring about the *person* or *time*
that the Spirit of Christ *within* them *indicated*
when it testified in *advance*
to the *sufferings* and the subsequent *glory* destined for *Christ*.

**The opening phrase is key; emphasize the word "you." Then speak in a more subdued voice, building in strength at the end.**

It was *revealed* to the *prophets*
that they were serving not *themselves* but *you*,
in regard to the things that have now been *announced* to you
through those who brought you *good news*
by the Holy *Spirit* sent from *heaven*
—things into which *angels* long to *look*!

---

opening scene with warmth and sensitivity. Jeremiah's own words are sincere, but God's reply is stronger. Speak with power and conviction.

**READING II** The first letter of Peter was written to Christians living in Asia Minor (modern Turkey), an area in which Paul was particularly active. It seeks to give them encouragement despite their sufferings. Government leaders were beginning to see that Christians were not simply a sect within Judaism, and the Christians' refusal to participate in the state cult made

them vulnerable to charges of treason and insubordination. The author writes to build up the community's hope and faith in a time of persecution, speaking of the joy that knowledge of Christ brings, despite adversity.

The Christian faith is characterized by newness in Christ. It is the equivalent of a new birth, with a future filled with hope and promise. That hope rests on a realization that Jesus is risen, an assertion that demonstrates God's tremendous mercy for humans and leads the author to break into praise of God.

Because of the victory of Jesus Christ over death, the Christian can look forward in

joy despite present trials, moving ever closer to the goal of salvation. The Christian loves Jesus despite having never seen him; the Christian believes in him, although he is no longer present on earth. The author knows that the Christian life is a paradox and continues to point out the intricacies of the faith throughout this passage and the entire letter.

The author asserts that even though the Hebrew prophets lived long before Jesus, they were really instructing believers about him. They prophesied about the sufferings that would befall Jesus, but they also predicted his glorification. They were able to

# BIRTH OF JOHN THE BAPTIST VIGIL ■ JUNE 23, 2001

Therefore prepare your *minds* for *action;*
*discipline* yourselves;
set all your *hope* on the *grace*
that Jesus Christ will *bring* you when he is *revealed.*

---

### GOSPEL    Luke 1:5–17

**A reading from the holy gospel according to Luke**

In the days of King *Herod* of *Judea,*
there was a priest named *Zechariah,*
who belonged to the priestly order of *Abijah.*
His *wife* was a descendant of *Aaron,*
and her name was *Elizabeth.*
Both of them were *righteous* before God,
living *blamelessly* according to all the *commandments*
and *regulations* of the *Lord.*
But they had no *children,* because Elizabeth was *barren,*
and both were getting *on* in *years.*

Once when Zechariah was serving as *priest* before *God*
and his section was on *duty,*
he was chosen by *lot,*
according to the custom of the *priesthood,*
to enter the *sanctuary* of the *Lord* and offer *incense.*
Now at the time of the *incense* offering,
the whole assembly of the *people* was praying *outside.*

Zechariah = zek-uh-RĪ-uh
Abijah = uh-BĪ-juh

**Speak firmly, then with a tone of regret as you mention their childlessness.**

do so precisely because the Holy Spirit spoke in them and inspired them. But now that same Spirit has been more fully revealed in the gospel of Jesus Christ.

As a result of the testimony from of old and their present hope, Christians are to put into action what their faith requires. The author advocates discipline and a constant focus on the further grace that will be theirs when Christ is fully revealed.

This selection is an appropriate one to address to Christians of all eras. Speak boldly of the joy that comes from believing in Jesus, despite our distance from him in

time and space. Although the author is probably speaking about the prophets of Israel, the passage is used today because John, the direct precursor of Jesus, is the last and greatest of the Hebrew prophets.

GOSPEL Only the gospel of Luke provides an account of John the Baptist's birth and of the visitation of Mary to Elizabeth. As he does throughout the gospel, the author begins by providing the historical setting for the events he describes, intimating that the events he recounts effect all of human history. The gospel writer places

John's conception during the reign of King Herod in Judea.

John, the author tells us, was born into a priestly family; both his father and mother were of priestly lineage and were righteous in God's sight. They upheld the law of Moses and presumably raised their son to respect it. Throughout the gospel, Jesus is presented as a fulfillment of God's promises to Israel; his precursor likewise stands within the tradition of Israel.

As in the case of many Hebrew women before her (such as Sarah, Rebecca, Rachel and Hannah), John's mother, Elizabeth, had

JUNE 23, 2001 ■ BIRTH OF JOHN THE BAPTIST VIGIL

Then there *appeared* to him an *angel* of the *Lord*,
standing at the *right* side of the altar of *incense*.
When Zechariah saw him, he was *terrified*;
and fear *overwhelmed* him.

**The angel speaks comfortingly.**

But the angel said to him,
"Do *not* be *afraid*, Zechariah,
for your *prayer* has been *heard*.
Your wife *Elizabeth* will bear you a *son*,
and you will name him *John*.

**Raise your voice in joy as you proclaim this promise.**

"You will have *joy* and *gladness*,
and many will *rejoice* at his birth,
for he will be *great* in the sight of the *Lord*.
He must never drink *wine* or strong *drink*;
even *before* his birth he will be *filled* with the Holy *Spirit*.

**Emphasize the mention of the Spirit and the power that will fill John.**

"He will turn many of the people of *Israel*
        to the *Lord* their *God*.
With the *spirit* and *power* of *Elijah* he will go *before* him,
to turn the hearts of *parents* to their *children*,
and the *disobedient* to the wisdom of the *righteous*,
to make ready a *people* prepared for the *Lord*."

no children in her old age. Into this sad situation an angel appears. While in the sanctuary of the temple, where only priests could enter, John's father, Zechariah, receives a message from God, delivered by the angel Gabriel, announcing the birth of a child. As in the annunciation to Mary, the angel's presence instills fear, but Zechariah is told not to be afraid. Zechariah is dumbfounded, unable to speak until after the child's birth.

The angel indicates the mission and temperament of the child. He is to be no ordinary child, but one whose birth will bring joy and whose life will be modeled after that of the prophets of old. He will be dedicated to God in the manner of the nazirites, who devoted themselves wholeheartedly—and visibly, by not cutting their hair—to serving God. Just as Elijah turned the hearts of Israel toward God, so also this child will be filled with a power that will lead many to righteousness and prepare them for God's presence.

Even in this story of the announcement of John's birth, then, several key themes from the gospel are presented: These events have lasting impact and affect all of history; they fulfill the expectations of Israel; and the lives of Jesus and John are set squarely in the religious tradition of Jerusalem and the temple. Finally, the Holy Spirit enlivens John, even from the womb, preparing the people for the coming of the Messiah.

Summon your storytelling skills to offer this tale to your listeners with the joy and awe it is meant to evoke.

JUNE 24, 2001

# BIRTH OF JOHN THE BAPTIST

*Lectionary #587*

## READING I    Isaiah 49:1–6

**A reading from the book of the prophet Isaiah**

**Speak with tenderness and compassion.**

*Listen* to me, O *coastlands*,
pay *attention*, you peoples from far *away*!
The Lord *called* me before I was *born*,
while I was in my mother's *womb* he *named* me.

He made my *mouth* like a sharp *sword*,
in the shadow of his *hand* he *hid* me;
he made me a polished *arrow*,
in his *quiver* he hid me *away*.

**The identification of Israel as the servant comes as a surprise. Speak boldly.**

**There is regret and sadness in these lines.**

And the Lord said to me, "You are my *servant*, *Israel*,
in whom I will be *glorified*."
But I said, "I have *laboured* in *vain*,
I have spent my strength for *nothing* and *vanity*;
yet surely my *cause* is with the *Lord*,
and my *reward* with my *God*."

And now the Lord *says*,
who formed me in the *womb* to be his *servant*,
to bring Jacob *back* to him,
and that Israel might be *gathered* to him,

**Raise your voice now and until the end, closing on a strong note.**

for I am *honoured* in the sight of the *Lord*,
and my *God* has become my *strength*.

READING I   The book of Isaiah contains several "servant songs" in which God's servant speaks of facing adversity while steadfastly serving the divine will. In today's selection from Isaiah, the servant describes being chosen by God and the mission that awaits God's messenger. But this passage also adds an interesting twist to the picture of an individual servant found elsewhere; in this passage, the servant is Israel.

In a beautiful description of the intimacy that exists between God and the servant, the servant recognizes having been called by God, even before birth. This is not simply a general call; God knows the servant by name and calls the servant specifically. God has chosen this one from all the rest and gives the servant a message so

sharp and true that it cuts like a sword. The servant is destined to draw the people into the relationship with God that is meant for them.

But the servant, Israel, has a bigger mission. Not only are God's chosen people to return to God, but Israel is to be a beacon for all the world to see. God's salvation is not for a chosen few but is available to all people. Israel must proclaim God's glory to the nations and thus draw all people to God.

JUNE 24, 2001 ■ BIRTH OF JOHN THE BAPTIST

The Lord says,
"It is too *small* a thing that you should be my *servant*
to *raise* up the tribes of *Jacob*
and to *restore* the survivors of *Israel*;
I will give you as a *light* to the *nations*,
that my *salvation* may reach to the end of the *earth*."

---

**READING II** Acts 13:22–26

**A reading from the Acts of the Apostles**

On the *sabbath*,
*Paul* and his companion went to the *synagogue*,
and the *officials* of the synagogue invited them
        to address the *people*.
So Paul stood up and began to *speak*.
"You *Israelites*, and all who *fear* God, *listen*.
God made *David king* of our *ancestors*.
In his *testimony* about him God said,
'I have found *David*, son of *Jesse*,
to be a man after my *heart*,
who will carry out all my *wishes*.'

"Of this man's *posterity*
God has brought to Israel a *Saviour*, *Jesus*, as he *promised*;
*before* the coming of *Jesus*
*John* had already proclaimed a baptism of *repentance*
to all the people of *Israel*.
And as John was *finishing* his work, he said,
'What do you suppose that I *am*?

---

Paul begins with a brief reference to Israel's history, then asserts that all history is directed to the appearance of Jesus.

Pause before mentioning John, then proceed to tell this story as an independent unit, in order to draw attention to the role of the Baptist.

---

We proclaim this passage in our celebration of the birth of John the Baptist because John was also a servant who sought to restore the people to God. He too had an intimate relationship with God, spoke the truth without flinching, and, as we know from the gospel, was chosen even before he was born. But the message is for all of us as well. We too are called by name and given the task of preaching God's message to all the earth. Proclaim this passage with an eye to the story of John but also as a challenge to your listeners to be a light to the nations.

READING II John was remembered by the early church as one who pointed toward Jesus as God's chosen one. There are hints of tension in the gospels between the followers of Jesus and the followers of John, who were at first rival groups. So the gospel writers make clear that John is the lesser of the two figures; it is Jesus who is the savior of Israel.

Jesus does not simply come on the scene unannounced or unexpected. As Paul makes clear in his speech in the synagogue, God chose David to carry out God's plan and promised him that one of his descendants would always reign over Israel. Paul proclaims that this promise is fulfilled in Jesus, David's descendant. Jesus is the rightful heir to the promises of God.

To prepare for Jesus, John arrived preaching a baptism of repentance. John's message was to the chosen people of Israel,

**210**

BIRTH OF JOHN THE BAPTIST ■ JUNE 24, 2001

*I* am not *he.*
No, but one is coming *after* me;
I am not *worthy* to untie the thong of the *sandals* on his *feet.'*

**Pause again after John's words, then proclaim Paul's final statement with confidence.**

"You descendants of Abraham's *family,*
and *others* who fear God,
to *us* the message of this *salvation* has been *sent.*"

---

**GOSPEL** Luke 1:57–66, 80

**A reading from the holy gospel according to Luke**

The time came for *Elizabeth* to give *birth,*
and she bore a *son.*
Her *neighbours* and *relatives* heard
that the Lord had shown his great *mercy* to her,
and they *rejoiced* with her.

**This unexpected gift of a child is a sign of God's tremendous love.**
**Zechariah = zek-uh-RĪ-uh**

On the *eighth* day they came to *circumcise* the child,
and they were going to name him *Zechariah* after his *father.*
But his mother said, "*No;* he is to be called *John.*"
They said to her, "None of your *relatives* has this name."
Then they began motioning to his *father*
to find out what name *he* wanted to give him.

**Speak Elizabeth's words firmly.**

He asked for a *writing* tablet and wrote,
"His *name* is *John.*"
And all of them were *amazed.*
*Immediately* his mouth was *opened* and his tongue *freed,*
and he began to *speak,* praising *God.*

**Give this line great emphasis. Then pause before recounting the amazing events that follow.**

---

and his task was to draw the people back into a right relationship with God.

Proclaim this speech in a straightforward manner, emphasizing the greatness of Jesus over John. But give due emphasis to the Baptist, who prepared the way for the one who was greater than he, and whose feast we celebrate today.

GOSPEL The story of the birth of John in the gospel of Luke parallels the infancy narrative of Jesus: An angel announces John's conception, name and mission; John's birth is greeted with great joy; and bystanders marvel at the events. But the events surrounding Jesus' birth surpass those surrounding John's, for John is the precursor. Even the stories of their births make clear that John is of lesser significance than Jesus, although he still has an important role to play in the events of salvation.

Elizabeth and Zechariah were devout Jews and circumcised their child on the eighth day, as required by the Mosaic law. The child was named in the same ceremony. Both his parents agree that the name announced by the angel should be given him, despite the objections of relatives. Zechariah had been unable to speak since his encounter with the angel in the temple. When the angel announced the impending birth of John, Zechariah had doubted, citing

JUNE 24, 2001 ■ BIRTH OF JOHN THE BAPTIST

**Speak with awe and wonder.**

*Fear* came over all their neighbours,
and all these things were *talked* about
throughout the entire *hill* country of *Judea*.
All who *heard* them *pondered* them and said,
*"What* then will this child *become?"*
For, indeed, the *hand* of the *Lord* was *with* him.

**Close with a firm tone.**

The child *grew* and became strong in *spirit*,
and he was in the *wilderness*
until the day he appeared *publicly* to *Israel*.

his and Elizabeth's advanced age. He was struck dumb because of his questioning and was allowed to speak only after obeying the angel's command to name the child John.

Zechariah's resolute stance and his renewed gift of speech inspire those present, who recognize that God's Spirit is upon this child. John grows strong in the Holy Spirit and lives a life set apart from others, a sign of his special status and mission. The wilderness is often a place of testing and strengthening, and John uses the time well, emerging from his self-imposed exile as a powerful messenger of God.

Proclaim the sense of inspiration in this gospel passage. Express the joy of the birth, the doubt of Zechariah's relatives, and Zechariah's stalwart resolve. Then speak with awe as it becomes evident to everyone that God's Spirit is guiding John.

JULY 1, 2001

# 13TH SUNDAY IN ORDINARY TIME

*Lectionary #99*

## READING I    1 Kings 19:16b, 19—21

**A reading from the first book of Kings**

Elijah = ee-LĪ-juh
Elisha = ee-LĪ-shuh
Shaphat = SHAY-fat

The Lord spoke to the prophet *Elijah* and said,
"You shall anoint *Elisha*, son of *Shaphat*,
as *prophet* in your *place*."

So Elijah set *out* from there, and found *Elisha*,
       who was *ploughing*.
There were twelve yoke of *oxen* ahead of him,
and he was with the *twelfth*.

Elijah passed *by* Elisha and threw his *mantle* over him.
Elisha left the *oxen*, ran *after* Elijah, and said,
"Let me kiss my *father* and my *mother*,
and *then* I will follow you."

**Elijah's response is cryptic; focus on the material following the semicolon.**

**Pause after "them."**

Then Elijah said to him,
"Go back again; for *what* have I done to you?"
Elisha *returned* from following Elijah,
took the yoke of *oxen*, and *slaughtered* them;
using the equipment from the *oxen*, he boiled their *flesh*,
and gave it to the people, and they *ate*.
Then Elisha set *out* and followed *Elijah*,
and became his *servant*.

READING I The call of a prophet often involves a direct encounter between human and divine. Sometimes the encounter involves a heavenly vision; at other times the prophet may hear the voice of God. For Elisha, the call to prophetic activity involves a period of apprenticeship under the tutelage of Elijah. Elijah, guided by God, chooses Elisha to assume the prophetic mantle. Elisha's task is to respond in trust.

The description of Elisha ploughing with twelve yoke of oxen, although probably an exaggeration, conveys how much he gave up in order to respond to God's call. But he does respond immediately, pausing only to notify his parents, thus fulfilling his family obligations. Inexplicably, Elijah seems to tell Elisha not to follow, but Elisha cannot be dissuaded.

Proclaim this story of Elisha's call with enthusiasm, emphasizing Elisha's willingness to follow Elijah without hesitation. It points forward to the lesson on discipleship in the gospel and is a fitting reminder to all of us that discipleship must be embraced wholeheartedly.

READING II Paul's letter to the Galatians is his treatise on Christian freedom. In it, he chastises, cajoles and rebukes the Galatians in order to bring them to accept the freedom that Christ has won for them. The central issue is circumcision and whether non-Jews, including the members of the Galatian community, were required to keep the Jewish law. Paul preaches the centrality of faith and presents the law as a burden that interferes with freedom in Christ. Paul argues that circumcision binds one to obey every aspect of the Jewish law, an obedience that is impossible to maintain and cannot bring salvation. Salvation is a

**213**

JULY 1, 2001 ■ 13TH SUNDAY IN ORDINARY TIME

---

**READING II** Galatians 5:1, 13–18

### A reading from the letter of Paul to the Galatians

> For *freedom* Christ has set us *free*.
> Stand *firm*, therefore,
> and do not submit again to a yoke of *slavery*.
> For you were called to *freedom*, brothers and sisters;
> only do not *use* your freedom
>         as an opportunity for self-*indulgence*,
> but through *love* become *slaves* to one another.
>
> For the whole *law* is summed up in a single *commandment*,
> "You shall love your *neighbour* as *yourself*."
> *If*, however, you *bite* and *devour* one another,
> take *care* that you are not *consumed* by one another.
>
> *Live* by the *Spirit*, I say,
> and do not *gratify* the desires of the *flesh*.
> For what the flesh desires is *opposed* to the Spirit,
> and what the *Spirit* desires is opposed to the *flesh*;
> for these are *opposed* to each other,
> to prevent you from *doing* what you *want*.
> But if you are led by the *Spirit*,
> you are not *subject* to the *law*.

*Proclaim this opening line with authority.*

*Love is central in any discussion of freedom. Speak this line in a firm rather than syrupy voice.*
*This, together with the command to love God, is what Jesus says is the sum of the law. Draw attention to it.*

*Throughout this section, emphasize the importance of the Spirit's guidance.*

---

**GOSPEL** Luke 9:51–62

### A reading from the holy gospel according to Luke

> When the days drew *near* for him to be taken *up*,
> Jesus set his face to go to *Jerusalem*.

---

gift offered in Christ; it is not something that can be earned with good behavior.

Today's passage does not deal directly with the question of circumcision but presents the issue of freedom in more general terms that are applicable today. Freedom is not simply the absence of law but the opportunity to act uprightly, to go beyond the letter of the law and truly love oneself and others. Real freedom is not freedom *from* responsibility but freedom *for* the responsibility of Christian life.

The Spirit provides the Christian with the moral guidance necessary to live in a

way that is truly free. Paul contrasts the Spirit with the desires of the flesh, another way of speaking of slavery to sin. The sins Paul has in mind are not simply "fleshly" in a sexual sense but include desires such as greed, jealousy and selfishness. These are not from the Spirit and are not the fruits of freedom in Christ but are the condition of enslaved, sinful humanity. The Spirit, however, guides the Christian beyond the law, for the Spirit knows what is right and good.

Reflect on actions or desires of your own that sometimes feel overpowering and enslaving. Keep them in mind as you read

this exhortation to freedom, and resolve to heed Paul's advice to be led by the Spirit.

GOSPEL   Jesus' journey in the gospel of Luke, which we follow throughout the rest of the liturgical year, is always directed toward Jerusalem and his death. Today's passage is found at a transition point in the gospel, when Jesus finishes his ministry in his home area of Galilee and begins his journey toward Jerusalem.

The journey from Galilee to Jerusalem often required passing through Samaritan territory. Although the Samaritans and Jews

**214**

13TH SUNDAY IN ORDINARY TIME ▪ JULY 1, 2001

And he sent *messengers ahead* of him.
On their *way* they entered a village of the *Samaritans*
to make *ready* for Jesus;
but the Samaritans did not *receive* him,
because his face was set toward *Jerusalem*.

When his disciples James and John *saw* it, they said,
"*Lord*, do you want us to command *fire*
        to come down from *heaven*
and *consume* them?"
But Jesus turned and *rebuked* them.
Then they went on to *another* village.

As they were going along the *road*, someone said to him,
"I will *follow* you wherever you *go*."
And Jesus said to him,
"*Foxes* have *holes*, and *birds* of the air have *nests*;
but the Son of *Man* has nowhere to lay his *head*."

To another Jesus said,
"*Follow* me."
But he replied,
"Lord, *first* let me go and bury my *father*."
But Jesus said to him,
"Let the *dead* bury their *own* dead;
but as for *you*, go and proclaim the *kingdom* of *God*."

Another said,
"I will *follow* you, Lord;
but let me *first* say *farewell* to those at my *home*."
Jesus said to him,
"*No* one who puts a hand to the *plough* and looks *back*
is *fit* for the kingdom of *God*."

**When Jesus meets with rejection, he simply continues on his way. There is no need for vengeance. Pause.**

**Read this as a direct response to the person's intent to follow wherever Jesus goes.**

**Is Jesus impatient here or resigned? Modify your voice according to your understanding.**

**Discipleship requires wholehearted focus on the goal ahead.**

shared many of the same traditions and beliefs, Samaritans rejected the centrality of Jerusalem and the temple cult. As a result, Jews and Samaritans were hostile to one another. The Samaritans in today's gospel selection reject Jesus precisely because he is on his way to Jerusalem.

When James and John (the "sons of thunder") want to call down fire from heaven, Jesus rebukes them. Their request is reminiscent of a similar incident in the life of Elijah, when Elijah did call down fire to demonstrate the superiority of Israel's God

to all others. But Jesus corrects his disciples; one cannot be a follower of Jesus and resort to violence.

The second half of the gospel selection presents Jesus' responses to those who wish to follow him. In the first, Jesus replies enigmatically to a would-be follower that the Son of Man has no place to lay his head. Following an itinerant preacher who advocates separation from the concerns of the world is not a life of leisure. To the second person, whose father has died, Jesus replies that discipleship involves ministry to the living. It is an active life of proclaiming

God's reign. Finally, in responding to the last would-be disciple, Jesus makes it clear that nothing—not even common family obligations—is more important than following Jesus. The call to discipleship is a demanding one.

Read this passage with attention to the two distinct sections that form the whole. The second section has three parts. Offer it to your community as a call to greater fidelity to Jesus and a summons to follow him on his path to Jerusalem and death.

## JULY 8, 2001

# 14TH SUNDAY IN ORDINARY TIME

*Lectionary #102*

### READING I    Isaiah 66:10–14c

**A reading from the book of the prophet Isaiah**

**Begin strongly, with a bright voice.**

*Rejoice* with Jerusalem,
and be *glad* for her,
all you who *love* her;
*rejoice* with her in *joy,*
all you who *mourn* over her—
that you may *nurse* and be *satisfied*
from her consoling *breast;*

**Lower your voice a bit and speak tenderly.**

that you may drink *deeply* with *delight*
from her glorious *bosom.*

**This is a promise. Deliver it with boldness.**

For *thus* says the *Lord*:
"I will extend *prosperity* to her like a *river,*
and the wealth of the *nations* like an overflowing *stream;*
and you shall *nurse* and be carried on her *arm,*
and *dandled* on her *knees.*
As a *mother* comforts her *child,*
so *I* will comfort *you;*
you shall be *comforted* in *Jerusalem.*

**Again, speak tenderly, then close with a confident declaration.**

"You shall *see,* and your heart shall *rejoice;*
your bodies shall *flourish* like the *grass;*
and it shall be *known*
that the *hand* of the Lord is with his *servants.*"

---

READING I The book of the prophet Isaiah is divided into two main sections, the first of which comes from the time of the prophet himself and the second (itself divided into two sections) from two centuries later, after the period of the Babylonian exile. Today's passage is from that latter half and celebrates the glory of Jerusalem. In the eyes of those who had longed for their beloved city and temple, both destroyed by the Babylonians, nothing could be more wonderful than witnessing Jerusalem's restoration.

Today's passage sings with joy at the prospect of the exiles being nurtured once again in their home. Previously they had mourned for Jerusalem and longed to see its splendor once again. The author depicts the city as a loving mother, providing for her beloved child's every need. Evoking the image of a nursing mother tenderly caressing her infant, the author speaks to the hearts of all who have known what it is to be away from home, to be lonely and heartbroken, and to return once again to a warm embrace.

The image changes as God promises a flood of prosperity to the holy city. Like a current that cannot be contained, all good things will come to Jerusalem. Once again she is a mother, playing with her children and holding them close. God is like a mother as well, comforting those who have been in mourning during the long exile and promising the renewal of the city. Every good will come to God's chosen ones.

Offer this beautiful declaration of God's love and care with gladness. Let your voice ring with joy and trust in God's goodness. If you are initially uncomfortable with the

**14TH SUNDAY IN ORDINARY TIME ■ JULY 8, 2001**

---

### READING II    Galatians 6:14–18

**A reading from the letter of Paul to the Galatians**

> *Speak firmly. Emphasize the word "cross" and speak the entire phrase with great conviction.*

May I never *boast* of *anything*
except the *cross* of our Lord Jesus *Christ*,
by which the *world* has been *crucified* to me,
and *I* to the *world*.
For neither *circumcision* nor *uncircumcision* is *anything*;
but a new *creation* is *everything*!

> *Let a freshness enter your voice as you speak about the new creation.*

As for those who will follow this *rule*—
*peace* be upon them, and *mercy*,
and upon the *Israel* of *God*.
From now *on*, let no one make *trouble* for me;
for I carry the marks of *Jesus* branded on my *body*.

> *Paul is proud of his sufferings.*

May the *grace* of our Lord Jesus *Christ*
be with your *spirit*, brothers and sisters. *Amen*.

---

### GOSPEL    Luke 10:1–12, 17–20

**A reading from the holy gospel according to Luke**

The Lord appointed seventy *others*
and sent them on *ahead* of him in *pairs*
to every town and place where he himself intended to *go*.

> *Speak this directly to your community. All Christians have a responsibility to labor in some way to help bring about the reign of God.*

He said to them,
"The *harvest* is *plentiful*, but the *labourers* are *few*;
therefore ask the *Lord* of the harvest

---

image of a woman nursing her child, practice the passage until you are confident that you can proclaim it as God's message of tender love. Speak God's words with confidence and hope.

**READING II** When Paul "boasts," he does not have in mind his own skills or triumphs. Instead he boasts about something that seems to make no sense: the cross of Jesus. Crucifixion was a means of torture and execution that was especially humiliating in the ancient world.

The Romans used it for condemned traitors and insurrectionists. For a Jew, it was a sign of being cursed by God. Yet Paul defiantly holds it up as the only reason for his boasting.

For Paul, the cross represents the only way salvation can come to the world. Because humans have chosen to reject the love God offers, because humans have chosen to act for their own glory rather than God's, because people have rejected the messenger of truth and Lord of justice, the cross is the sign of truth in a turbulent world. Jesus willingly gave himself for all humanity in order to right the wrongs of the world.

Embracing Jesus' cross means choosing the correct path to God and turning one's back on the falsehood of the world. Ordinary attitudes and expectations are turned upside down.

One of Paul's principal concerns was the acceptance of non-Jews into the Christian community. Some believed that everyone had to follow the Jewish law, which included circumcision of males, in order to follow Jesus. Paul emphatically rejects such an attitude and here considers it part of the folly of the world that has been

JULY 8, 2001 ■ 14TH SUNDAY IN ORDINARY TIME

to send out *labourers* into his *harvest*.
Go on your *way*.
*See*, I am sending you out like *lambs* into the midst of *wolves*.
Carry no *purse*, no *bag*, no *sandals*;
and greet *no* one on the *road*.

**Let a peacefulness enter your voice as you read this section. This is not, however, a sentimental peace but a serious, tough-minded realization of the truth.**

"Whatever house you *enter*,
first say, '*Peace* to this *house*!'
And if anyone is there who *shares* in peace,
your peace will *rest* on that person;
but if *not*, it will *return* to you.
*Remain* in the same house,
*eating* and *drinking* whatever they *provide*,
for the *labourer* deserves to be *paid*.
Do not move *about* from house to *house*.

"Whenever you *enter* a town and its people *welcome* you,
eat what is set *before* you;
cure the *sick* who are there, and say to them,
'The kingdom of *God* has come *near* to you.'

**This is Jesus' own message. Preach it as though you are one of the missionaries.**

"But whenever you enter a town
and they do *not* welcome you,
go out into its *streets* and say,
'Even the *dust* of your town that clings to our *feet*,
we wipe off in *protest against* you.
Yet know *this*: the kingdom of *God* has come *near*.'
I tell you,
on that *day* it will be more tolerable for *Sodom*
than for *that* town."

**God's judgment is harsh against those who refuse to listen.**

The seventy returned with *joy*, saying,
"Lord, in your *name* even the *demons* submit to us!"

**Express the disciples' joy and surprise.**

crucified on the cross. Everyone who recognizes God's openness to all will find peace.

Paul tells us elsewhere of some of the treatment he endured during his ministry, and the Acts of the Apostles confirms his sufferings. In today's reading, he defies anyone who would claim that his views make him a less-worthy follower of Christ and insists that the scars he bears as a result of his devotion to Jesus prove his faithfulness.

Paul had a strong personality and firm conviction. Try to express that as you read

this passage. Speak boldly and confidently, closing with a sincere offer of peace for all your listeners.

| GOSPEL | The mission of the seventy represents the spread of the good news to the entire world. Jewish tradition held that there were seventy nations in the world; that number came to represent all the peoples of the earth. The two-volume work of Luke-Acts is primarily concerned with the preaching of God's word to all the nations. Jesus' life and mission, while rooted

in the promises and opportunities of Judaism, has significance that extends beyond the twelve tribes of Israel. Israel had always seen itself as a "light to the nations," and the author of the gospel of Luke takes that mission seriously. There are many willing recipients of the gospel (a plentiful harvest) among the Gentiles and a great need for ministers who are willing to offer Jesus' message that the reign of God is near.

The missionaries are sent into the world with instructions: They are not to take

**14TH SUNDAY IN ORDINARY TIME ▪ JULY 8, 2001**

Jesus said to them,
"I watched *Satan* fall from *heaven* like a flash of *lightning*.
*See*, I have given you *authority* to tread
      on *snakes* and *scorpions*,
and over all the power of the *enemy*;
and nothing will *hurt* you.

"Nevertheless, do not rejoice at *this*,
that the spirits *submit* to you,
but *rejoice* that your names are written in *heaven*."

[Shorter: Luke 10:1–9]

**Build to this line. Speak slowly and with emphasis.**

any provisions with them, carrying only the knowledge of God and the peacefulness it brings. They are to offer peace to everyone in the homes they enter and are to be satisfied with whatever their hosts provide. If they are not welcomed, they are to leave, knowing that those who reject them face the judgment of God.

Although the ministry of the seventy is to consist of healing, thus continuing the work of Jesus, they return from their travels overjoyed with the power over demons that speaking Jesus' name provided them. To speak someone's name was to claim that person's authority. Jesus' confirms that all evil powers are overcome in the present reign of God. Even Satan has fallen. Jesus goes on to claim that nothing can harm God's messengers, not even poisonous snakes or any other evil power.

Surely this victory over evil is cause for rejoicing. But Jesus clarifies that the real reason for rejoicing lies not in the signs and wonders performed at the hands of the missionaries but in the mission itself; participating in it ensures the inscription of the disciple's name in heaven.

The most significant attributes of the mission given to the disciples in this passage can be applied today as well. Simplicity, detachment and peacefulness must describe our lives as well. Think of your own ministry and the work of your community as you share this message with the members of your assembly. Build in intensity until you reach the concluding statement that the goal of all ministry is beyond what we can see and know today.

JULY 15, 2001

# 15TH SUNDAY IN ORDINARY TIME

*Lectionary #105*

## READING I    Deuteronomy 30:10–14

**A reading from the book of Deuteronomy**

*Moses* spoke to the *people*, saying,
"*Obey* the Lord your *God*
by observing his *commandments* and *decrees*
that are *written* in this *book* of the *law*;
*turn* to the Lord your God with all your *heart*
and with all your *soul*.

"*Surely* this commandment that I am commanding you *today*
is not too *hard* for you,
nor is it too far *away*.
It is not in *heaven*, that you should say,
'*Who* will go up to *heaven* for us,
and *get* it for us so that we may *hear* it and *observe* it?'

"Neither is it beyond the *sea*, that you should say,
'Who will *cross* to the other side of the *sea* for us,
and *get* it for us so that we may *hear* it and *observe* it?'

"*No*, the word is very *near* to you;
it is in your *mouth* and in your *heart* for you to *observe*."

**Slow down as your proclaim this final phrase of the sentence. Speak clearly and forcefully.**

**This is meant to be reassuring; speak encouragingly.**

**Close with a tone that is at once comforting and challenging.**

READING I   Deuteronomy claims to contain the words of Moses addressed to the chosen people just before they entered the land of Canaan. The name of the book means "second law," and in it Moses proclaims the laws given by God at Mount Horeb (Sinai). He also reviews the history of Israel, offering the people motivation for keeping God's law.

In today's passage, Moses encourages Israel to take God's commandments to heart and observe them faithfully. But keeping the law involves more than simply adhering to a

set of rules. It enables the people to turn to God "with all your heart and all your soul." Faithfulness is a matter of constant conversion, continually approaching God in sincerity of heart.

A key feature of Israel's belief regarding the law, beautifully summed up in this passage, is the idea that God's commands can be kept; they are not overly burdensome or difficult. They are not a distant reality that must be sought in the heavens or in the sea but are near and dear to Israel, part of Israel's everyday life. Keeping the law expresses a heartfelt desire to serve the Lord in everything.

This reading is addressed to us as well as to Israel. As Christians, we do not strictly observe the Mosaic law, yet we too strive to keep the spirit of God's commands in our hearts, observing God's will in our actions. We also strive to turn to God continually and to work toward the day when God's word will be so truly written in our hearts that everything we do will reflect God's will. Proclaim this selection boldly, then, addressing it directly to your listeners.

**15TH SUNDAY IN ORDINARY TIME ■ JULY 15, 2001**

---

**READING II**   Colossians 1:15–20

**A reading from the letter of Paul to the Colossians**

Be sure you have the attention of the assembly before beginning. Then boldly proclaim this important first line.

*Christ* is the *image* of the invisible *God,*
the *firstborn* of all *creation;*
for in *him* all things in *heaven* and on *earth* were *created,*
things *visible* and *invisible,*
whether *thrones* or *dominions* or *rulers* or *powers—*
*all* things have been created *through* him and *for* him.

Pause briefly after "powers," then emphasize "all."

Christ is *before* all things,
and *in* him all things hold *together.*

He is the *head* of the *body,* the *church;*
he is the *beginning,* the *firstborn* from the *dead,*
so that he might come to have *first* place in *everything.*

Soften your voice a bit, as if you are sharing a meaningful confidence. Close strongly.

For in *Christ* all the fullness of *God* was pleased to *dwell,*
and *through* him God was pleased
     to *reconcile* to himself *all* things,
whether on *earth* or in *heaven,*
by making *peace* through the blood of his *cross.*

---

**READING II** The hymn from Colossians that you proclaim today presents Christ in the role occupied by Lady Wisdom in Hebrew wisdom literature. Just as Wisdom acts as cocreator with God in Proverbs, this letter presents Christ as the agent through whom everything has been made. He is above every other power and exists before everything else.

The author then turns to the question of Christ's redemptive work. Christ is the firstborn from the dead and thus brings life to all. He is also worthy of all praise because of his exalted status. Lest the hymn be understood to refer only to the exalted Christ in heaven, however, the author clarifies that "the body" over which Christ reigns is precisely the earthly Christian church.

The entire hymn proclaims boldly the preexistence of Christ. Although he came into the world at a particular time and place, he has always been with the Father. Indeed, God dwells so fully in Jesus that Jesus is the very manifestation of God in the world, the one through whom God can draw all people into a loving embrace. Yet the author stresses that it is through the painful reality of the cross that the reconciliation of the world with God is possible.

Offer this hymn of praise with a sense of awe as you sing the praises of Christ as the one exalted over every cosmic power. Let it be a reminder to your community that nothing is to be more important in the life of a Christian than God, who is manifest in Christ Jesus. Proclaim boldly the message that God is not distant but dwells fully in Christ, who has become one of us.

JULY 15, 2001 ■ 15TH SUNDAY IN ORDINARY TIME

## GOSPEL   Luke 10:25–37

**A reading from the holy gospel according to Luke**

A *lawyer* stood up to *test* Jesus.
"*Teacher*," he said, "what must I *do* to inherit
      eternal *life*?"

Jesus said to him,
      "What is *written* in the *law*?
What do you *read* there?"
The lawyer answered,
"You shall *love* the Lord your *God* with all your *heart*,
and with all your *soul*, and with all your *strength*,
and with all your *mind*;
and your *neighbour* as *yourself*."

And Jesus said to him,
"You have given the right *answer*;
*do* this, and you will *live*."
But wanting to *justify* himself, the lawyer asked Jesus,
"And *who* is my *neighbour*?"

Jesus replied,
"A *man* was going down from *Jerusalem* to *Jericho*,
and fell into the hands of *robbers*,
who *stripped* him, *beat* him, and went *away*,
leaving him half *dead*.

Now by chance a *priest* was going down that road;
and when he *saw* him, he passed *by* on the other *side*.
So likewise a *Levite*, when *he* came to the place and saw him,
passed *by* on the other *side*.

---

*Although the lawyer tests Jesus, he is not an entirely negative figure in this gospel; Jesus agrees with his understanding of the essential aspects of the law. Speak his question with sincerity.*

*Express the harshness of the beating.*

---

GOSPEL   Jesus' parable about the good Samaritan, found only in Luke's gospel, is one of the most beautiful and beloved parables of Jesus. In it, a lawyer—someone well versed in the Mosaic law—questions Jesus regarding eternal life. By linking Deuteronomy 6:4–5 and Leviticus 19:18, the lawyer asserts that the core of the Jewish legal tradition is summed up in the love of God and of neighbor. Jesus approves of his answer, but the lawyer presses him further. How far does this loving have to go? Jesus answers him by telling a story of how to act as a neighbor.

The story itself offers only tantalizing clues to questions we might bring to the text. We are not told the identity of the man who was beaten and robbed. Was he a trader, perhaps dishonest himself? Nor are we told what the priest and Levite were thinking as they passed him. Were they afraid that the man would die, making them unclean if they touched the corpse? Or were they afraid that they would be attacked, either by the man himself or by bandits waiting in ambush? Or were they simply unwilling to get involved?

## 15TH SUNDAY IN ORDINARY TIME ■ JULY 15, 2001

**Samaritan = suh-MAYR-uh-tuhn**
**Pause slightly before beginning to speak of the Samaritan. Emphasize the name in an attempt to shock your listeners, perhaps even speaking with a bit of disdain.**

"But a *Samaritan* while travelling came *near* him;
and when he *saw* him, he was moved with *pity*.
He *went* to him and bandaged his *wounds*,
having poured *oil* and *wine* on them.
Then he put him on his own *animal*,
brought him to an *inn*, and took *care* of him.

"The *next* day the Samaritan took out two *denarii*,
gave them to the *innkeeper*, and said,
'Take *care* of him;
and when I come *back*,
I will *repay* you whatever *more* you spend.'"

**Emphasize the word "neighbour."**

Jesus asked,
"*Which* of these three, do you think,
was a *neighbour* to the man
        who fell into the *hands* of the *robbers*?"
The lawyer said, "The one who showed him *mercy*."

**Address this to your assembly.**

Jesus said to him, "*Go* and do *likewise*."

---

Jesus does not address these questions or attempt to help his hearers understand the reasoning of the religious leaders, who pass on the other side of the road. Instead, he shocks his listeners by bringing in the figure of a Samaritan. Despite their common religious heritage, there was great animosity between Samaritans and Jews. The figure of the Samaritan introduces a religious and social enemy as the model of neighborliness and compassion.

In the end, the neighbor was not someone who had formal ties to the injured man but the one who saw to his needs. The one who showed mercy, the one who displayed kindness, is the neighbor. Neighborliness has nothing to do with kinship or being from the same town. It involves doing what is best for another, regardless of social responsibilities or position. The Samaritan, the outsider, was neighborly enough to have compassion and to recognize the need of the injured man.

Summon all your rhetorical skills to proclaim this passage effectively. Try to recapture some of the shock value that would have been present for Jesus' listeners. Then let the story itself inspire your listeners to identify with the Samaritan and to resolve to be people of action, getting involved in the lives of others and working for their welfare.

JULY 22, 2001

# 16TH SUNDAY IN ORDINARY TIME

*Lectionary #108*

## READING I    Genesis 18:1–10a

**A reading from the book of Genesis**

Mamre = MAHM-ray

The *Lord* appeared to *Abraham* by the oaks of *Mamre*,
as Abraham sat at the *entrance* of his *tent* in the heat of the *day*.
Abraham looked *up* and saw three *men* standing *near* him.
When he *saw* them,
he *ran* from the tent entrance to *meet* them,
and bowed down to the *ground*.

**Speak with excitement in order to convey Abraham's eagerness to honor the visitors.**

He said, "My *lord*, if I find *favour* with you,
do not *pass by* your servant.
Let a little *water* be brought, and wash your *feet*,
and *rest* yourselves under the *tree*.
Let me bring a little *bread*, that you may *refresh* yourselves,
and after *that* you may pass *on*—
since you have come to your *servant*."
So they said, "*Do* as you have *said*."

**Again, convey Abraham's haste and emphasize that he and Sarah are offering their finest foods to their guests.**

And Abraham *hastened* into the tent to *Sarah*, and said,
"Make ready *quickly* three measures of choice *flour*,
*knead* it, and make *cakes*."
Abraham ran to the *herd*,
and took a *calf*, tender and *good*,
and gave it to the *servant*, who hastened to *prepare* it.
Then he took *curds* and *milk* and the *calf* that he had prepared,
and set it *before* them;
and he stood *by* them under the *tree* while they *ate*.

---

READING I  In the ancient world, travel was risky, difficult and without many conveniences along the way, and hospitality was required of those who had the means to offer it. When the three men, presumably a manifestation of God, appear to Abraham, he instantly jumps up and greets them, offering refreshment and rest, and serving them the choicest foods. His is an example of true hospitality. The gratitude of the three visitors is shown when one of them promises that Abraham's wife Sarah will

bear a son. Abraham and Sarah had both given up hope for a child; in verses following those in today's passage, Sarah even laughs at the thought of bearing a child in her old age. But God's word is true and, through Isaac, Abraham and Sarah become the ancestors of a great people.

There are three points of emphasis in this passage: the hospitality Abraham and Sarah offer, the fact that they offer the very best that they have, and the promise that closes the story. Provide a rhythm to your proclamation that will allow these three points to stand out. Slow down near the end

so that the significance of God's promise can be fully appreciated.

READING II  Paul was prone to boasting. He boasts not of his talents or accomplishments but "of the Lord" and of his own sufferings for Christ. In the letter to the Colossians, an admirer of Paul writes in his name and continues Paul's emphasis on suffering. Suffering is cause for rejoicing because it draws one into closer imitation of Jesus and demonstrates the true nature of one's faith.

# 16TH SUNDAY IN ORDINARY TIME ■ JULY 22, 2001

Pause before this final scene. The tone changes. Speak God's promise with great solemnity.

They said to Abraham,
"Where is your wife *Sarah*?"
And he said, "*There*, in the *tent*."

Then one said,
"I will surely *return* to you in due *season*,
and your wife *Sarah* shall have a *son*."

---

**READING II**    Colossians 1:24–28

**A reading from the letter of Paul to the Colossians**

Speak with genuine joy but also with a tone of seriousness as you reveal the cause of the joy, namely, suffering.

I am now *rejoicing* in my *sufferings* for *your* sake,
and in my *flesh* I am completing
what is *lacking* in Christ's *afflictions*
for the sake of his *body*, that is, the *church*.

I became its *servant*
according to God's *commission* that was given to me for *you*,
to make the *word* of *God* fully *known*,
the *mystery* that has been hidden
throughout the *ages* and *generations*
but has now been *revealed* to his *saints*.

This sentence is long and complicated. Speak slowly and clearly. Emphasize the word "mystery."

To *them* God chose to make *known*
how *great* among the *Gentiles*
are the *riches* of the *glory* of this *mystery*,
which is *Christ* in *you*, the hope of *glory*.
It is *Christ* whom we *proclaim*,
*warning* everyone and *teaching* everyone in all *wisdom*,
so that we may present *everyone mature* in Christ.

Proclaim this with triumph, closing with firm conviction.

---

It is difficult to know precisely what is meant by the phrase "what is lacking in Christ's afflictions," but it might indicate that the sufferings of Christ are continued in those who suffer in his name. Although Jesus' passion and death were complete and need nothing added to them, Christians who continue to be persecuted for their faith make real his passion for the church in their own age. Paul's sufferings, then, incarnate in his body the passion of Jesus.

Central to today's reading is a discussion of ministry, which is a response to a call from God to reveal the mystery of God's

plan of salvation. This mystery must be carried to the Gentiles, a mission important to Paul, so that they might know Christ. The importance of each minister proclaiming Christ is something we should keep in mind as well, so that we might not become too burdened with concerns about how "successful" we are in our ministries. If we keep our eyes on Christ, we are following our calling.

Meditate on this reading until you are comfortable that you can convey the importance of suffering and the meaning of ministry that the author expresses. Speak slowly in

order to be clear, and proclaim the message with the same pride the author expresses.

GOSPEL  The story of Martha and Mary, like that of Abraham and the three visitors, is a story about hospitality. But it is also a story that is somewhat disturbing, for Jesus seems to rebuke his friend Martha for offering precisely the type of generosity and care that is usually required of a host.

Martha knows how to open her home to a guest. She knows that Jesus is tired and

JULY 22, 2001 ■ 16TH SUNDAY IN ORDINARY TIME

## GOSPEL  Luke 10:38–42

**A reading from the holy gospel according to Luke**

Now as *Jesus* and his *disciples* went on their *way*,
he entered a certain *village*,
where a woman named *Martha welcomed* him into her *home*.
She had a sister named *Mary*,
who sat at the Lord's *feet* and listened to what he was *saying*.

But Martha was *distracted* by her many *tasks*;
so she *came* to Jesus and asked,
"*Lord*, do you not *care*
that my sister has *left* me to do all the *work* by *myself*?
Tell her then to *help* me."

But the Lord answered her,
"*Martha, Martha*,
you are *worried* and *distracted* by many *things*;
there is need of only *one* thing.
Mary has chosen the *better* part,
which will *not* be taken *away* from her."

**Stress how welcoming Martha was. Mary is also introduced in a positive light.**

**Decide what emotions Martha is feeling and let that dictate your reading.**

**Jesus rebukes Martha, but it is a mild correction. Does he speak with resignation or with frustration? Speak the last line firmly.**

needs refreshment. She knows that offering care to another involves effort. Anyone who has ever prepared a large meal alone knows what Martha is experiencing and can understand her exasperation at being left to do all the work by herself.

But it is Mary who receives praise from Jesus. She too is offering hospitality, but of a different sort. What appears to Martha to be laziness and irresponsibility is accepted by Jesus as attentiveness and peacefulness. Mary offers her ear and succeeds in making the guest feel comfortable.

Perhaps the central message of this story is not so much the contrast between the active life and the contemplative life—with Mary's contemplation seen as clearly superior to Martha's action. Perhaps instead the placement of this story immediately after the narrative of the good Samaritan can help us to understand the need for a balance between action and prayer. Hospitality does not consist solely in listening (at the expense of meeting a guest's physical needs), nor is it solely found in constant activity. Loving others is complicated business and involves

taking action when necessary, but it also includes active listening.

Proclaim this story so that the three characters come alive. Determine what emotion lies behind the words of the speakers and give expression to it. Don't be afraid to portray any of the characters in what might at first appear to be a negative light. There is no question that there is conflict in the story. But the author clearly gives greater weight to the type of hospitality that Mary offers.

JULY 29, 2001

# 17TH SUNDAY IN ORDINARY TIME

*Lectionary #111*

## READING I    Genesis 18:20–21, 23–32

**A reading from the book of Genesis**

Mamre = MAHM-ray

Sodom = SOD-uhm
Gomorrah = guh-MOHR-ah

The Lord appeared to *Abraham* by the oaks of *Mamre*
and said,
"How *great* is the outcry against *Sodom* and *Gomorrah*
and how very *grave* their *sin*!
I must go *down*
and see whether they have done altogether
according to the *outcry* that has *come* to me;
and if *not*, I will *know*."

Use plenty of expression for Abraham's
words. Decide if he is shocked and
dismayed or simply being cunning.

Then Abraham came near and said,
"Will you *indeed* sweep away the *righteous* with the *wicked*?
Suppose there are *fifty righteous* within the city;
will you then sweep *away* the place
and not *forgive* it for the fifty *righteous* who are *in* it?
Far be it from *you* to do such a thing,
to slay the *righteous* with the *wicked*,
so that the *righteous* fare as the *wicked*!
Far be *that* from *you*!

Let your tone indicate how preposterous
it is to think that God would be unjust.

Shall not the Judge of all the *earth* do what is *just*?"
And the Lord said,
"If I find at Sodom *fifty righteous* in the city,
I will forgive the *whole place* for *their* sake."

READING I    God reveals to Abraham the fate of the wicked, sinful cities of Sodom and Gomorrah. The Lord announces the plan, but Abraham speaks boldly, questioning the wisdom of destroying cities that might still have righteous inhabitants within it.

What ensues is an almost comical exchange, as God and Abraham bargain over the price of salvation for the cities of Sodom and Gomorrah. The scene comes straight out of a Middle Eastern marketplace, in which bargaining over the correct price is an accepted—and expected—practice. The limits are set at the beginning: God intends to destroy everything; Abraham begs mercy for the cities if there are fifty innocent people within them. Between these positions, anything is possible. Abraham gradually adjusts the figure until, by the end of the conversation, God has come around to a far more merciful position.

But the back-and-forth haggling is not simply a humorous means of dragging out the story. There is real risk involved for Abraham. Just as a buyer in the marketplace must take care not to push too much lest the seller take offense, so also Abraham needs to be cautious. He cannot risk offending God by reducing the number too quickly, lest God become angry and destroy the cities regardless of the number of righteous people.

JULY 29, 2001 ■ 17TH SUNDAY IN ORDINARY TIME

**Abraham speaks humbly here.**

Abraham answered,
"Let me take it upon *myself* to speak to the *Lord,*
*I* who am but *dust* and *ashes.*
Suppose *five* of the fifty righteous are *lacking?*
Will you destroy the *whole city* for lack of *five?*"
And the Lord said,
"I will *not destroy* it if I find forty-*five* there."

Again Abraham spoke to the Lord,
"Suppose *forty* are found there."
He answered,
"For the sake of *forty* I will not *do* it."

Then Abraham said,
"Oh do not let the Lord be *angry* if I speak.
Suppose *thirty* are found there."
The Lord answered,
"I will not *do* it, if I find *thirty* there."

Abraham said,
"Let me take it upon *myself* to speak to the *Lord.*
Suppose *twenty* are found there."
The Lord answered,
"For the sake of *twenty* I will not *destroy* it."

Then Abraham said,
"Oh do not let the Lord be *angry* if I speak just *once* more.
Suppose *ten* are found there."
The Lord answered,
"For the sake of *ten* I will not *destroy* it."

**Although you may choose to express God's earlier words with different emphases, in this case be sure to speak with patience, devotion and love.**

The real message of the tale, however, is the mercy of God. Although God is portrayed here with human emotions, there is truth to the assertion that God has the right to punish the wicked. The author of goodness is also judge of the world. But God is a righteous judge and does not wish to take the lives of the innocent, even if it means that the wicked majority receives mercy as well. God allows the many to go unpunished for the sake of the few.

Allow yourself to be playful with this story without losing the central message of forgiveness. If the seriousness of the conversation inhibits you from seeing the humor in the piece, imagine haggling at a local flea market or garage sale instead. It might help to add in your mind the word "say" before each number ("Suppose there are, say, *fifty* righteous") in order to draw emphasis to each of the numbers Abraham proposes. Let Abraham's attitude change as you see fit: Is he being sneaky, insistent, cajoling or subservient? Let God's responses also change: God might be resigned, angry, impatient or annoyed. Speak the final line with great seriousness and certainty, so that your listeners will be left with the sense that God's mercy is sure.

**17TH SUNDAY IN ORDINARY TIME ■ JULY 29, 2001**

---

**READING II**    Colossians 2:6–14

**A reading from the letter of Paul to the Colossians**

*God is made known to the world through Jesus, the incarnate Son. Exult in this proclamation.*

Brothers and sisters,
as you have *received* Christ *Jesus* the *Lord*,
continue to live your *lives* in him,
*rooted* and built *up* in him and *established* in the *faith*,
just as you were *taught*, abounding in *thanksgiving*.
For in *him* the whole fullness of *deity* dwells *bodily*,
and you have come to *fullness* in *him*,
who is the *head* of every *ruler* and *authority*.

*Lift your voice as you proclaim God's tremendous power.*

In him *also* you were *circumcised* with a *spiritual* circumcision,
by putting *off* the body of *flesh* in the circumcision of *Christ*.
When you were *buried* with Christ in *baptism*,
you were also *raised* with him
through *faith* in the power of *God*,
who raised *Christ* from the *dead*.

*Speak firmly and with gratitude for God's forgiveness.*

And when you were *dead* in *trespasses*
and the *uncircumcision* of your *flesh*,
God made you *alive* together *with* him,
when he *forgave* us all our *trespasses*,
*erasing* the record that stood *against* us with its legal *demands*.
He set this *aside*, *nailing* it to the *cross*.

---

**READING II** The letter to the Colossians was written to believers who respected the authority of Paul but who had been led astray by the teachings of unknown preachers. The author wrote in Paul's name to instruct the Colossians in the correct understanding of the gospel.

The letter begins with instruction to be Christ-centered, for in Christ God is revealed to the world. The author then highlights three of Paul's favorite themes: baptism, the rejection of circumcision, and the centrality of the cross.

For Paul, initiation involves a baptism into the death of Christ with a hope for future resurrection. Here, baptism is understood as burial with Christ but also resurrection with him. Paul always insists that the resurrected life is in the future; believers must strive to be worthy of it. Colossians' author agrees with Paul that the Christian life requires moral living but understands the new life to have already begun.

Like Paul, the author does not think that circumcision is necessary for salvation, as some Jewish Christians insisted. The proof of this lies in the fact that the Colossians became believers and began their new life in Christ even when they were sinful and without benefit of circumcision. Because God forgives sin, its presence in someone's life does not deter that person from trusting completely in Christ and the efficacy of his death and resurrection.

JULY 29, 2001 ■ 17TH SUNDAY IN ORDINARY TIME

## GOSPEL    Luke 11:1–13

**A reading from the holy gospel according to Luke**

Jesus was *praying* in a certain *place*,
and after he had *finished*, one of his disciples said to him,
"*Lord*, teach *us* to *pray*,
as *John* taught *his* disciples."

He said to them, "When you *pray*, say:
'*Father*, *hallowed* be your *name*.
Your kingdom *come*.
Give us *each* day our daily *bread*.
And *forgive* us our *sins*,
for we *ourselves* forgive everyone *indebted* to us.
And do not *bring* us to the time of *trial*.'"

And Jesus said to the disciples,
"Suppose *one* of you has a *friend*,
and you go to him at *midnight* and say to him,
'*Friend*, lend me *three* loaves of *bread*;
for a *friend* of mine has arrived,
and I have nothing to set *before* him.'
And your friend answers from within,
'Do not *bother* me;
the door has already been *locked*,
and my *children* are with me in *bed*;
I cannot get *up* and give you *anything*.'

"I *tell* you,
even though he will *not* get up and give him anything
because he is his *friend*,
at least because of his *persistence*
he will get *up* and give him *whatever* he *needs*.

---

*This version of the Lord's Prayer is somewhat different from the one most familiar to us. Pause after each line so that the force of the words can sink in.*

*Pause before beginning. The tone becomes lighter as you tell this story.*

---

Because the Colossians had lived in sin and had not known the truth of God's message, the author likens them to prisoners who have a bail note or bond written against them. But Jesus' death on the cross cancels that bond, freeing believers of the "debts" of sin, which have been symbolically nailed to the cross with Jesus.

The central message of this selection is the importance of Christ's saving actions. Draw attention to the new life offered in him. Speak slowly and carefully, so that the message will not be lost on your listeners.

GOSPEL    The gospel of Luke portrays Jesus at prayer, especially at crucial points in his ministry. Prayer gives him strength and provides him with the guidance he needs on his journey. In response to a request from his disciples, Jesus teaches them to pray in a way that will identify them as his followers, just as John's disciples had adopted unique prayers. The prayer Jesus gives his disciples has become the unifying and identifying prayer of Christians.

The Lord's Prayer begins by acknowledging God's sovereignty and moves to petitions for the community. Far from being a private prayer, the Lord's Prayer expresses the petitions in the plural. *We* pray for *our* bread and ask forgiveness for *our* sins. As a community, we approach God in need and beg for mercy, while striving to offer mercy to others.

Jesus' instruction on prayer continues with a humorous story about the bothersome neighbor. Just as Abraham is persistent in

**230**

17TH SUNDAY IN ORDINARY TIME ■ JULY 29, 2001

**Speak solemnly and with encouragement.**

"So I *say* to you: *Ask*, and it will be *given* you;
*search*, and you will *find*;
*knock*, and the door will be *opened* for you.
For everyone who *asks receives*,
and everyone who *searches finds*,
and for everyone who *knocks*, the door will be *opened*.

**Pause again.**

"Is there *anyone* among you who,
if your *child* asks for a *fish*,
will give a *snake instead* of a fish?
Or if the child asks for an *egg*, will give a *scorpion*?

**Close with a tone of sincerity and trust.**

"If *you* then, who are *evil*,
know how to give *good* gifts to your *children*,
how much *more* will the heavenly *Father*
give the Holy *Spirit* to those who *ask* him!"

his dealings with God in today's first reading, so also each of us should be persistent
with God in times of need. Such requests
demonstrate our dependence on the divine.
And, just as the homeowner in the gospel
finally gets annoyed and grants his friend's
request, so also God just might give in out of
sheer fatigue!

The final story, of the father and child,
tempers the lesson of the previous story. Our
petitions are not simply to be self-centered
demands. God desires what is good for us.
And God grants us the most profound gift of

all, the Holy Spirit, who guides our prayer
and brings us all that we need.

Treat each of these three sections separately, giving voice to the different lessons
each offers. There is hyperbole in the stories; allow yourself to exaggerate along
with the author. Give special emphasis to
the final line concerning the Holy Spirit.

AUGUST 5, 2001

# 18TH SUNDAY IN ORDINARY TIME

*Lectionary #114*

## READING I    Ecclesiastes 1:2; 2:21–23

**A reading from the book of Ecclesiastes**

*Cry out with desperation in these opening lines.*

*Vanity* of *vanities*, says the Teacher,
*vanity* of *vanities*! All is *vanity*.

*Let sadness fill your voice as you describe the situation.*

Sometimes one who has toiled
        with *wisdom* and *knowledge* and *skill*
must leave *all* to be enjoyed by *another*
who did not *toil* for it.
This also is *vanity* and a great *evil*.

*There is deep pain in these words. Close with a sense of futility.*

What do mortals *get* from all the *toil* and *strain*
with which they *toil* under the *sun*?
For all their *days* are full of *pain*,
and their *work* is a *vexation*;
even at *night* their minds do not *rest*.
This *also* is *vanity*.

READING I  Hebrew wisdom literature attempts to give direction on how to live daily life. The author of Ecclesiastes finds much of life to be futile, for the same fate awaits both the wicked and the righteous: death. Written before belief in an afterlife developed, the book does not look to a future vindication for the righteous but recognizes that life can be unfair. The author concludes that the answer is to live well and be happy.

Today's passage is a mournful lament about the "vanity" or futility of life. As the author has observed, those who work hard often do not get to enjoy the fruits of their labor. Someone else, one who did not engage in the work, will enjoy the benefits of the other's labor. In fact, the reward for hard work is really just pain and frustration.

This selection highlights a reality that we would probably prefer to avoid. Far from being encouraging or joyous, it leaves us with a deep sense of sadness. The author appears to be disillusioned and tired. Only faith in God's goodness can provide peace for such a troubled soul.

Do not shy away from the pain the author expresses here. Start with a cry of anguish, then speak in a subdued voice and with a sense of futility.

READING II  The author of Colossians writes as an admirer of Paul to the early community in Colossae. The Colossian church was not founded by Paul, but the author clearly holds the community in high esteem. The author hopes that, by writing in Paul's name, Paul's influence will be felt in a community that had received some misguided teachings.

18TH SUNDAY IN ORDINARY TIME ▪ AUGUST 5, 2001

## READING II    Colossians 3:1–5, 9–11

**A reading from the letter of Paul to the Colossians**

*Lift your voice and speak brightly and encouragingly.*

So if you have been *raised* with *Christ*,
seek the things that are *above*,
where *Christ* is, seated at the right *hand* of *God*.

Set your minds on things that are *above*,
not on things that are on *earth*,
for you have *died*,
and your life is *hidden* with Christ in *God*.
When *Christ* who is your *life* is *revealed*,
then you *also* will be revealed with him in *glory*.

*Continue to speak with a strong voice but with disdain for the impure thoughts and actions these words describe.*

Put to *death*, therefore, whatever in you is *earthly*:
*fornication, impurity, passion,*
evil *desire*, and *greed*, which is *idolatry*.

Do not *lie* to one another,
seeing that you have stripped *off* the *old* self with its *practices*
and have clothed yourselves with the *new* self,
which is being *renewed* in *knowledge*
according to the image of its *creator*.

*Let your voice brighten again; end with a stirring announcement that Christ is everything.*

In that *renewal* there is no longer *Greek* and *Jew*,
*circumcised* and *uncircumcised*,
*barbarian, Scythian,*
*slave* and *free*;
but *Christ* is *all* and *in* all!

---

Although Paul always speaks of dying with Christ and asserts that the resurrected life lies in the future, the author of Colossians indicates that Christians have been raised already, just as Christ has been. Because the new life has already begun, we are to live as inhabitants of a heavenly order rather than be ruled by the spirits of the temporal world. Always keeping our eyes on the exalted Christ, we are to live lives worthy of him. Our heavenly, glorified life will be revealed when Christ himself is revealed.

Since the glorified life is not fully revealed on earth, there are moral imperatives that Christians are to follow in the meantime. As true residents of heaven, we are to leave earthly things behind. All forms of sin and temptation are earthly, but the Christian is a new self, with new ways of living. In language reminiscent of the baptismal ritual, in which those to be initiated approach the water naked and are later clothed with pure, white garments, the author speaks of stripping off the old self and putting on the new.

The final paragraph recalls a baptismal formula found in a letter of Paul that was presumably used in the baptismal rituals of the Pauline churches. It affirms that Christian initiation erases all the divisions of the world. In baptism, all are united into one community regardless of the barriers that ordinarily separate people from one another. In the Christian church, Christ is everything; nothing else matters.

Proclaim this passage with an eye to the lofty ideas being expressed. Offer the instructions as sincere reminders of how best to live. Finally, close with a strong voice,

AUGUST 5, 2001 ■ 18TH SUNDAY IN ORDINARY TIME

## GOSPEL   Luke 12:13–21

### A reading from the holy gospel according to Luke

Someone in the crowd said to Jesus,
"*Teacher*, tell my brother
        to divide the family *inheritance* with me."
But Jesus said to him,
"*Friend*, who set *me* to be a *judge* or *arbitrator* over you?"

And Jesus said to the crowd,
"Take *care*! Be on your *guard* against all kinds of *greed*;
for one's *life* does not consist in the abundance of *possessions*."

Then Jesus told them a *parable*:
"The land of a *rich* man produced *abundantly*.
And he thought to himself,
'What should I *do*, for I have no *place* to store my *crops*?'
Then he said, 'I will do *this*:
I will pull *down* my barns and build *larger* ones,
and *there* I will store all my *grain* and my *goods*.
And I will say to my soul,
"*Soul*, you have ample *goods* laid up for many *years*;
*relax*, *eat*, *drink*, be *merry*."'

"But God said to him,
'You *fool*!
This very *night* your life is being *demanded* of you.
And the things you have *prepared*, whose will *they* be?'
So it *is* with those who store up treasures for *themselves*
but are not rich toward *God*."

---

**Jesus' rebuke is harsh. He has no desire to negotiate possessions in this world; his values are elsewhere.**
**Proclaim this with a strong voice, as if Jesus is speaking to the crowds.**

**Is the man wily or simply satisfied with his success? Let your answer determine your reading.**

**God's condemnation is strong.**

---

confident of the unity we have in Christ, who is all and in all.

GOSPEL   The question about inheritance leads Jesus to tell a story about greed. The death of a family member and the subsequent division of property often led, both in Jesus' time and today, to examples of the unhealthy significance that money and possessions have in people's lives.

The man in the parable is already blessed with great abundance. He plans to do precisely what the author of Ecclesiastes suggests is the only way to be happy in life: eat, drink and be merry. By relaxing and enjoying what he has accumulated, he hopes to have a good, long life. But before he can enjoy his wealth, he is told he will die. Clearly his many possessions will offer him no comfort in death.

It is not so much the possessions themselves that are the problem here. The issue is the desire to accumulate and hoard, making wealth one's highest priority. Jesus reminds his listeners that true wealth comes from knowing and trusting God.

This passage is especially appropriate for our society, in which accumulation of assets is often an all-consuming goal. Even when we do not have many possessions, the desire to have more can eat away at our souls. Offer this challenging gospel reading to your community as a call to return to what is central and an encouragement to reflect on the many blessings we already have. Read it as a straightforward story, giving plenty of expression to the attitudes of the man and the strong response of God.

AUGUST 12, 2001

# 19TH SUNDAY IN ORDINARY TIME

*Lectionary #117*

## READING I Wisdom 18:6–9

**Pause after "Egypt" to make the setting clear to your listeners.**

### A reading from the book of Wisdom

The night of the *deliverance* from *Egypt*
was made known *beforehand* to our *ancestors*,
so that they might *rejoice* in sure *knowledge* of the oaths
in which they *trusted*.

The *deliverance* of the *righteous*
and the *destruction* of their *enemies*
were expected by your *people*.
For by the *same* means
by which you punished our *enemies*
you called us to *yourself* and *glorified* us.

**Emphasize this line. The glorification of God's chosen people is central.**

For in *secret*
the holy children of *good* people offered *sacrifices*,
and with one *accord* agreed to the divine *law*,
so that the saints would share *alike* the same *things*,
both *blessings* and *dangers*;
and *already* they were singing the praises of the *ancestors*.

READING I The exodus from Egypt and all that surrounded it had a lasting impact on the Hebrew people and continues to inspire Jews today. Today's reading alludes to these events.

In the exodus, God repeatedly revealed that the Hebrew people were the chosen ones by offering protection and guidance through their trials. Before leaving Egypt, the Israelites celebrated the Passover, slaughtering a lamb and marking their doors with

its blood to safeguard their children from death. Then they fled their homes and, with God's help, crossed the Red Sea as their pursuers were engulfed by the water.

The author suggests that the Hebrew people knew about the divine victory of the Exodus before it happened; they were long aware of their special calling because of this knowledge. Knowing that God would prevail, they offered the Passover sacrifice, thereby assenting to the divine law even before it was formally given to Moses at Mount Sinai.

The context of this passage is not immediately apparent, making it a difficult reading to comprehend and proclaim. Emphasize "the night of the deliverance" in the hope that it might be clear that it is the night of the Passover. Speak clearly and strongly of God's wondrous works for Israel.

AUGUST 12, 2001 ■ 19TH SUNDAY IN ORDINARY TIME

## READING II  Hebrews 11:1–2, 8–19

**A reading from the letter to the Hebrews**

Now *faith* is the assurance of things *hoped* for,
the *conviction* of things not *seen*.
Indeed, by *faith* our ancestors received *approval*.

By faith *Abraham* obeyed
when he was *called* to set out for a place
that he was to receive as an *inheritance*;
and he set *out*,
not *knowing* where he was *going*.
By *faith* he stayed for a *time*
in the land he had been *promised*,
as in a *foreign* land, living in *tents*,
as did *Isaac* and *Jacob*,
who were *heirs* with him of the same *promise*.

For Abraham looked forward to the *city* that has *foundations*,
whose *architect* and *builder* is *God*.
By faith Sarah *herself*, though *barren*,
received power to *conceive*, even when she was too *old*,
because she considered him *faithful* who had *promised*.

Therefore from *one* person,
and *this* one as good as *dead*,
*descendants* were born,
"as *many* as the *stars* of *heaven*
and as the *innumerable* grains of *sand* by the *seashore*."

*Begin with a strong voice. Pause at the end of the first sentence.*

*Stress the word "faith" wherever it is found in the reading.*

*Speak brightly as you recount this promise to Abraham.*

---

READING II  The reflection on faith in this chapter of Hebrews begins with a beautiful statement of its perspective: The author looks forward to something unknown, confident that it will become a reality. The text then reflects on several examples of faithfulness from Hebrew history, concentrating especially on the faith of Abraham. The examples are understood, however, entirely from a Christian perspective, as the reference to the binding of Isaac makes clear.

Abraham was an example of faithfulness throughout his lifetime. He left his homeland and set out for a land promised by God even though he did not know where he was going. Trusting in God's word, he lived as a foreigner in a foreign land and believed that more awaited him. Sarah, too, had faith that they could have a child, even though she and Abraham were both advanced in years ("as good as dead" is clearly an exaggeration!). Although they never saw their numerous descendants, they believed God and knew that they would have as many descendants as there are grains of sand. In

ancient Hebrew thought, the only concept of an afterlife was the hope of living on through one's descendants. The author of Hebrews accepts this, but alters it as well to conform to belief in a heavenly afterlife.

What characterizes the ancestors who are extolled in this passage is their willingness to believe in God's promises, even though they never saw their fulfillment. Only Abraham, in his offering of Isaac, was given immediate reward for his faithfulness when his son was returned to him alive.

# 236

19TH SUNDAY IN ORDINARY TIME ■ AUGUST 12, 2001

All of these *died* in *faith*
without having *received* the promises,
but from a *distance* they saw and *greeted* them.
They *confessed* that they were *strangers*
        and *foreigners* on the earth,
for people who speak in *this* way
make it *clear* that they are seeking a *homeland*.
If they had been thinking of the *land* that they had left *behind*,
they would have had opportunity to *return*.

But as it *is*, they desire a *better* country,
that is, a *heavenly* one.
Therefore God is not *ashamed* to be called their *God*;
indeed, he has prepared a *city* for them.

**Pause before beginning this important example of faithfulness.**

By faith *Abraham*, when put to the *test*,
offered up *Isaac*.
He who had received the *promises*
was ready to offer up his *only son*,
of whom he had been *told*,
"It is through *Isaac* that descendants shall be *named* for you."
Abraham *considered* the fact

**Speak of God raising someone from the dead as though you are sharing a great secret.**

that God is able even to *raise* someone from the *dead*—
and *figuratively* speaking, he *did* receive Isaac *back*.

[Shorter: Hebrews 11:1–2, 8–12]

---

The binding of Isaac is the example that is most useful to the author of Hebrews, for it points to the resurrection of Jesus. Abraham is anachronistically said to be able to see through the "raising" of his only son the fact that God can raise someone from the dead. Early Christians were fond of seeing in Isaac a precursor of Christ, the only Son who was brought back to life.

The image of the faithful ancestors is evoked here in order to provide inspiration to the community so that its members would hold fast to their faith, even if they did not immediately see its benefits. The hope in a heavenly future is projected back into the stories of the Hebrew forerunners to show that they too believed in promises that could not be fulfilled on earth. With such examples of confident trust, the author urges the community to pursue the goal that is ahead.

The reading itself is fairly straightforward. Begin on a strong note, then give honor to those faithful servants of God whose memory is evoked here, emphasizing always the centrality of faith in their decisions and actions. Close with a conscious allusion to the resurrection of Jesus, in whom all Christians have hope even though we have not seen him.

**237**

AUGUST 12, 2001 ■ 19TH SUNDAY IN ORDINARY TIME

### GOSPEL Luke 12:32–48

**A reading from the holy gospel according to Luke**

*Speak these words of Jesus with gentleness and encouragement.*

Jesus said to his disciples,
"Do not be *afraid*, little *flock*,
for it is your Father's good *pleasure* to give you the *kingdom*.
*Sell* your possessions, and give *alms*.
Make *purses* for yourselves that do not wear *out*,
an unfailing *treasure* in *heaven*,
where no *thief* comes *near* and no moth *destroys*.
For where your *treasure* is, there your *heart* will be *also*.

*Now your reading should become more urgent and forceful.*

"Be dressed for *action* and have your lamps *lit*;
be like those who are *waiting* for their *master*
to return from the *wedding* banquet,
so that they may open the *door* for him
as *soon* as he comes and *knocks*.
*Blessed* are those slaves
whom the master finds *alert* when he *comes*;
truly I *tell* you, he will fasten his *belt*
and have them sit down to *eat*,
and he will come and *serve* them.

If he comes during the middle of the *night*, or near *dawn*,
and finds them so,
*blessed* are those *slaves*.

*There is an ominous tone to these words.*

"But know *this*:
if the *owner* of the house
had known at what *hour* the thief was *coming*,
he would not have let his *house* be broken *into*.

You *also* must be *ready*,
for the Son of *Man* is coming at an unexpected *hour*."

---

GOSPEL Today's gospel reading continues the theme that was begun last Sunday. Possessions are of little use to one who is focused on a far greater treasure, a treasure that cannot be stolen or destroyed. The treasure is a royal possession, the reign of God.

The rest of the passage discusses the issue of preparedness. Slaves are to be alert as they await their master's return from the wedding feast. The master, too, needs to be prepared. Only those who are ready will receive the good things that are to come.

In this section, the author seeks to answer questions regarding Jesus' return to earth. The gospel was written several decades after Jesus' ministry and also after

Paul's letters, which display a fervent hope in the imminent return of the exalted Jesus. Some Christians must have been wondering when Jesus would come again and what signs would indicate that his coming was near. The author of Luke-Acts suggests that there is no need to watch for the time; rather, it is imperative to be always ready.

**238**

19TH SUNDAY IN ORDINARY TIME ■ AUGUST 12, 2001

**Peter's question is a practical one, and, as usual, Jesus does not answer directly but tells another story.**

*Peter* said,
"*Lord*, are you telling this parable for *us* or for *everyone*?"
And the Lord said,
"*Who* then is the *faithful* and prudent *manager*
whom his master will put in charge of his *slaves*,
to give them their allowance of *food* at the proper *time*?
*Blessed* is that slave
whom his master will find at *work* when he *arrives*.
Truly I *tell* you,
he will put *that* one in charge of *all* his *possessions*.
But if that slave says to *himself*,
'My master is *delayed* in *coming*,'

**Let your voice darken as you recount the viciousness of the irresponsible slave and the cruel fate that awaits such a person.**

and if he begins to *beat* the other slaves, *men* and *women*,
and to *eat* and *drink* and get *drunk*,
the *master* of that slave will come on a day
when he does not *expect* him
and at an *hour* that he does not *know*,
and will cut him in *pieces*,
and put him with the *unfaithful*.

"That slave who *knew* what his master wanted,
but did not *prepare* himself or *do* what was wanted,
will receive a severe *beating*.
But the one who did *not* know
and did what *deserved* a beating will receive a *light* beating.

**Pause before concluding on a strong, solemn note. Those of us who have been so richly blessed need to be ever mindful of this teaching.**

"From *everyone* to whom much has been *given*,
*much* will be *required*;
and from the one to whom *much* has been *entrusted*,
even *more* will be *demanded*."

[Shorter: Luke 12:35–40]

We are far removed from the situation that gave rise to this urgent expectation of Christ's coming. But we too know that we will be called to stand before our maker and judge. We can never know precisely when we will die, but we must be ever watchful, always faithful and ready so that we might be worthy to share in the heavenly banquet.

Peter's question and Jesus' response direct the issue especially to leaders in the community. Slaves are again symbolic of the servants of God, but these slaves have greater responsibility than others. They are to be especially prepared, for they are responsible for the care of others as well as themselves. And those who know what is expected of them will be held to a higher standard than those who act in ignorance.

The issue of preparedness is one that needs to be addressed by every member of the community, for we live in a society of distractions. Speak boldly, challenging your listeners and especially those in leadership positions to reflect on how well their hearts are attuned to the concerns that really matter. Emphasize the last few lines and encourage your listeners to reflect on the many gifts they have received from God, with the knowledge that such blessings require lives of even greater action.

# AUGUST 15, 2001

# ASSUMPTION

*Lectionary #622*

## READING I   Revelation 11:19a; 12:1–6a, 10ab

**A reading from the book of Revelation**

God's *temple* in *heaven* was *opened*,
and the *ark* of his *covenant* was seen within his *temple*.

A great *portent* appeared in *heaven:*
a *woman* clothed with the *sun*,
with the *moon* under her *feet*,
and on her head a *crown* of twelve *stars*.
She was *pregnant* and was crying out in *birth* pangs,
in the *agony* of giving *birth*.

Then *another* portent appeared in heaven:
a *great* red *dragon*, with seven *heads* and ten *horns*,
and seven *diadems* on his heads.
His *tail* swept down a *third* of the stars of *heaven*
and *threw* them to the *earth*.
Then the *dragon* stood before the *woman*
who was about to bear a *child*,
so that he might *devour* her child
as *soon* as it was *born*.

And she gave *birth* to a *son*, a *male* child,
who is to *rule* all the *nations* with a rod of *iron*.
But her child was snatched *away*
and taken to *God* and to his *throne;*
and the woman *fled* into the *wilderness*,
where she has a place *prepared* by *God*,

"Revelation," not "Revelations."

portent = POR-t*nt

The dragon is diabolical; speed up the tempo here in order to indicate the tensions inherent in the scene.
diadems = DĪ-uh-demz

This is the Messiah promised by the prophets.

Although there is still urgency in the "snatching" of the child and the flight of the woman, begin to calm your voice.

READING I The vision that the author of Revelation describes in this passage is one of a great battle between the forces of good and evil. The descriptions of the participants in the drama and the combat itself are drawn from both Greco-Roman and Jewish myths. The woman who gives birth appears to be Mary (or Israel) and the child is clearly the Messiah; elsewhere the woman seems to represent the church as her many offspring continue to be pursued by the dragon.

The apocalyptic imagery of this passage can be confusing. First, heaven is pictured as a great temple that contains the ark of the covenant, the ancient container that held the tablets of the Mosaic law. Then, as in a dream, the scene changes and the focus shifts to a woman about to give birth. She is beautifully clothed with the sun, moon and stars; she is the queen of heaven.

The dragon who earlier tried to grasp heavenly authority (by sweeping the stars out of heaven) now enters the scene, seeking to harm the woman's child. The appearance of the dragon (seven heads and ten

horns) comes from the depiction of the enemies of the righteous in the book of Daniel; the seven heads recall imperial Rome, the city on seven hills, which is here seen as the enemy of Christianity.

The child is born and taken to be with God. The woman now represents the church, cared for by God for a limited time (1260 days) until the dragon is defeated. During this time, however, the Messiah already reigns, as the voice from heaven proclaims.

This is a difficult but beautiful passage, chosen because of the imagery of the

# ASSUMPTION ■ AUGUST 15, 2001

**Proclaim this triumphant statement of divine rule with clarity and authority.**

so that there she can be *nourished*
for one *thousand* two *hundred* sixty *days.*

Then I heard a loud *voice* in heaven, *proclaiming,*
"*Now* have come the *salvation* and the *power*
and the *kingdom* of our *God*
and the *authority* of his *Messiah.*"

---

**READING II**     1 Corinthians 15:20–26

---

**A reading from the first letter of Paul to the Corinthians**

**Pause briefly at the end of this line.**

Brothers and sisters,
*Christ* has been *raised* from the *dead,*
the *first fruits* of those who have *died.*
For since *death* came through a human *being,*
the *resurrection* of the dead

**Pause.**
**Pause after "Adam."**

       has *also* come through a human *being;*
for as all *die* in *Adam,*
so all will be made *alive* in *Christ.*
But *each* in his own *order:*
*Christ* the first *fruits,*
*then* at his *coming* those who *belong* to Christ.

**Take a deep breath, and change your tone as you begin the next line. "Then" all things will be different and God will reign supreme. Celebrate this proclamation with joyful expectation in your voice.**

*Then* comes the *end,*
when he hands over the *kingdom* to *God* the *Father,*
after he has *destroyed* every *ruler*
and every *authority* and *power.*
For Christ must *reign*

**Your voice should be a bit more subdued but firm for this final line; pause after "destroyed."**

       until he has put all his *enemies* under his *feet.*
The *last* enemy to be destroyed is *death.*

---

woman. Mary has often been depicted as ruling the cosmos, and her Son is the one enthroned with God in heaven. Read the selection with awe at the heavenly vision and the beauty of the woman, and with compassion for her pain. In addition, convey the danger of the dragon's threat. Finally, close with the triumphant realization that all will be kept safe by God, who reigns in majesty.

| READING II | After rejecting the claim of some Christians that there is no resurrection of the dead, Paul develops

in this section the meaning of Christ's resurrection. In Jewish liturgical language, Christ is the "first fruits" of those who have died, the one who represents the whole. What he experienced in rising from the dead is available to all who die with faith in him.

Paul then alludes to his belief that death entered the world because of the sin of Adam. Christ—the second Adam—makes life possible both for Christians who have

already died and for those who remain alive at Christ's second coming. Finally, after overcoming death and all other hostile powers, Christ will turn over all rule to God.

We proclaim this reading on Assumption because of our belief that Mary has already followed her Son into heavenly glory. The tradition that she was taken into heaven after her death is a way of indicating that death was not the final word for her. Instead, she has already experienced a share in the resurrection promised to all who follow Jesus.

AUGUST 15, 2001 ■ ASSUMPTION

## GOSPEL    Luke 1:39–56

**A reading from the holy gospel according to Luke**

Judean = joo-DEE-*n
Zechariah = zek-uh-RĪ-uh

*Mary* set *out* and went with *haste*
to a Judean town in the *hill* country,
where she entered the house of *Zechariah* and greeted *Elizabeth*.

When Elizabeth heard Mary's *greeting*,
the child *leaped* in her *womb*.
And Elizabeth was *filled* with the Holy *Spirit*
and *exclaimed* with a loud *cry*,
"*Blessed* are you among *women*,
and *blessed* is the *fruit* of your *womb*.
And *why* has this happened to *me*,
that the *mother* of my *Lord comes* to me?
For as *soon* as I heard the sound of your *greeting*,
the *child* in my womb *leaped* for *joy*.
And *blessed* is she who *believed*
that there would be a *fulfilment*
of what was *spoken* to her by the *Lord*."

**Proclaim Elizabeth's words with sincerity and wonder. In order to avoid rattling through the familiar words, consciously try to slow down your diction, dwelling on every phrase.**

And Mary said,
"My *soul magnifies* the *Lord*,
and my spirit *rejoices* in God my *Saviour*,
for he has looked with *favour* on the lowliness of his *servant*.
Surely, from now on all *generations* will call me *blessed*;
for the *Mighty* One has done great *things* for me,
and *holy* is his *name*.
His *mercy* is for those who *fear* him
from *generation* to *generation*.

**Mary picks up the tone of praise.**

**Speak this and the following lines with a bit of disbelief in your voice; Mary must surely have been amazed at God's favor toward her.**

---

The beginning of the passage is difficult. Proclaim it slowly, emphasizing the contrasts between death and resurrection, between Adam and Christ. The second half of the reading is a proclamation of God's reign and can be read as a word of praise.

GOSPEL  The gospel of Luke is known for the hymns it contains, and the Magnificat, spoken by Mary in today's gospel, is one of the most beautiful. Although the hymn itself clearly draws on

material from the Hebrew tradition, it is the longest passage attributed to Mary in any gospel. It is not difficult to imagine a poor, unwed pregnant girl proclaiming these words, a celebration of God's compassion for the lowly and ability to humble the proud.

The context of the hymn is Mary's visit to Elizabeth. The mothers of two future itinerant preachers are brought together as friends and relatives. Since there was some tension between the followers of John and those of Jesus during their ministries and

afterward, the author here makes it clear that Jesus is the greater, and the unborn John and his mother rejoice at and are humbled by Mary's visit. Elizabeth utters a cry honoring Mary for her trust in God's promise to her.

Mary's response is a joyful, trusting song of reversal that celebrates God's activity in her life and in Israel's. While the hymn is a song of praise to God, it is fitting for a Marian feast since it illustrates Mary's humility and faith, including her belief in a righteous God who acts on behalf of the lowly.

**ASSUMPTION ■ AUGUST 15, 2001**

**With this line, let your voice become firmer and more insistent. The words Mary proclaims are those of upheaval; nothing is as it seems.**

"He has shown *strength* with his *arm*;
he has *scattered* the proud in the thoughts of their *hearts*.
He has brought down the *powerful* from their *thrones*,
and lifted up the *lowly*;
he has *filled* the hungry with *good* things,
and sent the *rich* away *empty*.
"He has *helped* his servant *Israel*,
in *remembrance* of his *mercy*,
according to the *promise* he made to our *ancestors*,
to *Abraham* and to his descendants *forever*."

**Pause before continuing in a subdued but clear voice.**

And Mary *remained* with *Elizabeth* about three *months*
and then returned to her *home*.

The first half of the hymn discusses the favor God has bestowed on Mary. Although she proclaims herself a handmaid or servant, one of the lowly ones, she will be called blessed because of the great things God has done for her and through her. In this way, the first half of the hymn foreshadows what follows: God deals with the individual servant Mary in much the same way as God has dealt with servant Israel. Both are blessed beyond measure, recipients of God's protection, compassion and lavish graciousness.

Not only is there divine favor for the lowly, but God acts decisively to eliminate systems of power and inequity. The haughty and proud, who have placed themselves on a level with God as they scorn the less fortunate, are shown their rightful place. The images are of political leaders; the message is that the land of Israel, occupied by a foreign power, will be vindicated. But Israel has within it also the individual poor, the hungry; they too shall be cared for.

Sing with Mary this song of praise and thanksgiving. Read the passage as a way of honoring her, especially easy to do when quoting the words of Elizabeth. But read it also as a celebration of God's righteousness, the triumph of the poor and humble over the proud and strong. Then work to make the words a reality in your own community wherever there are discrepancies—whether ecclesiastical, political, social or economic in nature—between the proud and the lowly, the hungry and the rich.

AUGUST 19, 2001

# 20TH SUNDAY IN ORDINARY TIME

*Lectionary #120*

| READING I | Jeremiah 38:1–2ab, 4–6, 8–10 |

**A reading from the book of the prophet Jeremiah**

Zedekiah = zed-uh-KĪ-uh

The officials of King *Zedekiah* heard the words
that *Jeremiah* was saying to all the *people*:
"Thus says the Lord:
'Those who *stay* in the city shall *die*;
but those who go out to the *Chaldeans* shall *live*.'"

Chaldeans = kahl-DEE-uhnz

Speak in a strong, angry voice.

Then the *officials* said to the king,
"This *man* ought to be put to *death*,
because he is *discouraging* the soldiers who are *left* in this *city*,
and *all* the *people*,
by speaking such *words* to them.
For this man is not seeking the *welfare* of this people,
but their *harm*."

King Zedekiah said,
"Here he *is*; he is in your *hands*;
for the *king* is powerless *against* you."

Malchiah = mal-KĪ-uh
Jeremiah's fate seems sure.

So they took *Jeremiah*
and threw him into the *cistern* of *Malchiah*, the king's *son*,
which was in the court of the *guard*,
letting Jeremiah down by *ropes*.
Now there was no *water* in the cistern, but only *mud*,
and Jeremiah *sank* in the *mud*.

---

**READING I** Jeremiah was a prophet in the southern kingdom of Judah in the late seventh and early sixth centuries BCE. Despite some beautiful messages about God's love and care for Israel, Jeremiah is often remembered as a prophet of doom who foretold the fall of Jerusalem and the monarchy. He often opposed other prophets (whom he considered "false") who tried to reassure the people and the king that God would save them.

During a time of political upheaval and threat from the powerful Babylonian empire, Jeremiah preached the necessity of submitting to Babylonian rule, arguing that Judah was not strong enough to withstand the threat. If Judah submitted, he reasoned, it might at least continue to exist, even if not as a completely independent nation. This was quite unpopular with those in power in the royal court. Such pessimism caused discouragement and was considered dangerous to the city and state. Jeremiah's words, however, proved to be true, and Judah fell to the Babylonian empire.

In today's reading, Jeremiah is treated badly for speaking the truth but is saved from death by the intervention of one of the king's servants. Proclaim this story with an eye to the exciting drama that it is.

**READING II** A great cloud of witnesses who trusted in God's promises surrounds us; some of them were mentioned in last week's reading from Hebrews. Their examples of faith have inspired Christians throughout the ages and continue to inspire us today.

## 20TH SUNDAY IN ORDINARY TIME ■ AUGUST 19, 2001

Ebed-melech = EH-bid—MEH-lik

Ebed-melech speaks with respect but boldness as he challenges the wrong that was done to Jeremiah.

So Ebed-*melech* the *Ethiopian*, an *officer* in the king's *house*,
*left* the king's house and *spoke* to the king,
"My lord *king*,
these *men* have acted *wickedly*
in all they did to the prophet *Jeremiah*
by throwing him into the *cistern* to *die* there of *hunger*,
for there is no *bread* left in the *city*."
Then the king commanded Ebed-*melech* the *Ethiopian*,
"Take three *men* with you from *here*,
and pull the prophet *Jeremiah up* from the cistern
before he *dies*."

---

## READING II  Hebrews 12:1–4

**A reading from the letter to the Hebrews**

Allow a tone of wonder to enter your voice.

Draw attention to Jesus' actions and central role in inspiring faith. This sentence is long; prepare it well.

Since we are *surrounded* by so great a cloud of *witnesses*,
let us also lay *aside* every *weight*
and the *sin* that clings so *closely*,
and let us *run* with *perseverance* the race that is set *before* us,
looking to *Jesus* the *pioneer* and *perfecter* of our *faith*,
who for the sake of the *joy* that was set *before* him
endured the *cross*,
*disregarding* its shame,
and has taken his *seat* at the right hand of the *throne* of *God*.

---

The author employs the image of a race to describe the Christian life. Full of eager longing, we are urged to set our sights on our goal and pursue it with all our energy. And our goal is precisely Jesus, who is both the inspiration for our faith and the one who gives us the strength to continue to believe.

Jesus himself is an example of such faithfulness, for he endured the pain and humiliation of death on a cross, trusting that God's righteousness would prevail. Because

of his faithfulness, Jesus is now glorified with God. We who have not had to suffer as Jesus did should look to him for strength.

This short passage contains several long sentences that will have to be prepared well in advance. Begin by urging your listeners to persevere, but close with a tone of comforting encouragement.

GOSPEL Far from the frail, syrupy Jesus of so many movies and much preaching, the Jesus of today's gospel is harsh and demanding, speaking of a great conflagration and an immersion into his death. The fire he brings is a purifying one; it will burn away all imperfection. For this reason Jesus longs for it. Fire is often associated with the day of judgment, when the righteous will be gathered into God's reign and the wicked cast into the

AUGUST 19, 2001 ■ 20TH SUNDAY IN ORDINARY TIME

Consider *Jesus*
    who endured such *hostility* against himself from *sinners*,
so that you may not grow *weary* or lose *heart*.
In your *struggle* against *sin*
*you* have not yet *resisted* to the point of shedding your *blood*.

---

### GOSPEL   Luke 12:49–53

**A reading from the holy gospel according to Luke**

*Jesus' words are fiery and strong. Speak them as such.*

Jesus said to his disciples:
"I came to bring *fire* to the *earth*,
and how I *wish* it were already *kindled*!
I have a *baptism* with which to be *baptized*,
and what *stress* I am under until it is *completed*!

*Do not shy away from these harsh words.*

"Do you think that I have come to bring *peace* to the earth?
*No*, I tell you, but rather *division*!
From now *on five* in one household will be *divided*,
*three* against *two* and *two* against *three*;
they will be *divided*:
*father* against *son* and *son* against *father*,
*mother* against *daughter* and *daughter* against *mother*,
*mother*-in-law against her *daughter*-in-law
and *daughter*-in-law against *mother*-in-law."

---

fires of damnation. This image of impending judgment recalls last week's gospel theme of preparedness.

Jesus also anticipates the terror and anguish of the "baptism" of his death. He does not shy away from it but in fact longs for its completion. Surely he wants it to be over, but he also knows it is necessary. And his disciples must share the baptism Jesus will undergo, suffering rejection as well as physical pain. In this gospel there are no shortcuts to discipleship.

Jesus goes on to describe the division his followers will experience. In recent weeks, we have seen that discipleship involves letting go of possessions and even the desire to possess. It requires sharing with those in need. It means being watchful and ready, always alert for the return of the master. And today we learn that discipleship will bring dissension, pitting family members against one another.

Proclaim this difficult reading with all the fire that burns in your soul. Do not quench the flames, but let the harshness of Jesus' words ring out. Although the radical message might make some uncomfortable, it is important for us to reflect on the demands of the Christian life. Are we ready to commit ourselves so totally to following Jesus that we will go wherever he goes, forsaking all we have and creating division?

# AUGUST 26, 2001

# 21ST SUNDAY IN ORDINARY TIME

*Lectionary #123*

### READING I   Isaiah 66:18–21

**A reading from the book of the prophet Isaiah**

**Open with a tone of majesty.**

Thus says the Lord:
"For I know their *works* and their *thoughts*,
and I am coming to gather all *nations* and *tongues*;
and they shall *come* and shall see my *glory*,
and I will set a *sign* among them.

Tarshish = TAHR-shish
Put = p<u>oo</u>t
Lud = luhd
Tubal = T<u>OO</u>-bahl
Javan = JAY-vuhn

"From *them* I will send *survivors* to the *nations*,
to *Tarshish*, *Put*, and *Lud*—which draw the *bow*—
to *Tubal* and *Javan*,
to the coastlands far *away*
that have not *heard* of my fame or seen my *glory*;
and they shall declare my *glory* among the *nations*.

**Imagine a colorful procession coming from the four corners of the earth and converging at the center of the world, the city of Jerusalem. Proclaim this vision with wonder.**

"They shall bring *all* your *kindred* from all the *nations*
as an *offering* to the *Lord*,
on *horses*, and in *chariots*,
and in *litters*, and on *mules*, and on *dromedaries*,
to my holy mountain *Jerusalem*," says the Lord,
"just as the *Israelites* bring a *grain* offering
in a clean *vessel* to the *house* of the *Lord*."

"And I will also take *some* of them as *priests* and as *Levites*,"
says the *Lord*.

---

**READING I** The book of Isaiah closes with a vision of a glorious Jerusalem, which will be a haven not only for the Jewish people but even for people of all nations. With the long exile in Babylon over, Jerusalem will be restored, and the people will once again rest in her arms. Jerusalem will be vindicated and will lead the world in singing praises to God.

Today's verses, close to the end of the book of Isaiah, form part of this vision. The passage itself is a bit unclear; there are references to the scattered members of the house of Israel and to those outside Israel, the Gentiles. All peoples will be gathered together and will know God's greatness.

Jews throughout the Diaspora will declare God's glory to those who do not know it. The cities and regions mentioned represent much of the known world, from North Africa to Asia Minor, perhaps extending westward to Spain or eastward to India. God's message will reach even the farthest ends of the world.

In a procession that recalls the return of the exiles to Jerusalem, the passage asserts that the Gentiles will bring back the descendants of Israel to the holy city. It is not entirely clear if the last line refers to these Diaspora Jews, who are worthy to serve in the temple despite having been dispersed, or if even the Gentiles will be allowed to serve as priests and Levites. What is clear is that all the nations will come to honor God.

Read this selection as a message of hope and encouragement, recognizing God's tremendous glory.

AUGUST 26, 2001 ■ 21ST SUNDAY IN ORDINARY TI

### READING II     Hebrews 12:5–7, 11–13

**A reading from the letter to the Hebrews**

And you have *forgotten* the exhortation
    that addresses you as *children*—
"My *child*, do not regard lightly the *discipline* of the *Lord*,
or lose *heart* when you are *punished* by him;
for the Lord *disciplines* those whom he *loves*,
and *chastises* every child whom he *accepts*."

*Endure* trials for the sake of *discipline*.
God is treating you as *children*;
for what *child* is there whom a parent does not *discipline*?

Now, discipline *always* seems *painful*
rather than *pleasant* at the *time*,
but *later* it yields the peaceful fruit of *righteousness*
to those who have been *trained* by it.

Therefore *lift* your drooping *hands*
and *strengthen* your weak *knees*,
and make straight *paths* for your *feet*,
so that what is *lame* may not be put out of *joint*,
but rather be *healed*.

*These words are meant to be reassuring. Read them forcefully, but with a tone of comfort.*

*Pause before these final lines. Speak with sincere encouragement.*

### GOSPEL     Luke 13:22–30

**A reading from the holy gospel according to Luke**

Jesus went through one *town* and *village* after *another*,
*teaching* as he made his way to *Jerusalem*.

---

READING II  In a beautiful passage that recalls the anguish of every parent who wants to teach a child what is right, the author extols the need for discipline and compares God with a parent. The author exhorts the readers to accept the necessary discipline that comes from God, who offers it out of love. God uses adversity to teach Christians; it is to be understood, then, as a loving corrective, despite how unpleasant it may feel. In the end, a person is stronger for having endured it.

The passage provides encouragement to people who have been Christians for some time and have experienced persecution. They are encouraged to hold fast to their faith and to rely on one another when faced with outside threats or internal fatigue. Although they may be weary, they should recognize that they can be healed and strengthened.

Many times our own communities are like the one Hebrews addressed. We grow tired and need encouragement. We also need to hear that the trials we face are for our benefit, if we but endure. Address this to your community, then, keeping in mind especially those who are struggling. Offer it as a message of hope to a sometimes weary people.

GOSPEL  The gospel of Luke does not mince words in demanding the wholehearted devotion of every Christian, a devotion first and foremost to following the path that Jesus walks, accompanying him on his journey to suffering and death. Discipleship requires a focus on what lies ahead and a willingness to endure trials for the sake of the good news. Today's gospel

**248**

21ST SUNDAY IN ORDINARY TIME ■ AUGUST 26, 2001

Someone asked him,
"*Lord*, will only a *few* be *saved*?"

Jesus said to them,

**Passing through the narrow door requires effort. Speak Jesus' words forcefully.**

"*Strive* to enter through the *narrow* door;
for *many*, I tell you, will *try* to enter and will not be *able*.

"When once the *owner* of the house has got *up* and *shut* the door,
and you begin to stand *outside*
and to *knock* at the door, saying,
'*Lord*, *open* to us,'
then in reply he will say to you,
'I do not *know* where you *come* from.'

**There is desperation in their voices. Jesus' response is harsh.**

"Then you will begin to say,
'We *ate* and *drank* with you,
and you taught in our *streets*.'
But the Lord will say,
'I do not *know* where you *come* from;
go *away* from me, all you *evildoers*!'

"There will be *weeping* and gnashing of *teeth*
when you see *Abraham* and *Isaac* and *Jacob*
and all the *prophets* in the kingdom of *God*,
and you *yourselves* thrown *out*.

**Allow your voice to be a bit gentler as you envision this procession of peoples. Close slowly, on a solemn note.**

Then people will come from *east* and *west*,
from *north* and *south*,
and will *eat* in the kingdom of *God*.

"*Indeed*, some are *last* who will be *first*,
and some are *first* who will be *last*."

reading indicates that few will have the strength necessary to be so single-minded.

Jesus uses the image of a house, with himself as the owner, to make his point. The door is not wide for the masses to enter but narrow, and only the most faithful and noble may pass. Once the door is closed, there is no way to force it open. It will not be enough to have known Jesus or heard his message; the follower of Jesus must demonstrate total commitment to him.

Although the door is closed, those waiting outside are able to catch a glimpse of the wonders within, including the presence of Israel's righteous ones. Although the patriarchs and prophets have entered the kingdom of God, the chosen people of old do not have exclusive claim to it. People from every nation will be able to enter if they wholeheartedly devote themselves to Jesus' message.

This harsh and challenging passage contains good news as well as rebuke. It was intended to remind Israel that Gentiles

will also find God's favor. But it is important for us to hear as well, lest we become complacent in our lives of faith. Offer this message to your listeners (and yourself!) as a challenge to be ever more faithful, unwilling to be complacent or self-satisfied.

# SEPTEMBER 2, 2001

# 22ND SUNDAY IN ORDINARY TIME

*Lectionary #126*

### READING I  Sirach 3:17–20, 28–29

**Sirach = SEER-ak**

**Although the theme is humility, the words are offered as loving instruction. Speak with encouragement.**

**Speak of God's might with forcefulness.**

**Close with a quiet, reflective tone.**

**A reading from the book of Sirach**

My *child*, perform your tasks with *humility*;
then you will be *loved* by those whom God *accepts*.
The *greater* you are,
the more you must *humble* yourself;
so you will find *favour* in the sight of the *Lord*.
Many are *lofty* and *renowned*,
but to the *humble* the Lord reveals his *secrets*.
For *great* is the might of the *Lord*;
but by the *humble* he is *glorified*.

When *calamity* befalls the *proud*,
there is no *healing*,
for an evil *plant* has taken *root* in them.

The mind of the *intelligent* appreciates *proverbs*,
and an attentive *ear* is the desire of the *wise*.

---

READING I Jewish wisdom literature often seems disjointed, and today's selection is no exception. There are three proverbs here, and each deals with a separate issue.

The first and most important message concerns humility. Wisdom literature in general is directed toward the wealthy and educated, often members of the royal court or other leading citizens. But a lesson on the importance of humility could be addressed to anyone.

Everything should be done with humility, for this brings favor not only from God but

from those most attuned to God as well. The author recognizes that this message will be especially hard for those in positions of prominence to hear, but they are the ones most in need of it. And those who are most humble are those who give glory to the Lord, who is the greatest of all.

The second lesson is related to the first and discusses the opposite of humility: pride. Those who are puffed up with pride will have an especially difficult time dealing with adversity. It is as though an evil plant is growing within them. The plant must be pulled

out by its roots; only then will it be possible to accept whatever life brings with humility.

Finally, there are still things that even the most educated and respected will not be able to understand. Humility remains necessary, but it is also helpful to turn to the wisdom of others in order to learn. The proverbs found in wisdom literature are a good place to start, since they offer practical, everyday lessons about life.

Proclaim this short passage slowly and carefully. Provide lengthy pauses between the three sections so that each can be understandable to your listeners.

**250**
22ND SUNDAY IN ORDINARY TIME ■ SEPTEMBER 2, 2001

### READING II    Hebrews 12:18–19, 22–24a

**A reading from the letter to the Hebrews**

*Begin strongly. The first line is extremely important; everything that follows it is parenthetical.*

You have not come to something that can be *touched*,
a blazing *fire*, and *darkness*, and *gloom*,
and a *tempest*, and the sound of a *trumpet*,
and a *voice* whose words made the hearers *beg*
that not another *word* be *spoken* to them.

*There is both promise and fulfillment in these words. Proclaim them with confidence.*

But *you* have come to Mount *Zion*
and to the *city* of the living *God*, the heavenly *Jerusalem*,
and to innumerable *angels* in festal *gathering*,
and to the assembly of the *firstborn* who are enroled in *heaven*,
and to *God* the judge of *all*,
and to the *spirits* of the *righteous* made *perfect*,

*Pause briefly before the mention of Jesus, then close firmly.*

and to *Jesus*, the mediator of a new *covenant*.

### GOSPEL    Luke 14:1, 7–14

**A reading from the holy gospel according to Luke**

*The first few lines are introductory. Read them as such, then begin afresh with Jesus' words.*

On one *occasion*
when Jesus was going to the house of a *leader* of the *Pharisees*
to eat a *meal* on the *sabbath*,
the *lawyers* and *Pharisees* were watching him *closely*.
When Jesus *noticed* how the guests chose the places of *honour*,
he told them a *parable*.

---

READING II  The letter to the Hebrews celebrates and builds on the experiences of the Jewish people and God's revelation to them. Hebrews recalls the holy people of old and their righteousness, looks back at God's saving works on behalf of the Israelites, and reflects on the superiority of Christ's sacrifice to the temple cult. In today's passage, the author contrasts two mountains, first recalling the encounter between God and Israel at Sinai. That experience pales in comparison with the Christian's approach to another holy mountain: the heavenly Jerusalem.

At Sinai, only Moses was able to approach and commune with God. The experience was too powerful for the rest of the community. The Israelites recognized the awesome majesty of God in the fire, darkness, storms and trumpet blasts that announced the divine presence.

Christians, too, recognize the glory of God—symbolized by angels and the appearance of God as judge—and yet need not be afraid to approach God's throne because Jesus mediates a new covenant between God and humankind. We need no longer cower in fear but can be confident that God

will judge us favorably because of the saving action of Jesus, who with his blood has ratified a new covenant with God.

The sentences in this passage are long and difficult. Emphasize the first line of each and then speak parenthetically as you finish the description. The final line of the selection should also be emphasized; it is because of Jesus' role in establishing the new covenant that the author can contrast these two mountaintop experiences.

SEPTEMBER 2, 2001 ■ 22ND SUNDAY IN ORDINARY TIME

**Is the host speaking harshly, or warmly and apologetically? Let your answer inform your reading.**

"When you are *invited* by someone to a *wedding* banquet,
do *not* sit down at the place of *honour*,
in case someone more *distinguished* than you
has been *invited* by your *host*;

and the host who invited *both* of you
may come and *say* to you,
'Give *this* person your place,'
and then in *disgrace* you would start to take the *lowest* place.

"But when you are *invited*,
*go* and sit down at the *lowest* place,
so that when your *host* comes,
he may say to you, '*Friend*, move up *higher*';
then you will be *honoured*
in the presence of *all* who sit at the table *with* you.
For all who *exalt* themselves will be *humbled*,
and those who *humble* themselves will be *exalted*."

**Let this sentence resound; it is the key to Jesus' teaching today.**

Jesus said *also* to the Pharisee who had *invited* him,
"When you give a *luncheon* or a *dinner*,
do not invite your *friends* or your *brothers* or *sisters*
or your *relatives* or rich *neighbours*,
in case they may invite *you* in *return*,
and you would be *repaid*.
But when you give a *banquet*,
invite the *poor*, the *crippled*, the *lame*, and the *blind*.
And you will be *blessed*, because they *cannot* repay you,
for you will be *repaid* at the *resurrection* of the *righteous*."

**Slow down here to make the meaning clear. True generosity does not expect repayment.**

---

**GOSPEL** The gospel of Luke repeatedly reverses the expected social order. From the Magnificat, in which Mary proclaims that God will exalt the lowly while humbling the mighty, to the crucifixion, in which the king of the cosmos is reviled and nailed to a cross, the author turns all expectations upside down. In today's passage, Jesus equates the desire of guests to find comfortable seating near the host with arrogance. Even the host should not invite friends but should instead welcome those who were excluded from ritual meals and forbidden to worship at the temple.

As is so often true in this gospel, the story operates on two levels. It is a story about both human relationships and the need for humility. On the level of relationships, it challenges all who have been blessed with plenty to reach out in concern to those who are struggling. Gift-giving takes on a new dimension if we are generous to those who really need assistance, rather than to those who return our favors. On the level of humility, those who strive for honor in this life are missing something of far greater significance. Only by acting in humility and a spirit

of true generosity can we hope to be honored at the "resurrection of the righteous."

The message of this passage needs to be heard again and again. Meditate on it and strive to live your life in accordance with it. Then offer it as both a challenge to the members of your community and as a promise that there is more to life than what we now know.

SEPTEMBER 9, 2001

# 23RD SUNDAY IN ORDINARY TIME

*Lectionary #129*

## READING I   Wisdom 9:13–18

**A reading from the book of Wisdom**

Let a tone of incredulity enter your voice. Of course no one can really do these things!

For who can *learn* the counsel of *God*?
Or who can *discern* what the Lord *wills*?
For the reasoning of *mortals* is *worthless*,
and our *designs* are likely to *fail*;
for a perishable *body* weighs down the *soul*,
and this earthy *tent burdens* the thoughtful *mind*.

Change your voice to reflect the inadequacies of human beings.

We can hardly *guess* at what is on *earth*,
and what is at *hand* we find with *labour*;
but *who* has traced out what is in the *heavens*?
*Who* has learned your *counsel*,
unless you have given *wisdom*
and sent your holy *spirit* from on *high*?

The final sentence provides an answer to all the questions. It is through wisdom that "the paths of those on earth" are made straight.

And thus the paths of those on *earth* were set *right*,
and people were taught what *pleases* you,
and were *saved* by *wisdom*.

---

**READING I** Today's selection is part of a larger prayer to God that asks for wisdom. The author praises Lady Wisdom and reflects on Wisdom's presence with God in creation. The present passage appears in this context.

The reading opens with what the author considers to be rhetorical questions. After describing Wisdom's greatness and asking for her guidance, the author expresses the obvious: No human can discern the mind of God without the counsel of Wisdom. Human beings are simply unable to comprehend

God's majesty without the assistance of one who can teach and direct their thoughts.

The Greek philosopher Plato taught that the soul is imprisoned in the body and must be released; human beings must flee the body and everything material. Similarly, the author of the book of Wisdom declares that the body weighs down the soul and impedes the mind. It is impossible for humans to understand God because of the body; we have trouble understanding even what we can see and know. Only those endowed with wisdom and given the spirit of God can begin to comprehend God's ways.

The concluding line of the passage actually begins a section of the book that reflects on Lady Wisdom's role in salvation history. As it stands in today's reading, it is a fitting conclusion to the assertion that humanity needs Wisdom. The assistance she has given in the past is still available for those who seek her today.

Proclaim the lofty ideas of this reading with a sincere and passionate tone. Read the questions in such a way as to make clear that the answer to each is "no one." Close with a tone of finality.

SEPTEMBER 9, 2001 ■ 23RD SUNDAY IN ORDINARY TIME

## READING II    Philemon 9b–10, 12–17

**A reading from the letter of Paul to Philemon**

*Paul writes as a respected leader. Speak with solemnity and authority.*

I, *Paul*, do this as an old *man*,
and now also as a *prisoner* of Christ *Jesus*.
I am *appealing* to you for my child, *Onesimus*,
whose *father* I have become during my *imprisonment*.

*Express Paul's fervent plea with a tone of longing.*

I am *sending* him,
that is, my own *heart*,
*back* to you.
I wanted to *keep* him with *me*,
so that he might be of *service* to me in your *place*
during my *imprisonment* for the *gospel*;
but I preferred to do *nothing* without your *consent*,
in order that your good *deed* might be *voluntary*
and not something *forced*.

*Speak with dignity. Paul wants cooperation, not capitulation.*

Perhaps *this* is the reason
        he was *separated* from you for a *while*,
so that you might have him back *forever*,
no longer as a *slave* but *more* than a slave,
a beloved *brother*—
especially to *me* but how much *more* to *you*,
both in the *flesh* and in the *Lord*.

*Let your voice be filled with warmth.*

So if you consider me your *partner*,
*welcome* him as you would welcome *me*.

*Onesimus is to be treated with the same honor and respect as Paul himself.*

---

READING II  The letter to Philemon is unique among Paul's correspondence. It is not a general letter, as are Paul's other writings to the communities he had founded or visited, but is addressed to three people and the church that meets in their house. Paul writes in a very personal tone, appealing to have the slave Onesimus freed and sent back to him.

Onesimus had fled from his master and turned to Paul, accepting Christianity. Paul sends him back to his owner but also writes this letter subtly asking for the return of Onesimus. He had found the slave particularly helpful in his ministry and knows that Philemon, who owned Onesimus, owes a debt to Paul for having led him to Christ. By referring to this debt of gratitude and comparing Onesimus to himself, Paul hopes to win freedom for Onesimus and gain an assistant for himself.

It is clear that Paul is asking for the slave's freedom, but he does not challenge the legality of slavery itself in doing so. In fact, he actually returns Onesimus to his owner as the law requires. Speak with sensitivity to the tensions that may exist in your community with regard to this issue but also with the same boldness and compassion that Paul displays.

GOSPEL  The gospel of Luke is subversive. The author does not mince words when it comes to what discipleship entails. The same author speaks of bringing down the powerful and exalting the homeless, the poor and the most sinful. This gospel often makes us squirm.

Being a disciple of Jesus involves leaving everything behind. Human relationships

# 23RD SUNDAY IN ORDINARY TIME ■ SEPTEMBER 9, 2001

## GOSPEL   Luke 14:25–33

**A reading from the holy gospel according to Luke**

*The demands of discipleship are great. Do not attempt to lessen them.*

Large *crowds* were *travelling* with Jesus;
and he turned and *said* to them,
"Whoever *comes* to me and does not *hate father* and *mother*,
*spouse* and *children*, *brothers* and *sisters*,
yes, and even life *itself*,
*cannot* be my *disciple*.
Whoever does not carry the *cross* and *follow* me
*cannot* be my *disciple*.

*The questions here are rhetorical. Give them full expression, then offer the alternatives with a tone of regret.*

"For *which* of you,
intending to build a *tower*,
does not *first* sit down and estimate the *cost*,
to see whether he has enough to *complete* it?
*Otherwise*, when he has laid a *foundation*
        and is not able to *finish*,
all who *see* it will begin to *ridicule* him,
saying, '*This* fellow began to *build* and was not able to *finish*.'

"Or what *king*,
going out to wage *war* against *another* king,
will not sit down *first*
        and consider whether he is able with *ten* thousand
to oppose the one who comes *against* him
        with *twenty* thousand?
If he *cannot*, *then*, while the other is still far *away*,
he sends a *delegation*
and asks for the terms of *peace*.

*Pause before this final sentence, then close strongly.*

"So *therefore*, none of *you* can become my *disciple*
if you do not give *up* all your *possessions*."

---

and responsibilities, even one's own life, cannot get in the way of devotion to Jesus and his message. The Greek word for "hate" in the opening lines is a strong one. How strange that the one who commands us to love our enemies and act compassionately toward our neighbors asks us to despise our families!

What Jesus demands is not that his followers act without justice or compassion but that commitment to him must take precedence over everything else. Discipleship involves forsaking anything that might get in the way of focusing on the goal ahead.

This idea of striving toward a goal clarifies the two examples that Jesus offers. In both instances, the protagonist must carefully consider what is necessary to reach the goal and prepare accordingly.

In the same way, the followers of Jesus must prepare for a life of discipleship by freeing themselves from any obstacles that might impede their progress. Chief among these are possessions. Throughout this gospel, the author argues that wealth and possessions can take hold of a person, rendering one bound to them. Only by being freed of the

entrapments of worldly goods can we truly follow Jesus.

Speak boldly, and do not try to soften the message of this text. It is not easy to hear these words, and we often fail. But offer Jesus' demands to the members of your assembly as a challenge to turn their lives ever more fully over to God. Stress especially the opening and closing sections, reading the two middle sections as examples of preparedness.

# SEPTEMBER 16, 2001

# 24TH SUNDAY IN ORDINARY TIME

*Lectionary #132*

## READING I    Exodus 32:7–11, 13–14

**A reading from the book of Exodus**

At the top of Mount *Sinai*, the *Lord* said to *Moses*,
"Go down at *once*!
Your *people*, whom you brought up out of the land of *Egypt*,
have acted *perversely*;
they have been *quick* to turn *aside*
        from the way that I *commanded* them;
they have *cast* for themselves an image of a *calf*,
and have *worshipped* it and *sacrificed* to it,
and said, '*These* are your *gods*, O Israel,
who brought you *up* out of the land of *Egypt*!'"

The Lord said to *Moses*,
"I have *seen* this people,
how stiff-*necked* they are.
Now let me *alone*,
so that my *wrath* may burn *hot against* them
and I may *consume* them;
and of *you* I will make a great *nation*."

But Moses *implored* the Lord his God, and said,
"O *Lord*, *why* does your wrath burn *hot* against your *people*,
whom you brought out of the land of *Egypt*
with great *power* and with a mighty *hand*?

**God is angry. Speak forcefully.**

**Speak with scorn as you recount God's quotation of Israel's words. How ironic that God, the one who brought Israel out of Egypt, must give voice to this idolatry.**

**Speak with anger and impatience.**

**Moses is bold but respectful.**

---

READING I │ The famous incident of the golden calf, recounted in this reading, comes after Moses has been on Mount Sinai for a very long time. The people were told not to attempt to look upon God; instead all communication between God and Israel was to be mediated by Moses. During Moses' time on the mountain, God gave instructions for proper living (both general and specific) and told Moses how to build the ark of the covenant that was to serve as a visible reminder of God's presence and guidance.

Moses remained on the mountain for such a long time that the people must have thought he was deserting them. They rebel, building an image of a calf, a sign of youthfulness and strength. While their true God and deliverer is giving the law to Moses, the people proclaim that the calf—which they have fashioned—is the god who brought them out of Egypt.

God observes the people's idolatry and sends Moses down to intervene. God, portrayed here with human emotions, is furious.

Although Moses and God had just been discussing the covenant God wants to establish with Israel and how Israel should live as God's chosen people, God is now willing to abandon them and establish a covenant with Moses and his descendants. Moses must defend the people against God's wrath.

Moses reminds God of the promises made to Abraham, Isaac and Israel (Jacob). God had promised lasting fidelity and had even sworn allegiance to this people. God is convinced by Moses' plea and abandons the punishment planned for the people.

**24TH SUNDAY IN ORDINARY TIME** ■ SEPTEMBER 16, 2001

**Speak with sincerity.**

Remember *Abraham, Isaac,* and *Israel,* your *servants,*
how you *swore* to them by your own *self,* saying to them,
'I will *multiply* your *descendants* like the *stars* of *heaven,*
and *all* this land that I have *promised*
I will give to your *descendants,*
and they shall *inherit* it *forever.*'"

**Pause before the final sentence, then proclaim it with certainty.**

And the Lord changed his *mind*
about the *disaster* that he planned to *bring* on his *people.*

---

### READING II ´ 1 Timothy 1:12–17

**A reading from the first letter of Paul to Timothy**

**Speak with a deep sense of gratitude.**

I am *grateful* to Christ *Jesus* our *Lord,*
who has *strengthened* me,
because he judged me *faithful* and appointed me to his *service,*
even though I was formerly a *blasphemer,*
a *persecutor,* and a man of *violence.*

**The tone changes here to one of apology.**

But I received *mercy*
because I had acted *ignorantly* in *unbelief,*
and the *grace* of our Lord *overflowed* for me
with the *faith* and *love* that are in Christ *Jesus.*

**Stress the overwhelming nature of God's grace.**

The saying is *sure* and worthy of full *acceptance,*
that Christ *Jesus* came into the world to save *sinners*—
of whom I am the *foremost.*

**Speak with humility.**

---

In many ways, Moses is the true hero in this story, and it is no wonder that he has long been held in high esteem by the Jewish people. He rejects having his own posterity be the sole recipients of the promises made to Abraham, Isaac and Jacob, in order to hold God to the earlier covenant.

Proclaim this selection with vigor. Speak God's words forcefully and angrily. Moses responds sincerely but also insistently. The last line should be spoken calmly

but firmly; the theme of God's forgiveness will continue through all the readings today.

READING II  The present passage offers an account of Paul's life before his call to serve Christ. But the personal nature of the account does not detract from our ability to identify with its content.

The Acts of the Apostles and Paul's own letters reveal that Paul had once zealously persecuted the early followers of Christ. But he had an experience of the risen Christ's presence and was called not only to be a

disciple but to serve the Lord by proclaiming the gospel to the Gentiles. He applied the same energy and zeal to spreading the good news as he had to persecuting Christians.

The present passage is a reflection on Paul's life, but one to which any Christian can relate. Only by receiving mercy and being strengthened by God can we serve Christ. Although not all of us formerly persecuted others, we know that we have done what is

SEPTEMBER 16, 2001 ■ 24TH SUNDAY IN ORDINARY TIME

But for that very *reason* I received *mercy*,
so that in *me*, as the *foremost*,
Jesus *Christ* might display the utmost *patience*,
making me an *example*
to those who would come to *believe* in him for eternal *life*.

**Raise your voice in praise to God!**

To the *King* of the *ages*,
*immortal*, *invisible*, the only *God*,
be *honour* and *glory* forever and *ever*. Amen.

---

**GOSPEL** Luke 15:1–32

**A reading from the holy gospel according to Luke**

All the *tax* collectors and *sinners*
          were coming near to *listen* to Jesus.
And the *Pharisees* and the *scribes* were *grumbling* and saying,
"This fellow welcomes *sinners* and *eats* with them."

**Imagine a famous person—especially a well-known teacher or religious leader—who socializes with criminals. How would you respond? Express your response accordingly.**

So Jesus told them a *parable*:
"Which *one* of you,
          having a hundred *sheep* and losing *one* of them,
does not leave the ninety-*nine* in the *wilderness*
and go after the one that is *lost* until he *finds* it?
When he has *found* it,
he lays it on his *shoulders* and *rejoices*.
And when he comes *home*,
he calls together his *friends* and *neighbours*, saying to them,
'*Rejoice* with me,
for I have found my *sheep* that was *lost*.'

**Express the shepherd's joy and excitement.**

---

wrong, thus harming ourselves and others, and turning away from God's love. But there is hope, for Jesus came to save sinners. With the author, we can each hope that God will continue to work in our lives, forgiving us even when we sin repeatedly.

Reflect on this selection before attempting to read it in the assembly. Think of your own life and the mistakes you have made, then consider God's abundant grace, in which you have been offered mercy and called to a

life of faithful service. Attempt to make the words your own as you share this message with your community. Speak with humility but certainty, and close with a fervent prayer of praise.

GOSPEL | Today's gospel divides up neatly into two sections. The first has to do with questions of value: What are things really worth to us? The second section is the much-loved tale of the prodigal son, a story found only in the gospel of Luke. Both sections take our assumptions

about life and our dealings with others and turn them on their heads. Nothing is ever as simple as it seems.

The passage opens with a complaint from the religious leadership. Jesus was fraternizing with despicable people: tax collectors, who were widely reviled as cheats; and "sinners," probably those who could or would not keep the law of Moses. Adhering to the proverb "You are known by the company you keep," the Pharisees speak disparagingly of Jesus. In typical fashion, Jesus responds with parables.

**258**

24TH SUNDAY IN ORDINARY TIME ■ SEPTEMBER 16, 2001

Just *so*, I tell you,
there will be more *joy* in *heaven* over one sinner who *repents*
than over ninety-nine *righteous* persons who need *no* repentance.

"Or what *woman* having ten silver *coins*,
if she loses *one* of them,
does not light a *lamp*, *sweep* the *house*,
and search *carefully* until she *finds* it?
When she has *found* it,
she calls together her *friends* and *neighbours*, saying,
'*Rejoice* with me,
for I have found the *coin* that I had *lost*.'

**Again, speak with exuberance.**

Just *so*, I tell you,
there is *joy* in the presence of the *angels* of *God*
over one *sinner* who *repents*."

Then Jesus said,
"There was a *man* who had two *sons*.
The *younger* of them said to his *father*,
'*Father*, give me the share of the *property*
that will *belong* to me.'
So the father divided his property *between* them.

**Start fresh here, reading slowly and with expression, as though reading this story for the first time.**

"A few days *later* the *younger* son gathered all he *had*
and travelled to a distant *country*,
and there he *squandered* his property in dissolute *living*.
When he had spent *everything*,
a severe *famine* took place throughout that *country*,
and he began to be in *need*.
So he *went* and hired himself *out*
to one of the *citizens* of that country,
who sent him to his *fields* to feed the *pigs*.

---

The parables of the lost sheep and the lost coin challenge the Pharisees' value system—and ours. The shepherd, in an attempt to save one lost sheep, risks the safety of the rest of the fold. The woman turns her house upside down in hopes of finding her lost coin. Is it really worth it to risk so much in order to gain so little?

Jesus makes clear that he is really speaking of the value of a single human life. It is easy to affirm in theory that each life matters, that each person is worthy of being saved. But isn't it easier to focus on serving the needs of an entire group—whether a parish community, a class of students, a group of colleagues—than to focus on one demanding individual? Jesus' words challenge us to see the needy person, the nuisance or the incorrigible delinquent as worthy of our time and effort.

The story of the prodigal son illustrates in concrete terms the importance of forgiveness. The relationships described—family members, siblings competing with one another—are so common that it is easy to identify with the story. The author uses it to respond further to the Pharisees' question about Jesus' association with sinners.

The story opens with arrogance. The younger son, who clearly was living a comfortable life in his father's home, demands his inheritance. In Jesus' day, as now, it was unusual for a parent to divide an estate before death, although it did occasionally occur. The son's question, then, displays not only his greed for the wealth he hoped to obtain but also his complete disregard for his father. It is as though he wishes his father were dead.

SEPTEMBER 16, 2001 ■ 24TH SUNDAY IN ORDINARY TIME

The young man would *gladly* have filled *himself*
with the *pods* that the pigs were *eating*;
and *no* one gave him *anything*.

"But when he came to *himself* he said,
'How *many* of my father's hired *hands*
     have bread *enough* and to *spare*,
but here *I* am dying of *hunger*!
I will get *up* and go to my *father*, and I will *say* to him,
"*Father*, I have *sinned* against *heaven* and before *you*;
I am no longer *worthy* to be called your *son*;
*treat* me like one of your hired *hands*."'

**Speak with sincere humility.**

"So he set *off* and went to his *father*.
But while he was still far *off*,
his father *saw* him and was filled with *compassion*;
he *ran* and put his arms *around* him and *kissed* him.
Then the son said to him,
'*Father*, I have sinned against *heaven* and before *you*;
I am no longer *worthy* to be called your *son*.'

**The father is ecstatic.**

**Again, speak sincerely.**

"But the *father* said to his *slaves*,
'*Quickly*, bring out a *robe*—the *best* one—and put it *on* him;
put a *ring* on his *finger* and *sandals* on his *feet*.
And get the fatted *calf* and *kill* it,
and let us *eat* and *celebrate*;
for this son of mine was *dead* and is *alive* again;
he was *lost* and is *found*!'
And they began to *celebrate*.

**Express the father's excitement and love.**

"Now his *elder* son was in the *field*;
and when he came and approached the *house*,
he heard *music* and *dancing*.
He called one of the *slaves* and asked what was going *on*.

**The tone changes as the older son enters the scene.**

As if the younger son's arrogance were not enough, he has the audacity to take his inheritance and waste it. The older son later tells us that his brother not only "squandered" his wealth, but spent it on "loose women," adding insult to injury. As so often happens, however, his behavior catches up with him, and he soon hits rock bottom. Jesus' listeners would have recognized this when they learned he was living with pigs, which made one ritually unclean according to Jewish law.

In desperation, the son reflects on his former life and regrets what he has done. But he still has some pride. The younger son realizes that he has wronged his father and resolves to demand nothing of him. Yet he also knows his father's kind, loving nature, expressed even to servants, and turns to him in humility. The son's sincerity is evident when he sticks to his resolve and asks to be treated as a servant, even after his father warmly embraces him.

The older son, who had faithfully stayed by his father's side while his brother acted irresponsibly, now emerges as resentful and obstinate. Although his attitude is understandable, the contrast with his father's response to the younger son is striking. The older son was not wronged, yet he refuses to forgive his brother. The father was treated despicably, yet he opens his heart and his home, and lavishly celebrates the return of his beloved son. The older son's refusal to forgive makes one wonder if there is still, indeed, a lost son.

24TH SUNDAY IN ORDINARY TIME ▪ SEPTEMBER 16, 2001

**Speak with a righteous indignation. Everything the older son says is true.**

The slave replied, 'Your *brother* has come,
and your *father* has killed the fatted *calf*,
because he has got him back *safe* and *sound*.'
Then the *elder* son became *angry* and refused to go *in*.
His *father* came out and began to *plead* with him.
But he answered his father,
'*Listen*! For all these *years*
I have been working like a *slave* for you,
and I have *never* disobeyed your *command*;
yet you have never given *me* even a young *goat*
so that I might *celebrate* with my *friends*.
But when this *son* of yours came *back*,
who has *devoured* your property with *prostitutes*,
you *killed* the fatted *calf* for *him*!'

**Is the father impatient, sad or tender? Let your answer determine your tone. Close with a sense of peaceful joy.**

"Then the father said to him,
'*Son*, you are *always* with me,
and all that is *mine* is *yours*.
But we had to *celebrate* and *rejoice*,
because this *brother* of yours was *dead*
and has come to *life*;
he was *lost* and has been *found*.'"

[*Shorter: Luke 15:1–10*]

On one level, the story deals with human relationships and the importance of forgiveness. On another level, of course, the father represents God's loving embrace of sinners and gentle rebuke of the self-righteous. The religious leaders who had questioned Jesus' behavior must have been squirming at the implications of this parable. Could God really grant the same forgiveness and favor to cheats and sinners as to them?

This final parable, then, affirms the truth found in the first two stories. God forgives the sinner, and all of heaven rejoices when one person repents. But the story of the prodigal son also challenges all of us to act with the wronged father's compassion, forgiveness and generosity. It is a demanding lesson.

Although the reading is long, it is well worth the time you will need to devote to it. Do not rush through it, but savor the stories, letting each one sink in before turning to the next. Give plenty of expression to the characters in the final parable, and close with a tone of joy and compassion.

# SEPTEMBER 23, 2001

# 25TH SUNDAY IN ORDINARY TIME

*Lectionary #135*

## READING I    Amos 8:4–7

**A reading from the book of the prophet Amos**

**Begin strongly. Amos is angry.**

Hear *this*, you that *trample* on the *needy*,
and bring to *ruin* the *poor* of the *land*,
saying, "*When* will the new moon be *over*
      so that we may sell *grain*;
and the *sabbath*, so that we may offer *wheat* for *sale*?
We will measure out *less* and charge *more*,
and *tamper* with the *scales*,
buying the *poor* for *silver*
and the *needy* for a pair of *sandals*,
and selling the *sweepings* of the *wheat*."

The *Lord* has *sworn* by the pride of *Jacob*:
"*Surely* I will *never* forget *any* of their *deeds*."

**Allow a tone of whining and greed to enter your voice. Pause briefly after "sabbath."**

**Speak with arrogance toward the poor.**

**Let your voice thunder with divine wrath.**

---

READING I  The prophet Amos preached to the people of the northern kingdom of Israel in the eighth century BCE, spreading a message of justice and compassion. Today's passage is a stinging rebuke of those who are cheating and oppressing the poor for their own gain.

Amos was active during a time of great prosperity for Israel. There was relatively little threat from foreign powers (although a short time later the northern kingdom of Israel did fall to the Assyrians) and this, combined with agricultural success, resulted in a flourishing economy. Many of the leading citizens were growing gluttonous and lazy, often at the expense of the poor.

Each new moon and each Sabbath was a religious holiday during which no business could be conducted. Amos chastises the storeowners not only for their greed but also for their religious insincerity. They pretended to observe feasts but were really contemplating their future sales. Even on the Sabbath, they plotted to cheat others in order to fatten themselves. They had no concern for the poor and needy but intended to take advantage of them in order to make more money. God swears that these deeds will not be forgotten.

This is an especially appropriate message for us in our affluent society. Especially during times of widespread prosperity, when we hear how strong our economy is, we tend to forget the truly needy in our communities. Not everyone is enjoying abundance or is able to take long, leisurely vacations (or any vacation at all). Despite apparently widespread wealth, the gap between rich and poor grows greater all the time. Proclaim this passage, then, as an urgent reminder to the members of your community to practice

**25TH SUNDAY IN ORDINARY TIME ■ SEPTEMBER 23, 2001**

| | |
|---|---|
| | **READING II** 1 Timothy 2:1–7 |

**A reading from the first letter of Paul to Timothy**

**Read slowly through the list of prayers.**

My dearly *beloved*,
I urge that *supplications*, *prayers*,
*intercessions*, and *thanksgivings* be made for *everyone*,
for *kings* and all who are in high *positions*,
so that we may lead a *quiet* and *peaceable* life
in all *godliness* and *dignity*.
This is *right* and is *acceptable* in the sight of *God* our *Saviour*,
who desires *everyone* to be *saved*
and to come to the *knowledge* of the *truth*.

**Pause before this line, then speak decisively.**

For there is *one* God;
there is also one *mediator* between *God* and the human *race*,
Christ *Jesus*, *himself* human,
who *gave* himself a ransom for *all*;
this was *attested* at the right time.

**Speak with pride in this ministry.**

For *this* I was appointed a *herald* and an *apostle*,
a teacher of the *Gentiles* in *faith* and *truth*.
I am telling the *truth*, I am not *lying*.

---

fairness in all transactions, to be sincere in their religious practices, and to have compassion for those in need. Do not try to soften the message but proclaim it forcefully.

| | |
|---|---|
| READING II | The "pastoral letters" (First and Second Timothy, and |

Titus) were written by an admirer of Paul to deal with concerns that Paul himself had never faced. The present passage from First Timothy gives instructions on prayer, discusses God's relationship with the human

race through the person of Jesus, and reflects on Paul's own ministry.

The author begins by urging constant prayer, a theme that resonates throughout much of the Pauline correspondence. A unique aspect of the prayer enjoined here is that it is to be offered for kings and government officials. The relationship between Christians and the government in the early centuries after Jesus' death was varied. Some civil authorities violently persecuted Christians and denied them the right to worship freely. Sometimes Christians resisted; at other times, however, Christians sought to

endear themselves to the authorities in the hope that they would be able to practice their new religion in peace.

Paul, like Jesus, seems to have had a somewhat ambivalent attitude toward civil authorities. He did not advocate active resistance but was concerned about order within the Christian community, regardless of its wider environment. It is surprising, then, that this author speaks confidently about praying for civil leaders.

SEPTEMBER 23, 2001 ■ 25TH SUNDAY IN ORDINARY TIME

## GOSPEL  Luke 16:1–13

**A reading from the holy gospel according to Luke**

Jesus said to the *disciples*,
"There was a *rich* man who had a *manager*,
and charges were *brought* to him
that the manager was *squandering* his *property*.

So the rich man *summoned* him and said to him,
'What is this that I *hear* about you?
Give me an *accounting* of your *management*,
because you cannot be my *manager* any *longer*.'

"Then the manager said to himself,
'What will I *do*,
now that my *master* is taking the position *away* from me?
I am not *strong* enough to *dig*,
and I am *ashamed* to beg.
I have *decided* what to do so that,
when I am *dismissed* as manager,
people may *welcome* me into their *homes*.'

"*So*, summoning his master's *debtors* one by *one*,
he asked the *first*,
'How *much* do you owe my *master*?'
He answered, 'A *hundred* jugs of *olive* oil.'
He said to him,
'Take your *bill*, sit down *quickly*, and make it *fifty*.'
Then he asked *another*, 'And how much do *you* owe?'
He replied, 'A *hundred* containers of *wheat*.'
He said to him, 'Take your *bill* and make it *eighty*.'

*The man speaks firmly, in a demanding tone.*

*He is a bit frantic, but also shrewd.*

*Surely the recipients of his dishonest acts of generosity would have been grateful, as he had hoped.*

The author's point is that all people have the capacity to know God. There is one God, and God wants everyone to be saved. That is accomplished through Jesus, who is the mediator between the God and humanity precisely because he is both human and divine. His life was given for all people, including those in positions of authority.

The mention of Jesus' role and his saving death prompt the author to reflect on the ministry of Paul, whose role was to preach the cross of Christ to the Gentiles. Sent by God, he preached in the hope of bringing as many people as possible into the fold by

teaching them about God's tremendous love revealed in Christ.

Proclaim this passage as an urgent reminder to your listeners of the importance of prayer. Because Jesus has already bridged the gap between God and humankind, we can approach God freely, turning over everything in our hearts to the one who loves us beyond our imagining.

GOSPEL The parable of the unjust steward is sometimes difficult to read, much less proclaim in the

assembly. Jesus actually seems to praise the steward for his dishonesty or "shrewdness." This is especially surprising to find in the gospel of Luke, which preaches the necessity of giving up possessions and even family relationships in order to follow Jesus. But perhaps the message of the story is even more radical than we first expect.

Because he was either incompetent or dishonest with his master's property, the steward loses his job. He first responds with panic but then realizes he can turn the situation to his advantage. As the one responsible for holding the receipts indicating

**25TH SUNDAY IN ORDINARY TIME ■ SEPTEMBER 23, 2001**

**Let surprise be heard in your voice.**

"And his master *commended* the dishonest manager
because he had acted *shrewdly*;
for the *children* of this *age* are more *shrewd*
in dealing with their own *generation*
than are the children of *light*.

"And I *tell* you,
make *friends* for yourselves by means of dishonest *wealth*
so that when it is *gone*,
they may *welcome* you into the *eternal* homes.

"Whoever is faithful in a very *little*
is faithful also in *much*;
and whoever is *dishonest* in a very little
is dishonest also in *much*.
*If* then you have not been faithful with the *dishonest* wealth,
who will entrust to you the *true* riches?
And if you have not been *faithful* with what belongs to *another*,
who will give you what is your *own*?

**Proclaim the final paragraph in a strong voice.**

"No *slave* can serve two *masters*;
for a slave will either *hate* the one and love the *other*,
or be *devoted* to the one and *despise* the other.
You cannot serve *God* and *wealth*."

*[Shorter: Luke 16:10–13]*

the amounts of money owed by each of his master's debtors, he still wields power. He instructs the debtors, each of whom is no more honorable than he, to rewrite the terms of their agreement with his master. The steward hopes they will be indebted to him when he is unemployed.

Perhaps the most surprising line in the entire passage is Jesus' recommendation of friendship with such dishonest wealth. Is this the same Jesus who demands that people leave everything behind in order to follow him? But Jesus says that even the proper

use of dishonest wealth can ensure heavenly blessings. The disciple must be so completely detached from money that its presence or absence is insignificant. What matters is that what is accomplished—with or without wealth—is of such quality that it will reap an eternal reward.

All the riches of the world seem to fall under the title "dishonest wealth" in this story. Dealing with wealth—unimportant though it is in itself—can prepare one for truly significant responsibilities. In the end, though, as the final section makes clear, it is important to be detached from the wealth

one uses in this world. The purpose of using it is to serve God. Any other goal is idolatrous, placing something material above God.

Proclaim this passage boldly, trusting that the message of detachment from wealth will be heard. Do not shy away from the difficulties, but draw special attention to the final section in order to clarify the main point of the passage.

SEPTEMBER 30, 2001

# 26TH SUNDAY IN ORDINARY TIME

*Lectionary #138*

## READING I  Amos 6:1a, 4–7

**A reading from the book of the prophet Amos**

The message is dire. Begin in a booming voice.

Thus says the *Lord*, the God of *hosts*:
"*Alas* for those who are at *ease* in *Zion*,
and for those who feel *secure* on Mount *Samaria*!

Let contempt fill your voice.

"*Alas* for those who lie on beds of *ivory*,
and *lounge* on their *couches*,
and eat *lambs* from the *flock*,
and *calves* from the *stall*;
who sing idle *songs* to the sound of the *harp*,
and like *David improvise* on instruments of *music*;
who drink *wine* from *bowls*,
and *anoint* themselves with the finest *oils*,

Fairly shout the final line.

but are not *grieved* over the ruin of *Joseph*!

Speak this word of judgment with finality but also with sadness.

"*Therefore* they shall now be the *first* to go into *exile*,
and the *revelry* of those who lie in *ease* shall pass *away*.

---

**READING I** The prophet Amos lived in the eighth century BCE and preached to the people of the northern kingdom of Israel. His was a message of righteousness, calling the people to do justice to one another. Amos often speaks with anger and sarcasm, chastising the wealthy for their treatment of the poor.

The complacency of the wealthy is particularly irksome to Amos. Oblivious to the needs of the poor, they lounge in luxury and eat the choicest foods. In utter self-indulgence, they idly make music, drink sumptuously from bowls rather than cups, and anoint themselves with perfume.

The prophet was especially concerned with how the wealthy treated the poor. Here the wealthy appear much like the rich man in today's gospel—unconcerned with the poor outside their very doors—that is, until they suffer the consequences of their greed and complacency.

In an ominous warning, Amos seems to predict the fall of Israel and the exile of its people. In fact, Assyria did conquer Israel later in the eighth century BCE. It is not entirely clear if Amos anticipated the strength of that foreign power or if he simply knew that Israel's wickedness would be punished. He speaks ironically of the prominent and wealthy members of the community, unconcerned as they are about the impending demise of the nation, who will retain their foremost positions when the country is defeated: They who were first in luxury will be first in exile!

Proclaim this reading as a wake-up call to your community. Do not be afraid to speak forcefully and with a note of disdain in your voice. Close with a sense of doom.

**26TH SUNDAY IN ORDINARY TIME ■ SEPTEMBER 30, 2001**

---

### READING II    1 Timothy 6:11–16

**A reading from the first letter of Paul to Timothy**

As for *you*, Timothy, man of *God*;
pursue *righteousness*, *godliness*, *faith*,
*love*, *endurance*, *gentleness*.
Fight the *good* fight of the *faith*;
take *hold* of the eternal *life*, to which you were *called*
and for which you made the good *confession*
in the presence of many *witnesses*.

In the presence of *God*, who gives *life* to all *things*,
and of Christ *Jesus*,
who in his *testimony* before Pontius *Pilate*
        made the good *confession*,
I *charge* you to keep the *commandment* without *spot* or *blame*
until the *manifestation* of our Lord Jesus *Christ*,
which he will bring *about* at the right *time*.
He is the *blessed* and only *Sovereign*,
the King of *kings* and Lord of *lords*.

It is he *alone* who has *immortality*
and *dwells* in unapproachable *light*,
whom no one has ever *seen* or *can* see;
to *him* be *honour* and eternal *dominion*. *Amen*.

---

*Pause after each item in the list, in order to give each its due weight.*

*Speak fervently.*

*Lift your voice boldly and direct this challenge to your community.*

*The last six lines should be spoken as a sincere word of praise. Let your voice build in intensity through the entire section.*

---

READING II The first letter to Timothy was written as a letter of support from a wise older teacher to a younger minister. It provides encouragement, instruction and hope as the author urges Timothy to remain faithful in his own life and true to his calling as a minister of Christ.

The reference to Timothy's "good confession" of faith is probably intended as an allusion to his initiation. His baptismal confession in front of many witnesses opens for him the possibility of eternal life. Christ's testimony before Pilate is called by the same name—"good confession"—suggesting

that what Timothy has confessed is of the highest quality, although it also demands much of him. There is no hint that he will be asked to give his life as Jesus did, but he has been called to offer his life in service to others in the faith.

The letter, although not written by Paul, appeals to Paul's authority by using his name and upholding Paul's teachings. The reference to the "commandment" is unclear but may refer to a teaching of Paul, to the call to serve the community in active ministry, or to

the baptismal pledge. Whatever it is, Timothy is to preserve it until the coming of Jesus.

The mention of Jesus inspires the author to burst into a beautiful hymn of praise. Jesus is extolled as the King of Kings and Lord of Lords. Although last week's passage from the same letter instructs Christians to pray for civil rulers, the author here makes it clear that there is really only one king and Lord.

Concentrate on the members of your community as you share this passage with them. Think especially of those in leadership positions in the community and address it to them as you speak words of encouragement.

SEPTEMBER 30, 2001 ■ 26TH SUNDAY IN ORDINARY TIME

## GOSPEL   Luke 16:19–31

**A reading from the holy gospel according to Luke**

Jesus told this *parable*
to those among the *Pharisees* who loved *money*:

> **Let your voice be filled with mock admiration for the extravagance.**

> **The tone changes. Speak woefully about the plight of Lazarus.**

"There was a *rich* man who was dressed in *purple* and fine *linen*
and who feasted *sumptuously* every day.
And at his *gate* lay a *poor* man named *Lazarus*,
     covered with *sores*,
who *longed* to satisfy his *hunger*
with what fell from the rich man's *table*;
even the *dogs* would come and *lick* his *sores*.

"The poor man *died*
and was carried away by the *angels* to be with *Abraham*.
The *rich* man *also* died and was *buried*.
In *Hades*, where he was being *tormented*,
he looked *up* and saw *Abraham* far *away*
with *Lazarus* by his *side*.
He called out,

> **Raise your voice to express a petition from afar.**

'Father *Abraham*, have *mercy* on me,
and send *Lazarus* to dip the tip of his *finger* in *water*
and cool my *tongue*;
for I am in *agony* in these *flames*.'

"But Abraham said,

> **Abraham speaks warmly but firmly.**

'*Child*, remember that during your *lifetime*
you received *your* good things,
and *Lazarus* in *like* manner *evil* things;
but now *he* is comforted *here*,
and *you* are in *agony*.

**Lift your voice in the final section and sing out your praises to Jesus the exalted Lord.**

GOSPEL | The gospel of Luke is filled with teachings about wealth and the proper attitude toward money. Today's parable contrasts extreme wealth with absolute poverty. As so often happens in this gospel, while Jesus' teaching pertains primarily to the life anticipated after death, it also applies to attitudes and actions that are necessary in this life.

The beginning of the story is not that hard to imagine. The rich man of the parable lives in comfort, dressed in finery and enjoying his wealth, completely oblivious to the destitute beggar outside his door. Many of us can observe in our own cities the striking contrast between the terrible living conditions of the poor and the extravagance of the rich, who live only a short distance from each other. When we are in the comfort of our own homes, it is easy to forget the struggles of our neighbors. The story has a ring of truth to it, even if the situations of the protagonists are exaggerated for greater effect.

But the situation becomes more complicated after each man dies. Each receives his just reward, but the rich man, now in torment, wants to change his situation. After all, he had always had the means to do so in life. But he is not overly demanding; he does not ask to join Lazarus in the comforting bosom of Abraham. He desires only a drop of water to soothe his suffering and begs Abraham to send Lazarus to deliver it to him.

In the standard mode of this gospel, everything one usually expects is turned upside down. The rich man was accustomed

**268**

26TH SUNDAY IN ORDINARY TIME ■ SEPTEMBER 30, 2001

*Besides* all this,
between *you* and *us* a great *chasm* has been fixed,
so that those who might want to pass from *here* to *you*
cannot *do* so,
and no one can cross from *there* to *us*.'

"The man who had been *rich* said,
'*Then*, father, I *beg* you to *send* Lazarus to my *father's* house—
for I have five *brothers*—
that he may *warn* them,
so that they will not *also* come into this place of *torment*.'

**The law of Moses and the prophetic teachings stress justice for the downtrodden and care for the poor.**

"Abraham replied,
'They have *Moses* and the *prophets*;
they should listen to *them*.'
He said,
'*No*, father Abraham;
but if someone goes to them from the *dead*,
they will *repent*.'
Abraham said to him,
'If they do not listen to *Moses* and the *prophets*,
*neither* will they be convinced
even if someone *rises* from the *dead*.'"

**Speak sadly but with conviction. Surely the author wants us to think of what happened to Jesus himself.**

to making demands of others. Now he is told that he has already received more than his share of good things; it is Lazarus's turn. The gulf that separates the heavenly abode from the realm of fire contrasts with the proximity of the rich man and Lazarus on earth. When he had the chance, the rich man did not help Lazarus; now Lazarus is unable to help him.

The rich man generously thinks of others, hoping to help them, although he thinks only of his family members, wanting them to avoid a similar fate. He does not consider first and foremost the plight of the poor. In telling words, Abraham asserts that the rich

man's family members—and the rich man himself, while he was alive—have all the instructions they need to live a righteous life. They have the law of Moses and the teachings of the prophets, both of which demand justice for the oppressed.

The final exchange serves to alert the reader to the main point of the gospel message. The rich man says that his brothers would listen to someone who came to them from the dead. The author has Abraham disagree with the man's assertion, well aware that people continued to reject the Christian message that Jesus has conquered death.

Nothing, not even someone rising from the dead, will be able to convince the obstinate. Faith is essential in order for people to open their hearts and allow themselves to be guided by God in service to their neighbor.

Offer this message to your listeners as a challenge to resolve to follow Jesus, keeping wealth in its proper place and serving the poor and needy. Give plenty of expression to the various characters in the reading, while remembering also that the author is using hyperbole to make a point.

OCTOBER 7, 2001

# 27TH SUNDAY IN ORDINARY TIME

*Lectionary #141*

**READING I**   Habakkuk 1:2–3; 2:2–4

Habakkuk = HAB-uh-kuhk

Speak with heartfelt longing.

This is a genuine question. Habakkuk cannot understand how God can allow this.

Speak God's words firmly but calmly.

The final line is key. Emphasize it strongly, especially the word "faith."

**A reading from the book of the prophet Habakkuk**

*Habakkuk* called out to the *Lord*:
"O *Lord*, how *long* shall I cry for *help*,
and you will not *listen*?
Or cry to you '*Violence!*'
and you will not *save*?
*Why* do you make me see *wrong*doing
and look at *trouble*?
*Destruction* and *violence* are *before* me;
*strife* and *contention arise*."

Then the Lord *answered* me and said:
"Write the *vision*;
make it *plain* on *tablets*,
so that a runner may *read* it.
For there is still a *vision* for the appointed *time*;
it speaks of the *end*, and does not *lie*.
If it seems to *tarry*, *wait* for it;
it will surely *come*, it will not *delay*.
Look at the *proud*!
Their *spirit* is not *right* in them,
but the *righteous* live by their *faith*."

**READING I**   Habakkuk expresses a concern common to many people of faith, both in the Bible and elsewhere: the apparent absence of God and the injustice of life. How can a good God allow violence and injustice to occur? Where is God when the suffering cry out?

Habakkuk preached at a time when a foreign army was threatening the southern kingdom of Judah; the Babylonians eventually conquered the tiny state. But Habakkuk's complaints do not always refer to threats from outside. It is possible that the prophet refers to the unjust actions of the king of Judah himself.

God responds to Habakkuk's complaints with an answer that is commonly given to prophets: Write down what you know. The content of Habakkuk's vision concerns the time when God will intervene: It is coming soon. The promise of God's intervention is a message of judgment for the proud but one of hope for those who walk in justice. These righteous ones live by faith, absolutely confident in God's reliability. Habakkuk has complained about God's absence, and God responds by saying that those who are righteous should trust in God's presence and love.

There is a timeless quality to the words of Habakkuk. Express his exasperation and longing with sincerity and heartfelt pleading. God answers firmly and reassuringly. Close on a strong note as you describe the faith of the righteous.

**READING II**   First and Second Timothy, and Titus, referred to as the "pastoral letters," were written in Paul's

**27TH SUNDAY IN ORDINARY TIME ■ OCTOBER 7, 2001**

Speak confidently and boldly.

> **READING II** 2 Timothy 1:6–8, 13–14

**A reading from the second letter of Paul to Timothy**

I *remind* you, Timothy, to *rekindle* the gift of *God*
that is *within* you through the laying on of my *hands*;
for God did not give us a spirit of *cowardice*,
but rather a spirit of *power*
and of *love* and of self-*discipline*.
Do not be *ashamed*, then,
of the *testimony* about our *Lord* or of me his *prisoner*,
but join *with* me in suffering for the *gospel*,
*relying* on the power of *God*.

*Hold* to the standard of sound *teaching*
      that you have *heard* from me,
in the *faith* and *love* that are in Christ *Jesus*.
Guard the good *treasure entrusted* to you,
with the help of the Holy *Spirit* living *in* us.

name and encourage fidelity to his teachings. They are addressed to individuals but express concern for the entire community.

Based on the two letters that bear his name, it seems that Timothy was a leader in his community. He apparently looked to Paul for advice, and Paul had encouraged him as he began his ministry. The mention of Paul laying hands on Timothy in today's reading suggests an ordination rite. It also points to a period after Paul's life and ministry, since such practices developed only later. The pastoral letters were actually written by an

admirer of Paul seeking to preserve Paul's teachings and style of ministry.

Today's selection could be addressed to anyone involved in serving the Christian community, but especially those in leadership. The author seeks to inspire greater devotion to service and greater zeal for the gospel. God provides the courage to face adversity; to give in to fear is to be ashamed of the gospel, an attitude the author deplores. Despite hardship, the Christian is to press on, relying on divine assistance.

The author reminds the young minister of the truths that have been passed on to him.

Pastoral leadership—indeed the Christian faith itself—is not an individual matter. The teachings of the faith are part of a treasure that is entrusted to each community and generation of Christians. This precious tradition is to be safeguarded. But the Christian faith is not static. The Holy Spirit lives within each believer, actively guiding the church.

Reflect on those in leadership positions in your community as you share this message with your listeners. But address it as well to the entire assembly, encouraging

OCTOBER 7, 2001 ■ 27TH SUNDAY IN ORDINARY TIME

## GOSPEL    Luke 17:5–10

**A reading from the holy gospel according to Luke**

The apostles said to the Lord,
"*Increase* our *faith!*"
The Lord replied,
"If you had *faith* the size of a *mustard* seed,
you could say to this *mulberry* tree,
'Be *uprooted* and planted in the *sea,*'
and it would *obey* you.

"Who *among* you would say to your *slave*
who has just come in
        from *ploughing* or tending *sheep* in the *field,*
'Come here at *once* and take your place at the *table*'?
Would you not *rather* say to him,
'Prepare *supper* for me,
put on your *apron* and *serve* me while I *eat* and *drink;*
*later you* may eat and drink'?
Do you *thank* the slave for doing what was *commanded*?
So you *also,*
when you have done *all* that you were ordered to *do,* say,
'We are worthless *slaves;*
we have done only what we *ought* to have done!'"

**Speak slowly but with confidence.**

**Imagine yourself in charge of a work crew, and speak as one insisting that your employees put in a good day's work. Speak kindly but firmly.**

each person to be courageous in proclaiming the love of God for all to hear. Speak warmly and reassuringly.

GOSPEL   Jesus' disciples, recognizing the importance of faith, ask for more. Jesus responds with a teaching about the strength of even a little faith. The tiniest amount can work wonders. More importantly, Jesus' message teaches that the gift of faith, like any other gift, cannot be demanded; it can only be appreciated.

The parable that follows teaches a similar lesson. One who is working in service to another cannot expect a reward. Service is a requirement of discipleship.

It is difficult for many of us to hear this story. We react with horror at the thought of owning another human being; we deplore the lack of gratitude and appreciation shown by the master. The author does not question the institution of slavery, however, but simply lays out its rules. And they apply particularly to service for the gospel.

When applied to the Christian life, the meaning of the parable is clear. Those serving God cannot simply stop working and expect gratitude. Rather, out of gratitude to God for the gift of faith and for God's tremendous love, we must share our faith with others and strive to bring God's justice to reality on earth. We do not minister for the sake of ourselves; instead, we act out of gratitude for the undeserved gifts we have already received.

Proclaim this passage with boldness in order to convey the importance of faith and service to the gospel. But be sensitive to the emotions that Jesus' example might stir.

# OCTOBER 14, 2001

# 28TH SUNDAY IN ORDINARY TIME

*Lectionary #144*

## READING I  2 Kings 5:14–17

**A reading from the second book of Kings**

Naaman = NAY-uh-muhn
Aram = AYR-uhm
Elisha = ee-LĪ-shuh

**Speak with wonder.**

*Naaman*, commander of the *army* of the king of *Aram*
and a mighty *warrior, obeyed* Elisha:
he went down and *immersed* himself seven times in the *Jordan*,
according to the *word* of the man of *God*;
his flesh was *restored* like the flesh of a young *boy*,
and he was *clean*.

**Naaman speaks humbly and gratefully.**

Then he *returned* to the man of God,
*he* and all his *company*;
Naaman *came* and stood before *Elisha* and said,
"Now I *know* that there is no God in all the *earth*
except in *Israel*;
please accept a *present* from your *servant*."

**Read Elisha's words with stubborn pride.**

But Elisha said,
"As the Lord *lives*, whom I *serve*,
I will accept *nothing*!"
Naaman urged Elisha to *accept*,
but he *refused*.

**With Naaman, resolve to serve God faithfully, then speak his closing words with conviction.**

Then Naaman said,
"If *not*, please let two *mule*-loads of *earth*
be given to your *servant*;
for your *servant* will no longer offer burnt *offering* or *sacrifice*
to any *god* except the *Lord*."

---

READING I  Today's passage begins mid-way through the story of Naaman and Elisha. Naaman the Syrian was an important and powerful man, but he was stricken with leprosy. He heard that there was a prophet in Israel named Elisha who could cure him, and so he approached Elisha for help. But he arrogantly turned away when Elisha sent a servant to talk with him rather than coming himself. Although Naaman began to leave, he reconsidered and agreed to Elisha's cure—immersing himself in the waters of the Jordan—which is where today's story begins.

Naaman is proud, but he is not ignorant. When his flesh is cleansed he recognizes the greatness of the prophet Elisha and the superiority of Israel's God. In gratitude, he offers a gift to Elisha from the wealth he had brought with him, but Elisha refuses.

Naaman's response seems odd at first. He asks Elisha for some dirt to take back with him, declaring that he will sacrifice only to the Lord. The idea behind this is that

a god could be worshipped only in the land of the people who worshiped that god. To worship the God of Israel, Naaman must take some of Israel's earth back with him.

When you understand the context of this reading, you will be able to proclaim it as the interesting story of healing and conversion that it is. Express amazement at the miracle that occurs, and stress the conviction of both Naaman and Elisha. Naaman is sincere in his gratitude, and Elisha is equally serious. Speak the final line expressing Naaman's devotion to God with forcefulness.

OCTOBER 14, 2001 ■ 28TH SUNDAY IN ORDINARY TIME

## READING II    2 Timothy 2:8–13

**A reading from the second letter of Paul to Timothy**

**Be sure you have the attention of the assembly before you begin, then proclaim this message in a strong voice.**

Remember Jesus *Christ*,
raised from the *dead*, a descendant of *David*—
*that* is my *gospel*,
for which I suffer *hardship*,
even to the point of being *chained* like a *criminal*.
But the word of *God* is *not* chained.

**Speak harshly of the hardships of ministry. Then pause, lower your voice, and quietly but firmly proclaim the line about God's word.**

*Therefore* I endure *everything* for the sake of the *elect*,
so that they may *also* obtain the *salvation* that is in Christ *Jesus*,
with eternal *glory*.

**Slow down and proclaim each line separately, in order to avoid becoming sing-song. Build in intensity to the end.**

The saying is *sure*:
If we have *died* with him,
we will also *live* with him;
if we *endure*,
we will also *reign* with him;
if we *deny* him,
he will also deny *us*;
if we are *faithless*,
he remains *faithful*—
for he *cannot* deny *himself*.

READING II The second letter to Timothy was written by an admirer of Paul many years after Paul's death. The author writes as if Paul is still alive and refers to events in Paul's life. The author also upholds Pauline teaching and encourages faithfulness to Paul's preaching.

Paul was often imprisoned for the sake of the gospel during his missionary travels, and the author alludes to his suffering. While in prison, Paul wrote letters to the churches he had founded and others he had visited.

Even while imprisoned, he worked to spread the gospel to the Gentiles—who were his special responsibility—and to build up the communities of Christians he had known. Today's reading opens with a reference to Paul's imprisonment and to his evangelism while in chains. In a powerful statement of the force of the gospel despite all human efforts to squelch it, the author claims that the word of God cannot be chained. It has a life of its own.

The author emphasizes key Pauline themes: the hope in Christ's resurrection; the significance of suffering for the gospel; and

the eagerness to endure whatever is necessary in order to bring others to salvation.

The last few verses of the passage are taken from an ancient Christian hymn. The Christian has died with Christ (in the waters of baptism) but has hope of living with him. The Christian life involves endurance, but we can also look forward to the fulfillment of God's promises. God's love is eternal.

Reflect on your own ministry as you read these words. Although you might not be asked to witness to your faith from prison, think of the suffering you have endured for

**28TH SUNDAY IN ORDINARY TIME ■ OCTOBER 14, 2001**

## GOSPEL  Luke 17:11–19

**A reading from the holy gospel according to Luke**

On the way to *Jerusalem*
Jesus was going through the region between *Samaria* and *Galilee.*

As he entered a *village,*
ten *lepers approached* him.
Keeping their *distance,*
they called *out,* saying,
"*Jesus, Master,* have *mercy* on us!"

When Jesus *saw* them, he said to them,
"Go and *show* yourselves to the *priests.*"
And as they *went,* they were made *clean.*
Then *one* of them, when he saw that he was *healed,*
turned *back,* praising *God* with a loud *voice.*
He prostrated himself at Jesus' *feet* and *thanked* him.
And he was a *Samaritan.*

Then Jesus asked,
"Were not *ten* made clean?
But the other *nine,* where are *they?*
Was *none* of them found to *return*
and give praise to God except this *foreigner?*"

Then Jesus said to Samaritan,
"Get *up* and go on your *way;*
your *faith* has made you *well.*"

---

*Because of the contagious nature of skin diseases, lepers were required to keep their distance and call out to others to stay away. These lepers instead call out for mercy.*

*Jews were suspicious of Samaritans. This one displays knowledge of and gratitude for God's work in him.*

*Speak gently and kindly.*

---

your principles. Then speak confidently as you share this message with your assembly.

GOSPEL  The gospel story today has many similarities with the first reading. Both include a cure of leprosy, thankfulness for God's goodness, and a foreigner who expresses faith and gratitude.

The law of Moses indicates that a cure of leprosy is to be confirmed by a priest. Jesus sends the lepers he encounters to the priests; on the way they are cured. Nine

continue their journey, but one, a Samaritan, returns to thank Jesus and praise God.

Samaritans and Jews were at odds with one another, despite a common heritage. They differed over the contents of scripture and over the proper place and manner of worship. Jews were suspicious of Samaritans and tried to avoid contact with them whenever possible.

The author of this gospel repeatedly surprises the reader by suggesting that unexpected people prove to be truly righteous. Surely no Jew would have expected the single righteous leper to be a Samaritan.

Jesus emphasizes the importance of the man's faith. True healing and well-being go beyond the merely physical.

In our own day, the Samaritan in this story would be someone from a religious background or ethnic group different from our own, or perhaps a drug addict or convict. Keep that image in mind as you tell this story with enthusiasm. Speak Jesus' words clearly, so that your listeners can join with the Samaritan leper in praising God.

OCTOBER 21, 2001

# 29TH SUNDAY IN ORDINARY TIME

*Lectionary #147*

## READING I     Exodus 17:8–13

**A reading from the book of Exodus**

Amalek = AM-uh-lek
Rephidim = REH-fih-dim

*Amalek* came and fought with *Israel* at *Rephidim*.
*Moses* said to *Joshua*,
"Choose some *men* for us and go *out*, fight with *Amalek*.
*Tomorrow* I will *stand* on the top of the *hill*
with the staff of *God* in my *hand*."

So Joshua did as Moses *told* him,
and fought with *Amalek*,
while *Moses, Aaron,* and *Hur* went up to the top of the *hill*.

Hur = her

Whenever Moses held up his *hands*, Israel *prevailed*;
and whenever he *lowered* his hands, *Amalek* prevailed.
But Moses' hands grew *weary*;
so they took a *stone* and put it *under* him,
and he *sat* on it.
*Aaron* and *Hur* held up his *hands*,
one on *one* side, and the other on the *other* side;
so his hands were *steady* until the sun *set*.

Speak this final line quietly. The real point of the story has already been made.

And Joshua *defeated* Amalek and his *people* with the *sword*.

---

READING I  The battle between Israel and the Amalekites takes place while the Israelites are wandering in the desert after their flight from Egypt. Shortly before Israel arrived at Mount Sinai—where Moses conversed with God and received instructions for the people—Amalek and his warriors attacked the Israelites. In the account that forms today's first reading, Israel is victorious because of the intervention of God through Moses.

Moses is clearly the authority not only when it comes to prophecy but even in military matters. Although Joshua is here and elsewhere the general in charge of the troops, Moses gives instructions and presides over the events.

The image of Moses holding the staff of God and standing with outstretched arms suggests that he was acting as a military standard. Ancient peoples would often go into battle with a statue of their god as a standard in order to inspire courage in the troops. Since Israel's God cannot be depicted, Moses acts in God's place, representing God's presence and power. With the assistance of other leaders of the community, Moses is able to withstand weariness, staunchly remaining in his designated position for the entire day. As a result, Israel overcomes its adversaries.

It can be difficult to read about a military victory with enthusiasm. But the point of this story is Moses' steadfastness and God's faithful protection of Israel. Proclaim the narrative in a straightforward manner.

# 29TH SUNDAY IN ORDINARY TIME ■ OCTOBER 21, 2001

> **READING II**    2 Timothy 3:14—4:2

**A reading from the second letter of Paul to Timothy**

*This sentence is long. Practice it well so that you know when to pause, then speak slowly.*

*Continue* in what you have *learned* and firmly *believed*,
knowing from whom you *learned* it,
and how from *childhood* you have known the sacred *writings*
that are able to *instruct* you for *salvation*
through *faith* in Christ *Jesus*.

All *scripture* is inspired by *God*
and is useful for *teaching*,
for *reproof*, for *correction*, and for training in *righteousness*,
so that everyone who *belongs* to God may be *proficient*,
equipped for every good *work*.

*Pause briefly after "you," then announce firmly, "proclaim the message." This line needs to be stressed more than any other in this passage.*

In the presence of *God* and of Christ *Jesus*,
who is to *judge* the living and the *dead*,
and in view of his *appearing* and his *kingdom*,
I solemnly *urge* you:
*proclaim* the *message*;
be *persistent* whether the time is *favourable* or *unfavourable*;
*convince, rebuke,* and *encourage*,
with the utmost *patience* in *teaching*.

---

**READING II** We do not come before God alone but as part of a community. If it were not for our parents, family, teachers and others, we might not know anything about God. The author of today's selection recognizes the importance of instruction and encourages the members of the community to cling to the faith that has been passed on to them.

Especially important among the religious traditions that are handed from generation to generation is scripture. For the author, "scripture" means the Hebrew scriptures. The stories of Israel's journey toward greater understanding of God, the prophetic messages, and the instruction in right living that characterizes Hebrew wisdom literature can all form the Christian in righteousness.

Finally, the author begins to look forward to the future, to the time when Jesus will return as judge and ruler of the world. In a bold statement, the author encourages the readers to proclaim their faith in all situations, even when it is not easy, and to instruct others with patience.

This passage can be directed to all the members of your assembly since its message is timeless. In proclaiming it, you do precisely what the author says to do: You encourage a respect for God's word in scripture, and you instruct your own community to hold fast to the faith and to proclaim it with enthusiasm. Read with encouragement and patience in your voice.

**GOSPEL** The first line of the passage states Jesus' message in today's parable: Pray always. The story of the unjust judge illustrates the importance of persistence in prayer.

OCTOBER 21, 2001 ■ 29TH SUNDAY IN ORDINARY TIME

## GOSPEL    Luke 18:1–18

**A reading from the holy gospel according to Luke**

Jesus told the disciples a *parable* about their need to pray *always* and not to lose *heart*.

He said,
"In a certain *city* there was a *judge*
who neither feared *God* nor had respect for *people*.
In that city there was a *widow*
who kept *coming* to him and saying,
'Grant me *justice* against my *opponent*.'

"For a *while* the judge *refused*;
but *later* he said to himself,
'Though I have no fear of *God* and no respect for *anyone*,
yet because this *widow* keeps *bothering* me,
I will grant her *justice*,
so that she may not wear me *out* by continually *coming*.'"

And the Lord said,
"*Listen* to what the unjust *judge* says.
Will not *God* grant justice to his *chosen* ones
who *cry* to him *day* and *night*?
Will he delay *long* in *helping* them?
I *tell* you, God will *quickly* grant *justice* to them.
"And *yet*, when the Son of *Man* comes,
will he find *faith* on *earth*?"

*It appears that he was corrupt, caring only for himself and his own benefit.*

*Resolve in your heart that the answer to this question is a resounding "Yes!"*

Jesus is not afraid to use a dishonorable figure to illustrate his point. In another parable, he even praises the shrewdness and dishonesty of a steward who falsifies the notes of debt owed to his master. Rather than excoriate the judge in today's story, Jesus compares him with God! Although he is a poor excuse for a judge, he illustrates the faithfulness and devotion of the judge of the world.

The judge is clearly not fulfilling his duties on a regular basis. He does not care about God nor is he concerned about other members of his community. He does not seek justice or uphold what is right. Yet a poor, powerless widow is able to turn him around with her irritating persistence.

Widows in antiquity—women without a husband or family to care for and protect them—often faced danger and had few resources. They were among the downtrodden, depending on the kindness of strangers to meet their needs. You may decide for yourself if the widow in this story is meek and quiet (although persistent!) or if she is assertive and demanding. Either way, it is her unwillingness to give up that finally makes a difference.

Just as the widow refused to give up in asking for what she needed, so also the Christian can turn to God in everything, unwilling to stop asking and trusting in God's mercy and love.

Give plenty of expression to the characters in this story as you encourage the members of your assembly to pray always. The final line is spoken directly to each of us. If we take the message of the parable to heart, we will be able to affirm that we can indeed trust completely in God.

## OCTOBER 28, 2001

# 30TH SUNDAY IN ORDINARY TIME

*Lectionary #150*

### READING I    Sirach 35:15–17, 20–22

**A reading from the book of Sirach**

The *Lord* is the *judge*,
and with *him* there is no *partiality*.
He will not show *partiality* to the *poor*
but he will *listen* to the *prayer* of one who is *wronged*.
The Lord will not *ignore* the supplication of the *orphan*,
or the *widow* when she pours out her *complaint*.

The one whose service is *pleasing* to the Lord will be *accepted*,
and the *prayer* of such a person will *reach* to the *clouds*.

The prayer of the *humble pierces* the clouds,
and it will not *rest* until it reaches its *goal*;
it will not *desist* until the Most High *responds*
and does *justice* for the *righteous*,
and executes *judgment*.
*Indeed*, the Lord will not *delay*.

**Wait until you have the attention of your listeners, then begin boldly.**

**Pause before turning to the next point.**

**Close with conviction.**

---

**READING I** The book of Sirach is a relatively late book of Jewish wisdom literature, a body of texts offering advice about right living. The present passage reflects on the proper attitude of the human person before God and how that posture affects God's response to prayer. First, however, the author discusses God's response to human social and economic positions, and to those who are less fortunate than others.

God is fair to all, whether rich or poor, powerful or powerless, strong or weak. But God also recognizes that some people suffer disadvantage in society and need special protection. Orphans and widows, two categories of people who had little legal protection or wealth in Hebrew society, are singled out. But they represent all the disadvantaged and oppressed. God listens and responds willingly to the poor and powerless when they cry out in need.

The passage then moves to the type of person whose prayer is most favorable to God. The one who serves God with enthusiasm and prays with humility will be heard. If we look ahead to the gospel reading, we see the same message expressed in a different way: The Pharisee's prayer, filled with self-righteousness for his many accomplishments, is not as pleasing to God as the sincere supplication of the humble tax collector, who recognizes his unworthiness before God.

The message of this passage is timeless. Reflect on your own attitudes, and then offer this reading to your community with sincerity and humility. Speak with conviction but also with compassion.

**READING II** The author of the second letter to Timothy recalls the suffering Paul endured before his death. Yet

OCTOBER 28, 2001 ■ 30TH SUNDAY IN ORDINARY TIME

---

**READING II**   2 Timothy 4:6–8, 16–18

**A reading from the second letter of Paul to Timothy**

*Speak solemnly and slowly.*

As for *me*,
I am *already* being poured out as a *libation*,
and the time of my *departure* has *come*.
I have *fought* the *good* fight,
I have *finished* the *race*,
I have *kept* the *faith*.

From now *on*
there is *reserved* for me the crown of *righteousness*,
which the *Lord*, the righteous *judge*,
will *give* me on that *day*,
and not only to *me*
but also to *all* who have longed for his *appearing*.

*Let your voice be filled with regret rather than anger.*

At my *first* defense *no* one came to my *support*,
but all *deserted* me.
May it *not* be counted *against* them!

*Proclaim this with strength and conviction. Close with joyful confidence.*

But the *Lord* stood by me
and gave me *strength*,
so that through *me* the message might be fully *proclaimed*
and all the *Gentiles* might *hear* it.
So I was *rescued* from the lion's *mouth*.

The Lord will *rescue* me from every evil *attack*
and *save* me for his heavenly *kingdom*.
To *him* be the *glory* forever and *ever*. *Amen*.

---

the author speaks with hope and confidence, looking forward to life with God in glory. Throughout, Paul's experiences reflect those of Jesus.

Just as Jesus spoke of the wine as his blood at the Last Supper, so also the author characterizes his life as a libation, a drink offering poured out during worship. Early Christians suffering persecution often connected their bodies and their lives with the eucharist, an offering to God that could also give life to others.

Using image of an athlete, the author speaks with satisfaction of having endured

to the end. Just as winning athletes received a victor's crown, so also God reserves a crown of righteousness for the victorious Christian. It will be given on the day when Christ is revealed as judge of the world.

In very personal terms, the author alludes to having been abandoned at his trial, just as Jesus was. But, like Jesus, he prays for others even as he approaches death himself. He relies on God's strength to support him through his tribulations, knowing that he can proclaim the gospel even from prison.

Proclaim this text solemnly and with a bit of sadness. But do not lose sight of the

firm faith that undergirds the author's words. Even when speaking of the abandonment the author expresses, proclaim his belief in God's mercy. The closing verses express the hope of one who is certain to die soon but still trusts in God and looks forward to joining God in eternity; such hope causes the author to break into praise. Join with him in lifting your voice to God.

| GOSPEL | The story of the Pharisee and the tax collector in the gospel of Luke is a tale that hits home, if we let it. It is a story of righteousness and sin,

30TH SUNDAY IN ORDINARY TIME ■ OCTOBER 28, 2001

### GOSPEL  Luke 18:9–14

**A reading from the holy gospel according to Luke**

Jesus told this *parable*
to some who trusted in *themselves* that they were *righteous,*
and regarded *others* with *contempt:*

"Two *men* went up to the *temple* to *pray,*
one a *Pharisee* and the other a *tax* collector.
The *Pharisee,* standing by *himself,* was praying *thus,*
'God, I *thank* you that I am not like *other* people:
*thieves, rogues, adulterers,*
or even like this *tax* collector.
I *fast* twice a *week;*
I give a *tenth* of all my *income.*'

"But the *tax* collector, standing far *off,*
would not even look up to *heaven,*
but was beating his *breast* and saying,
'God, be *merciful* to me, a *sinner*!'

"I *tell* you,
this man went down to his home *justified* rather than the *other;*
for all who *exalt* themselves will be *humbled,*
but all who *humble* themselves will be *exalted.*"

---

**Do not give away the conclusion of the parable with your voice. Speak the Pharisee's words sincerely and genuinely.**

**The tax collector speaks simply and sorrowfully. Pause.**

**Speak Jesus' words forcefully.**

---

but not in the places we usually expect to see them.

Since the gospels often portray Jesus in conflict with Pharisees, we can sometimes forget that the Pharisees were concerned with proper living, extending the legal precepts of the temple to all of life. They taught that people should live holy lives in their homes and daily affairs. Pharisees also believed in the resurrection of the dead, in contrast to the Sadducees, the priestly caste of the Jerusalem temple.

Jesus had much in common with the Pharisees but also found them prone to self-righteousness. The Pharisee in the story has devoted himself to God and has even gone beyond what the law requires. But he is also proud of his good behavior and consequently looks down on others.

Tax collectors were known as cheaters, often charging more than was required in order to line their own pockets. The tax collector in the story seems to acknowledge that his actions have been less than admirable. He knows he is a sinner. Yet Jesus claims that the tax collector demonstrates the proper attitude of one approaching God in prayer! As is typical in the gospel of Luke, all expectations are turned upside down. The religious leader is criticized, while the sinner is praised.

Anyone who seeks to live the moral life can fall into the same trap that snared the Pharisee. We sometimes find it easy look down others whom we presume to be sinners. Yet Jesus' challenge falls directly on us. While not advocating sinful behavior, he insists on honesty and humility before God.

Do not be afraid of the shock that should accompany this story. Share its challenge with your listeners so that all in the assembly can together grapple with its meaning.

# NOVEMBER 1, 2001

# ALL SAINTS

*Lectionary #667*

## READING I   Revelation 7:2–4, 9–14

"Revelation," not "Revelations."

### A reading from the book of Revelation

I, *John*, saw an *angel*
ascending from the *rising* of the *sun*,
having the *seal* of the living *God*,
and he called with a loud *voice* to the *four angels*
who had been given *power* to damage *earth* and *sea*, saying,
"Do *not* damage the *earth* or the *sea* or the *trees*,
until we have marked the *servants* of our God
with a *seal* on their *foreheads*."

And I heard the number of those who were *sealed*,
one *hundred* forty-four *thousand*,
sealed out of *every tribe* of the people of *Israel*.

After this I looked, and there was a great *multitude*
that no one could *count*, from every *nation*,
from all *tribes* and *peoples* and *languages*,
standing before the *throne* and before the *Lamb*,
robed in *white*, with *palm* branches in their *hands*.

Pause before reading the words of
the crowd, then proclaim them loudly
and clearly.

They cried out in a loud *voice*,
"*Salvation* belongs to our *God* who is *seated* on the *throne*,
and to the *Lamb*!"

And all the *angels* stood around the *throne*,
around the *elders* and the four living *creatures*;
they fell on their *faces* before the *throne*
and *worshipped* God, singing,

READING I   The visionary John tells of his experience of being taken before the throne of God, where he sees angels and a lamb (Christ) who has been slain. After the lamb opens a sealed scroll, an angel bears the instrument for the final seal, the seal of God. In antiquity, seals were used to close documents and to mark possessions. Here the divine seal, a sign of ultimate authority, is used to mark those faithful to God.

Those eligible for marking with the seal are a vast number. The number 144,000 is intended to signify the complete nation of Israel. Not only the Israelites, but Gentiles of every race and nation are included among the chosen ones of God. The number of Gentiles is so great that it cannot be determined. Although these numbers are sometimes used to justify exclusion and the superiority of a few, the idea is really one of inclusion: Anyone faithful to God is worthy to be counted as one of God's servants.

The faithfulness of this crowd becomes evident as the vision continues. The white robes and palm branches indicate those martyred for their faith. This is confirmed by the elder, who tells John that these faithful have "washed their robes . . . in the blood of the Lamb." They cry out with the angels before the throne of God.

The purpose of apocalyptic writing is to encourage those who are struggling and who might even face persecution for the faith. Just as those dressed in white have been vindicated and now bask in God's presence, so also anyone who faithfully endures trial now will be justified by God and made to share in the heavenly glory.

Today's feast is a feast of memories, family stories and inspiring saints. As we remember today all the saints—those widely

**ALL SAINTS ■ NOVEMBER 1, 2001**

**Read this quotation slowly and with great emphasis on each term of honor. Pause slightly after "God" and be sure not to swallow the final "Amen."**

"*Amen*! *Blessing* and *glory* and *wisdom*
and *thanksgiving* and *honour* and *power* and *might*
be to our *God forever* and *ever*! *Amen*."

Then one of the elders *addressed* me,
"Who are *these*, robed in *white*,
and where have they *come* from?"
I said to him, "Sir, *you* are the one that *knows*."
Then he said to me,

**Speak this as the message of comfort it was intended to be.**

"*These* are they who have come *out* of the great *ordeal*;
they have *washed* their *robes*
and made them *white* in the blood of the *Lamb*."

---

### READING II    1 John 3:1–3

**A reading from the first letter of John**

**Speak tenderly and lovingly throughout this selection. Read slowly.**

See what *love* the Father has *given* us,
that we should be called *children* of *God*;
and that is what we *are*.
The reason the world does not *know* us
is that it did not know *him*.

**Pause briefly before and after this line. Read it with conviction.**

*Beloved*, we are *God's* children now;
what we *will* be has not yet been *revealed*.
What we *do* know is *this*:
when he is *revealed*, we will be *like* him,
for we will *see* him as he *is*.

**This is both a statement of reality and an exhortation to your listeners to be pure.**

And *all* who have this hope in *God purify* themselves,
just as *he* is pure.

---

recognized for their holiness and those known only to a few—we realize that we belong to a community of faith. We recall those who have instilled faith in us, those who have gone ahead to experience the full revelation of God. We would not be here, would not be joining our voices in praise of God, were it not for them. And so we take comfort in knowing that they are part of that multitude standing before the throne of God, free of all pain and anxiety.

READING II Building on the promise of today's first reading, this

passage from the Johannine correspondence is addressed both to the recipients of the letter and to us. It affirms the tremendous love bestowed on us by God. We are not simply God's creatures, nor are we recipients from afar of God's goodness. Rather, we are part of the family of God, heirs to all God's blessings. The great chasm that divides imperfect mortals from the magnificent, immortal God is bridged, and we are called children of God.

The author offers this message, just as the mystic John did in the first reading, to

encourage those who are facing adversity. "The world" does not recognize the identity of these children of God, but that does not change the reality. But there is still more: The final outcome for our lives is still shrouded in mystery. The author makes two claims about that future reality: On that day we shall be like God, and we shall share in the beatific vision of a God fully revealed.

This is a message of hope for the future and encouragement for the present. The final line makes it clear that those who hope to become like God and to see God must now live lives of purity worthy of their calling.

NOVEMBER 1, 2001 ■ ALL SAINTS

## GOSPEL  Matthew 5:1–12a

**A reading from the holy gospel according to Matthew**

When Jesus saw the *crowds*, he went up the *mountain*;
and after he sat *down*,
his disciples *came* to him.
Then he began to *speak*, and *taught* them, saying:

"*Blessed* are the *poor* in *spirit*,
for *theirs* is the kingdom of *heaven*.
Blessed are those who *mourn*,
for they will be *comforted*.

"Blessed are the *meek*,
for they will *inherit* the *earth*.
Blessed are those who *hunger* and *thirst* for *righteousness*,
for they will be *filled*.

"Blessed are the *merciful*,
for they will *receive* mercy.
Blessed are the *pure* in *heart*,
for they will see *God*.

"Blessed are the *peacemakers*,
for they will be called *children* of *God*.
Blessed are those who are *persecuted* for *righteousness*' sake,
for *theirs* is the kingdom of *heaven*.

"Blessed are *you* when people *revile* you
and *persecute* you and utter all kinds of *evil*
against you *falsely* on *my* account.
*Rejoice* and be *glad*,
for your reward is *great* in *heaven*."

---

**Do not try to rush through the beatitudes. Speak each one as a distinct unit before moving on to the next. If it seems right to you to emphasize "blessed" more than is indicated here, feel free to do so. But be careful not to make each line sound exactly the same.**

**Direct this line to your listeners.**

**The final sentence indicates the attitude that is to greet adversity; there is a promise of good things yet to come.**

---

This selection requires a slow, sincere and thoughtful rendering. Although the term "child of God" might be familiar, meditate on its significance and proclaim it to the assembly.

GOSPEL   The beatitudes in Matthew "spiritualize" the concerns expressed also in the beatitudes in Luke. In Luke the needs are concrete: the poor are really poor, the hungry are really starving. Here, however, the ones who are blessed are not only those struggling to survive or

those mistreated by the powerful but anyone who loves righteousness and is willing to suffer for it. Each beatitude tells of a present reality and offers a promise for the future that turns the present experience upside down or bestows a reward of heavenly magnitude. What we know now is not all that there is to know.

The beatitudes offer an assurance that the pilgrims who have preceded us on this journey, having steadfastly endured the trials of their age, now enjoy peace and happiness in the presence of God. They are also a promise to us, living in a world filled with

sorrow and slander, that there is more to come. The beatitudes in Matthew in particular are a challenge to us who live in comfort to share in the struggle to create a just, compassionate world.

The natural rhythm of this passage makes it easy to proclaim but also offers pitfalls to the inattentive. Each blessing must be spoken sincerely and simply, with a pause before reading the "reward." Listen to your own words as though you are hearing the passage for the first time, so that they can truly provide comfort and challenge to your listeners.

## NOVEMBER 4, 2001

# 31ST SUNDAY IN ORDINARY TIME

*Lectionary #153*

## READING I    Wisdom 11:22—12:2

### A reading from the book of Wisdom

**Speak in awe and wonder, then change your tone to proclaim God's mercy.**

The whole *world before* you, O Lord,
is like a *speck* that tips the *scales*,
and like a drop of morning *dew* that falls on the *ground*.
But you are *merciful* to *all*,
for *you* can do all *things*,
and you *overlook* people's *sins*,
so that they may *repent*.

*Lord*, you *love* all things that *exist*,
and detest *none* of the things that you have *made*,
for you would not have *made* anything if you had *hated* it.
How would anything have *endured*
if you had not *willed* it?
Or how would anything *not* called *forth* by you
have been *preserved*?
You *spare* all things, for they are *yours*, O Lord,
*you* who *love* the *living*.

**Declare God's tremendous love with certainty and gratitude.**

**Although you are speaking of divine correction, it is given gently. Speak encouragingly.**

For your immortal *spirit* is in all *things*.
Therefore you *correct* little by little those who *trespass*,
and you *remind* and *warn* them of the things
        through which they *sin*,
so that they may be *freed* from *wickedness*
and put their *trust* in *you*, O Lord.

---

READING I    The Wisdom of Solomon is a late work of Jewish wisdom literature (it does not actually claim to have been written by King Solomon). Wisdom literature teaches how one should live in order to merit the afterlife prepared for the righteous. But it also speaks eloquently of the nature of God. Today's selection reflects on God's relationship with the created world and especially with sinful humanity.

The passage begins by reflecting on God's majestic grandeur, with which nothing can compare. Insignificant as the universe is in God's eyes, God has created it and loves it. Everything that God has made is worthy of preservation, for God has willed its very existence.

Above all, God is able to forgive our sinfulness. God can do anything, of course, but human beings are especially singled out for mercy. Despite our many failings, we still have God's spirit. Yet God does not simply forgive sinful humanity without trying to make it better. God chastises and instructs so that we might learn to do what is right and be free from all sin, faithful to God.

This reading deserves to be proclaimed with special care. Reflect on the divine glory present in creation and especially on the tremendous love and forgiveness of God. Think about a time when you might have experienced God's gentle correction and its outcome. Then allow all the hope and gratitude in your heart to rise to your lips as you share with your community the splendor of God's creation and love. Read the closing sentence as an encouragement and a reminder that divine chastisement serves a greater purpose.

READING II    Paul opens each of his letters with a prayer. He was

NOVEMBER 4, 2001 ■ 31ST SUNDAY IN ORDINARY TIME

## READING II    2 Thessalonians 1:11—2:2

**A reading from the second letter of Paul to the Thessalonians**

**Let your voice be filled with love and encouragement.**

We always *pray* for you,
asking that our *God* will make you *worthy* of his *call*
and will fulfil by his *power* every good *resolve* and work of *faith*,
so that the name of our Lord *Jesus* may be *glorified* in you,
and *you* in *him*,
according to the *grace* of our *God* and the Lord Jesus *Christ*.

**Change your tone here to one that is firm and instructive.**

As to the *coming* of our Lord Jesus *Christ*
and our being gathered *together* to *him*,
we *beg* you, brothers and sisters,
not to be quickly shaken in *mind* or *alarmed*,
either by *spirit* or by *word* or by *letter*, as though from *us*,

**Speak the last line slowly.**

to the effect that the *day* of the *Lord* is already *here*.

---

particularly fond of the community at Thessalonica and speaks with joy and gratitude for them and for their faith. Although this letter may have been written by someone other than Paul himself, it admirably recounts Paul's values and teachings.

The author begins by praying that the Thessalonians may be worthy of what God asks of them. But the author is confident that God can work through them, acting with power to bring about what is good. Through their actions, Jesus will be glorified. The author also speaks of the Thessalonians being glorified in the Lord, apparently in a

new age. All of this is in accordance with God's grace.

The letter then turns to a problematic issue rooted in Paul's own teachings. In his earliest surviving correspondence, First Thessalonians, Paul expresses a fervent belief that Jesus will return soon. In today's passage from Second Thessalonians, the author has to temper the expectations of members of the community, who believed that Jesus' return was imminent.

Apparently, there were some members of the community who had prophesied about the immanent second coming of Jesus, and

others pointed to Paul's earlier letter to support the view. While upholding Pauline authority, the author modifies Paul's teaching, downplaying the possibility of Christ's imminent return, to make the gospel relevant to the contemporary Thessalonian community.

Speak fondly but powerfully as you offer the prayer in this passage, sincerely intending it for your own community. Continue to be sincere in the second half of the selection, knowing that Christians today should also guard against being too easily swayed by easy expectations of what is in store for us.

# 31ST SUNDAY IN ORDINARY TIME ■ NOVEMBER 4, 2001

## GOSPEL    Luke 19:1–10

**A reading from the holy gospel according to Luke**

Zacchaeus = zuh-KEE-uhs

Jesus entered *Jericho* and was passing *through* it.
A *man* was there named *Zacchaeus*;
he was a chief *tax* collector and was *rich*.
He was trying to see *who* Jesus *was*,
but on account of the *crowd* he could *not*,
because he was *short* in *stature*.

Express the eagerness of Zacchaeus.

So he ran *ahead* and climbed a *sycamore* tree to see *Jesus*,
because he was going to pass that *way*.
When Jesus came to the *place*,
he looked *up* and said to him,

Jesus speaks urgently but kindly.

"*Zacchaeus*, *hurry* and come *down*;
for I must stay at *your* house today."

So *Zacchaeus* hurried *down* and was *happy* to welcome Jesus.
All who *saw* it began to *grumble* and said,
"He has gone to be the *guest* of one who is a *sinner*."

Zacchaeus is sincere in his generosity.

Zacchaeus *stood* there and said to the Lord,
"*Look*, *half* of my *possessions*, Lord, I will give to the *poor*;
and if I have *defrauded* anyone of *anything*,
I will *pay* back *four* times as much."

Then Jesus *said* of him,
"*Today salvation* has come to this *house*,
because Zacchaeus *too* is a son of *Abraham*.

Close with conviction.

For the Son of *Man* came to seek *out* and to *save* the *lost*."

---

GOSPEL | The gospel of Luke is fond of tax collectors. Although such people were reviled in antiquity (and often today as well!), the author enjoys giving them important, positive roles in Jesus' ministry and stories. Tax collectors had the habit of charging taxpayers more than was actually required and then pocketing the difference. They had a well-deserved reputation for dishonesty.

Zacchaeus is a comical figure, so short that he needed to climb a tree to see the preacher everyone was talking about. Often in the gospels, sinful people approach Jesus with trembling, only to be praised for their faith. In this case, however, Jesus reaches out to Zacchaeus. Jesus did not simply tolerate the "scum" of society; he eagerly embraced them. No wonder his action was met with such disapproval.

Just by his presence, Jesus inspires Zacchaeus to do what is right. Zacchaeus eagerly announces that he will not only right any wrongs he has committed, but will go far beyond what is required, giving four times the necessary amount. He also intends to provide for the poor. Jesus declares that Zacchaeus is saved.

Reflect on your own ministry and that of your community. Do you reach out to those who have bad reputations, or do you try to avoid them? How can you seek them out lovingly, as Jesus did, without compromising your own ideals?

Proclaim this interesting story with plenty of expression. Speak the words of Zacchaeus with eagerness, and close with a solemn but caring pronouncement by Jesus.

NOVEMBER 11, 2001

# 32ND SUNDAY IN ORDINARY TIME

*Lectionary #156*

## READING I    2 Maccabees 7:1–2, 9–14

**A reading from the second book of Maccabees**

Antiochus = an-TĪ-uh-kuhs

It *happened* that seven *brothers* and their *mother* were *arrested*
and were being *compelled* by King *Antiochus*,
under *torture* with whips and *thongs*,
to partake of unlawful *swine's* flesh.
*One* of the brothers, speaking for *all*, said,
"What do you intend to *ask* and *learn* from us?
For we are ready to *die*
rather than transgress the laws of our *ancestors*."

Speak with great conviction and a tone of defiance.

After the *first* brother had died,
they brought forward the *second* for their sport.
And when he was at his last *breath*, he said to the King,
"You accursed *wretch*,
you dismiss us from this *present* life,
but the King of the *universe* will raise us *up*
to an *everlasting* renewal of *life*,
because we have *died* for his *laws*."

The brother speaks with disdain for the king but hope in God's promise of life.

After *him*, the *third* was the victim of their sport.
When it was *demanded*,
he quickly put out his *tongue*
and *courageously* stretched forth his *hands*,
and said *nobly*,

---

**READING I** The story of the torture and death of the seven brothers and their mother has served for centuries to inspire people in times of persecution. Today's passage is part of the story of Jewish resistance to persecution at the hands of Antiochus IV Epiphanes, the Seleucid king controlling Palestine at the time. Antiochus and his armies overran Palestine about 150 years before the time of Jesus, desecrating the temple in Jerusalem and forbidding fulfillment of the Jewish law. The Jews, led by

the Maccabean brothers, revolted and eventually drove the Seleucids out of the land, cleansing and rededicating the temple. The present story shows the tremendous courage of the brothers and expresses a belief in an afterlife, echoed in today's gospel.

The belief in resurrection developed relatively late in Jewish thought, during the persecution of Antiochus. While expressed in several writings from this period and later, it was still a matter of discussion and disagreement in Jesus' day. Initially, an afterlife was anticipated only for those who were righteous. The wicked were not expected to

suffer eternal punishment but would suffer a far worse fate. They would simply die and cease to exist.

Today's reading details only a small portion of the whole story told in Second Maccabees. Each brother courageously submits to the torture but resists attempts to make him violate God's law. The first brother asserts that he and his brothers are willing to die rather than break the Jewish law. The third brother willingly offers his tongue and

32ND SUNDAY IN ORDINARY TIME ■ NOVEMBER 11, 2001

"I got *these* from *Heaven*,
and because of God's *laws* I *disdain* them,
and from *God* I hope to get them *back* again."

**Express their surprise and admiration.**

As a *result* the king *himself* and those *with* him
were *astonished* at the young man's *spirit*,
for he regarded his *sufferings* as *nothing*.

After the *third* brother *too* had died,
they *maltreated* and tortured the *fourth* in the same *way*.
When he was near *death*, he said to his torturers,

**Proclaim the end of the reading with finality and hope.**

"One cannot but choose to *die* at the hands of *mortals*
and to *cherish* the hope *God* gives
of being *raised* again by him.
But for *you*, there will be *no* resurrection to *life*!"

---

**READING II**   2 Thessalonians 2:16—3:5

**A reading from the second letter of Paul to the Thessalonians**

**Plan your phrasing well. Speak with joy and peace.**

May our *Lord* Jesus Christ *himself*
and God our *Father*,
who *loved* us
and through *grace* gave us eternal *comfort* and good *hope*,
*comfort* your *hearts* and *strengthen* them
        in every good *work* and *word*.

**This is a sincere plea. Offer it to your listeners as such.**

Brothers and sisters, *pray* for us,
so that the *word* of the *Lord* may spread *rapidly*
and be glorified *everywhere*,
just as it is among *you*,

---

hands to be cut off, declaring that they have been given to him by God but keeping them is less important than keeping God's law. He declares his hope that God will restore what has been destroyed. Finally, the fourth brother makes clear the source of the hope and courage that inspires them. Although he chooses to die rather than to break the law, he has hope that he will be raised again. Yet he declares that his persecutors will know no afterlife but will simply perish.

The story of the torture and great courage of the brothers and their mother teaches a lesson about the importance of following

God's commands. It also instructs us about the source of their hope, as well as ours: There is more than this life; we trust that something greater awaits us. But the tale also serves to inspire all who might be forced to sacrifice their ideals. The courage of the brothers can be emulated by anyone who sincerely strives to do what is right.

Proclaim this fascinating story with plenty of expression. Speak the brothers' words clearly and firmly. Then let the story speak for itself.

READING II   Second Thessalonians was written to encourage the community to hold fast to the teachings its members had received from Paul and to continue to live responsibly. The present passage is a prayer of hope and encouragement.

The Christian faith is grounded in the love of God, who is revealed in Jesus. Only by relying on God will people truly receive strength and encouragement.

The author asks for prayer also for those who are involved in the ministry of

NOVEMBER 11, 2001 ■ 32ND SUNDAY IN ORDINARY TIME

and that we may be rescued from *wicked* and evil *people*;
for not *all* have *faith*.

But the *Lord* is *faithful*;
he will *strengthen* you and *guard* you from the *evil* one.
And we have *confidence* in the Lord *concerning* you,
that you are *doing* and will go *on* doing
the things that we *command*.
May the Lord direct your *hearts* to the love of *God*
and to the *steadfastness* of *Christ*.

**Read these final lines with a firm and reassuring voice.**

---

**GOSPEL**  Luke 20:27–38

**A reading from the holy gospel according to Luke**

Some *Sadducees*,
     those who say there is *no resurrection*,
*came* to Jesus and asked him a *question*,
"*Teacher*,
*Moses* wrote for us that if a man's *brother* dies,
leaving a *wife* but no *children*,
the man shall *marry* the widow
and raise up *children* for his *brother*.
Now there were seven *brothers*;
the *first* married, and died *childless*;
then the *second*
and the *third* married her,
and so in the *same* way all *seven* died *childless*.

**Sadducees = SAD-yoo-seez**
**The Sadducees are trying to trap Jesus; speak their words with mock sincerity.**

---

evangelization. Paul traveled throughout the Mediterranean region spreading the gospel, and this text claims that it was especially well received by the Thessalonians. In an ambiguous statement, the author refers to evil, faithless people who are apparently opposed to the gospel. It is not clear precisely who these evil ones were or what they taught.

But the author asserts that the Lord is faithful and will protect the community, and speaks confidently of the Thessalonians'

faith, praying fervently that they remain rooted in God's love, always trusting in Christ.

This selection is especially easy to proclaim to your community. Address the members of the assembly directly as you encourage them, alluding to their faith and good works. Conclude with a sincere prayer that your listeners will turn their hearts to God, always confident of Christ's faithfulness.

GOSPEL | In order to understand the present passage, one must remember that there was an active debate about the resurrection of the dead at the

time of Jesus. The belief in resurrection was a relatively new one, and the conservative faction in charge of the temple (the Sadducees) was slow to accept it. The Pharisees, on the other hand, believed in the resurrection, and Jesus agrees with them.

The other piece of information that is helpful in comprehending the question posed to Jesus is that the practice described in the question was indeed prescribed by the Mosaic law. In an era when there was no

32ND SUNDAY IN ORDINARY TIME ■ NOVEMBER 11, 2001

*Finally* the woman *also* died.
In the *resurrection*, therefore,
*whose* wife will the woman *be*?
—for the *seven* had *married* her."

Jesus said to them,
"Those who belong to *this* age *marry* and are given in *marriage*;
but those who are considered *worthy* of a place in *that* age
and in the *resurrection* from the *dead*
neither *marry* nor are *given* in marriage.

Indeed they cannot *die* any more,
because they are like *angels* and are *children* of *God*,
being children of the *resurrection*.

"And the fact that the dead are *raised*
Moses *himself* showed in the story about the *bush*,
where he speaks of the Lord as the God of *Abraham*,
the God of *Isaac*, and the God of *Jacob*.
Now he is God not of the *dead*, but of the *living*;
for to *him all* of them are *alive*."

[Shorter: Luke 20:27, 34–38]

**Jesus responds firmly and clearly. They entirely misunderstand the teaching about the afterlife. And they certainly underestimate him!**

**Proclaim this final sentence with firm conviction.**

belief in an afterlife, it was essential to have children in order to carry on one's name and heritage. Children were the closest thing to life after death. In that context, the practice of levirate marriage—in which the brother of a deceased, childless man married his brother's widow to produce heirs for the dead man—developed.

The question is clearly intended to trap Jesus, but Jesus refuses to be caught. Marriage itself does not apply in heaven.

Human existence and human relationships will be different than they are in this world. Jesus then reinforces his point by asserting that the God of Israel is the God of the living. Unfortunately, the story about the burning bush has nothing to do with the question of the resurrection of the dead. But the argument reflects a belief that the holy people of old live in heaven.

Although the practice of levirate marriage is foreign to us, the story provides an intriguing means of teaching about resurrection. Just as Jesus had hope in a future

resurrection, so also we trust that there is more to life than what we know now. Proclaim this story with enthusiasm, as you express the Christian hope that death is not the final word.

# NOVEMBER 18, 2001

# 33RD SUNDAY IN ORDINARY TIME

*Lectionary #159*

## READING I    Malachi 4:1–2

Malachi = MAL-uh-kī

**A reading from the book of the prophet Malachi**

The Lord says this:

Let your voice be filled with urgency.

"*See*, the *day* is *coming*, *burning* like an *oven*,
when all the *arrogant* and all *evildoers* will be *stubble*;
the *day* that *comes* shall burn them *up*," says the Lord of *hosts*,
"so that it will leave them neither *root* nor *branch*.

Lift your voice in hope and joy.

"But for *you* who revere my *name*
the *sun* of *righteousness* shall rise,
with *healing* in its *wings*."

## READING II    2 Thessalonians 3:7–12

**A reading from the second letter of Paul to the Thessalonians**

Brothers and sisters,

Offer this message with a tone of pride rather than arrogance. Sincerely strive to be a model for others in your life.

you *yourselves* know how you ought to *imitate* us;
we were not *idle* when we were with you,
and we did not eat anyone's *bread* without *paying* for it;
but with *toil* and *labour* we worked *night* and *day*,
so that we might not burden *any* of you.

---

READING I — As we draw to the end of the liturgical year, we reflect on the end times and the day of God's judgment. The end of the world is to be feared by wicked, but for those who delight in the Lord it will be a joyous day.

The Day of the Lord is often invoked by the Hebrew prophets as a day of judgment, when God will be fully revealed and will give each of us what we deserve. Malachi's vision of the day of judgment makes use of the image of fire. Fire is powerful and destructive, but it is also necessary, providing light and warmth.

The prophet first alludes to fire's ability to cause widespread devastation. Evoking the image of a wildfire sweeping over the land, the prophet speaks of the proud being swallowed up in an all-consuming conflagration. They are like the stubble from crops that is left in the field after the grain has been harvested, which farmers sometimes burn in order to clear the field of the residue from past years and to prepare the ground for a new planting. God's judgment of fire will consume the evildoers completely.

Those who do what is right, however, have nothing to fear. For them, the fire will bring not destruction but the warm glow of the sun, shining as righteousness. The sunrise of the Day of the Lord will bring healing, creating wholeness.

Do not shy away from Malachi's harsh message of judgment. At the same time, however, be sure to give emphasis to the hopefulness of the final sentence. Direct the prophet's message of hope to your listeners.

READING II — Paul believed that Jesus would return soon to bring God's judgment to the world. He also taught the communities he founded to look forward

**33RD SUNDAY IN ORDINARY TIME ■ NOVEMBER 18, 2001**

This was *not* because we do not have that *right*,
but in order to give you an *example* to *imitate*.
For even when we were *with* you,
we gave you this *command*:
"Anyone *unwilling* to *work* should not *eat*."

**Proclaim this with a sense of outrage and righteous concern. Close in a firm voice.**

For we hear that *some* of you are living in *idleness*,
mere *busybodies*, not doing any *work*.
Now *such* persons we *command* and *exhort*
in the Lord Jesus *Christ*
to do their work *quietly* and to *earn* their own *living*.

---

### GOSPEL    Luke 21:5–19

**A reading from the holy gospel according to Luke**

When *some* were speaking about the *temple*,
how it was *adorned* with beautiful *stones* and *gifts* dedicated
to *God*,
Jesus said,
"As for these things that you *see*,
the *days* will *come* when not one *stone* will be left upon *another*;
*all* will be thrown *down*."

**Does Jesus speak sadly or in an ominous tone? Reflect your opinion in your voice.**

They asked him,
"*Teacher*, when will this *be*,
and what will be the *sign* that this is about to take *place*?"

And Jesus said,
"*Beware* that you are not led *astray*;
for *many* will come in my *name* and say,
'I am *he*!' and, 'The *time* is *near*!'
Do *not* go *after* them.

**Now Jesus speaks a stern warning. Address his concerns to your assembly, then continue in a tone of warning.**

---

to Christ's second coming. Unfortunately, some Christians thought it was therefore unnecessary to work and were idly awaiting Jesus' return. They became a burden on the larger community and caused dissension with idle gossip.

This situation resulted in the message we read today. The author reprimands those who are unwilling to work. It is important to keep in mind, however, that the author is addressing a very specific situation. The instruction that those who are unwilling to work should not eat is not meant as an argument against food programs or government

services. It is directed to those who are fully capable of supporting themselves but who choose not to do so.

Paul often presents his own life and ministry as an example to the members of his fledgling communities. The present passage picks up that theme and suggests that the recipients of the letter look to their own ministers in order to see how to live genuine, faith-filled lives. A believer can fervently hope for Jesus' return while at the same time continuing to accept the daily responsibilities that life entails.

Emphasize for the members of your community the importance of honest work. But the most important theme is the disruption caused by the unwillingness of some to do their part, expressed in the final paragraph.

GOSPEL | The apocalyptic discourse in Luke's gospel describes what will happen in the end times. Even while predicting woes, the author also makes clear that catastrophe does not necessarily point to the end of the world. The

NOVEMBER 18, 2001 ■ 33RD SUNDAY IN ORDINARY TIME

"When you hear of *wars* and *insurrections*,
do not be *terrified*;
for these things must take place *first*,
but the *end* will not follow *immediately*."

Then Jesus said to them,
"*Nation* will rise against *nation*, and *kingdom* against *kingdom*;
there will be great *earthquakes*,
and in various places *famines* and *plagues*;
and there will be dreadful *portents*
and great *signs* from *heaven*.

**Pick up the tempo slightly, and let a note of terror enter your voice at this dire prediction.**

"But *before* all this occurs,
they will *arrest* you and *persecute* you;
they will hand you *over* to *synagogues* and *prisons*,
and you will be brought before *kings* and *governors*
because of my *name*.

"This will give you an *opportunity* to *testify*.
So make up your minds *not* to prepare your *defence* in *advance*;
for *I* will give you *words* and a *wisdom*
that *none* of your opponents
    will be able to *withstand* or *contradict*.

**There is comfort in these words. Suffering is not in vain, nor must the Christian endure it without assistance.**

"You will be *betrayed* even by *parents*,
by brothers and *sisters*,
and by relatives and *friends*;
and they will put *some* of you to *death*.
You will be hated by *all* because of my *name*.
But not a *hair* of your *head* will *perish*.
By your *endurance* you will gain your *souls*."

**Close with a tone of reassurance.**

most important message is the perseverance required of Jesus' followers, regardless of the situation that surrounds them.

The story opens with Jesus' proclamation that the temple in Jerusalem will be destroyed and a question about when the destruction will occur. Jesus' own relationship with the temple was mixed: Although he worshiped in the temple and revered it, he also questioned whether worship of God was properly understood by those who engaged in it. When the author of Luke was writing, the temple had already been destroyed by

the Romans after a period of resistance by the Jews to Roman rule.

Jesus then discusses the horrifying events that will precede the end of the world. His followers should not be misled by those who claim to know when the end will come, but they can be sure that it will be preceded by tribulation. Jesus' disciples will also suffer in some way for their faith. Jesus predicts persecution and imprisonment, events that will allow the gospel to be proclaimed even more broadly.

Because of our experience of history, the predictions in this passage do not seem

to apply to us. We know that the temple has been destroyed and has never been rebuilt. We know that there are wars and famines throughout the world, and often feel powerless to stop them. And few of us have had the experience of being thrown into prison or tortured. But we can respond to the challenge to preach the gospel in whatever circumstances we find ourselves.

Proclaim this reading forcefully, giving special emphasis to the teachings that will probably benefit your community the most: the need to resist deceivers, and the encouragement to persevere against all odds.

## NOVEMBER 25, 2001

# CHRIST THE KING

*Lectionary #162*

### READING I 2 Samuel 5:1–3

**Hebron = HEB-ruhn**

**The elders speak with gratitude and loyalty.**

**Speak triumphantly.**

**A reading from the second book of Samuel**

*All* the tribes of *Israel* came to David at *Hebron*, and said,
"*Look*, we are your *bone* and *flesh*.
For some *time*, while *Saul* was king over us,
it was *you* who led *out* Israel and brought it *in*.
The Lord said to you:
'It is *you* who shall be *shepherd* of my people *Israel*,
you who shall be *ruler* over Israel.'"

So all the elders of *Israel* came to the king at *Hebron*;
and King *David* made a *covenant* with them at Hebron
    before the *Lord*,
and they *anointed* David *king* over *Israel*.

---

**READING I** Today's story about David's encounter with the Israelite tribes at Hebron is a classic story of the establishment of a covenant, this time not between God and humankind but between a leader and his people. David was able to unite all of the tribes under a single monarchy, despite the strife that had characterized the reign of his predecessor, Saul, and the divisions that remained after Saul's death.

The union of the monarch with his people is expressed in the assurance the elders give that they are David's "bone and flesh." They pledge such great loyalty and devotion

to him that they consider themselves his body. They acknowledge as well that he will protect them. David had already distinguished himself while Saul was king, and the elders recognize him as God's chosen ruler.

David will later establish Jerusalem, on the border dividing the northern and southern tribes, as his capital. But for now it is to the southern city of Hebron (a city closely associated with Abraham) that the leaders of Israel come to forge a pact with David and anoint him as their king.

Proclaim this reading in a straightforward manner. Speak fondly of David and with a tone of triumph. This was the beginning of Israel's glory days.

**READING II** The beautiful hymn about Christ featured in our reading today is found near the beginning of the letter to the Colossians. The passage opens with the injunction to give thanks to God. The reason for the gratitude is the opportunity to live in the heavenly abode, a promise made possible by Christ's redemptive action.

NOVEMBER 25, 2001 ■ CHRIST THE KING

## READING II    Colossians 1:12–20

**A reading from the letter of Paul to the Colossians**

*Sincerely offer your own thanks to God, and invite your community to pray with you.*

Give *thanks* to the *Father*,
who has *enabled* you
to share in the *inheritance* of the *saints* in the *light.*

The Father has *rescued* us from the power of *darkness*
and *transferred* us into the *kingdom* of his beloved *Son,*
in whom we have *redemption,*
the forgiveness of *sins.*

*Pause before beginning the hymn. Then speak in a tone of wonder and conviction.*

Christ is the *image* of the invisible *God,*
the *firstborn* of all *creation;*
for in *him* all things in *heaven* and on *earth* were *created,*
things *visible* and *invisible,*
whether *thrones* or *dominions* or *rulers* or *powers—*
*all* things have been created *through* him and *for* him.
Christ is *before* all things,
and *in* him all things hold *together.*

Christ is the head of the *body,* the *church;*
he is the *beginning,* the *firstborn* from the *dead,*
so that he might come to have *first* place in *everything.*
For in *Christ* all the fullness of *God* was pleased to *dwell,*
and *through* him
God was pleased to *reconcile* to himself *all* things,
whether on *earth* or in *heaven,*
by making *peace* through the blood of his *cross.*

The mention of God's beloved Son inspires the author to launch into the hymn itself. Through Christ, human beings can see and know God. The invisible, ineffable God is made visible through him. He has been with God always, and through him the world was created. The author adopts language that was used in Hebrew wisdom literature to describe Lady Wisdom, who is depicted there as cocreator with God.

The author then builds on the Pauline image of the body and its many parts. In other passages, Paul compares members of the Christian community to body parts in order to argue that each person has an indispensable gift to offer to the rest of the community. This author presents Christ as the head of that body, its ruler and guiding force. Because of his role as the conqueror of death, who makes it possible for believers to experience life eternal (he is "firstborn" from the dead), Christ is to be given the foremost place in everything. He is first in death and in life, and is worthy to be honored in eternity.

The fundamental Christian belief that in Jesus God is revealed to the world is linked to the idea of salvation through the cross. The fullness of God dwells in Jesus, who is both divine and human. Because Jesus is both human and divine, he can bridge the gap between God and humanity, despite our propensity to turn away. Through his death, Jesus restored us to right relationship with God.

This selection is a joy to share with your community. Invite your listeners to give thanks with you as you proclaim the wondrous deeds of God in Jesus. Speak with a sense of awe.

## CHRIST THE KING ■ NOVEMBER 25, 2001

### GOSPEL    Luke 23:35–43

**A reading from the holy gospel according to Luke**

*Speak in a mocking tone.*

When Jesus had been *crucified*, the *people* stood by *watching;*
the leaders *scoffed* at him saying,
"He saved *others;*
let him save *himself* if he is the *Messiah* of *God*, his *chosen* one!"
The soldiers *also* mocked Jesus,
coming *up* and offering him sour *wine,*
and saying, "If *you* are the King of the *Jews, save* yourself!"
There was also an *inscription* over Jesus,
"*This* is the King of the *Jews.*"

*Proclaim this line with pride, although it was not intended to be understood this way by Jesus' persecutors.*

One of the *criminals* who were hanged there
kept *deriding* Jesus and saying,
"Are *you* not the *Messiah?*
*Save* yourself and *us!*"

*There is righteous indignation in this criminal's voice.*

But the other *rebuked* him, saying,
"Do you not fear *God,*
since you are under the same *sentence* of *condemnation?*
And *we* indeed have been condemned *justly,*
for *we* are getting what we *deserve* for our deeds,
but *this* man has done nothing *wrong.*"
Then he said,

*Speak with sincere humility.*

"*Jesus, remember* me when you come into your *kingdom.*"
Jesus replied,

*Jesus responds firmly but lovingly.*

"Truly I *tell* you, *today* you will be with me in *Paradise.*"

---

**GOSPEL**  The irony of reading about the crucifixion on the feast of Christ the King is overwhelming. Just as we are proclaiming that Jesus is the exalted Lord, the "firstborn of all creation," the fulfillment of the promises to David, we see him bruised and beaten, dying on the cross. It is indeed the supreme irony of the Christian faith that the one who is Lord of all was willing to give his life for us, suffering a lonely, painful and humiliating death.

The gospel of Luke is fond of presenting such paradoxes. All our expectations about society, personal responsibility and our relationship with the things of this world are turned on their head in this gospel. The lowly are exalted, sinners are called righteous, the one who dies gives life. We close this liturgical year with the ultimate paradox: The one to whom we offer all glory and honor and praise is lifted high for all to see—powerless, hanging on the cross.

The inscription on Jesus' cross proclaims that he is king of the Jews. What his tormentors thought was a joke or a condemnation, however, was indeed the truth. But, in another example of irony, a convicted criminal recognizes Jesus for who he is. He acknowledges his own guilt and Jesus' innocence, and confesses that Jesus will soon be entering his true realm.

Remember as you proclaim this passage that you are sharing it with your assembly on the feast that proclaims Christ as king. Read with an underlying note of triumph in your voice, despite the horrors you describe. Share the encounter of the just criminal and Jesus with a compassion.